Shojo Beat

Stepping on Roses

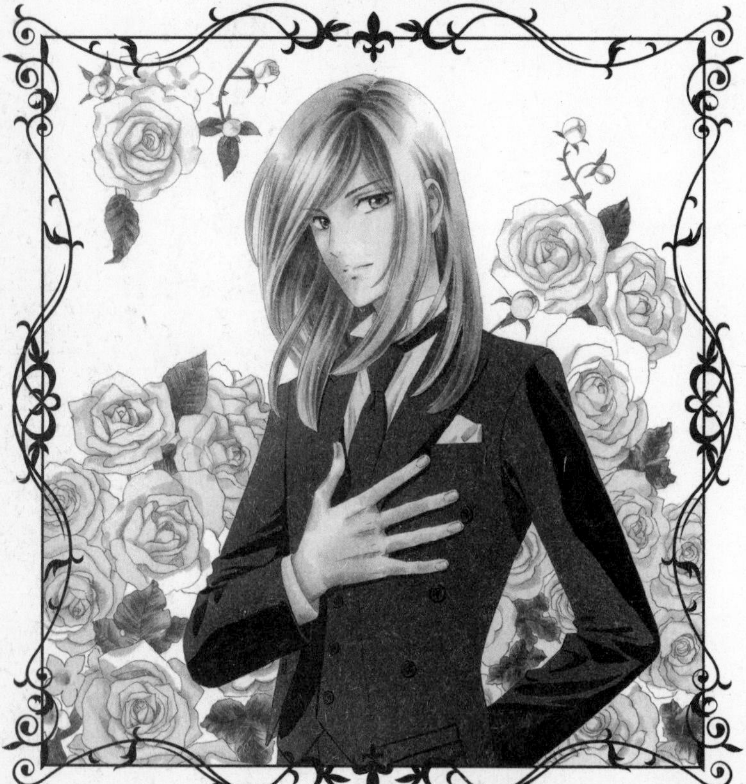

Vol. 6

Story & Art by

Rinko Ueda

Stepping on Roses

**Volume 6
CONTENTS**

Story Thus Far

During the Meiji Era, Sumi Kitamura was living a life of poverty and taking care of young orphans that her elder brother Eisuke brought home from the streets. Then, in order to pay off Eisuke's debts, she married Soichiro Ashida, the heir to a wealthy conglomerate. Even though this is a marriage of convenience, Soichiro and Sumi begin to have feelings for each other.

However, the couple have a fight one night, and Sumi goes after Soichiro in the rain. Soichiro's friend Nozomu offers Sumi shelter in his home, and she agrees to model for his painting. The next day, Soichiro discovers the painting at Nozomu's house and is shocked to learn that Nozomu is still in love with Sumi...

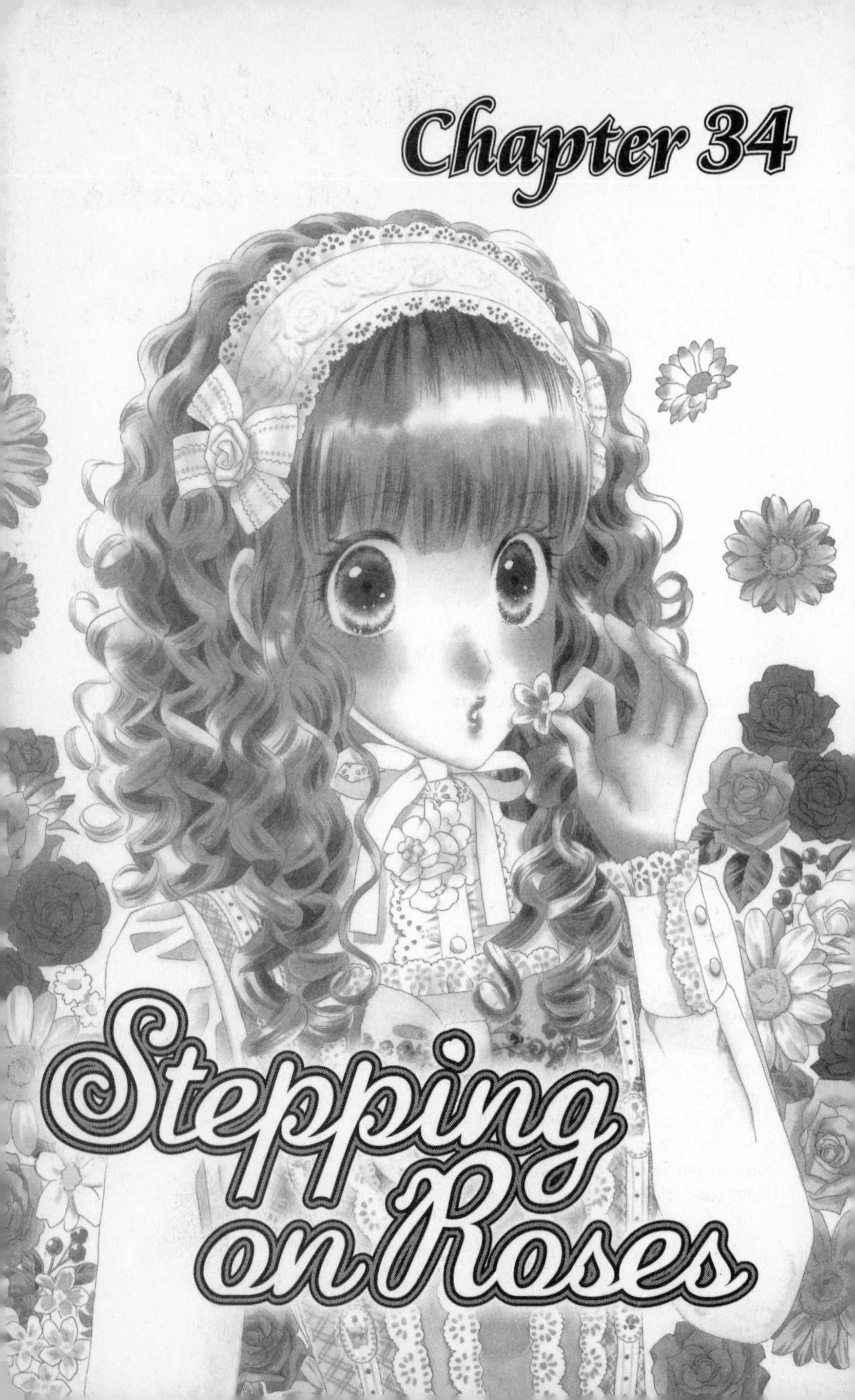
Chapter 34
Stepping on Roses

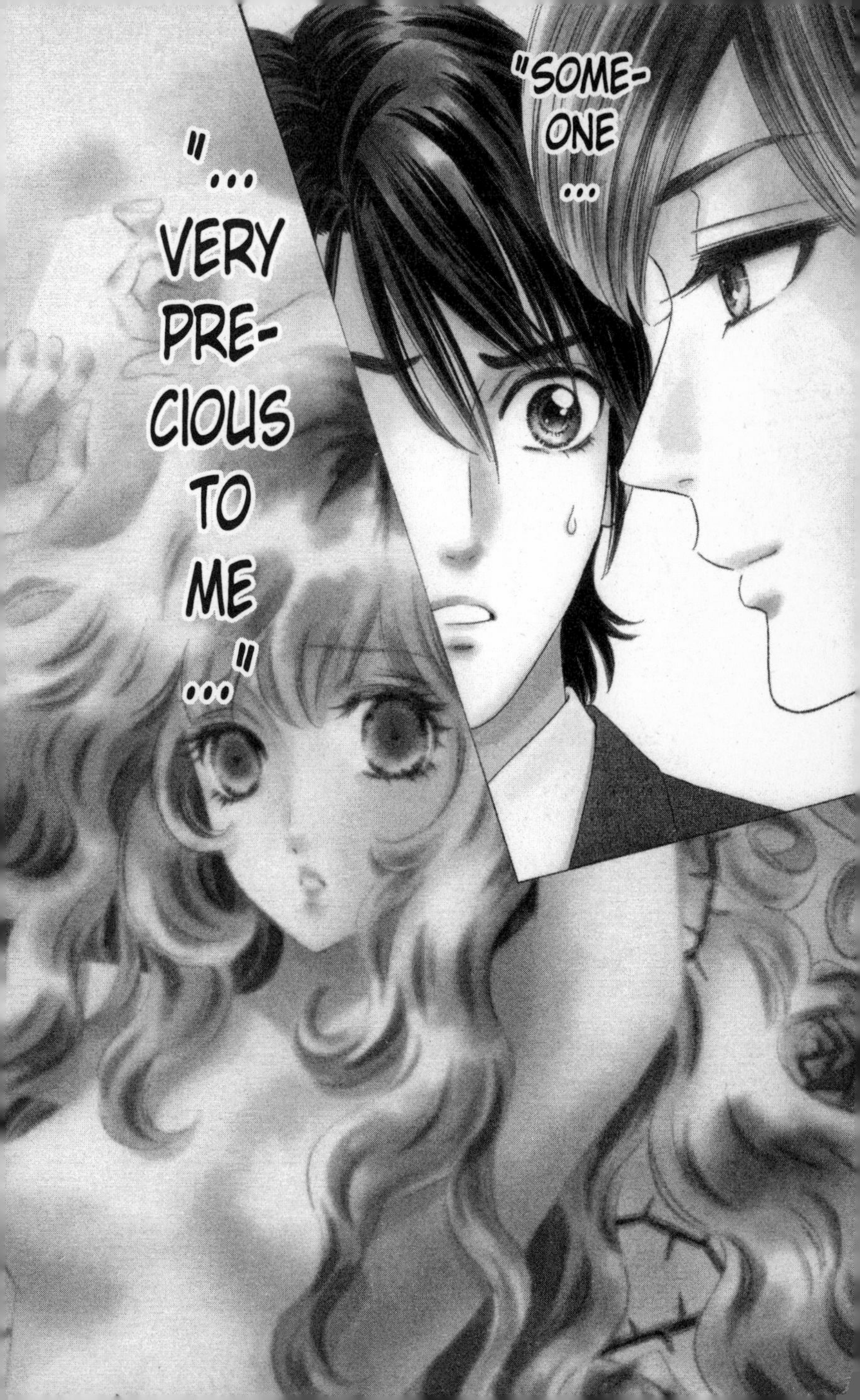
"SOME-ONE ...
"... VERY PRE-CIOUS TO ME ..."

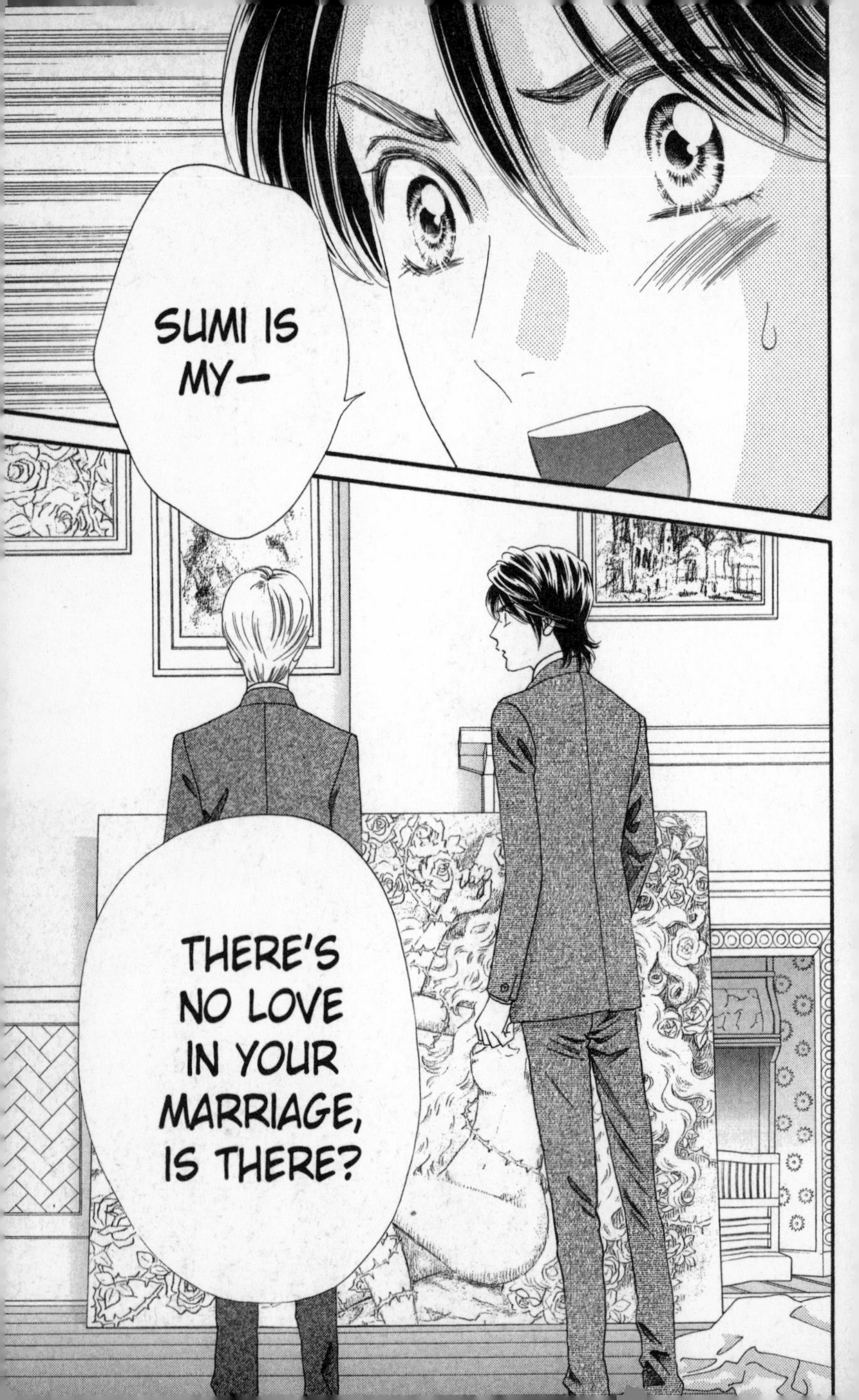
SUMI IS MY—
THERE'S NO LOVE IN YOUR MARRIAGE, IS THERE?

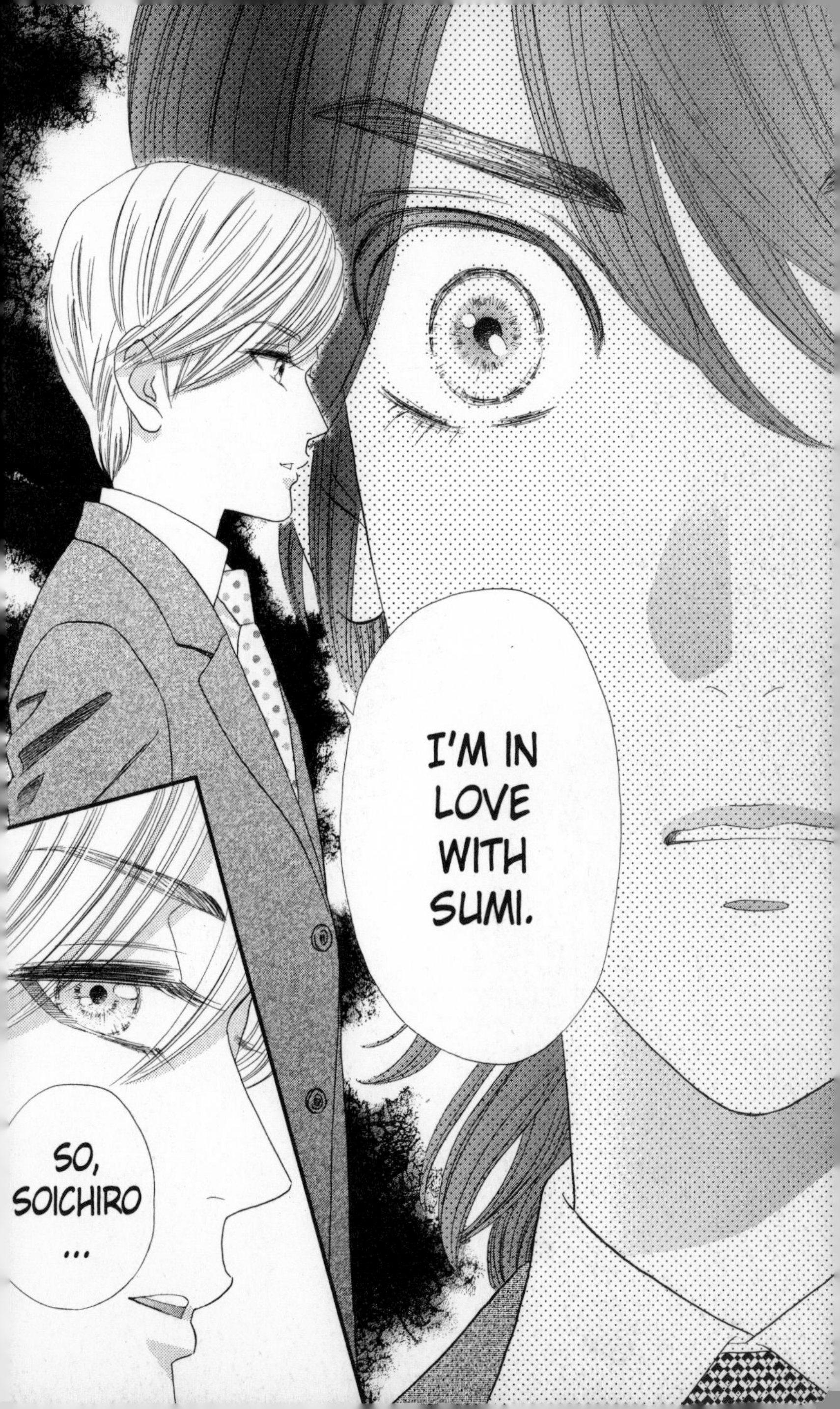
I'M IN LOVE WITH SUMI.
SO, SOICHIRO ...

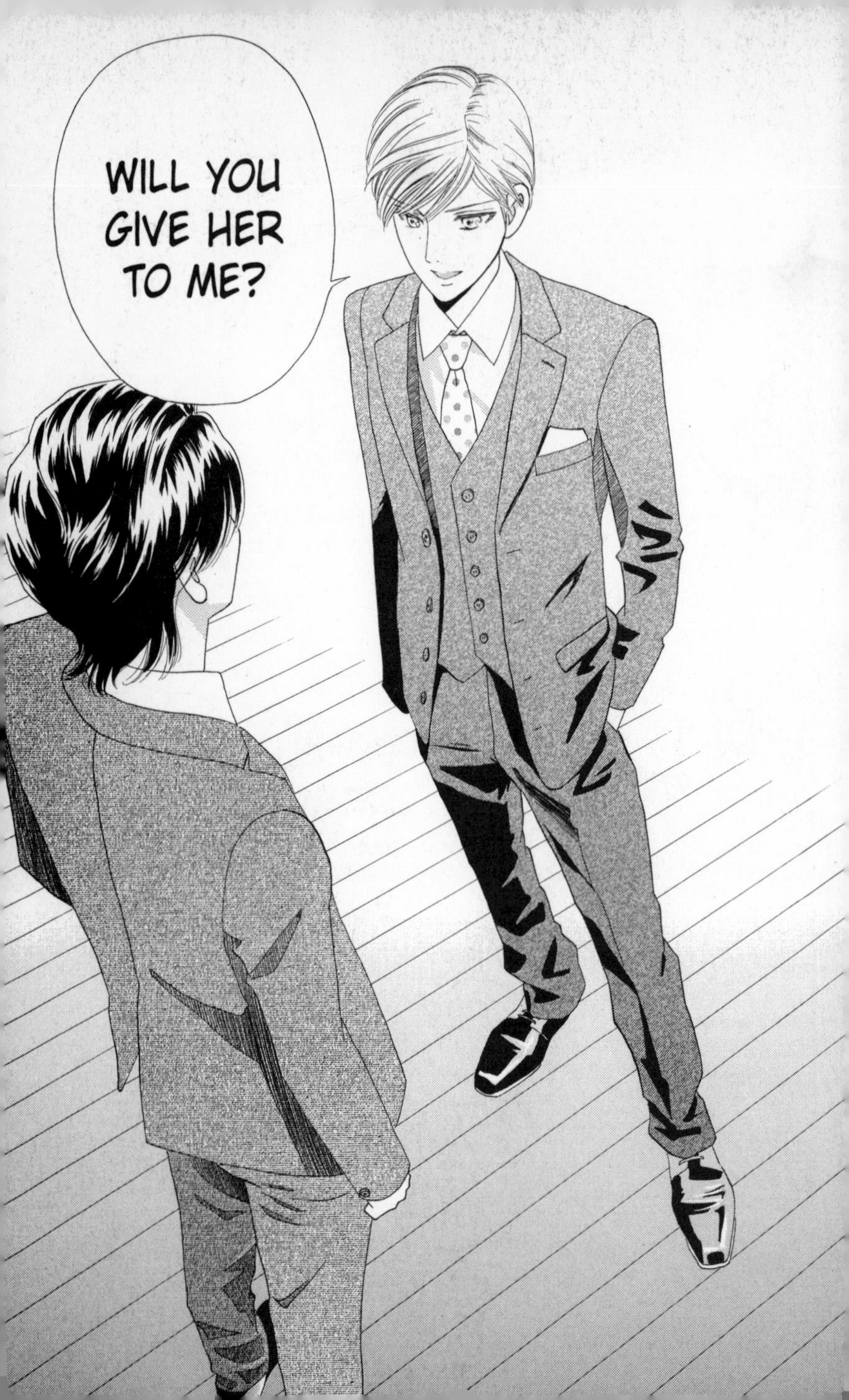
WILL YOU GIVE HER TO ME?

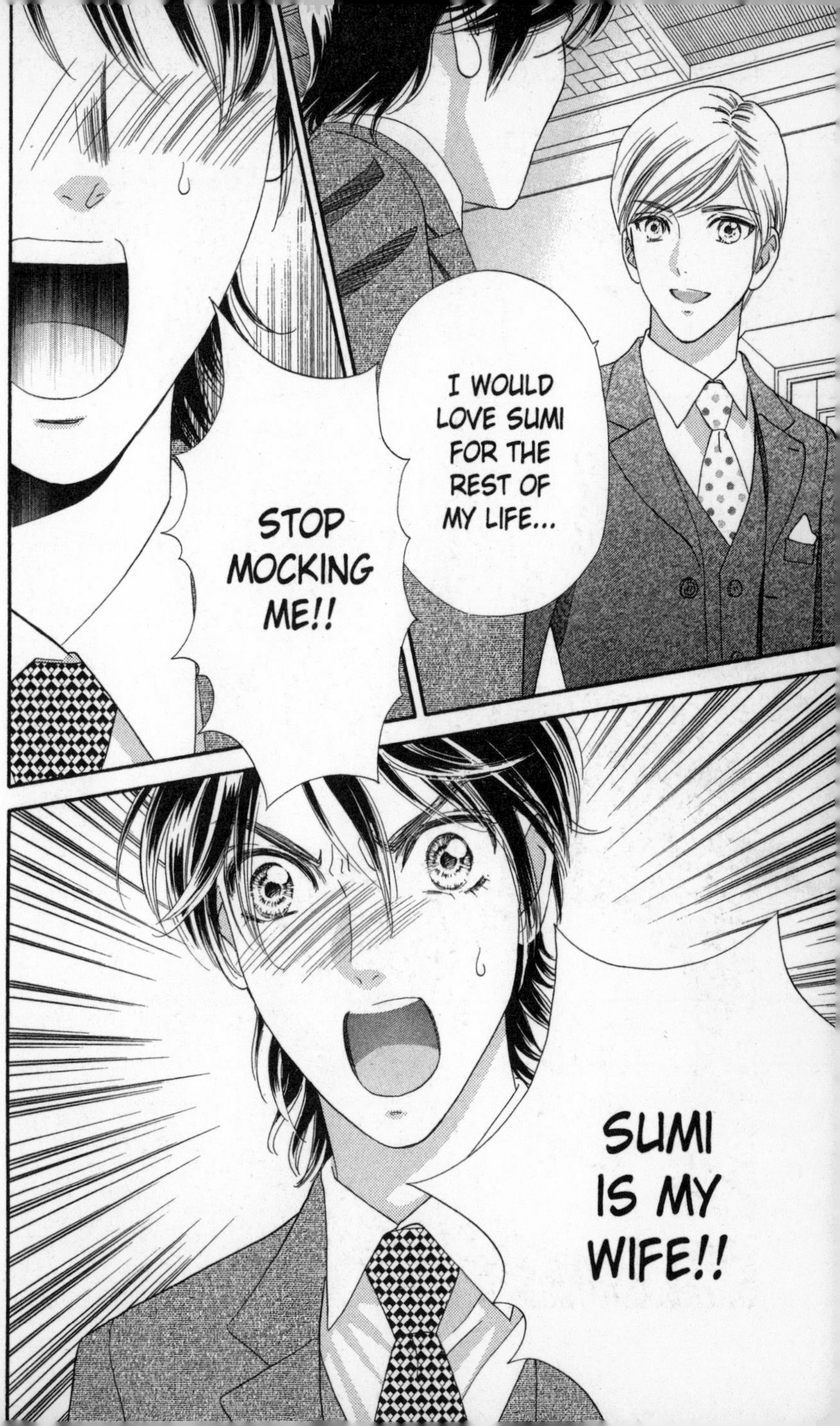
I WOULD LOVE SUMI FOR THE REST OF MY LIFE...
STOP MOCKING ME!!
SUMI IS MY WIFE!!

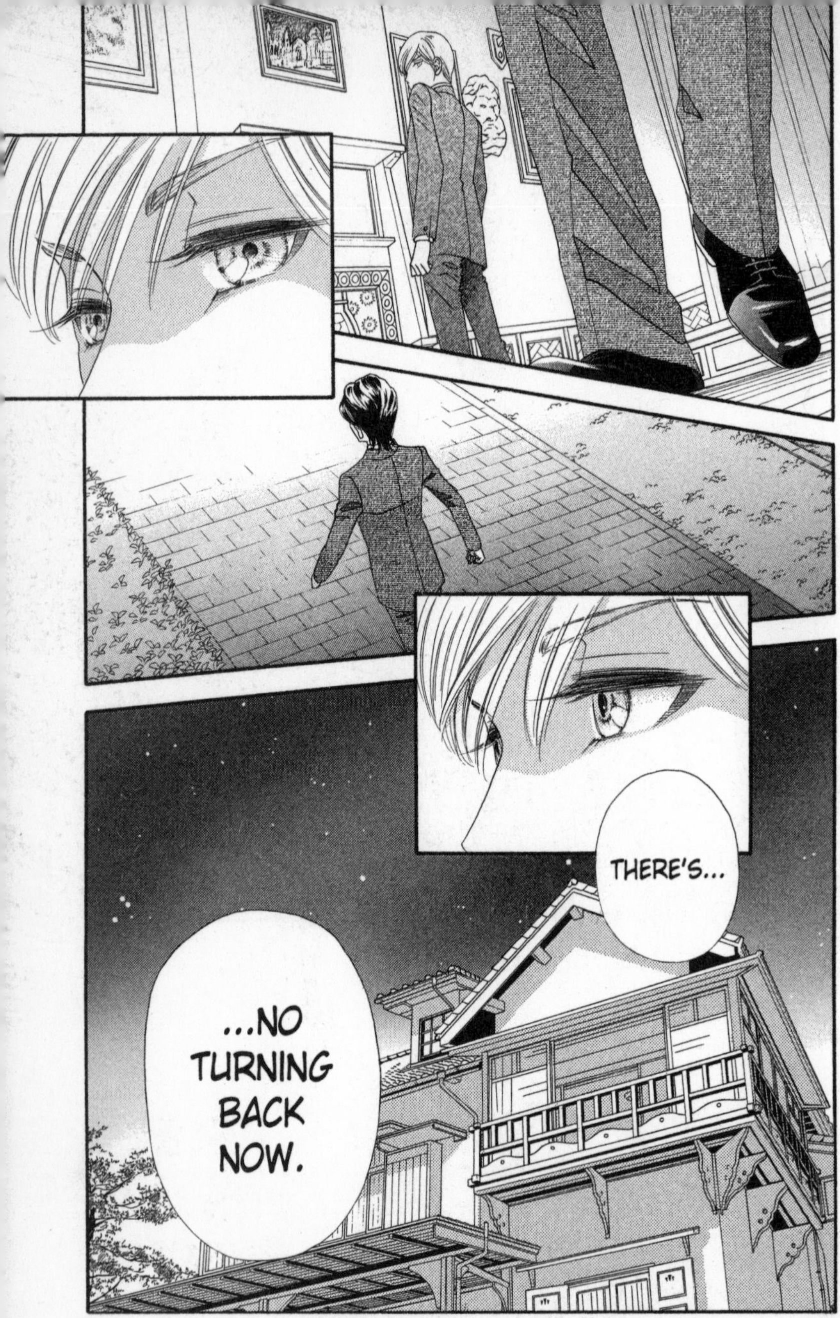
THERE'S...
...NO TURNING BACK NOW.

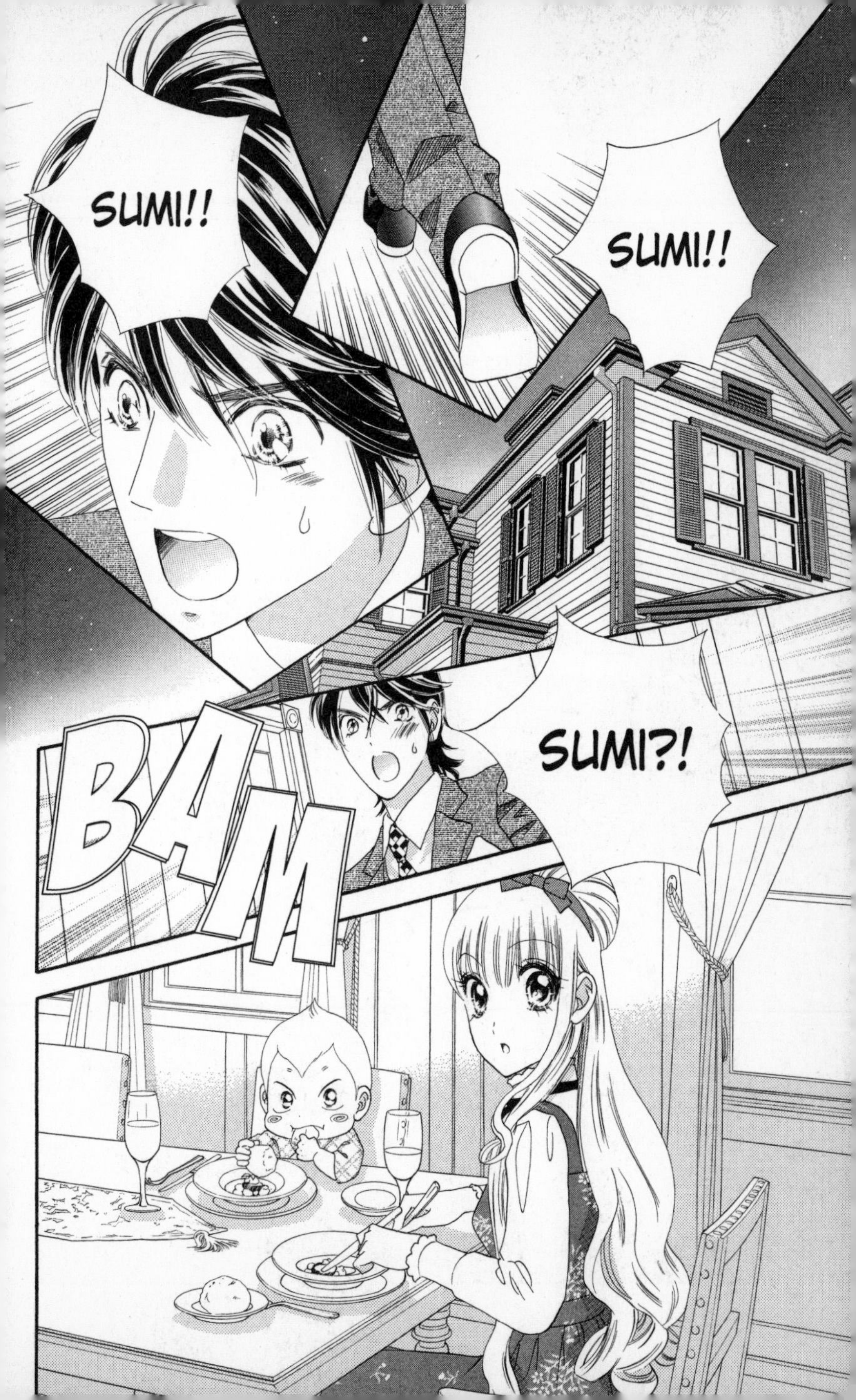
SUMI!!
SUMI!!
SUMI?!
BAM

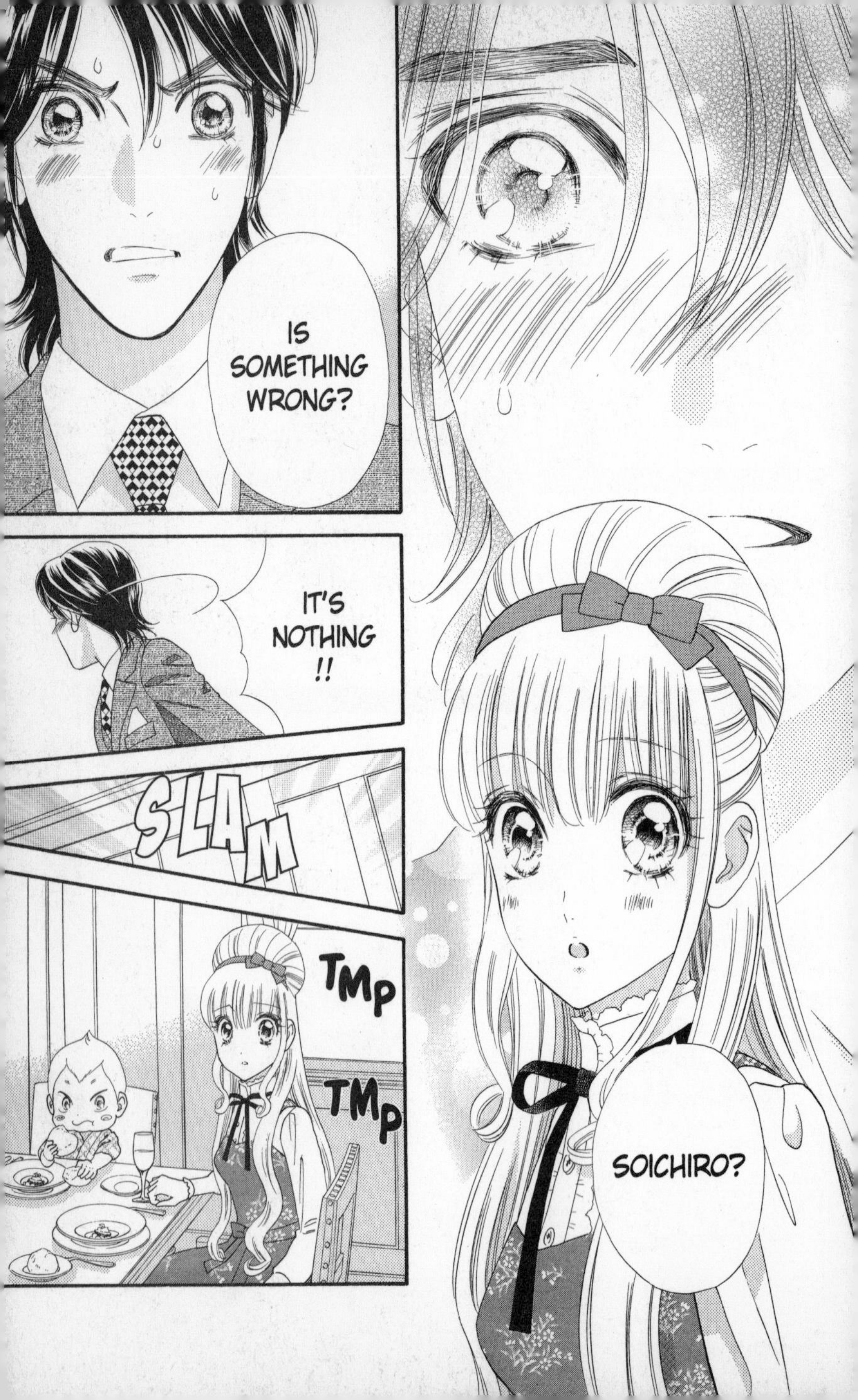
SOICHIRO?
IS SOMETHING WRONG?
IT'S NOTHING!!
SLAM
TMP
TMP

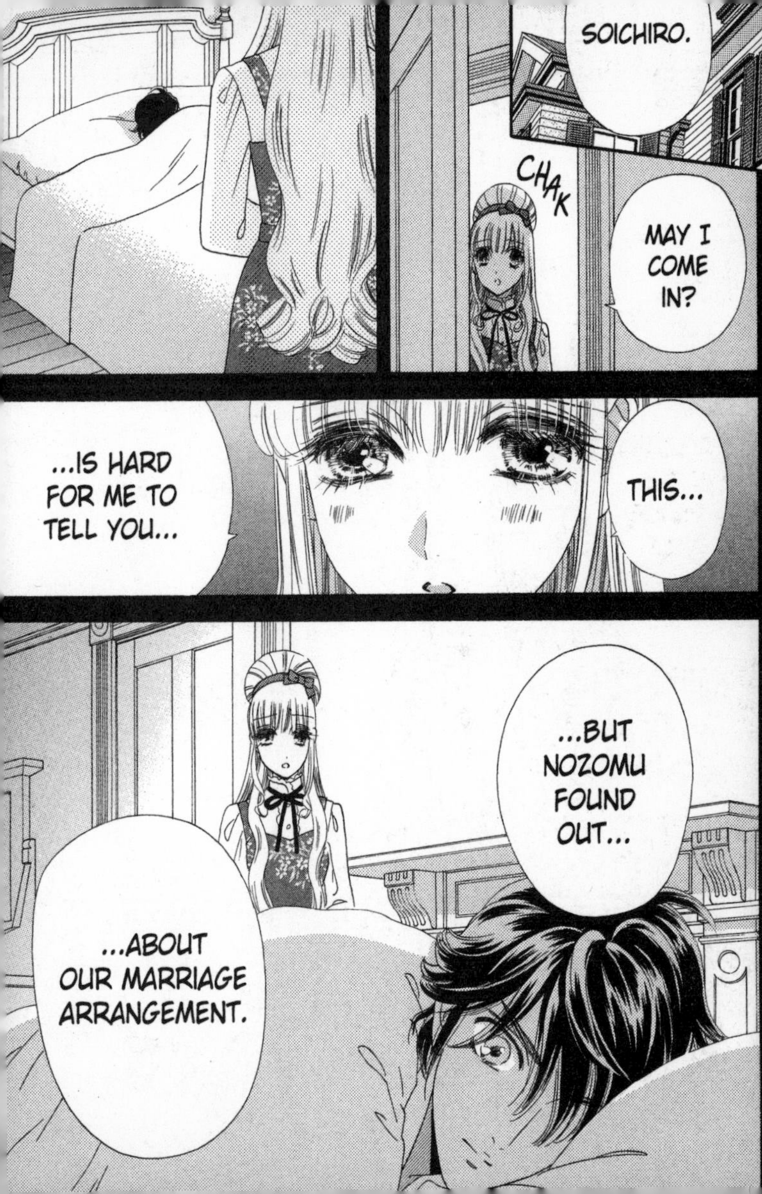
SOICHIRO.
CHAK
MAY I COME IN?
THIS...
...IS HARD FOR ME TO TELL YOU...
...BUT NOZOMU FOUND OUT...
...ABOUT OUR MARRIAGE ARRANGEMENT.

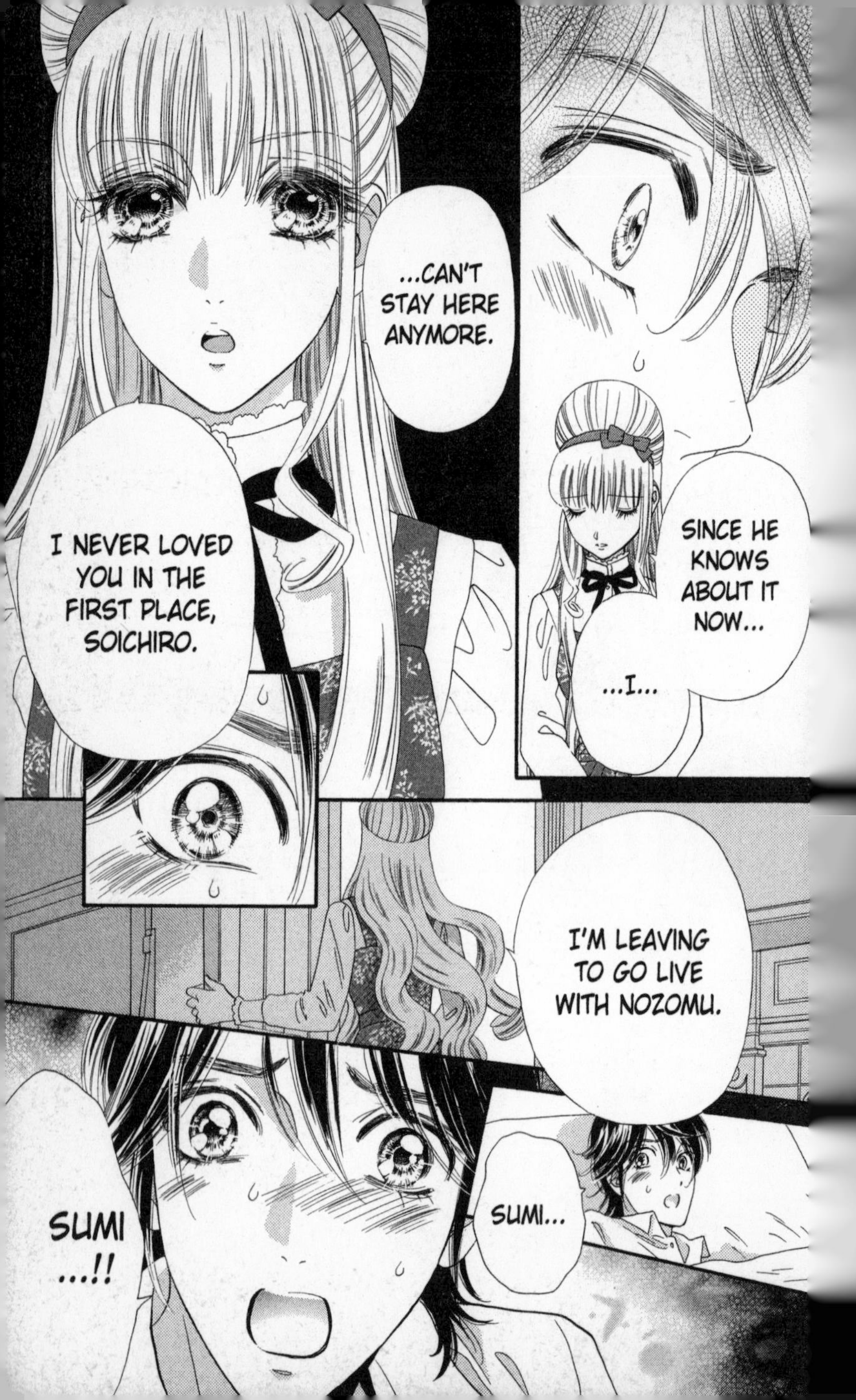
SINCE HE KNOWS ABOUT IT NOW...
...I...
...CAN'T STAY HERE ANYMORE.
I NEVER LOVED YOU IN THE FIRST PLACE, SOICHIRO.
I'M LEAVING TO GO LIVE WITH NOZOMU.
SUMI...
SUMI ...!!

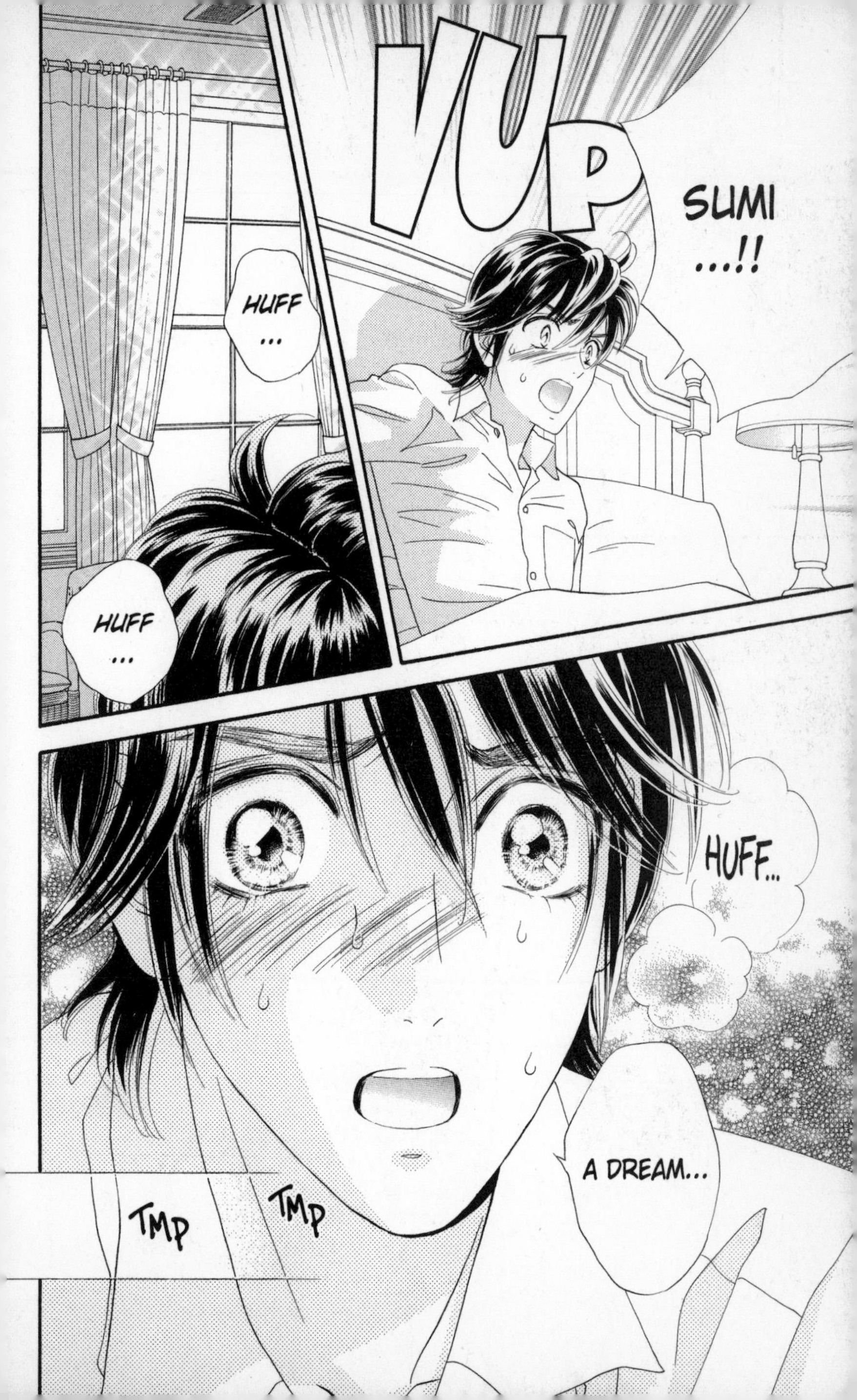
VUP
SUMI ...!!
HUFF ...
HUFF ...
HUFF...
A DREAM...
TMP
TMP

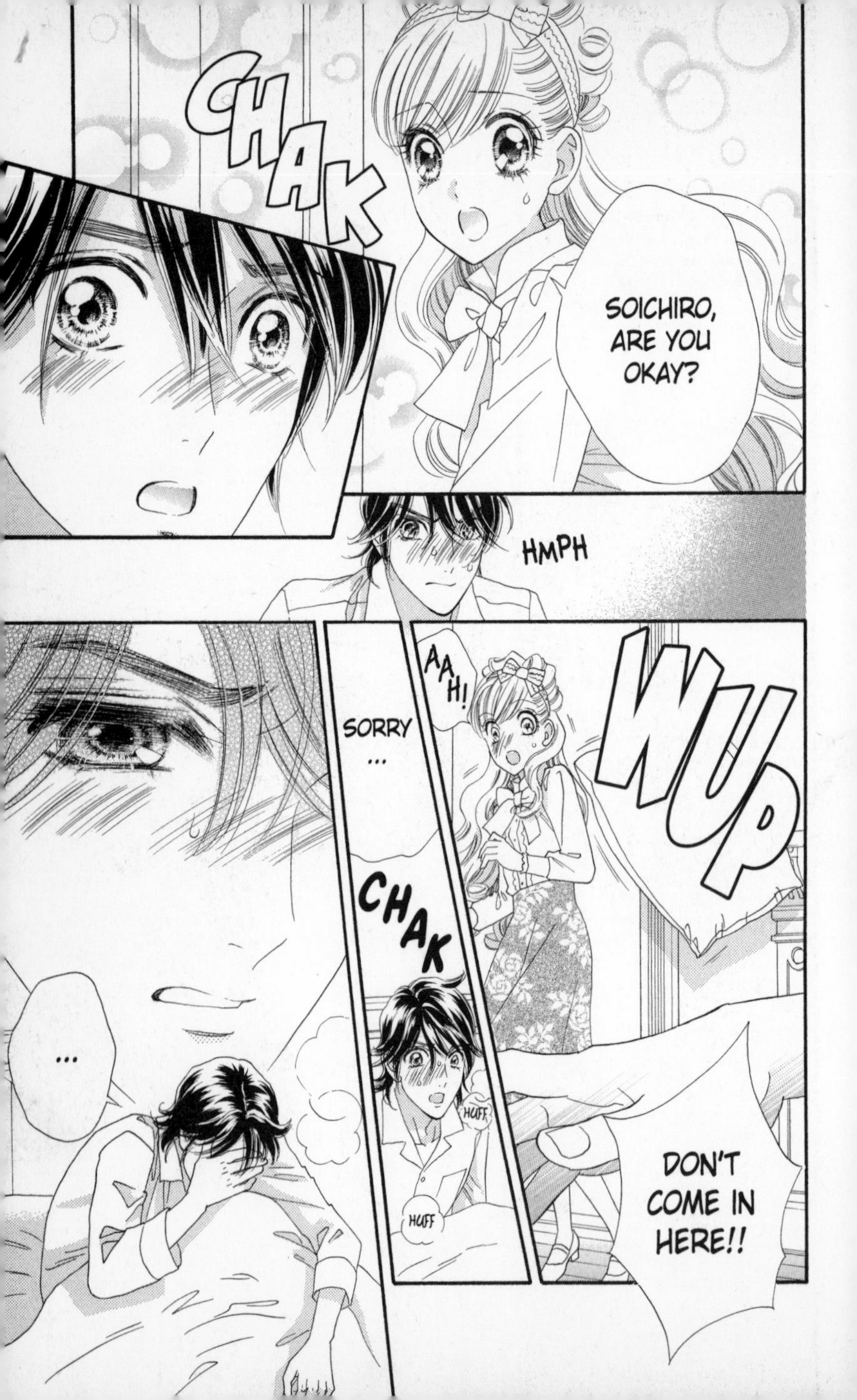
CHAK
SOICHIRO, ARE YOU OKAY?
HMPH
WUP
AAH!
DON'T COME IN HERE!!
SORRY ...
CHAK
HUFF
HUFF
...

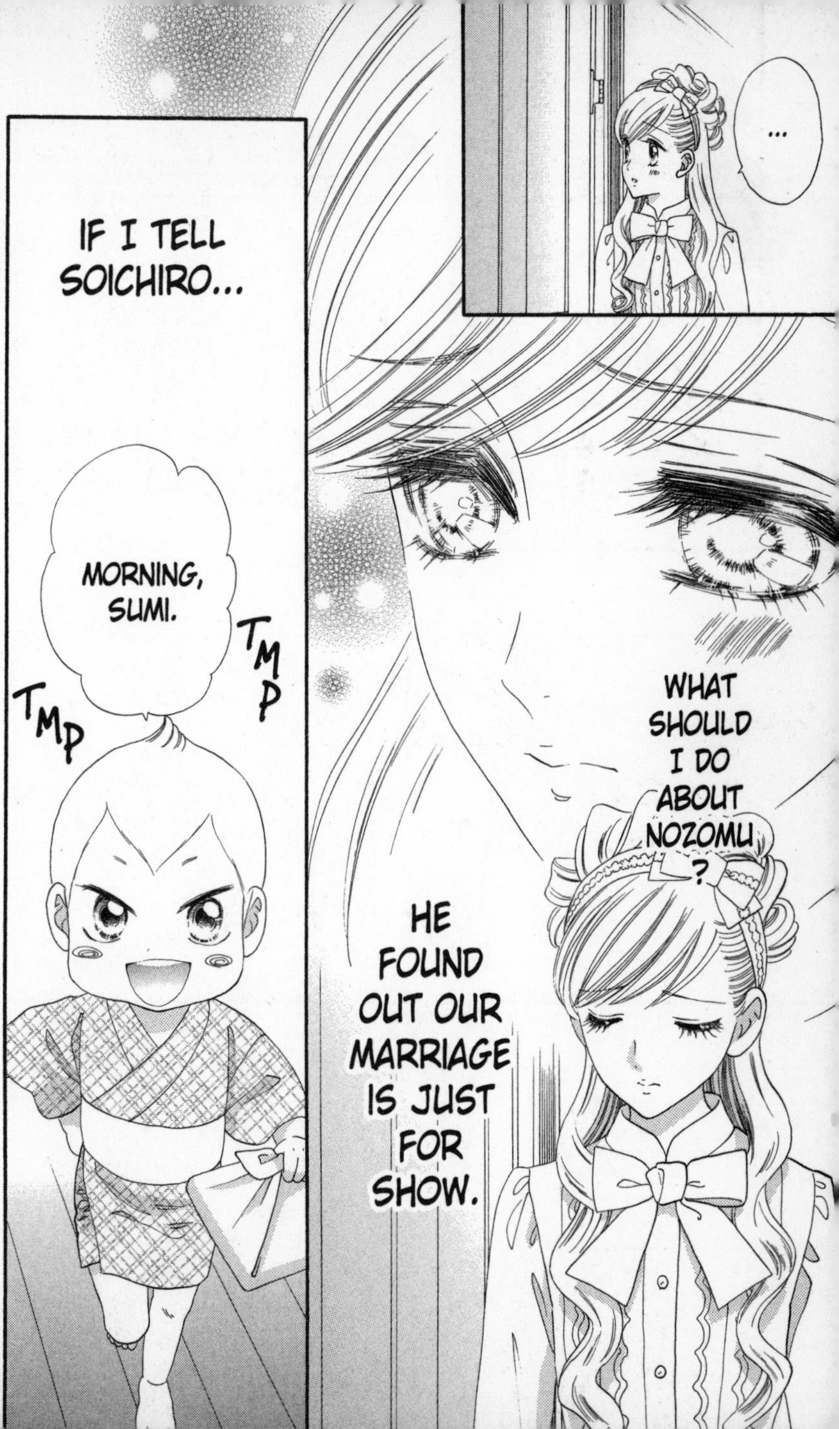
...
WHAT SHOULD I DO ABOUT NOZOMU?
HE FOUND OUT OUR MARRIAGE IS JUST FOR SHOW.
IF I TELL SOICHIRO...
MORNING, SUMI.
TMP
TMP

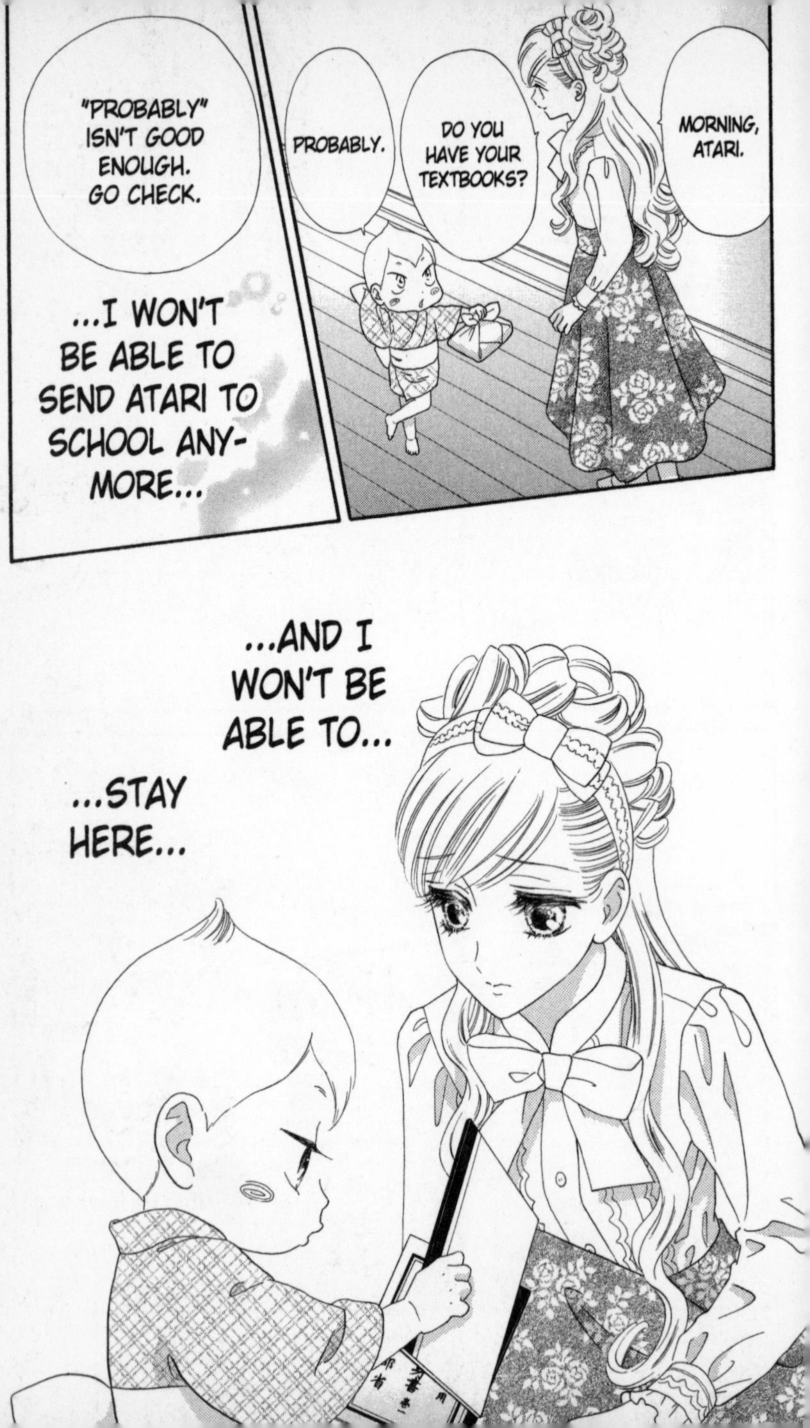
MORNING, ATARI.
DO YOU HAVE YOUR TEXTBOOKS?
PROBABLY.
"PROBABLY" ISN'T GOOD ENOUGH. GO CHECK.
...I WON'T BE ABLE TO SEND ATARI TO SCHOOL ANY-MORE...
...AND I WON'T BE ABLE TO...
...STAY HERE...

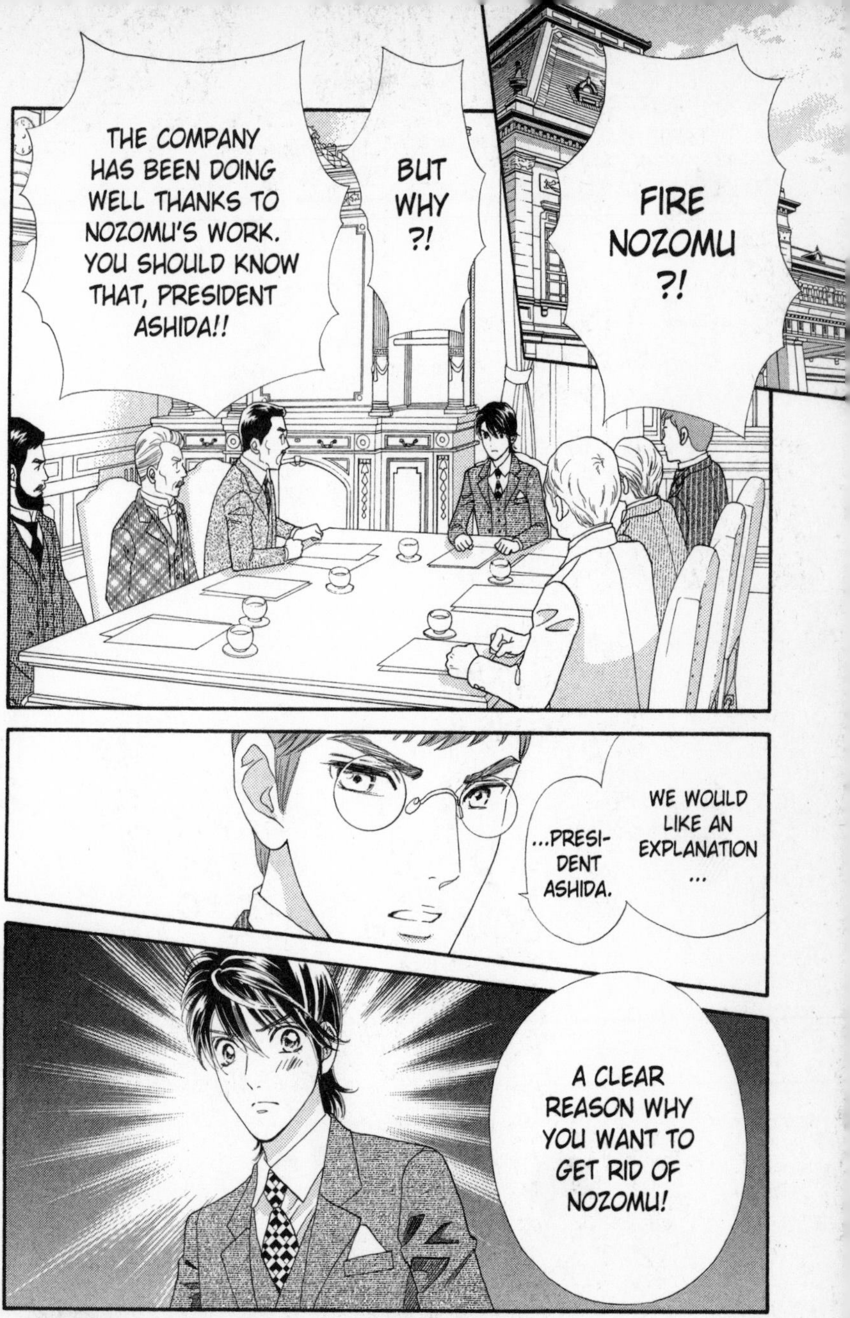
FIRE NOZOMU ?!
BUT WHY ?!
THE COMPANY HAS BEEN DOING WELL THANKS TO NOZOMU'S WORK. YOU SHOULD KNOW THAT, PRESIDENT ASHIDA!!
WE WOULD LIKE AN EXPLANATION ...
...PRESI-DENT ASHIDA.
A CLEAR REASON WHY YOU WANT TO GET RID OF NOZOMU!

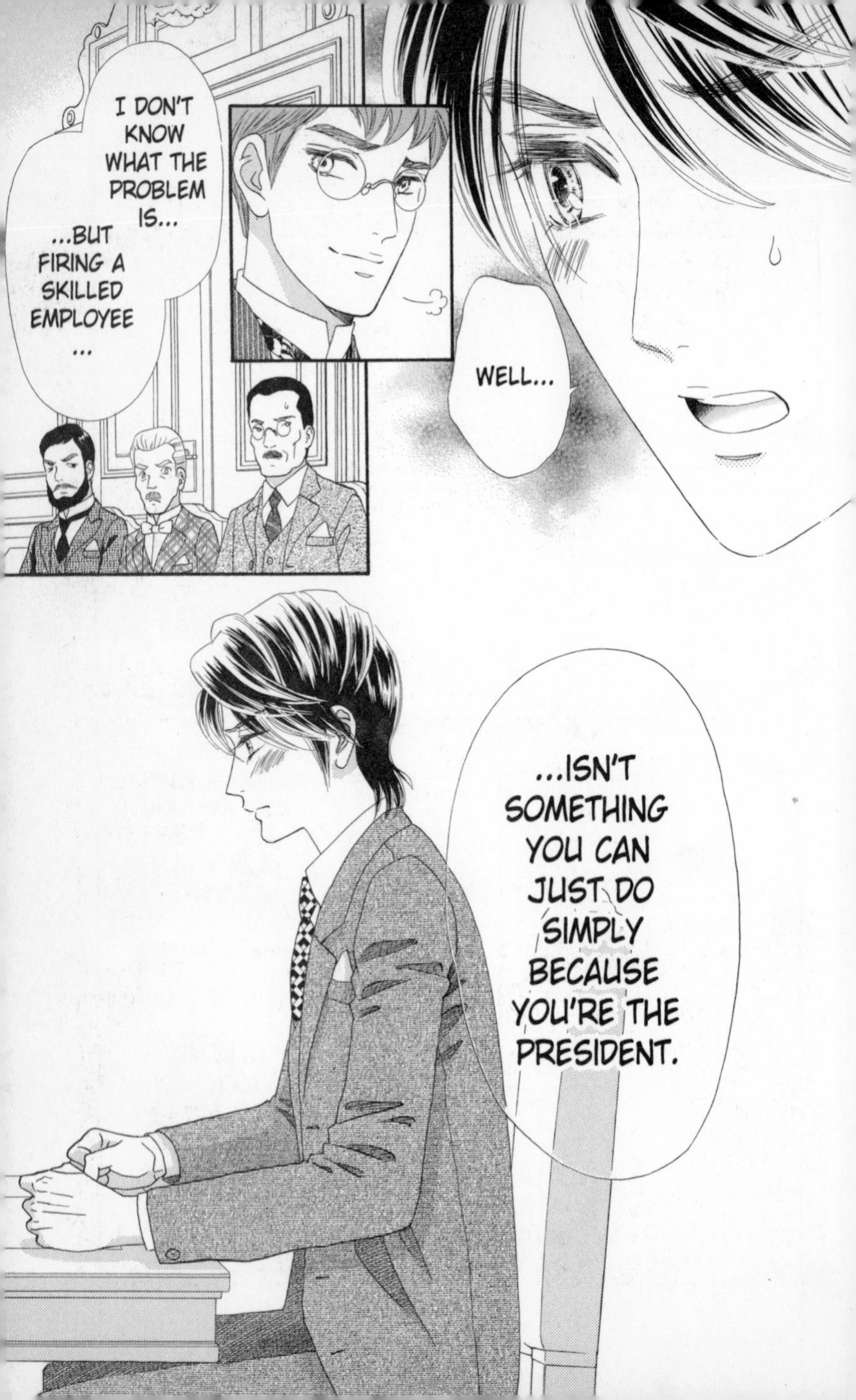
WELL...
I DON'T KNOW WHAT THE PROBLEM IS...
...BUT FIRING A SKILLED EMPLOYEE ...
...ISN'T SOMETHING YOU CAN JUST DO SIMPLY BECAUSE YOU'RE THE PRESIDENT.

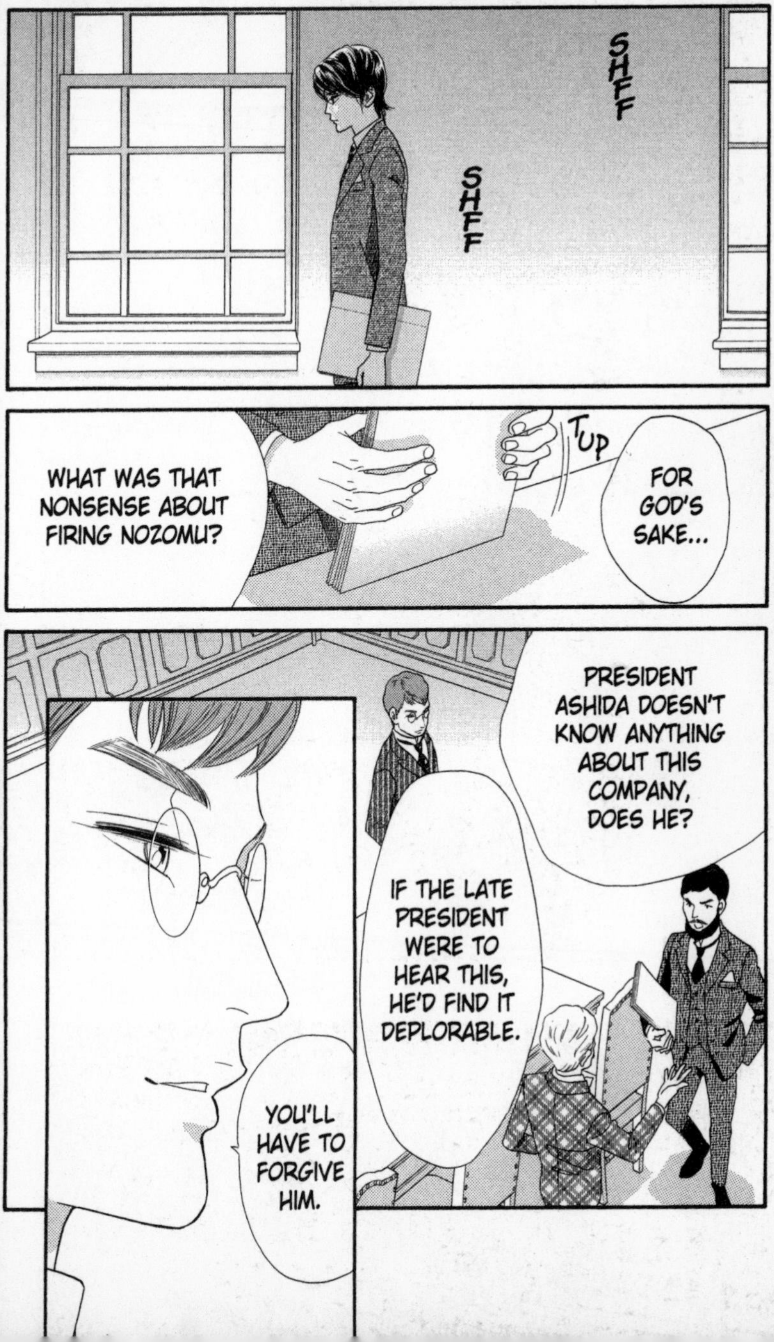
SHFF
SHFF
TUP
FOR GOD'S SAKE...
WHAT WAS THAT NONSENSE ABOUT FIRING NOZOMU?
PRESIDENT ASHIDA DOESN'T KNOW ANYTHING ABOUT THIS COMPANY, DOES HE?
IF THE LATE PRESIDENT WERE TO HEAR THIS, HE'D FIND IT DEPLORABLE.
YOU'LL HAVE TO FORGIVE HIM.

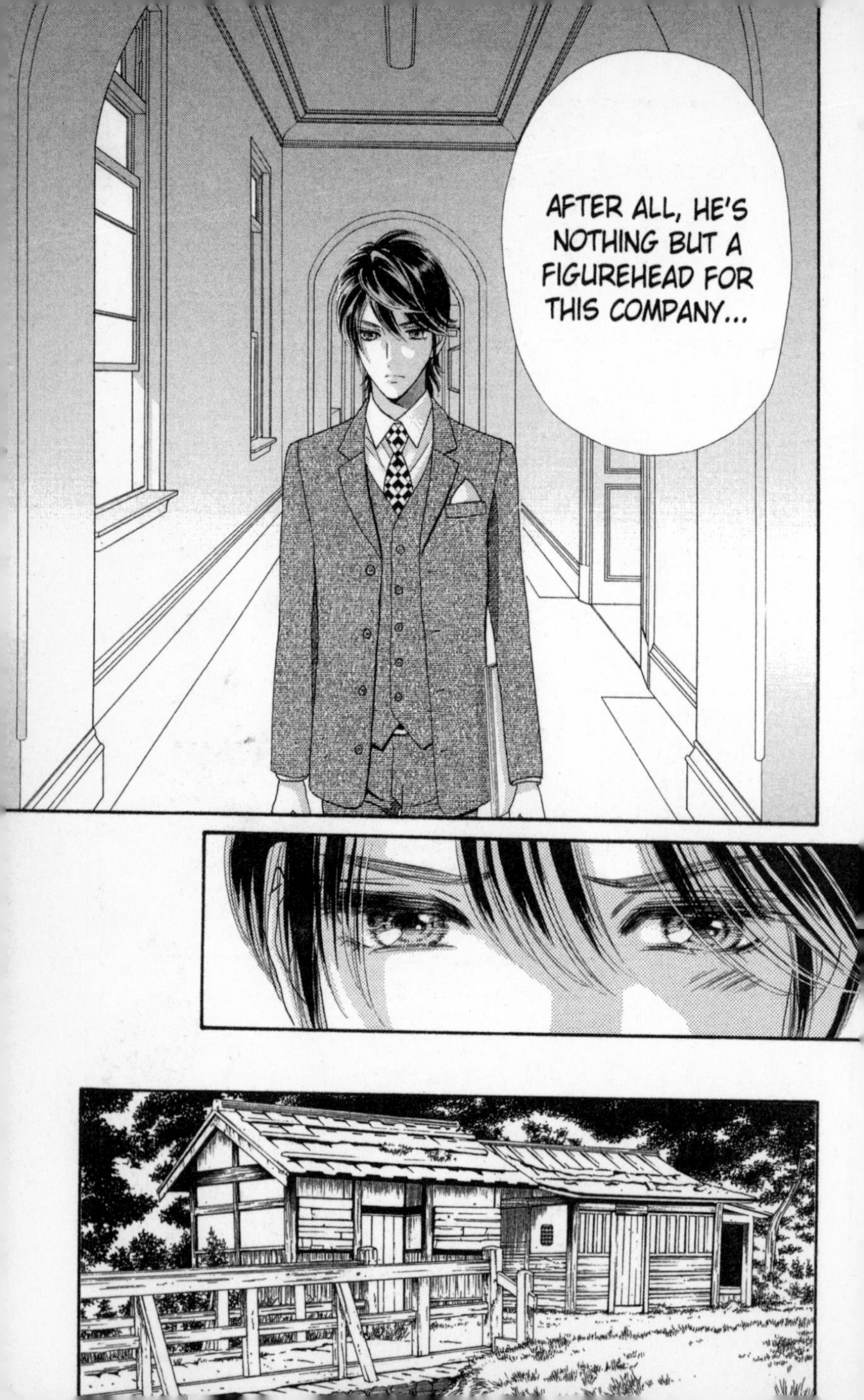
AFTER ALL, HE'S NOTHING BUT A FIGUREHEAD FOR THIS COMPANY...

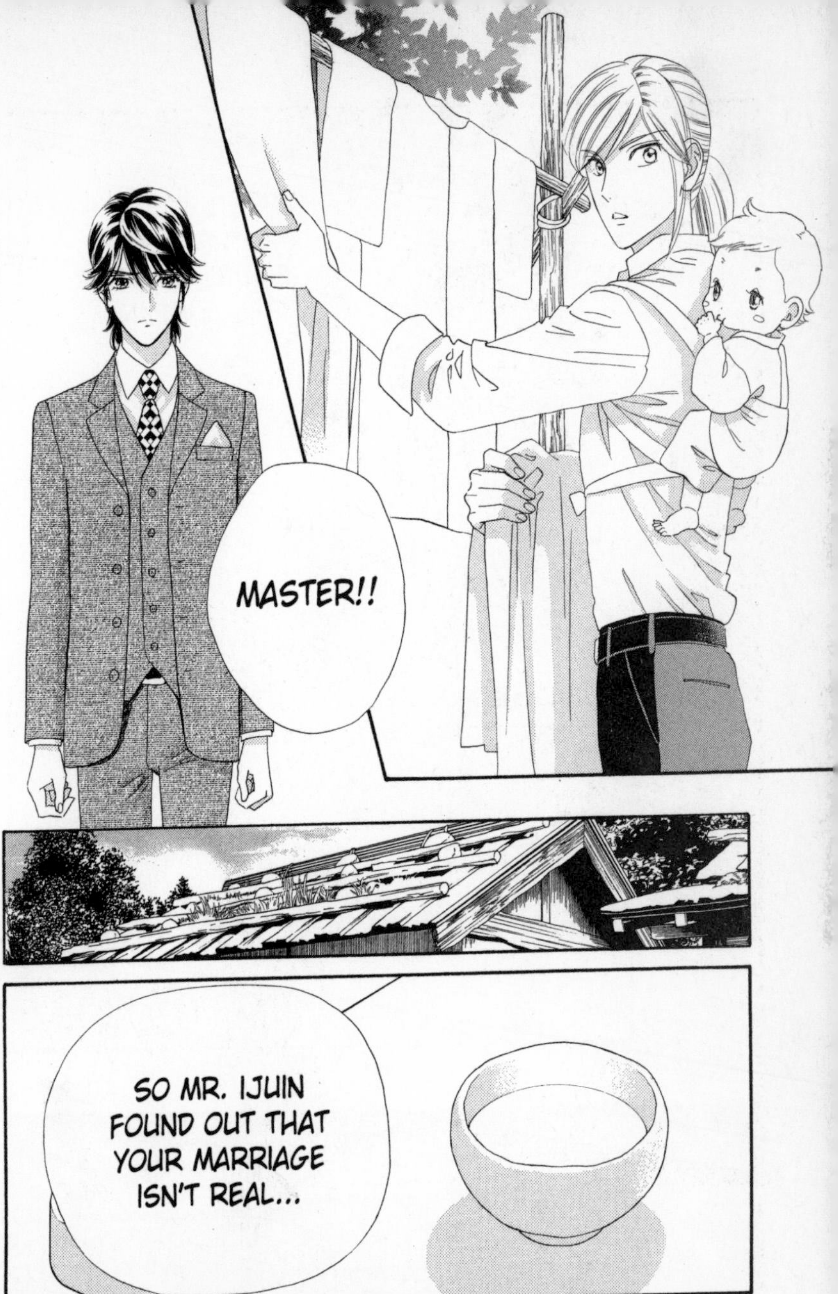
MASTER!!
SO MR. IJUIN FOUND OUT THAT YOUR MARRIAGE ISN'T REAL...

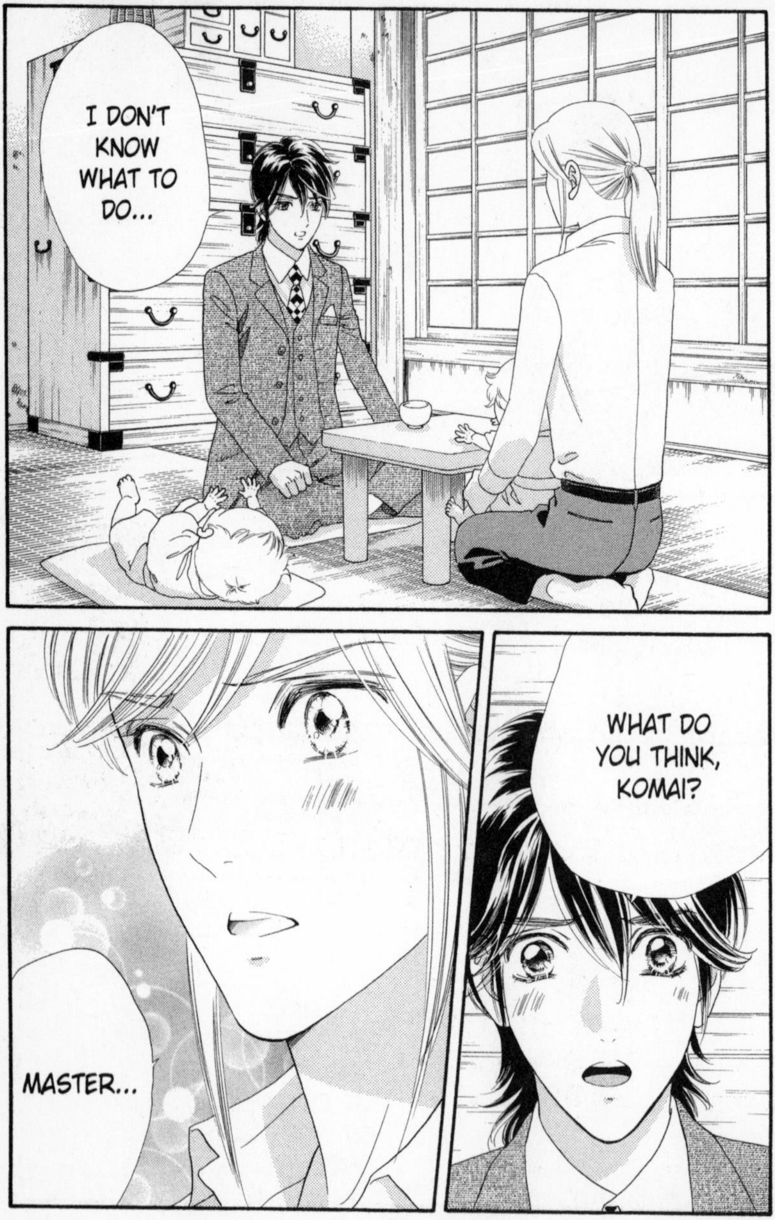
I DON'T KNOW WHAT TO DO...
WHAT DO YOU THINK, KOMAI?
MASTER...

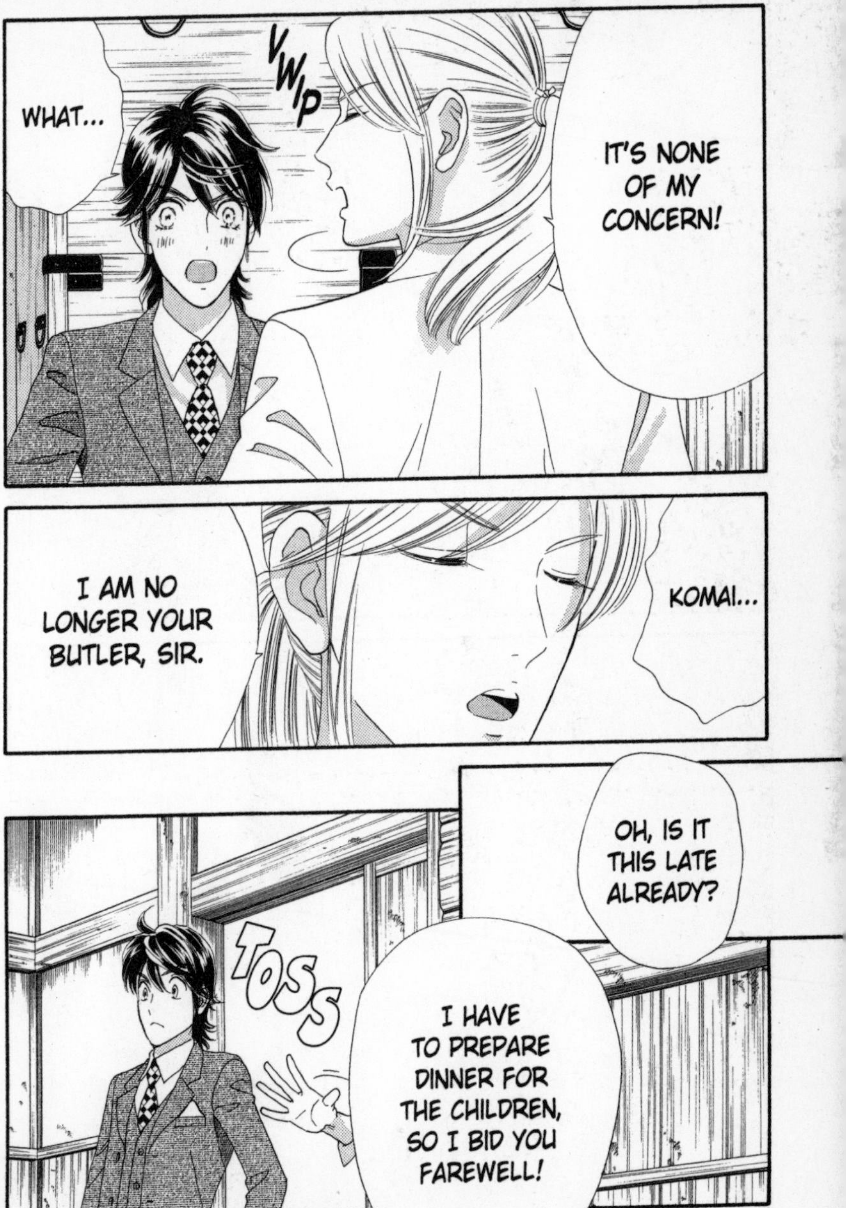
IT'S NONE OF MY CONCERN!
VWIP
WHAT...
KOMAI...
I AM NO LONGER YOUR BUTLER, SIR.
OH, IS IT THIS LATE ALREADY?
I HAVE TO PREPARE DINNER FOR THE CHILDREN, SO I BID YOU FAREWELL!
TOSS

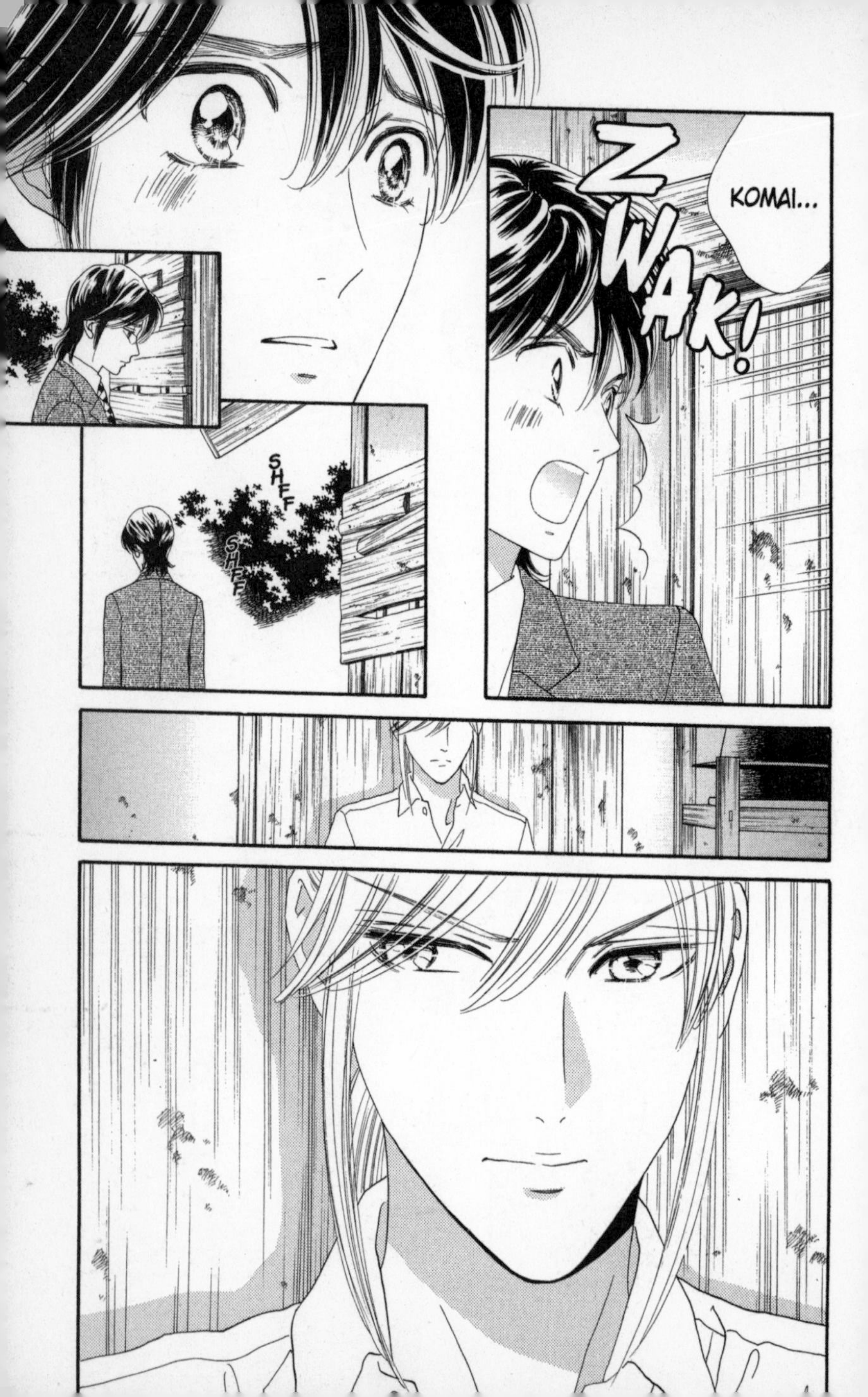
ZWAK!
KOMAI...
SHFF
SHFF

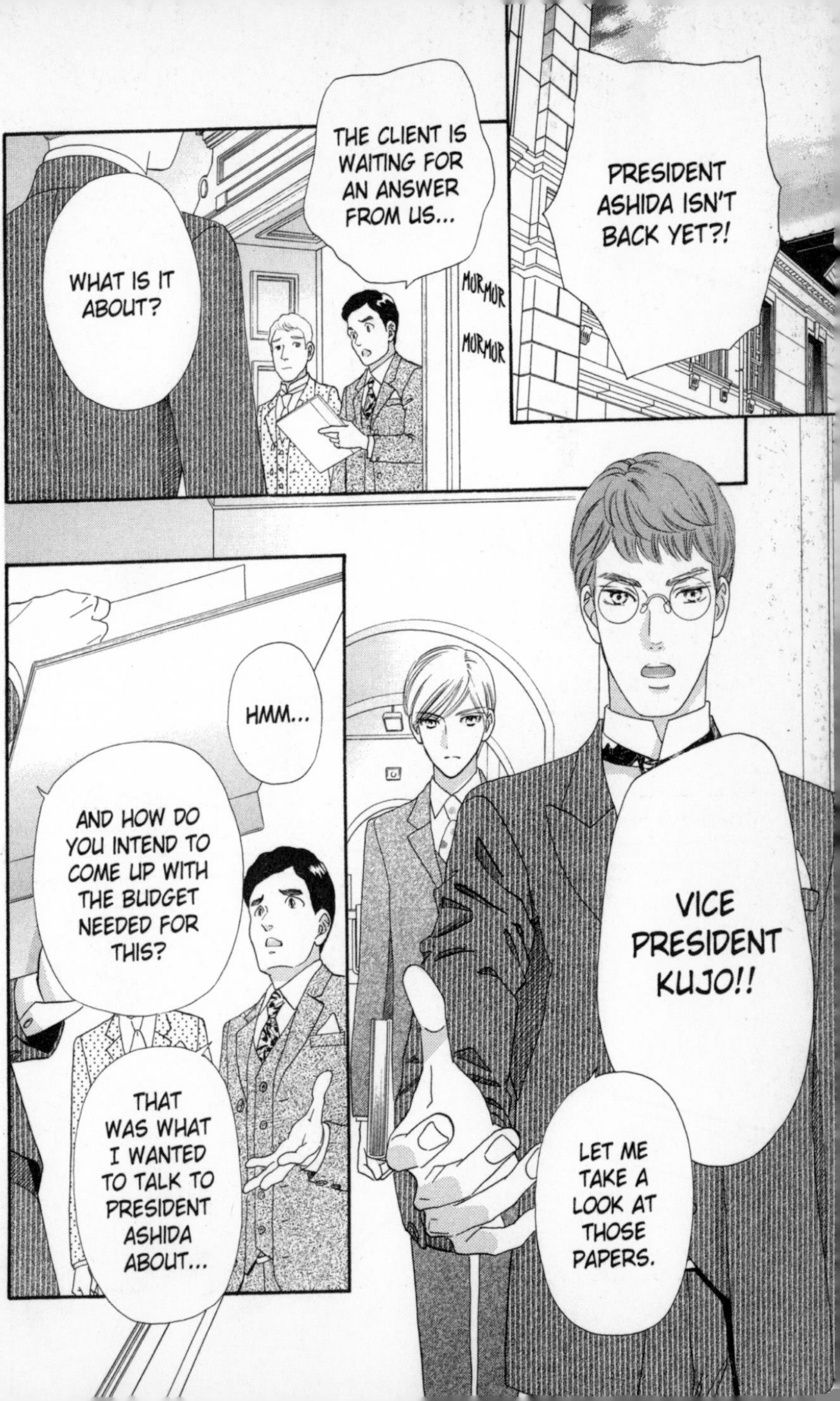
PRESIDENT ASHIDA ISN'T BACK YET?!
THE CLIENT IS WAITING FOR AN ANSWER FROM US...
MURMUR
MURMUR
WHAT IS IT ABOUT?
VICE PRESIDENT KUJO!!
LET ME TAKE A LOOK AT THOSE PAPERS.
HMM...
AND HOW DO YOU INTEND TO COME UP WITH THE BUDGET NEEDED FOR THIS?
THAT WAS WHAT I WANTED TO TALK TO PRESIDENT ASHIDA ABOUT...

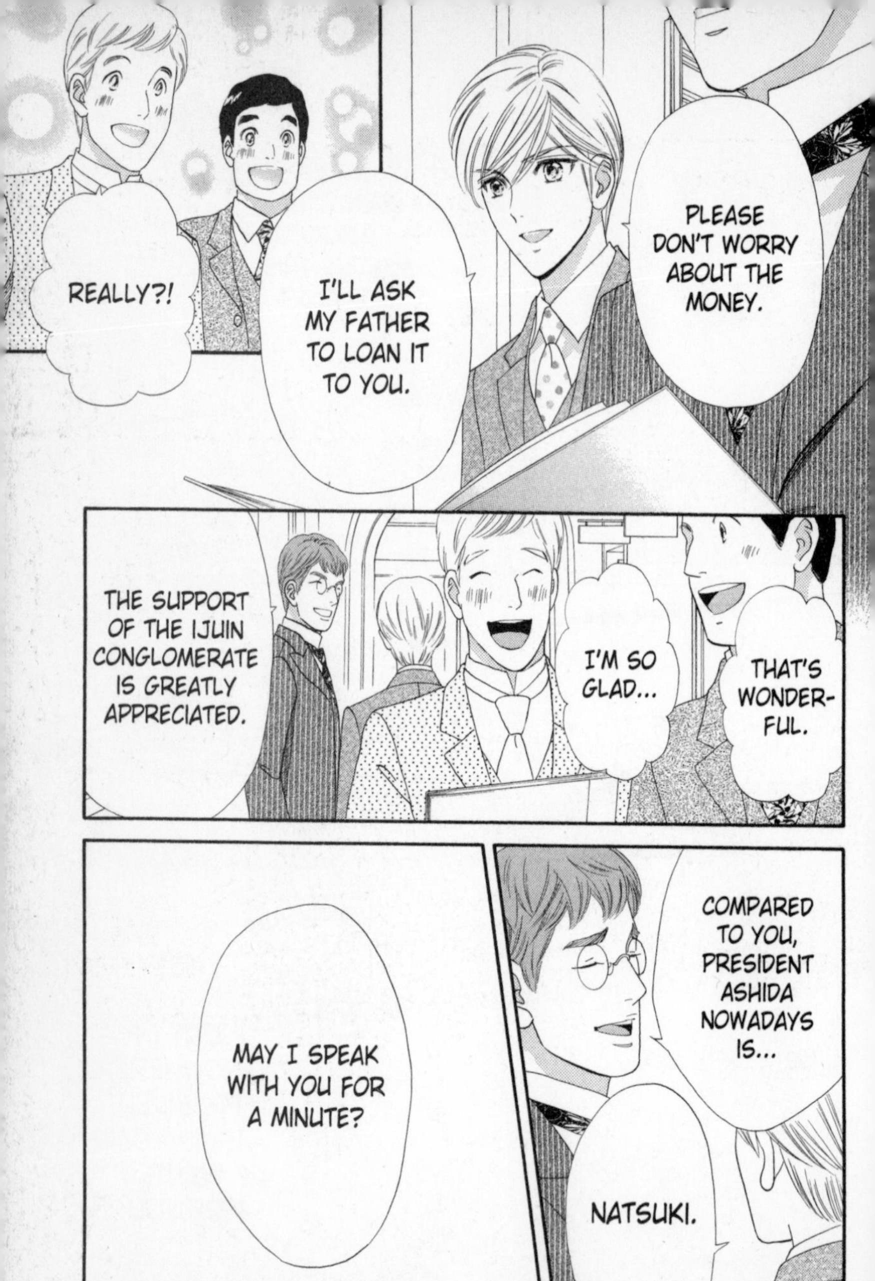
PLEASE DON'T WORRY ABOUT THE MONEY.
I'LL ASK MY FATHER TO LOAN IT TO YOU.
REALLY?!
THAT'S WONDER-FUL.
I'M SO GLAD...
THE SUPPORT OF THE IJUIN CONGLOMERATE IS GREATLY APPRECIATED.
COMPARED TO YOU, PRESIDENT ASHIDA NOWADAYS IS...
NATSUKI.
MAY I SPEAK WITH YOU FOR A MINUTE?

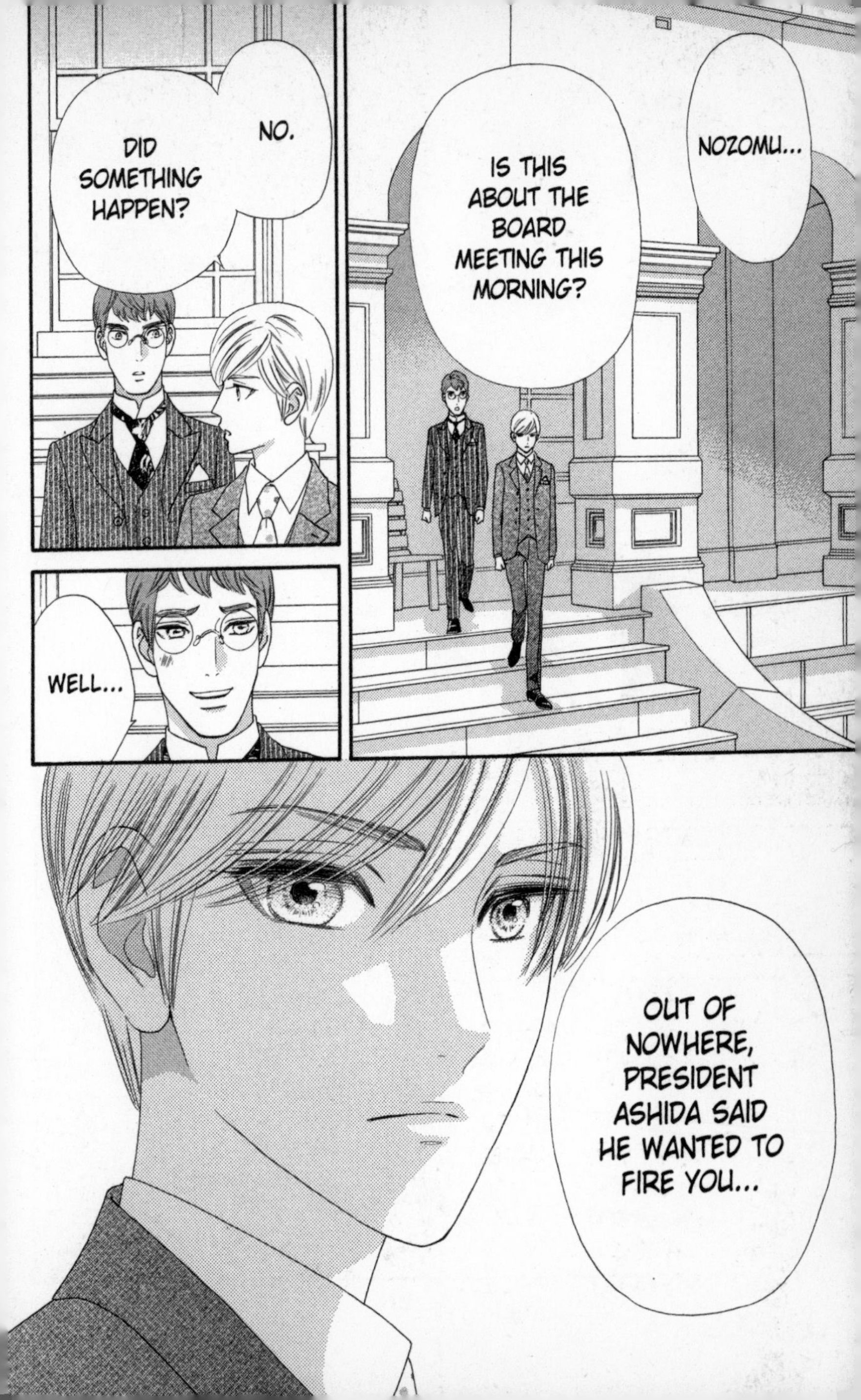
NOZOMU...
IS THIS ABOUT THE BOARD MEETING THIS MORNING?
NO.
DID SOMETHING HAPPEN?
WELL...
OUT OF NOWHERE, PRESIDENT ASHIDA SAID HE WANTED TO FIRE YOU...

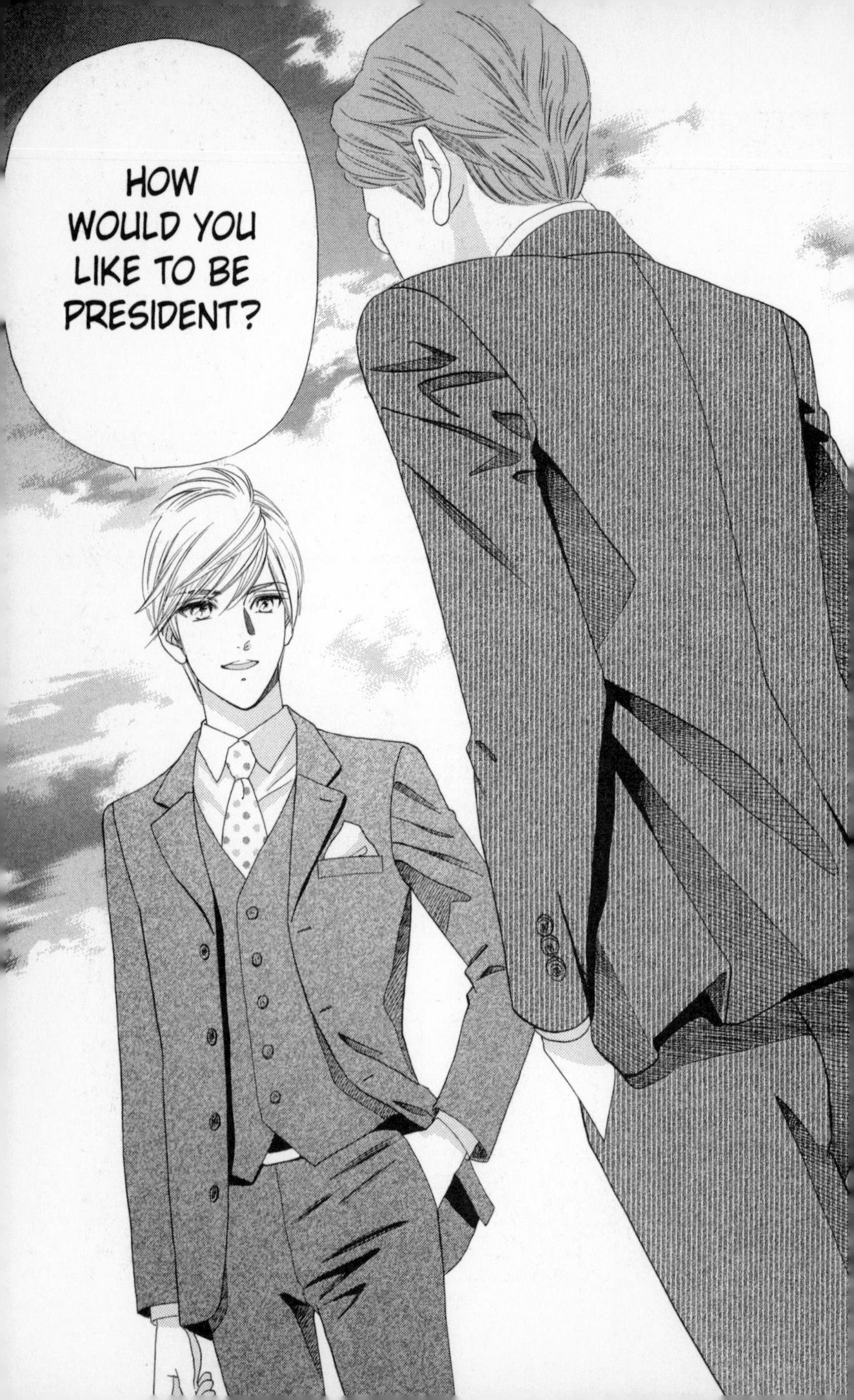
HOW WOULD YOU LIKE TO BE PRESIDENT?

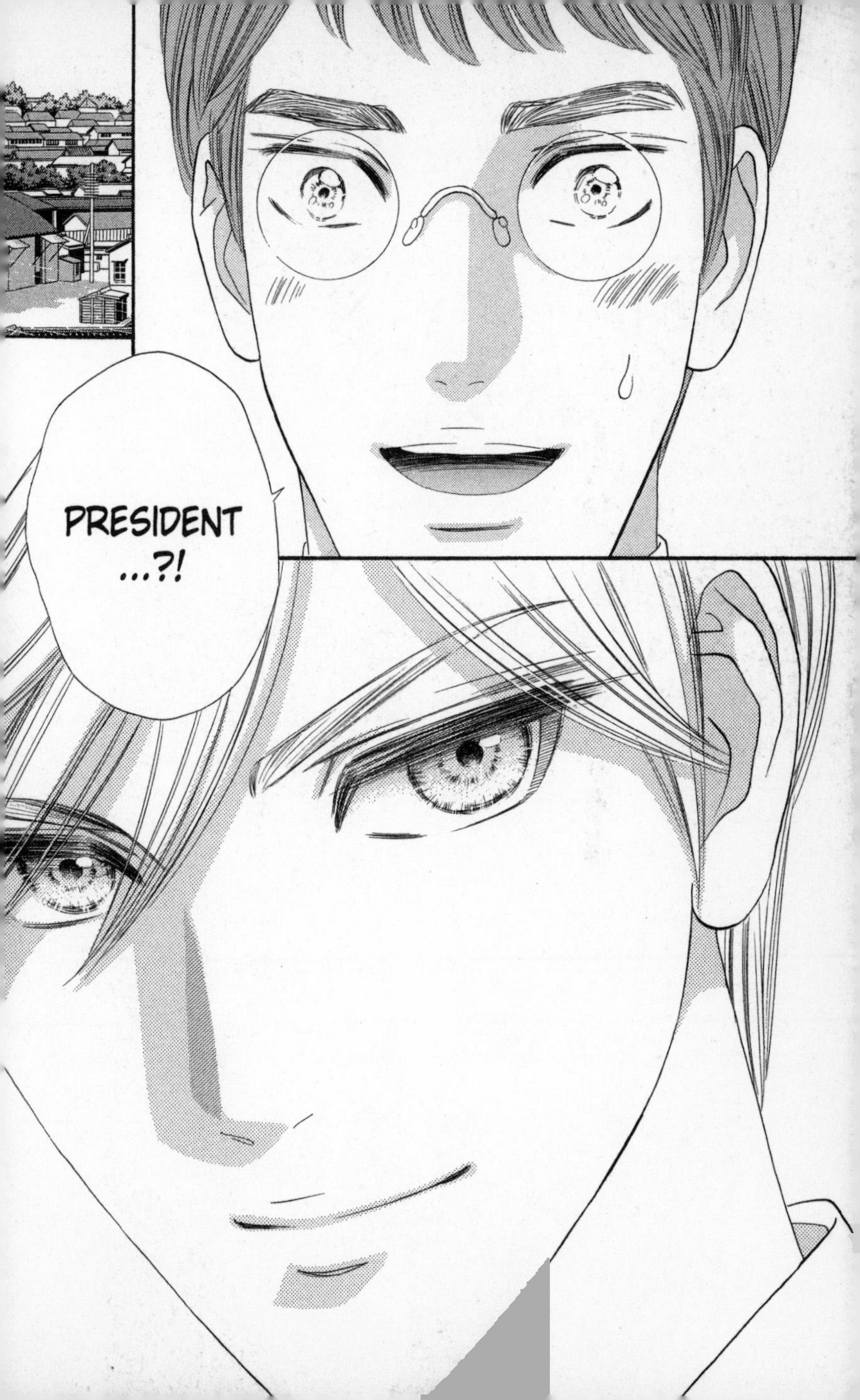
PRESIDENT ...?!

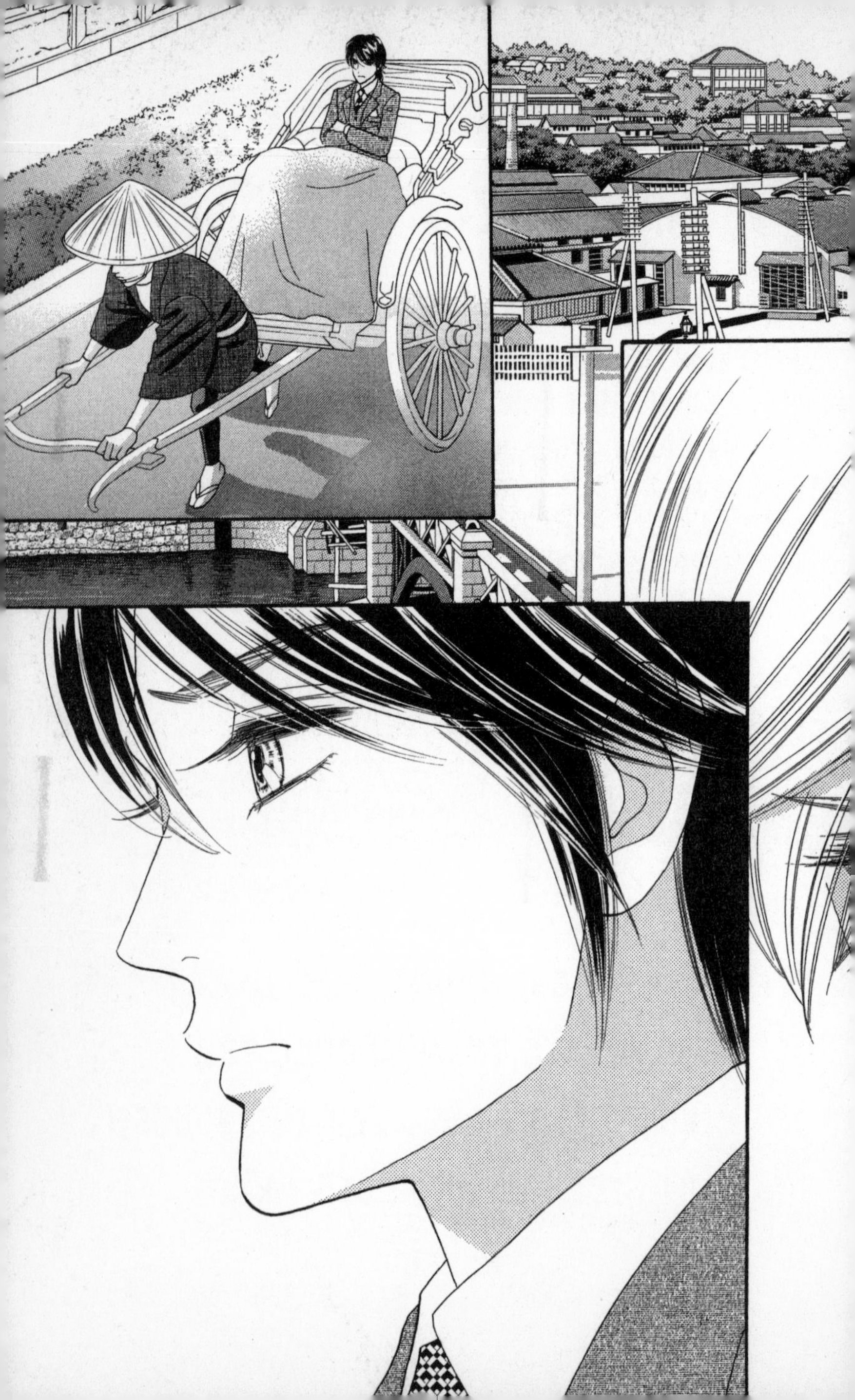

GREETINGS ~

✿ HELLO, IT'S UE-RIN.
MY DAUGHTER IS NOW A LITTLE OVER ONE.
NOW THAT SHE'S TODDLING AROUND,
I CAN'T TAKE MY EYES OFF HER.

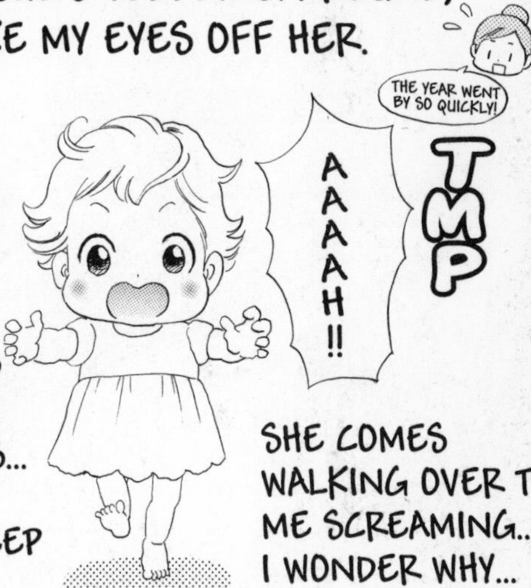
THE YEAR WENT BY SO QUICKLY!
TMP
AAAAAH!!
TMP

SHE HAS BOTH ARMS STRETCHED OUT BEFORE HER WHEN SHE WALKS... I WONDER WHY? MAYBE IT'S TO KEEP HER BALANCE.

SHE COMES WALKING OVER TO ME SCREAMING... I WONDER WHY...

✿ I DON'T EVEN HAVE TIME TO *FAINT*, SO I'D LIKE TO INTRODUCE THE LOCATIONS I USED FOR THE HOUSES IN *STEPPING ON ROSES* NEXT!!

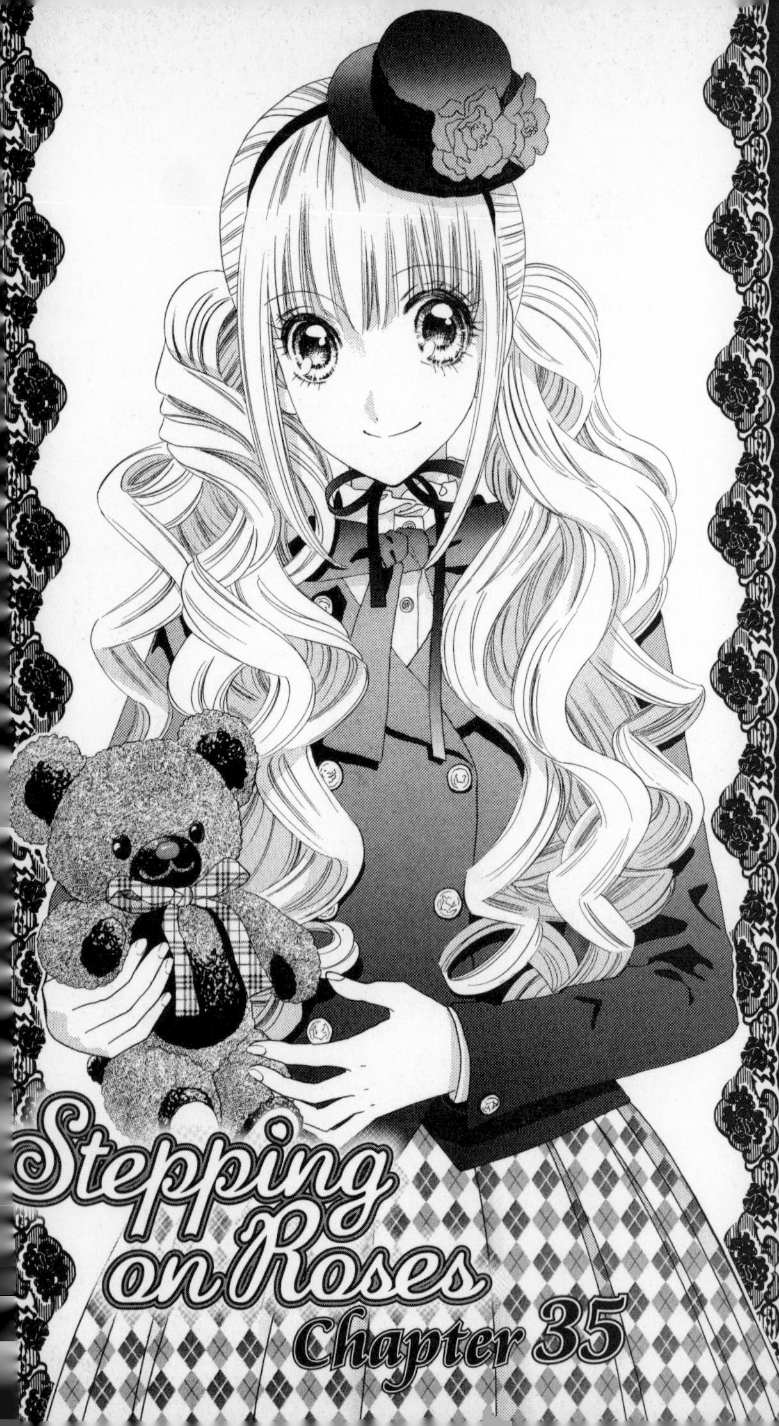
Stepping on Roses
Chapter 35

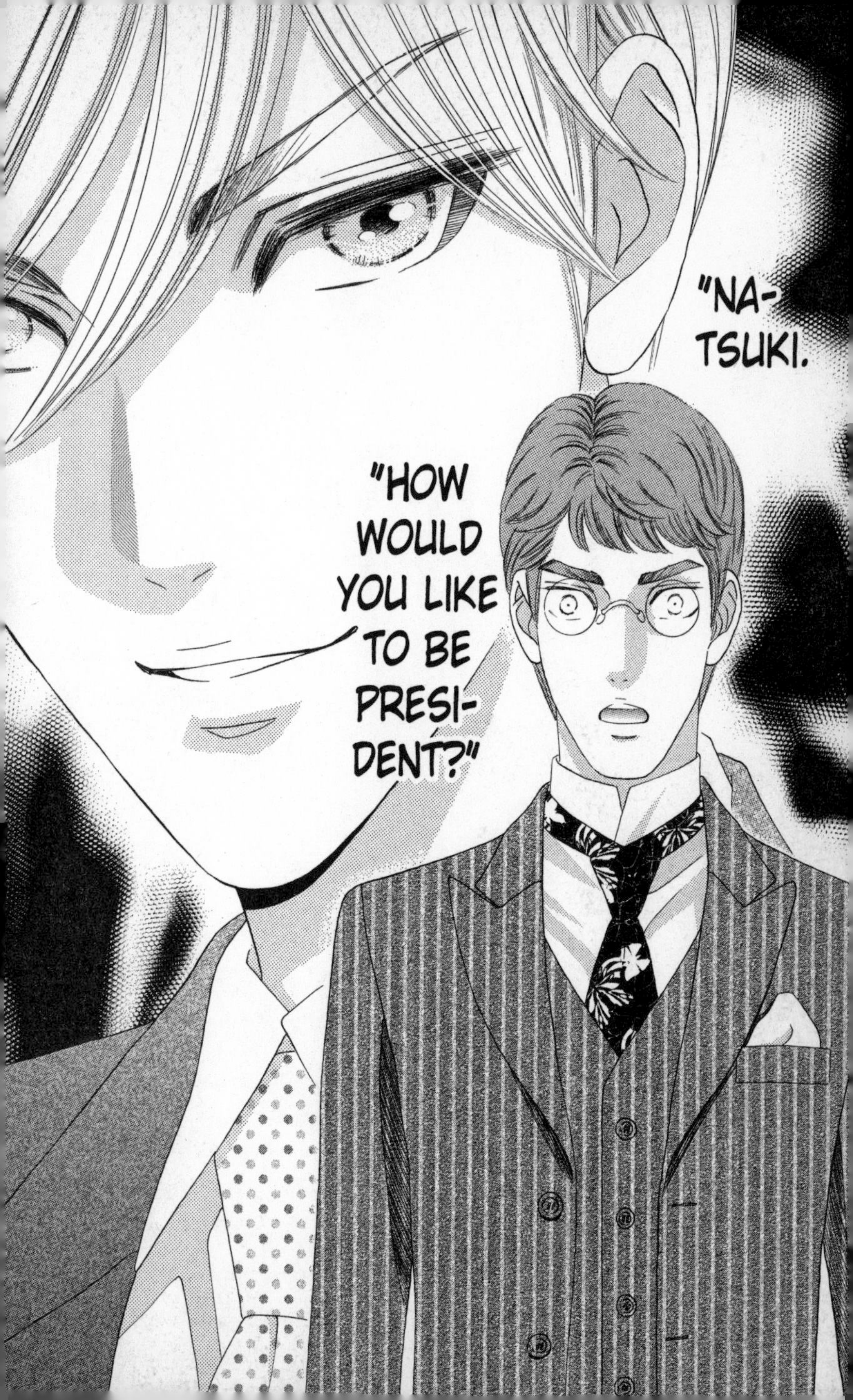
"NA-TSUKI.
"HOW WOULD YOU LIKE TO BE PRESI-DENT?"

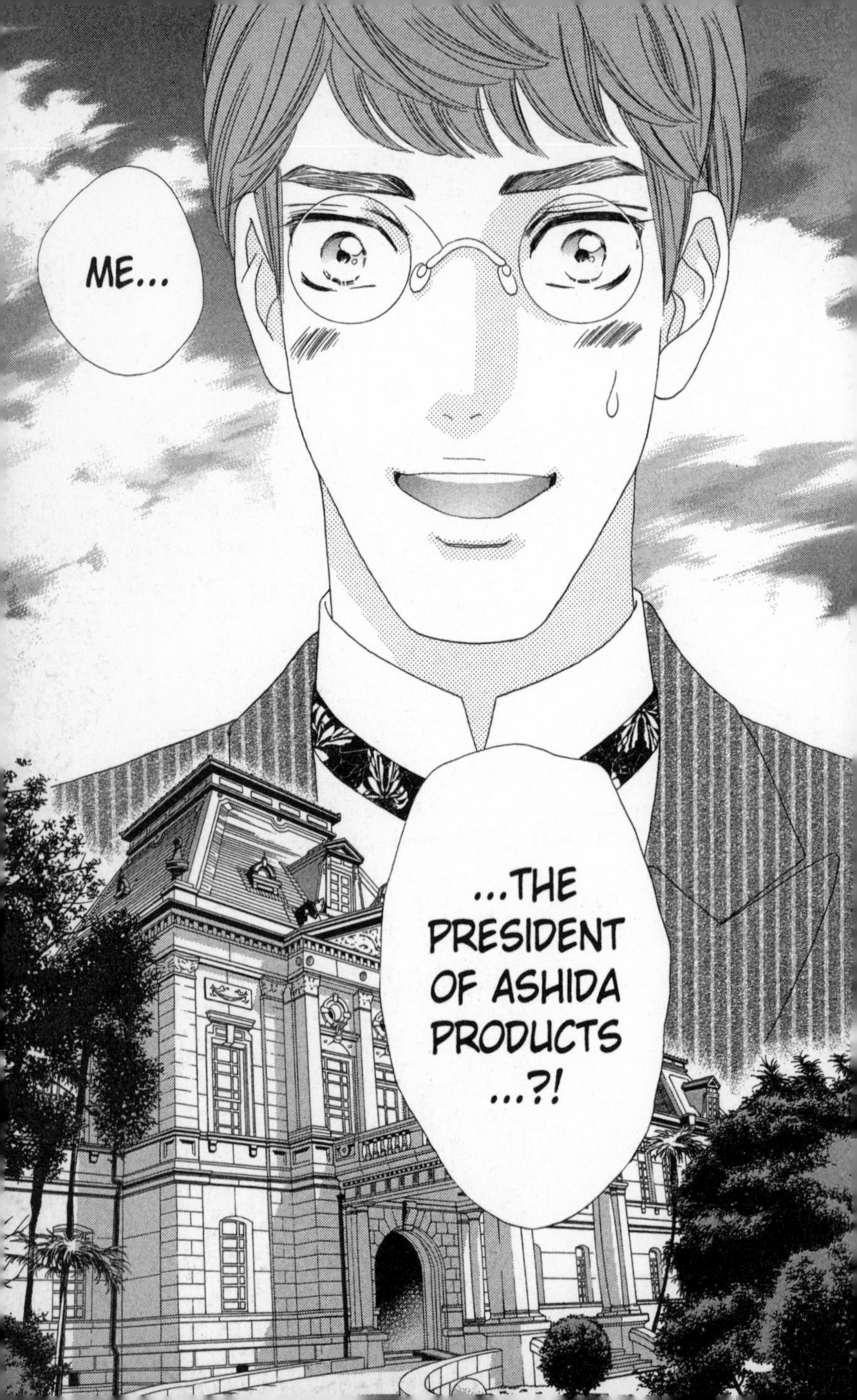
ME...
...THE PRESIDENT OF ASHIDA PRODUCTS ...?!

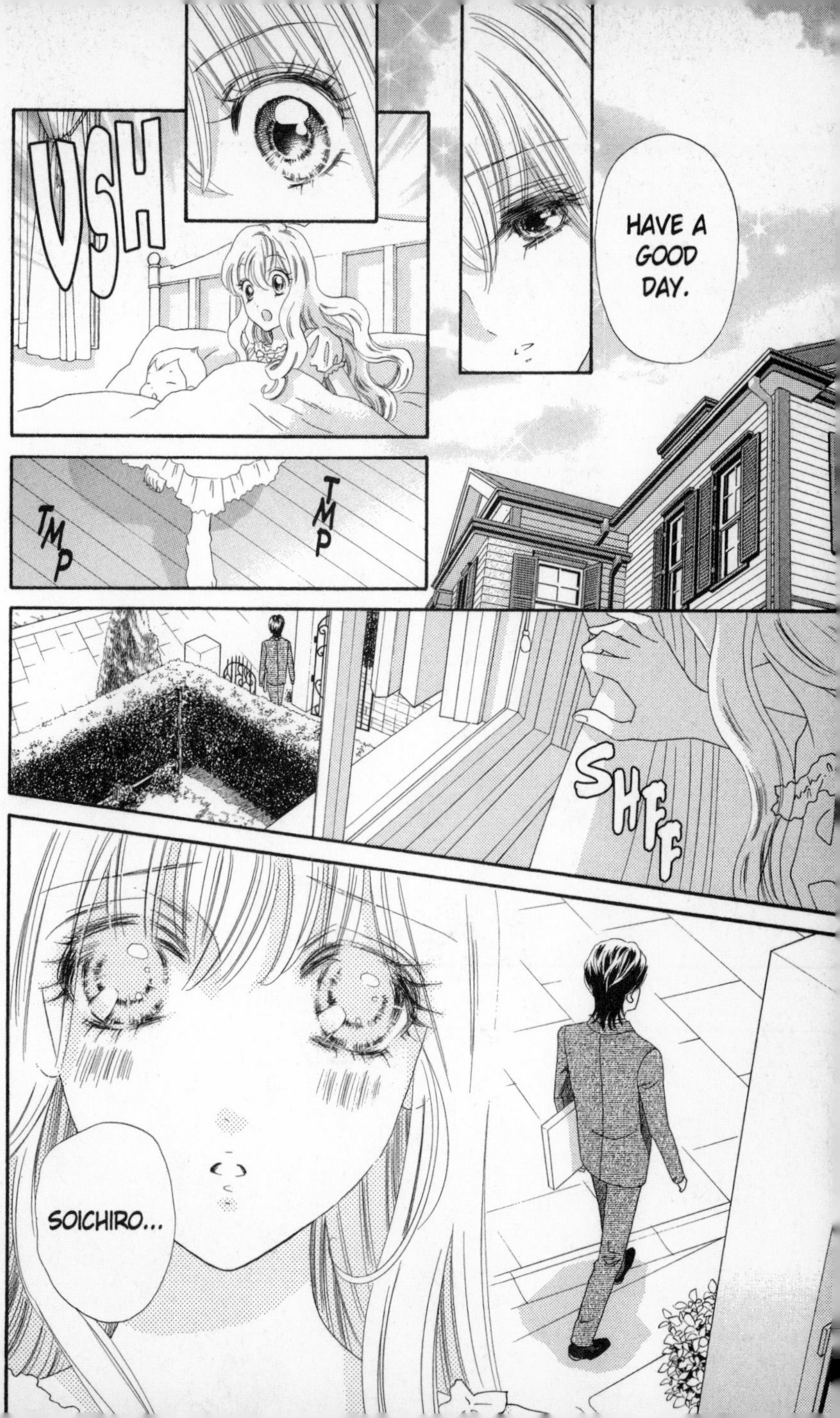
HAVE A GOOD DAY.
VSH
TMP TMP
SHFF
SOICHIRO...

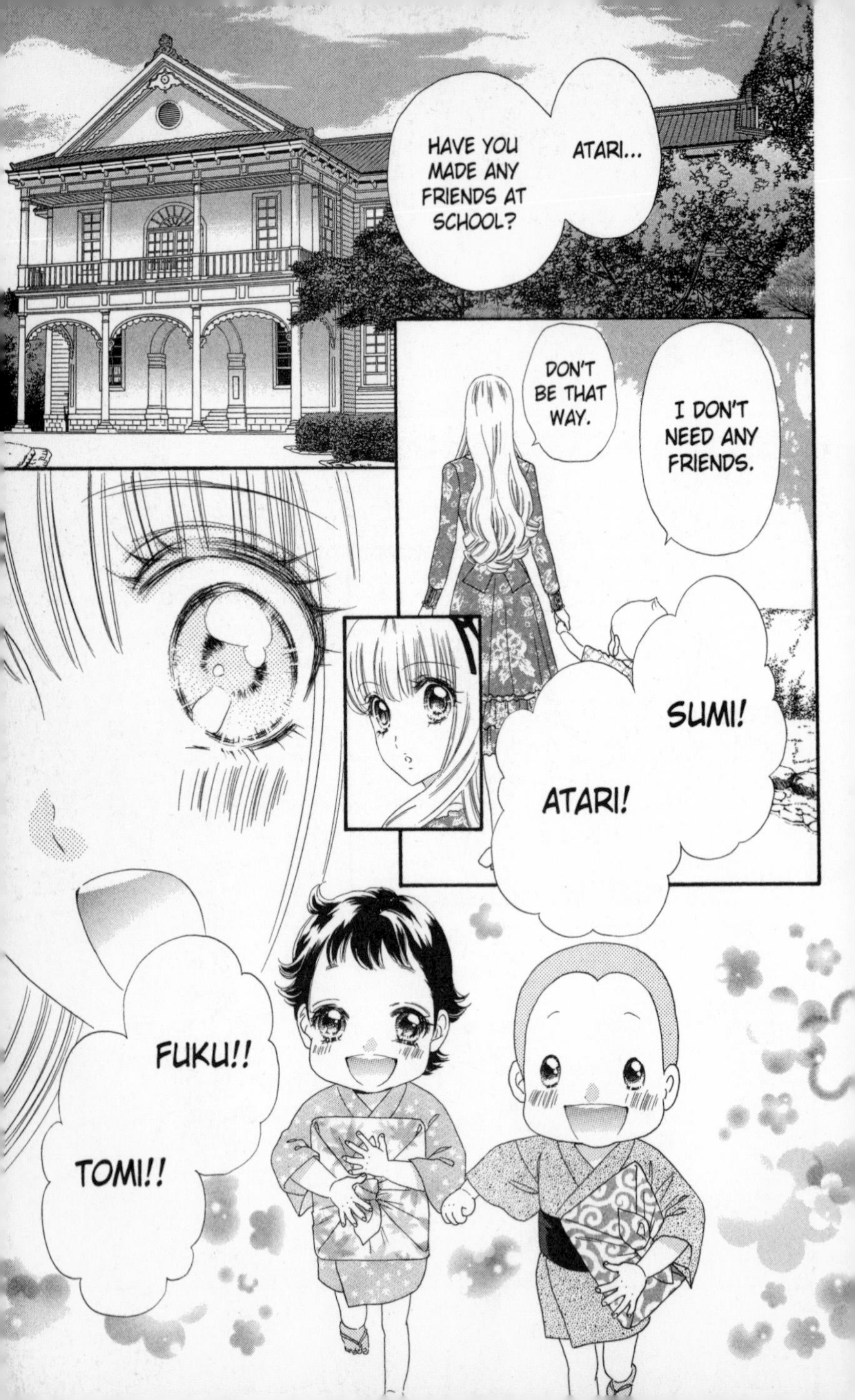
ATARI...
HAVE YOU MADE ANY FRIENDS AT SCHOOL?
I DON'T NEED ANY FRIENDS.
DON'T BE THAT WAY.
SUMI!
ATARI!
FUKU!!
TOMI!!

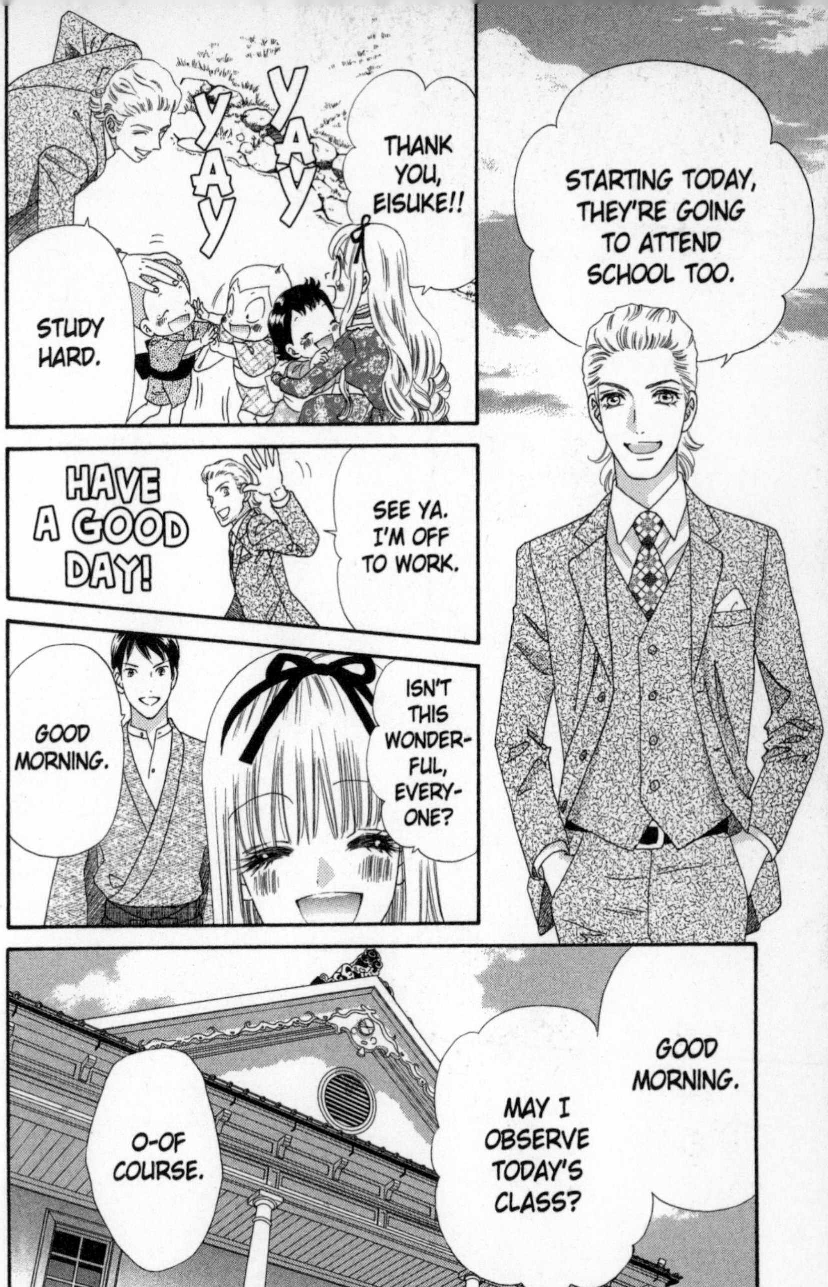
STARTING TODAY, THEY'RE GOING TO ATTEND SCHOOL TOO.
THANK YOU, EISUKE!!
YAY
YAY
STUDY HARD.
SEE YA. I'M OFF TO WORK.
HAVE A GOOD DAY!
ISN'T THIS WONDER-FUL, EVERY-ONE?
GOOD MORNING.
GOOD MORNING.
MAY I OBSERVE TODAY'S CLASS?
O-OF COURSE.

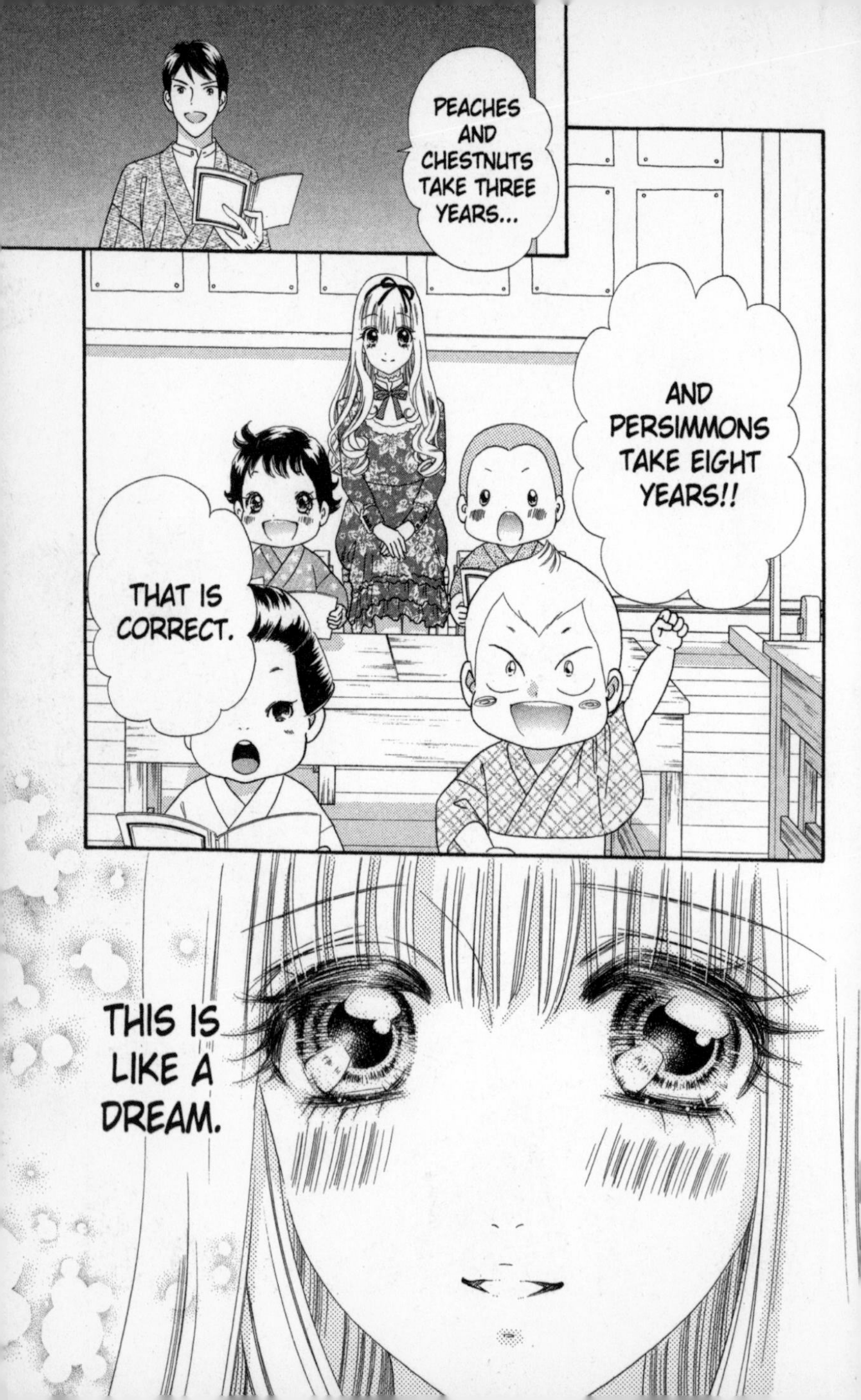
PEACHES AND CHESTNUTS TAKE THREE YEARS...
AND PERSIMMONS TAKE EIGHT YEARS!!
THAT IS CORRECT.
THIS IS LIKE A DREAM.

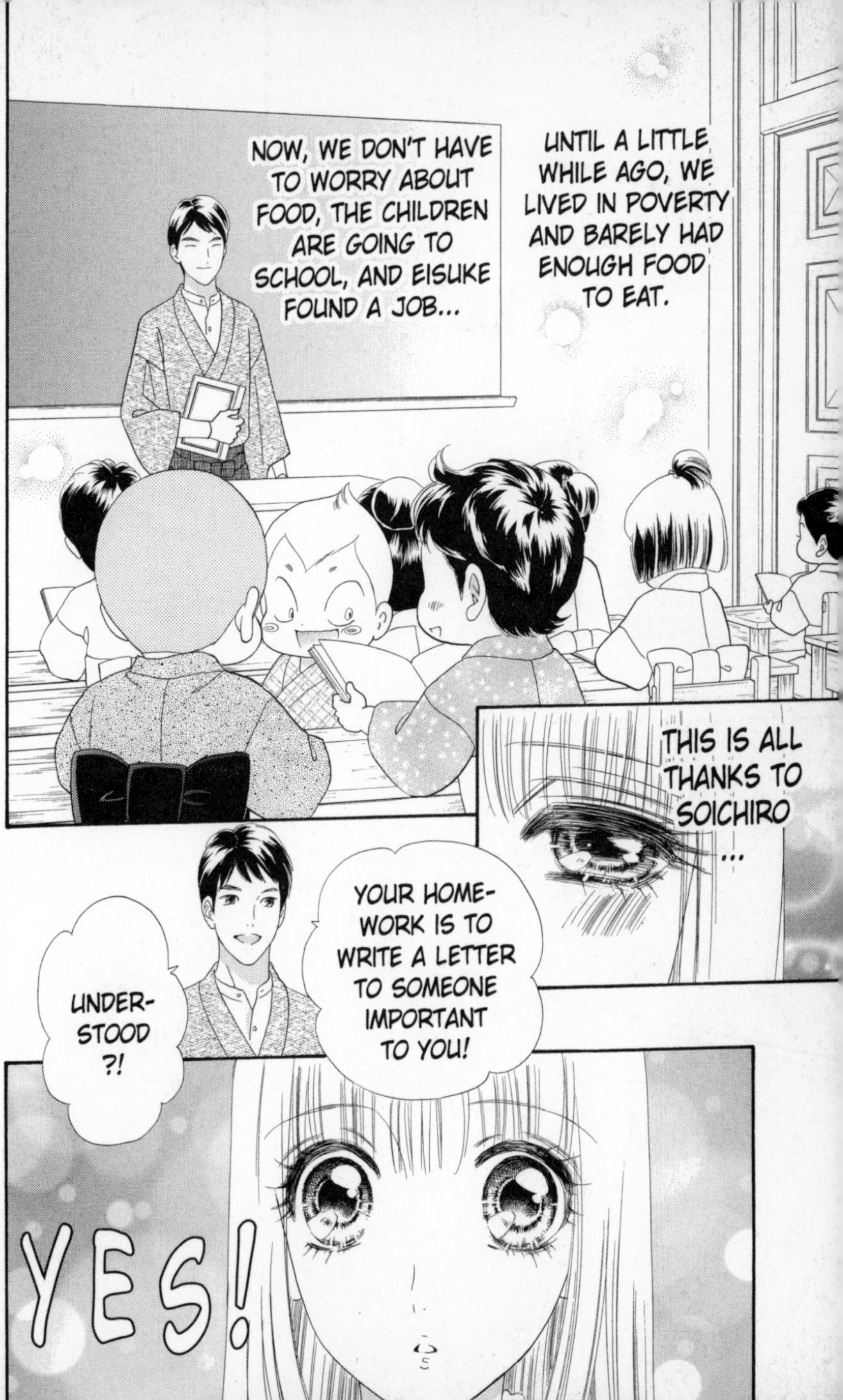
UNTIL A LITTLE WHILE AGO, WE LIVED IN POVERTY AND BARELY HAD ENOUGH FOOD TO EAT.
NOW, WE DON'T HAVE TO WORRY ABOUT FOOD, THE CHILDREN ARE GOING TO SCHOOL, AND EISUKE FOUND A JOB...
THIS IS ALL THANKS TO SOICHIRO ...
YOUR HOME-WORK IS TO WRITE A LETTER TO SOMEONE IMPORTANT TO YOU!
UNDER-STOOD ?!
YES!

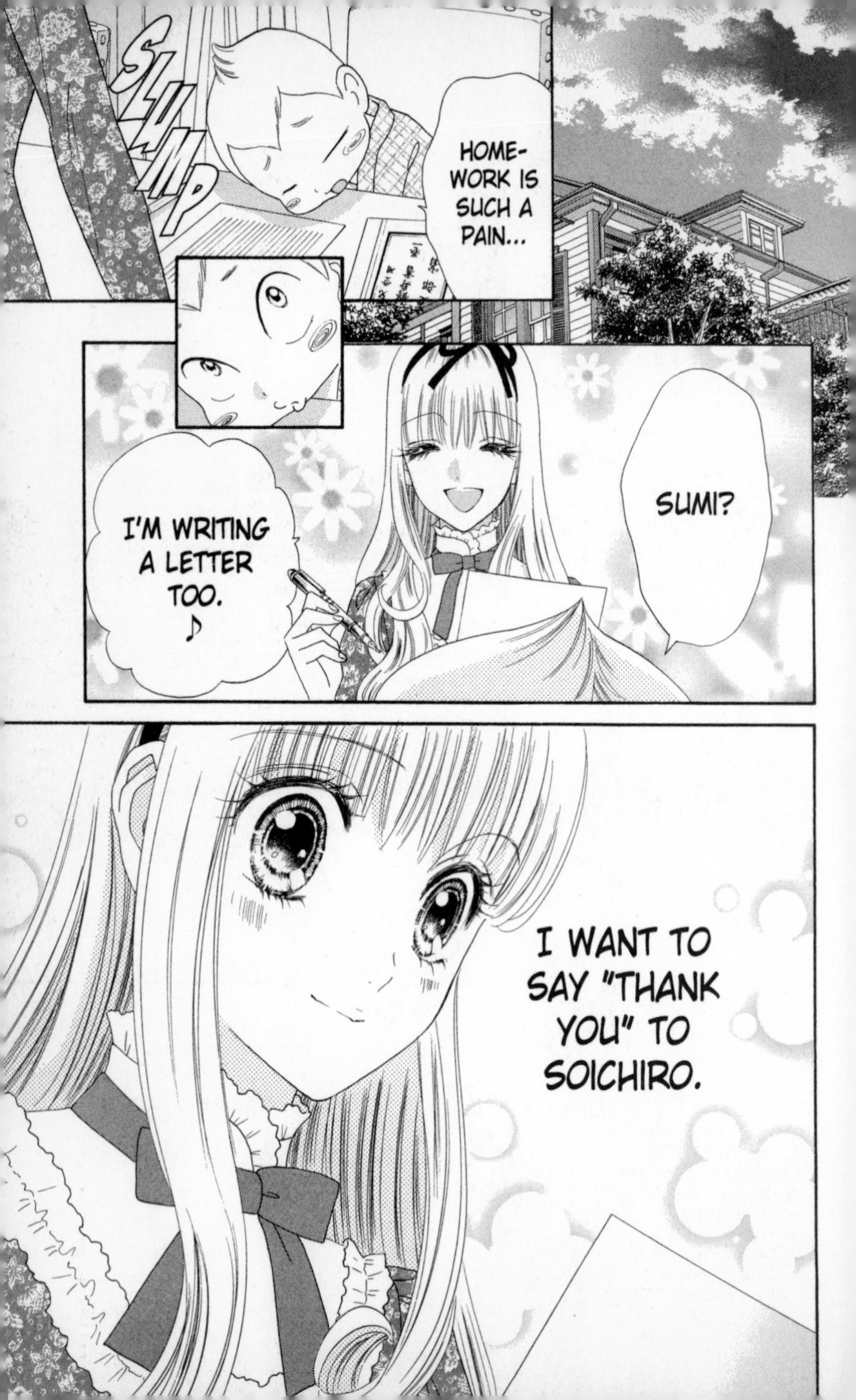
HOME-WORK IS SUCH A PAIN...
SLUMP
SUMI?
I'M WRITING A LETTER TOO. ♪
I WANT TO SAY "THANK YOU" TO SOICHIRO.

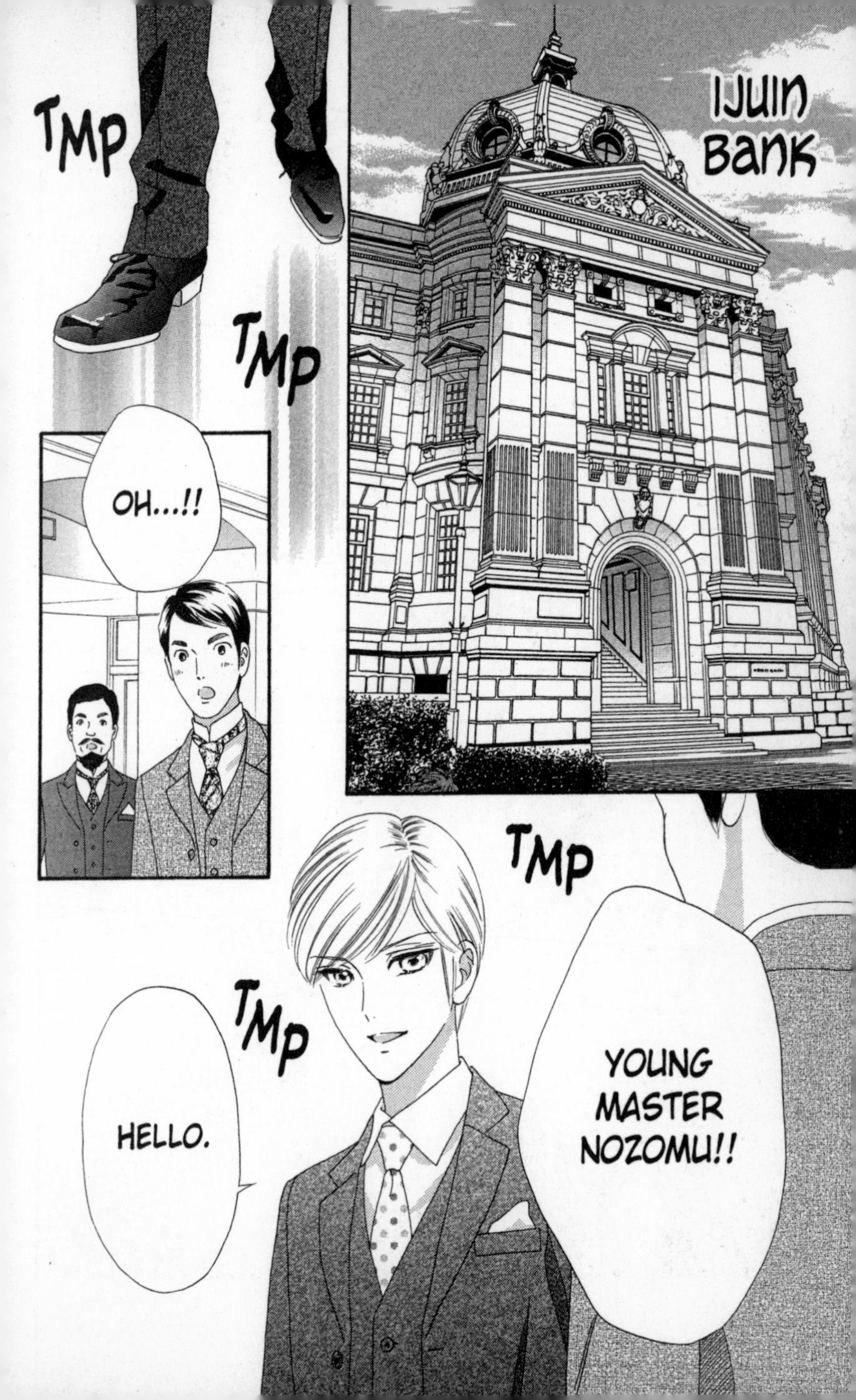
IJUIN BANK
TMP
TMP
OH...!!
TMP
YOUNG MASTER NOZOMU!!
TMP
HELLO.

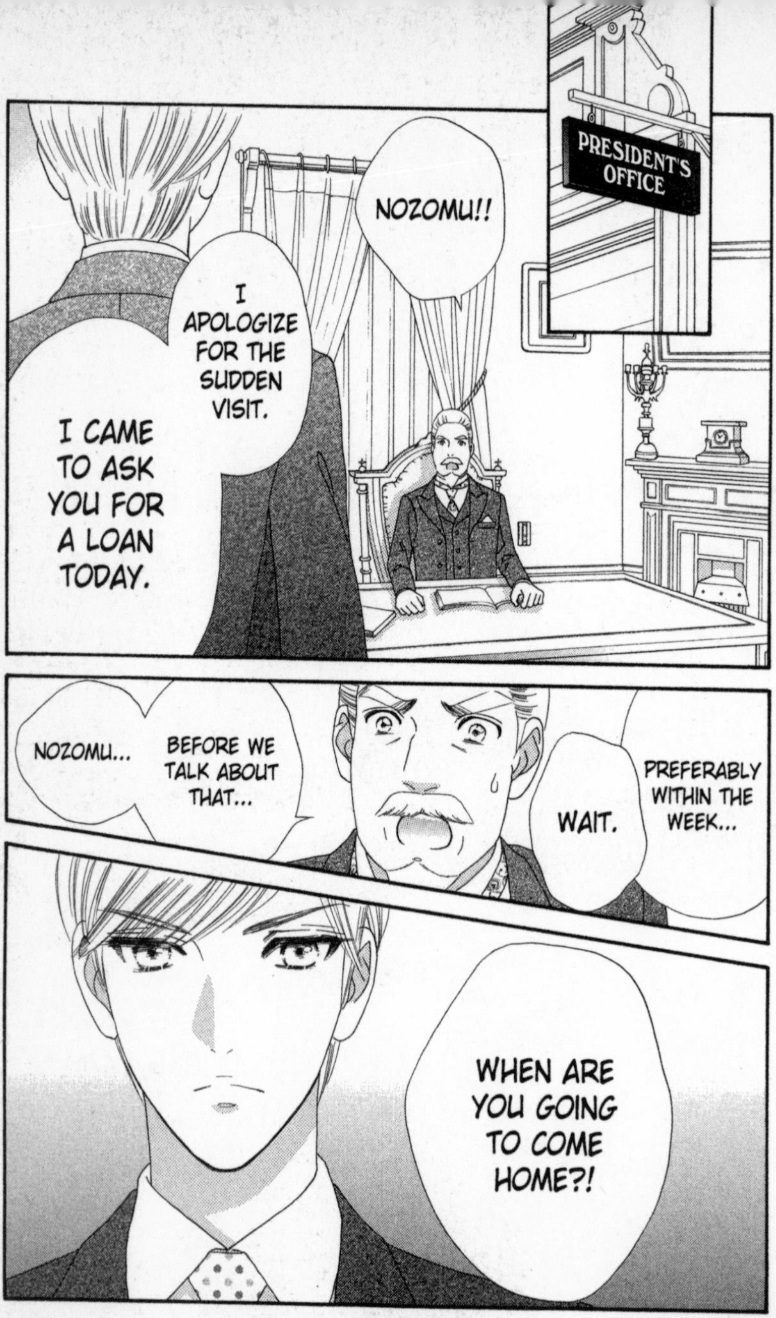
PRESIDENT'S OFFICE
NOZOMU!!
I APOLOGIZE FOR THE SUDDEN VISIT.
I CAME TO ASK YOU FOR A LOAN TODAY.
PREFERABLY WITHIN THE WEEK...
WAIT.
NOZOMU...
BEFORE WE TALK ABOUT THAT...
WHEN ARE YOU GOING TO COME HOME?!

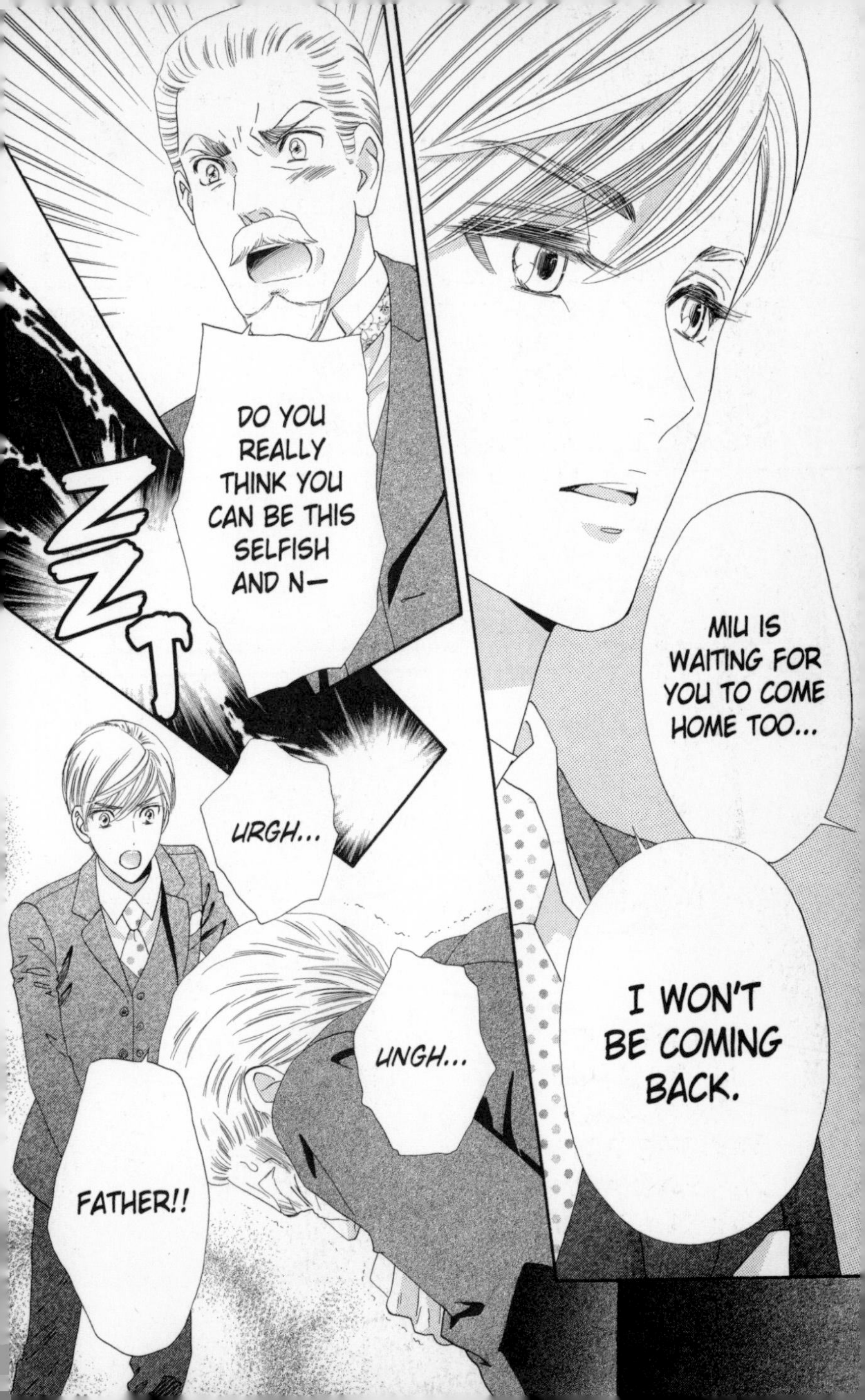
MIU IS WAITING FOR YOU TO COME HOME TOO...
I WON'T BE COMING BACK.
DO YOU REALLY THINK YOU CAN BE THIS SELFISH AND N—
URGH...
UNGH...
FATHER!!

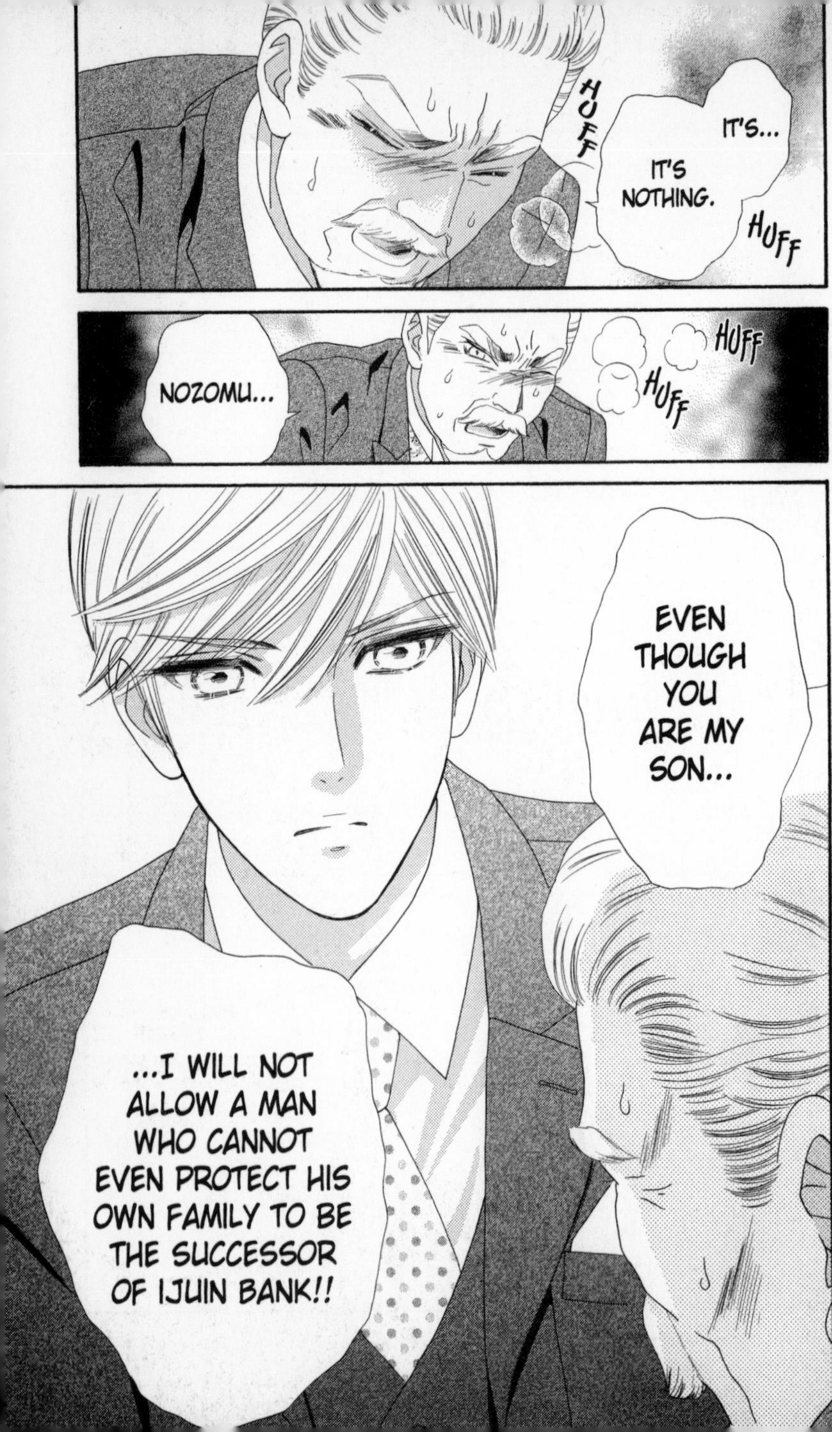
IT'S... IT'S NOTHING.
HUFF
HUFF
HUFF
HUFF
NOZOMU...
EVEN THOUGH YOU ARE MY SON...
...I WILL NOT ALLOW A MAN WHO CANNOT EVEN PROTECT HIS OWN FAMILY TO BE THE SUCCESSOR OF IJUIN BANK!!

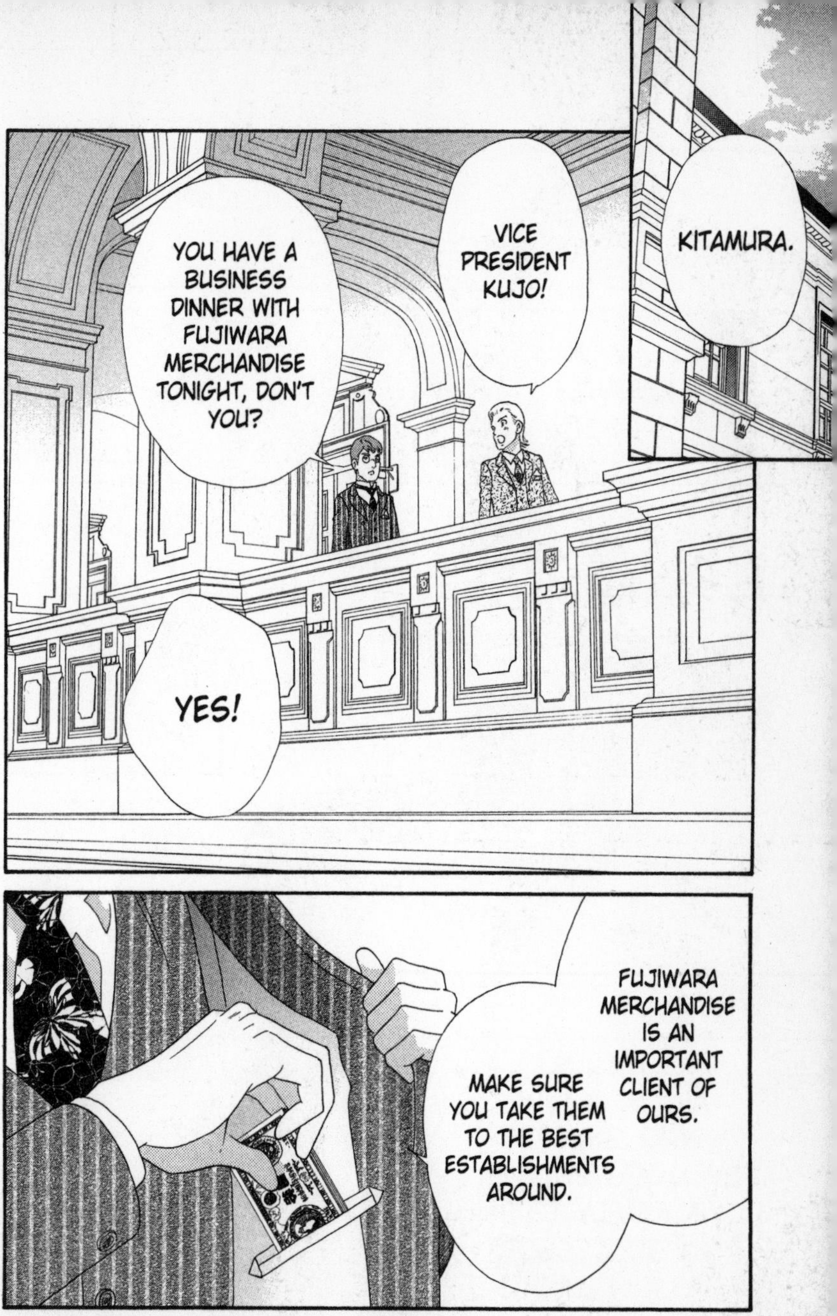
KITAMURA.
VICE PRESIDENT KUJO!
YOU HAVE A BUSINESS DINNER WITH FUJIWARA MERCHANDISE TONIGHT, DON'T YOU?
YES!
FUJIWARA MERCHANDISE IS AN IMPORTANT CLIENT OF OURS.
MAKE SURE YOU TAKE THEM TO THE BEST ESTABLISHMENTS AROUND.

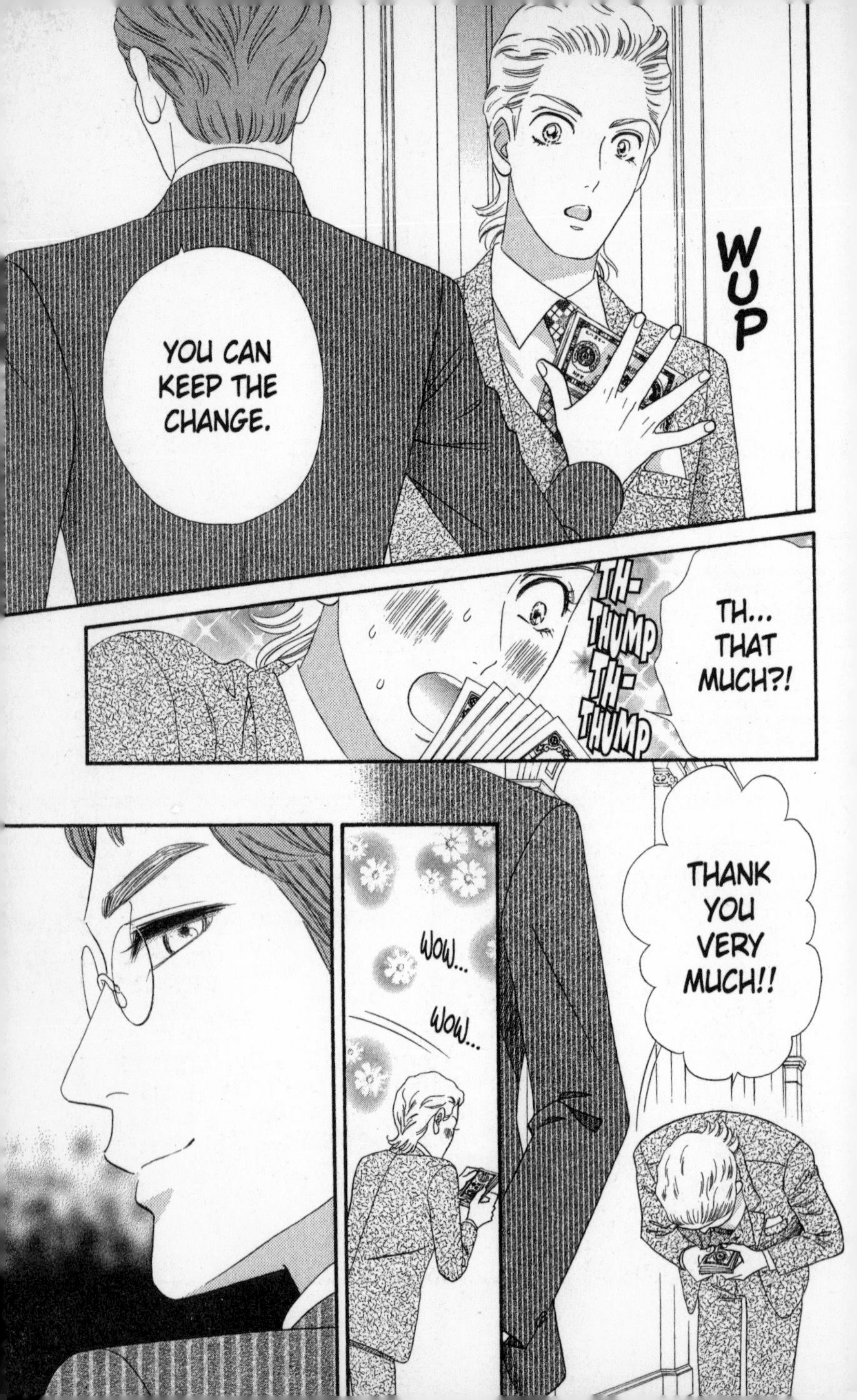
WUP
YOU CAN KEEP THE CHANGE.
TH... THAT MUCH?!
TH-THUMP TH-THUMP
THANK YOU VERY MUCH!!
WOW...
WOW...

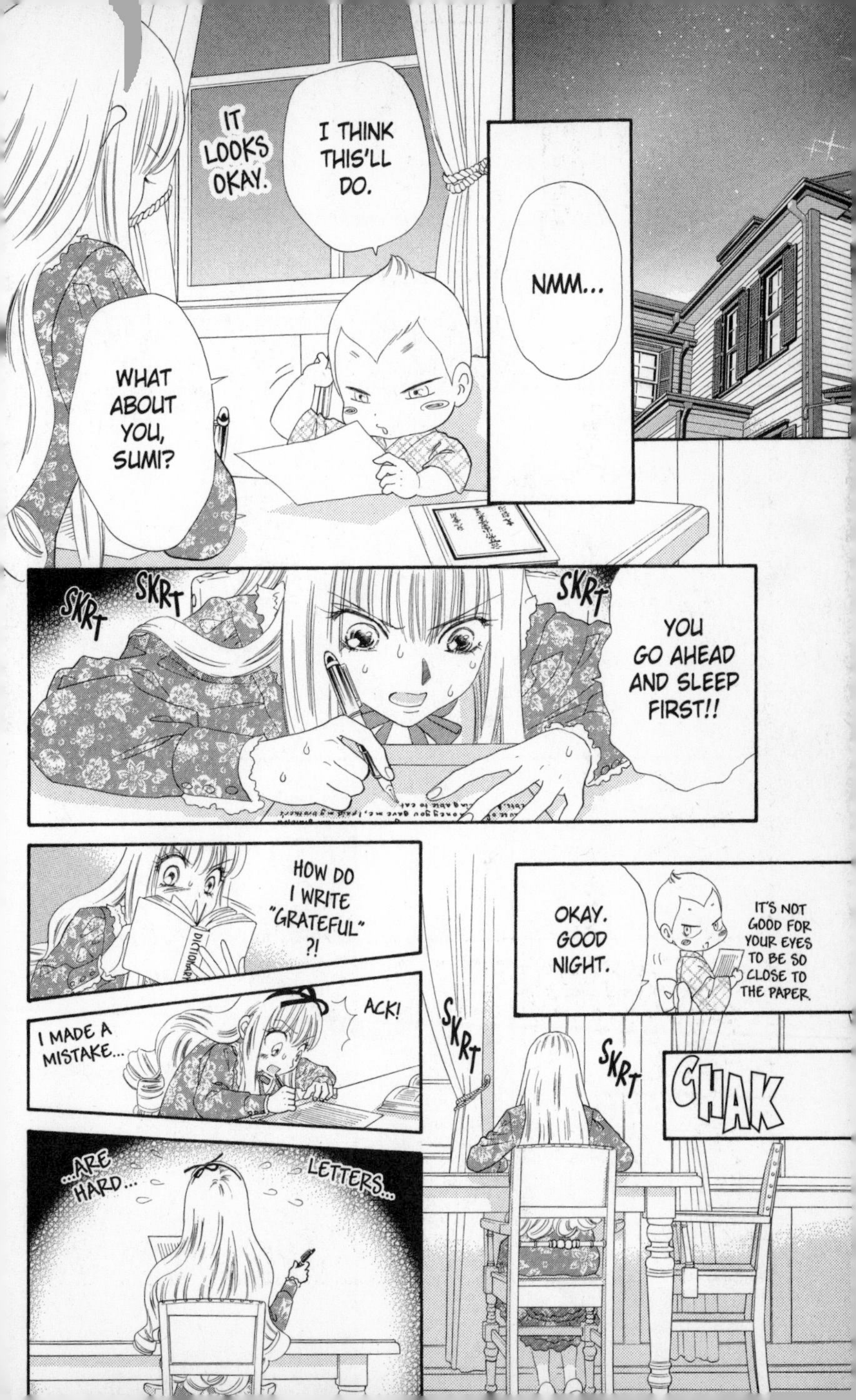
NMM...
I THINK THIS'LL DO.
IT LOOKS OKAY.
WHAT ABOUT YOU, SUMI?
SKRT
YOU GO AHEAD AND SLEEP FIRST!!
SKRT
SKRT
OKAY. GOOD NIGHT.
IT'S NOT GOOD FOR YOUR EYES TO BE SO CLOSE TO THE PAPER.
CHAK
SKRT
SKRT
HOW DO I WRITE "GRATEFUL"?!
DICTIONARY
ACK!
I MADE A MISTAKE...
LETTERS...
...ARE HARD...

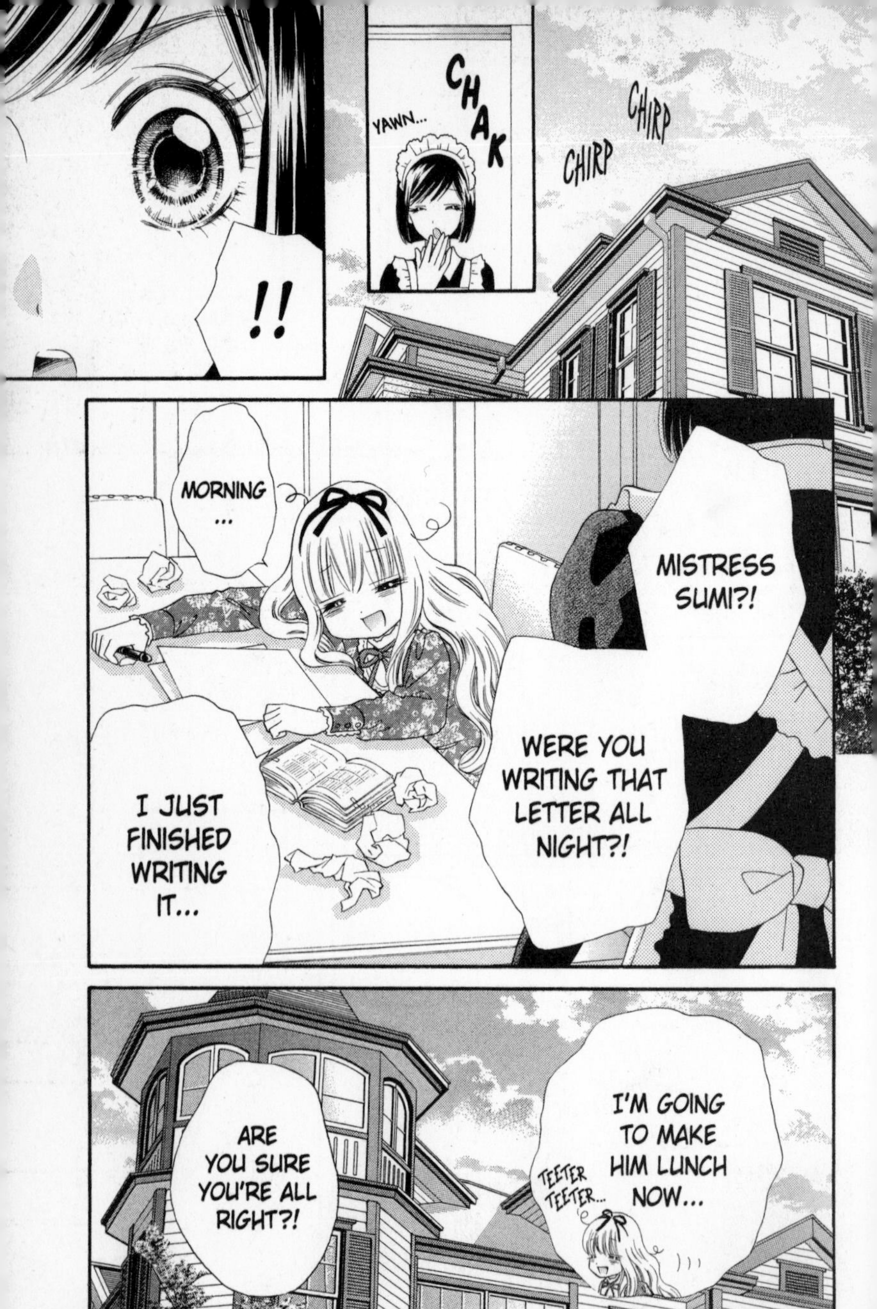
CHIRP
CHIRP
CHAK
YAWN...
!!
MISTRESS SUMI?!
MORNING...
WERE YOU WRITING THAT LETTER ALL NIGHT?!
I JUST FINISHED WRITING IT...
I'M GOING TO MAKE HIM LUNCH NOW...
TEETER TEETER...
ARE YOU SURE YOU'RE ALL RIGHT?!

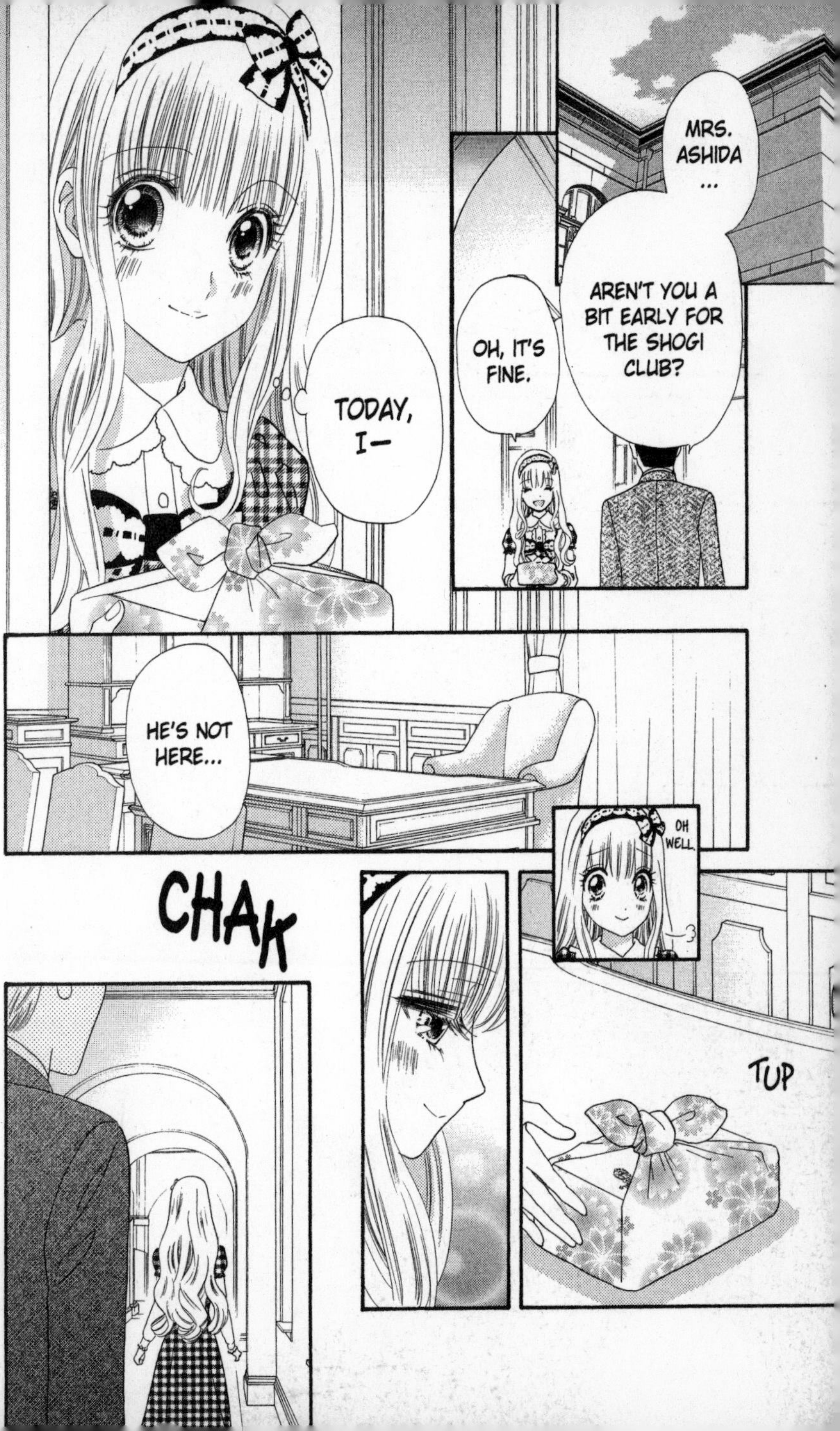
MRS. ASHIDA ...
AREN'T YOU A BIT EARLY FOR THE SHOGI CLUB?
OH, IT'S FINE.
TODAY, I—
HE'S NOT HERE...
OH WELL.
TUP
CHAK

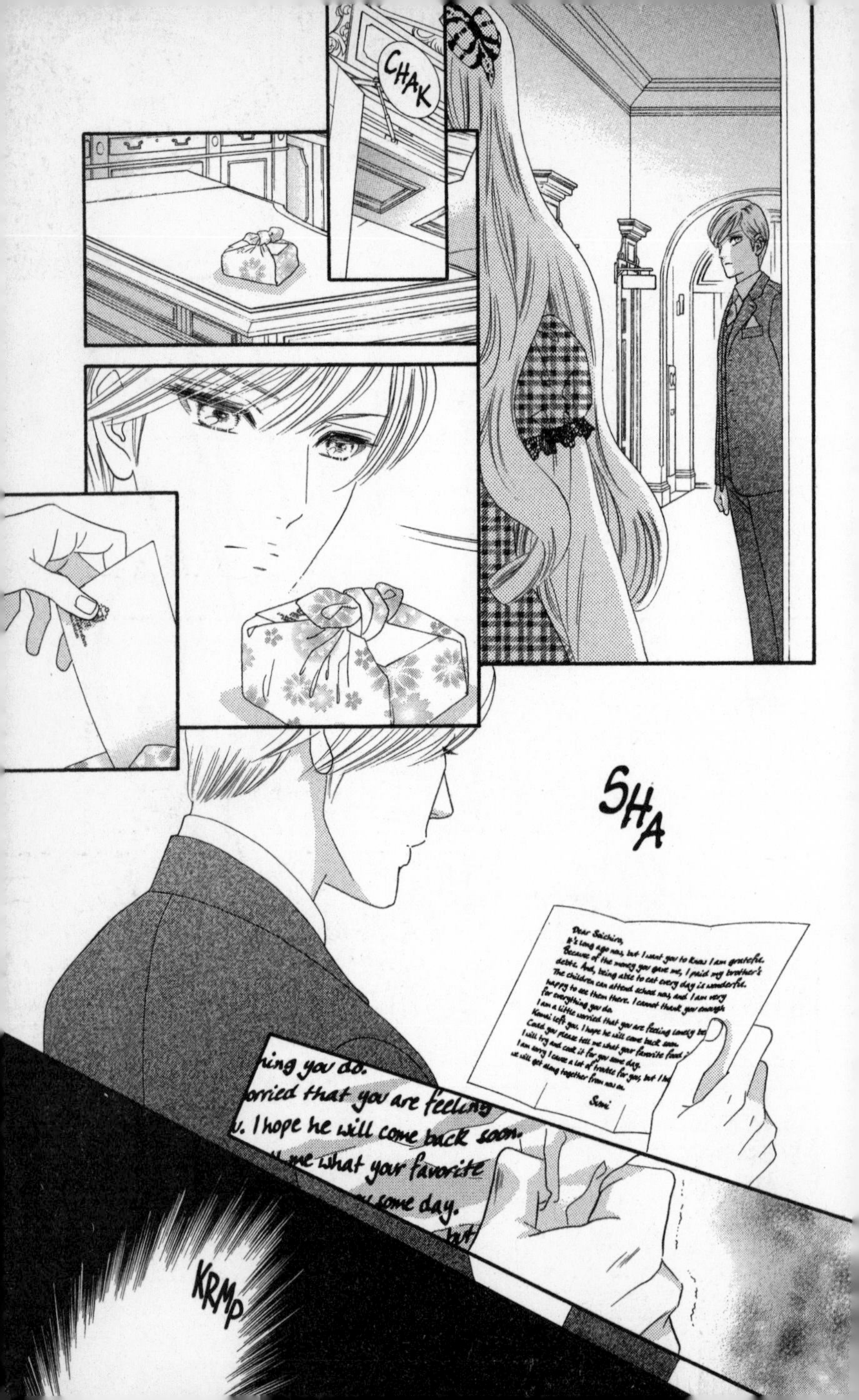
CHAK
SHA
Dear Seichiro,
It's long ago now, but I want you to know I am grateful.
Because of the money you gave me, I paid my brother's
debts. And, being able to eat every day is wonderful.
The children can attend school now, and I am very
happy to see them there. I cannot thank you enough
for everything you do.
I am a little worried that you are feeling lonely be
Kawai left you. I hope he will come back soon.
Could you please tell me what your favorite food
I will try and cook it for you some day.
I am sorry I cause a lot of trouble for you, but I h
we will get along together from now on.
Sumi
hing you do.
orried that you are feeling
u. I hope he will come back soon.
ll me what your favorite
u some day.
but
KRMP

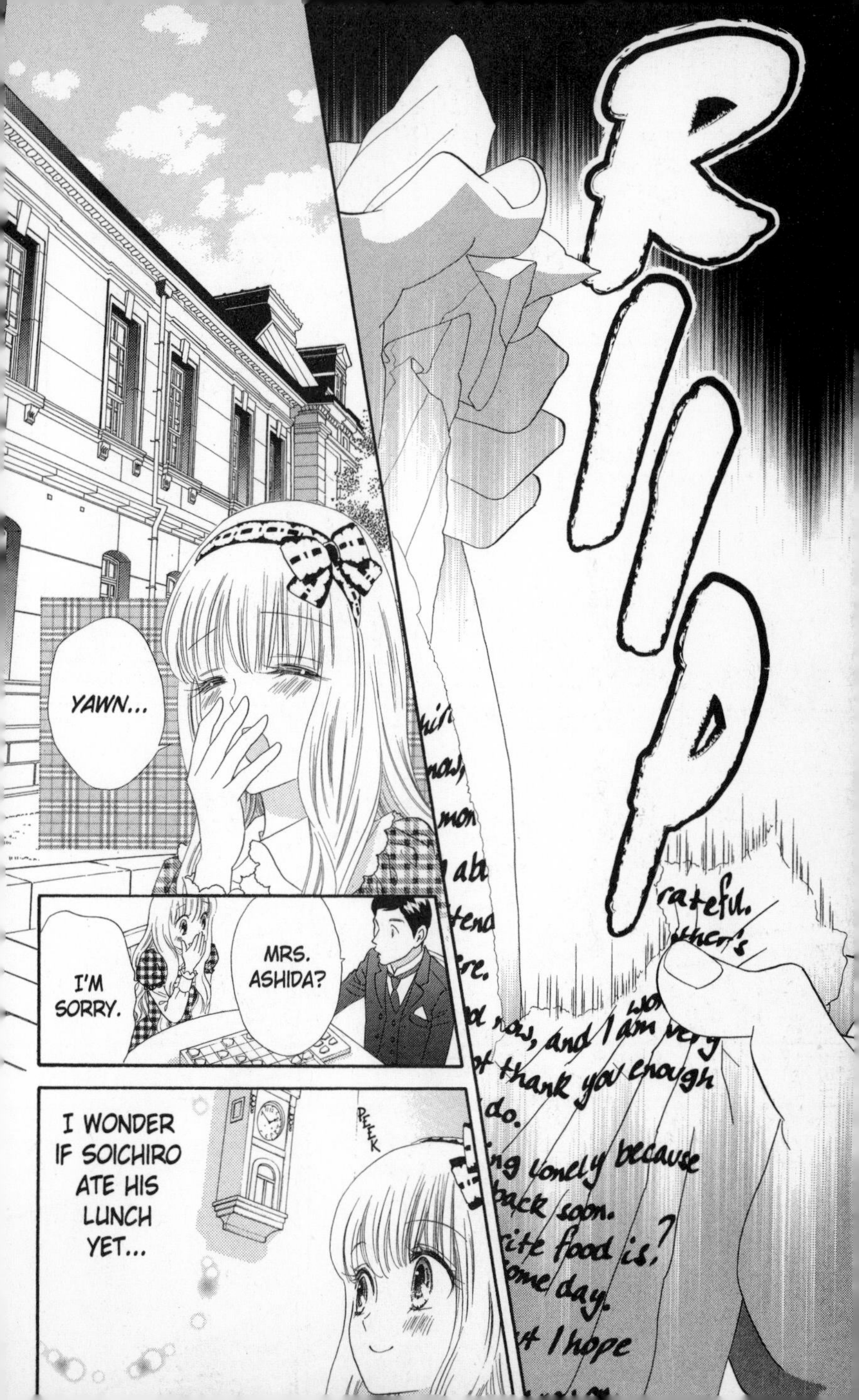
RIP
rateful.
now, and I am very
thank you enough
do.
ing lonely because
back soon.
rite food is?
ome day.
t I hope
YAWN...
MRS. ASHIDA?
I'M SORRY.
PEEK
I WONDER IF SOICHIRO ATE HIS LUNCH YET...

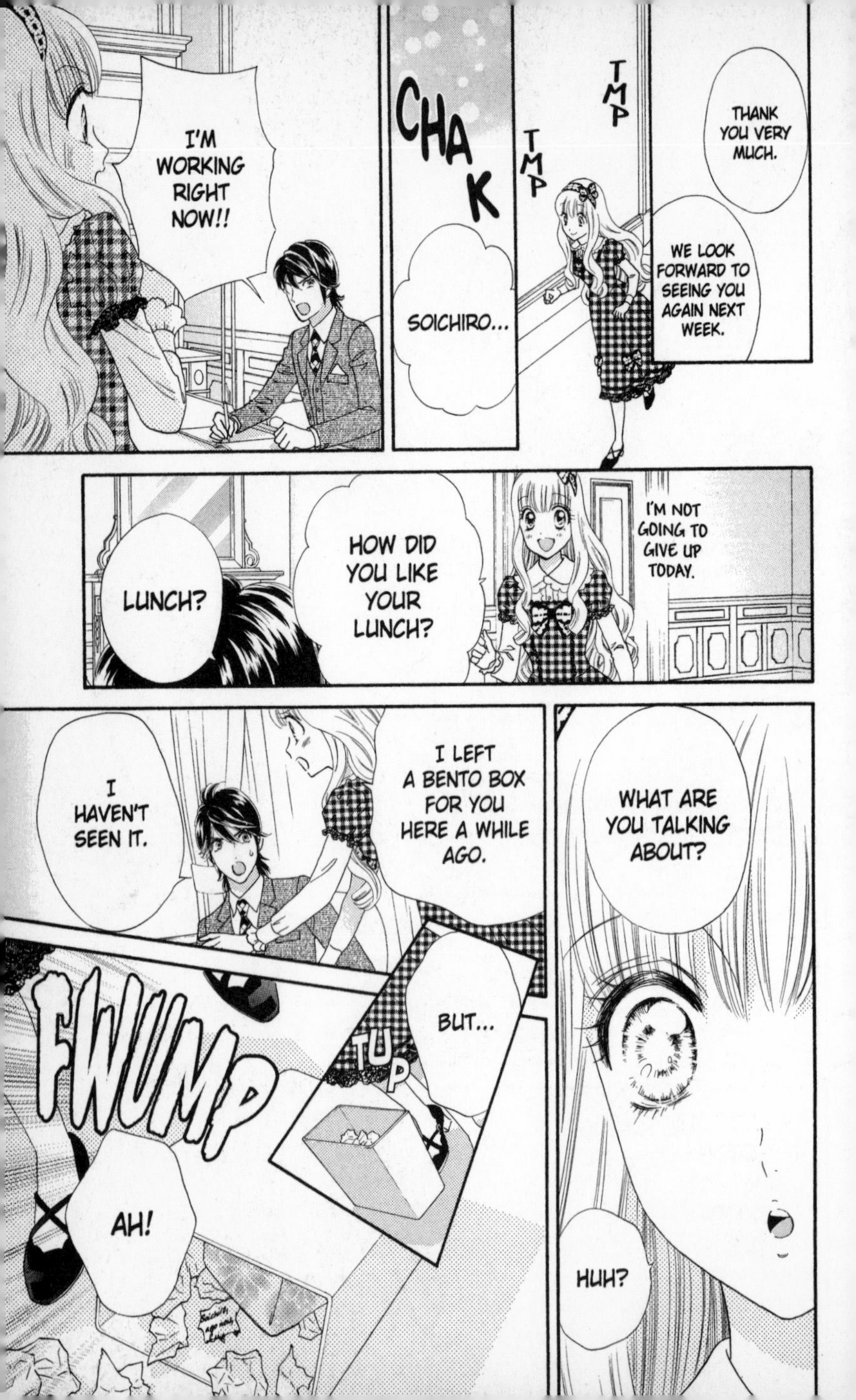
TMP
TMP
THANK YOU VERY MUCH.
WE LOOK FORWARD TO SEEING YOU AGAIN NEXT WEEK.
CHAK
SOICHIRO...
I'M WORKING RIGHT NOW!!
I'M NOT GOING TO GIVE UP TODAY.
HOW DID YOU LIKE YOUR LUNCH?
LUNCH?
WHAT ARE YOU TALKING ABOUT?
HUH?
I LEFT A BENTO BOX FOR YOU HERE A WHILE AGO.
I HAVEN'T SEEN IT.
BUT...
TUP
FWUMP
AH!

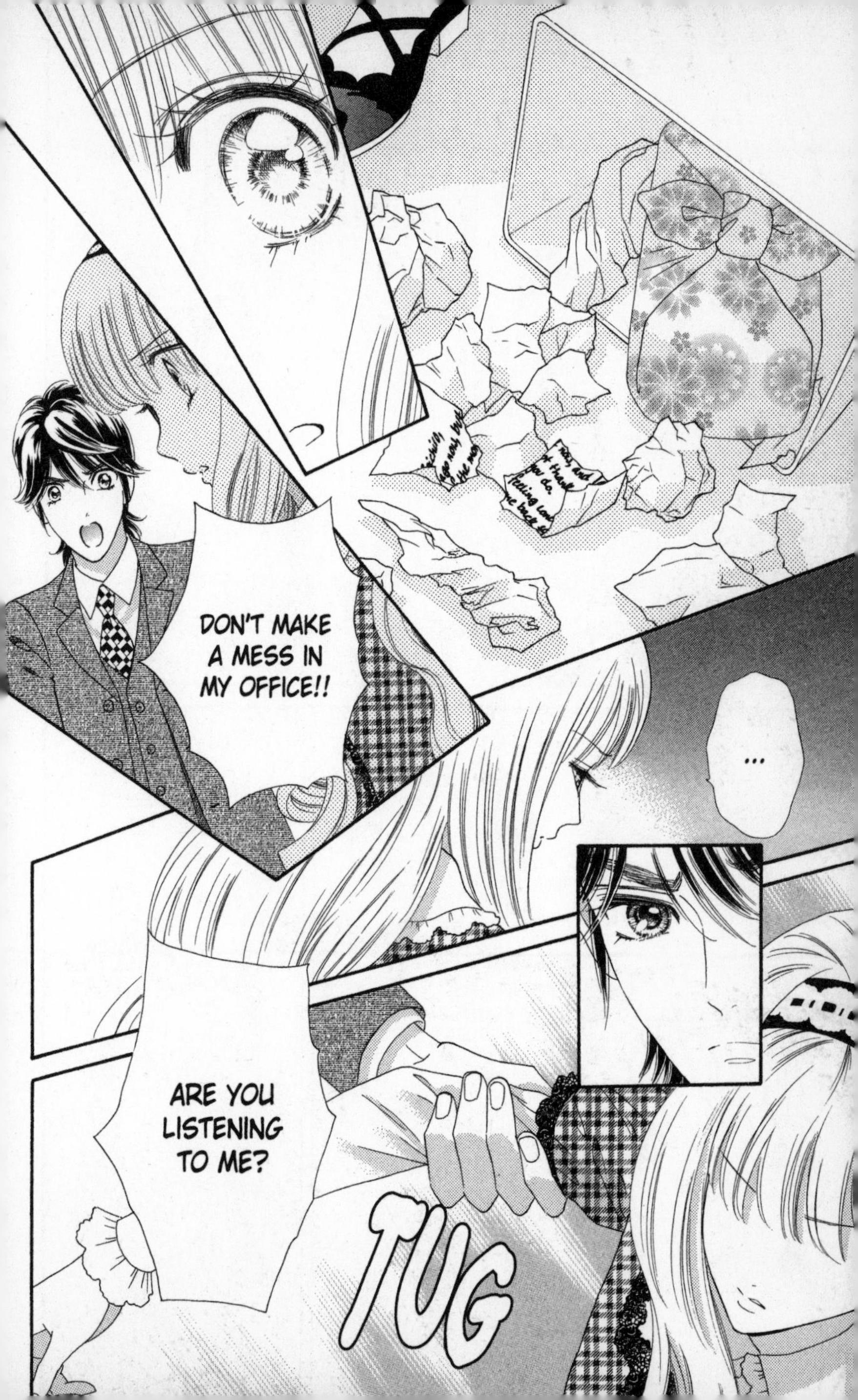

DON'T MAKE A MESS IN MY OFFICE!!
...
ARE YOU LISTENING TO ME?
TUG

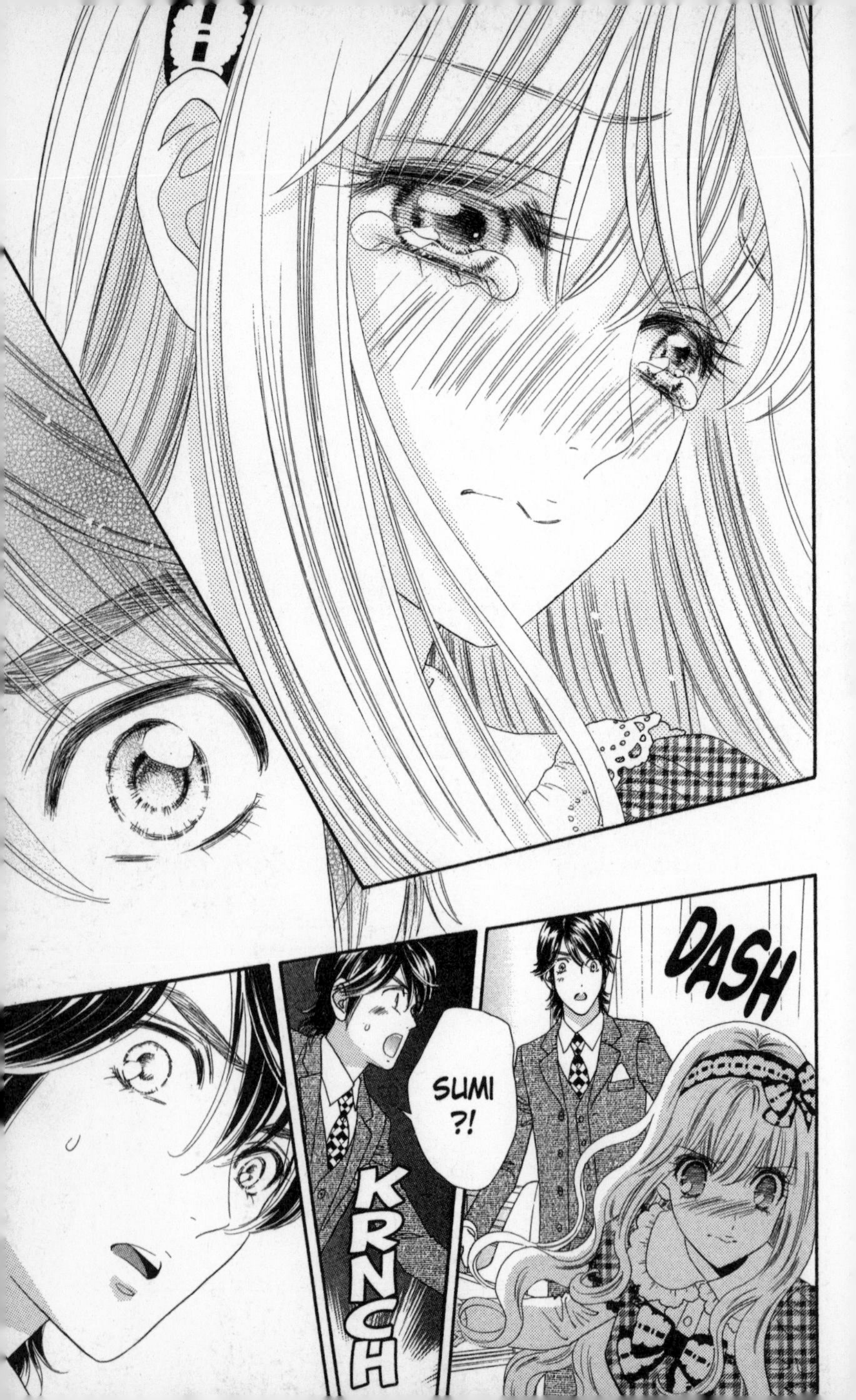
!
DASH
SUMI ?!
KRNCH

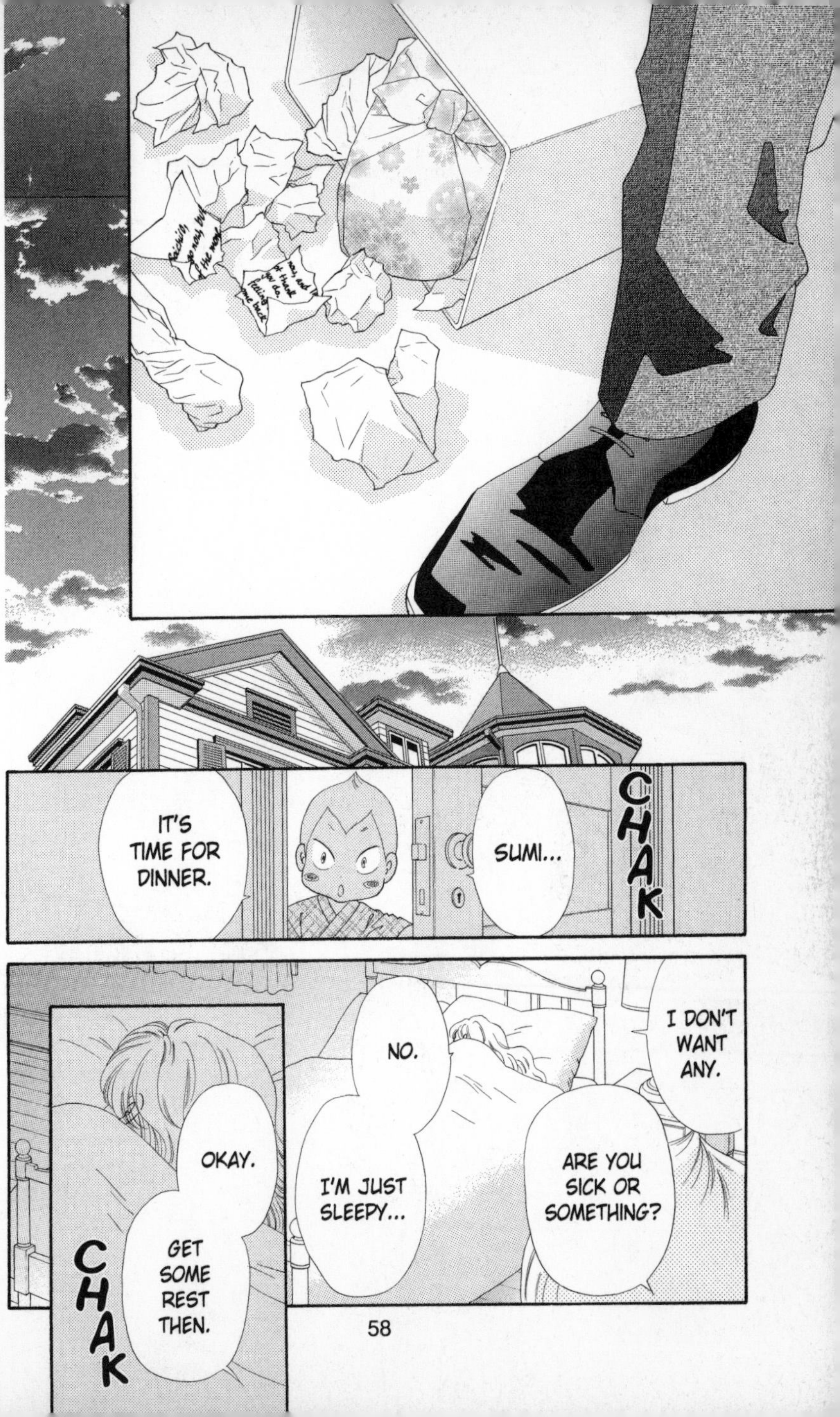

CHAK
SUMI...
IT'S TIME FOR DINNER.
I DON'T WANT ANY.
ARE YOU SICK OR SOMETHING?
NO.
I'M JUST SLEEPY...
OKAY.
GET SOME REST THEN.
CHAK

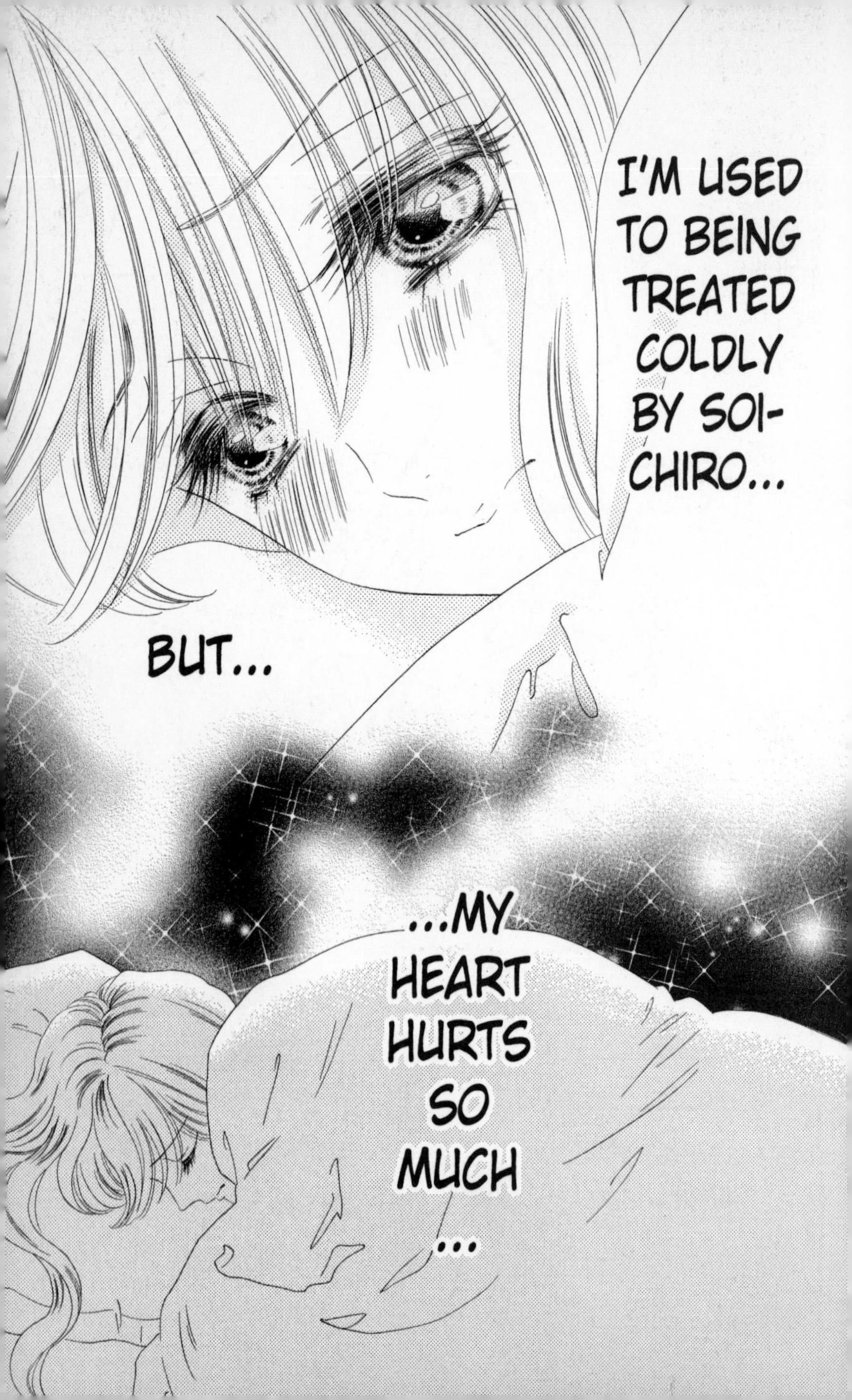

I'M USED TO BEING TREATED COLDLY BY SOI-CHIRO...
BUT...
...MY HEART HURTS SO MUCH ...

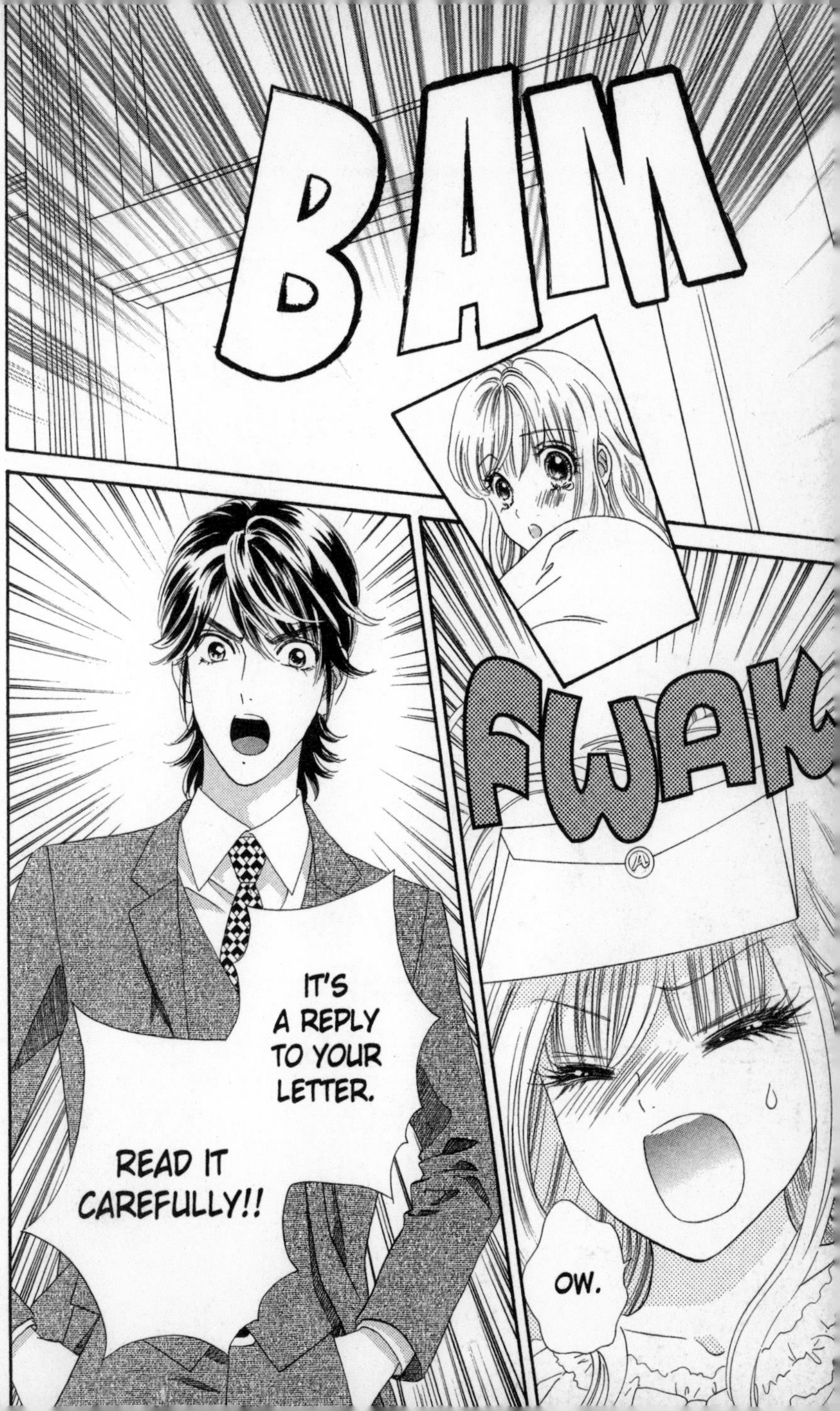
BAM
FWAK
OW.
IT'S A REPLY TO YOUR LETTER.
READ IT CAREFULLY!!

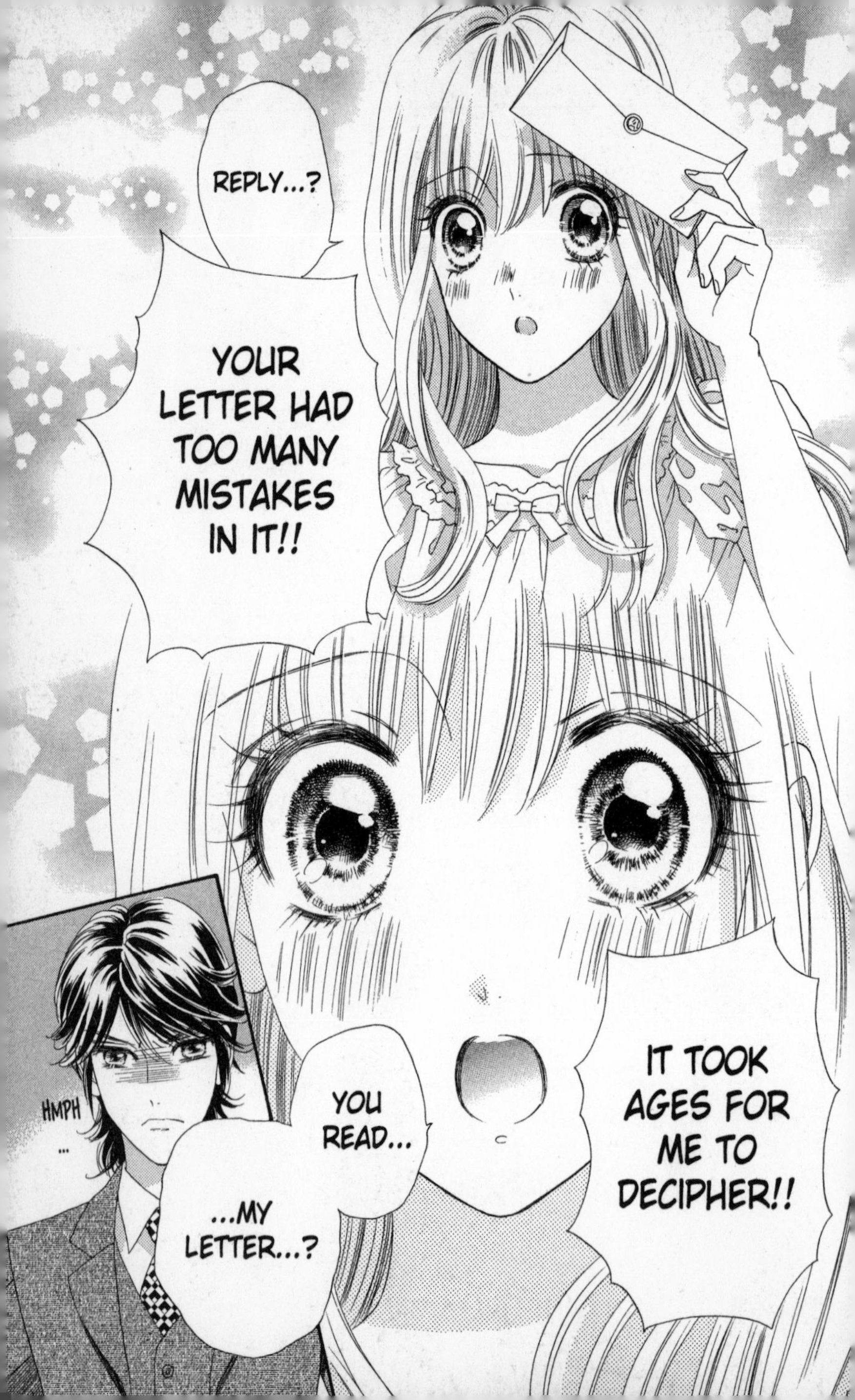
REPLY...?
YOUR LETTER HAD TOO MANY MISTAKES IN IT!!
IT TOOK AGES FOR ME TO DECIPHER!!
YOU READ...
...MY LETTER...?
HMPH...

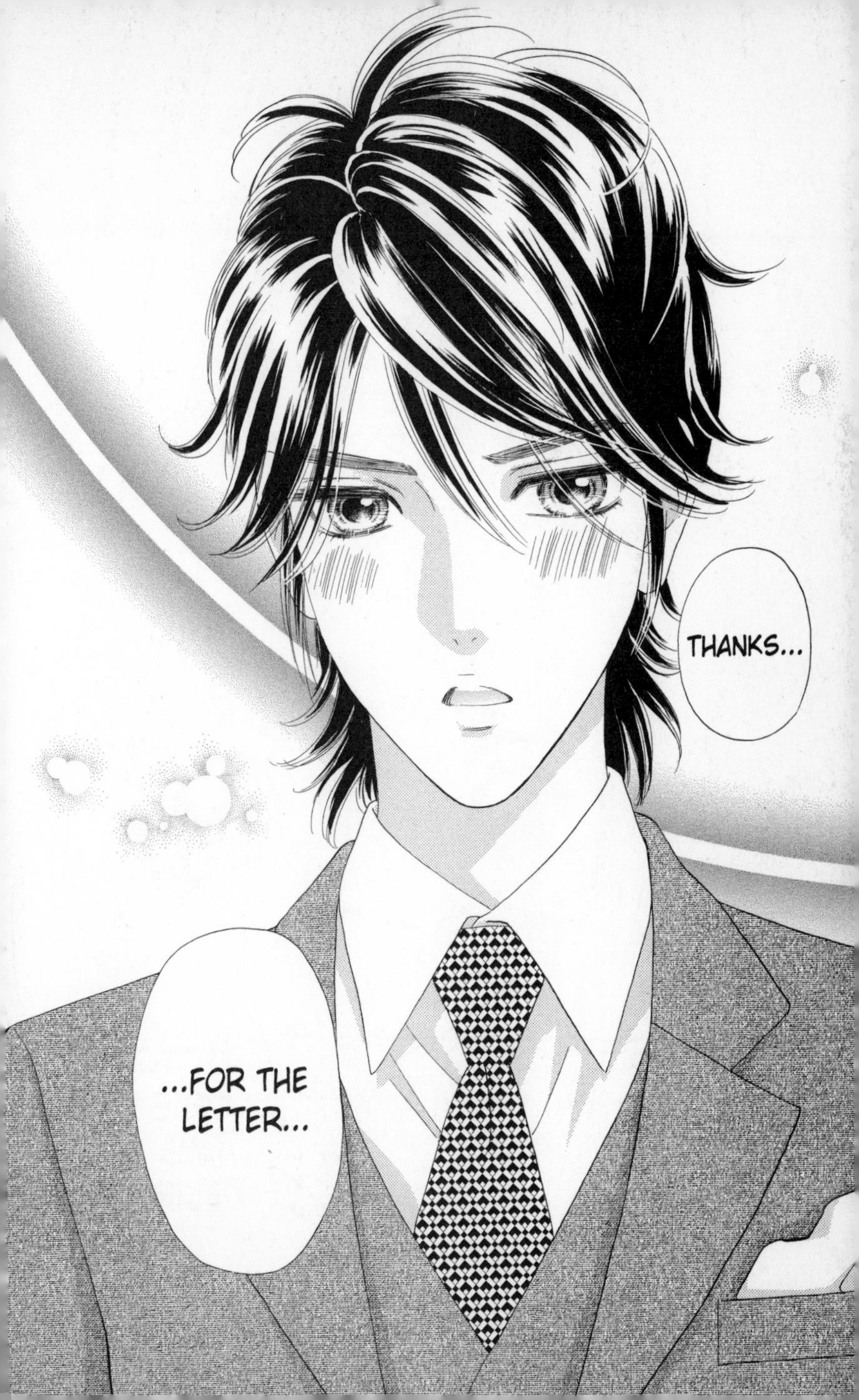
THANKS...
...FOR THE LETTER...

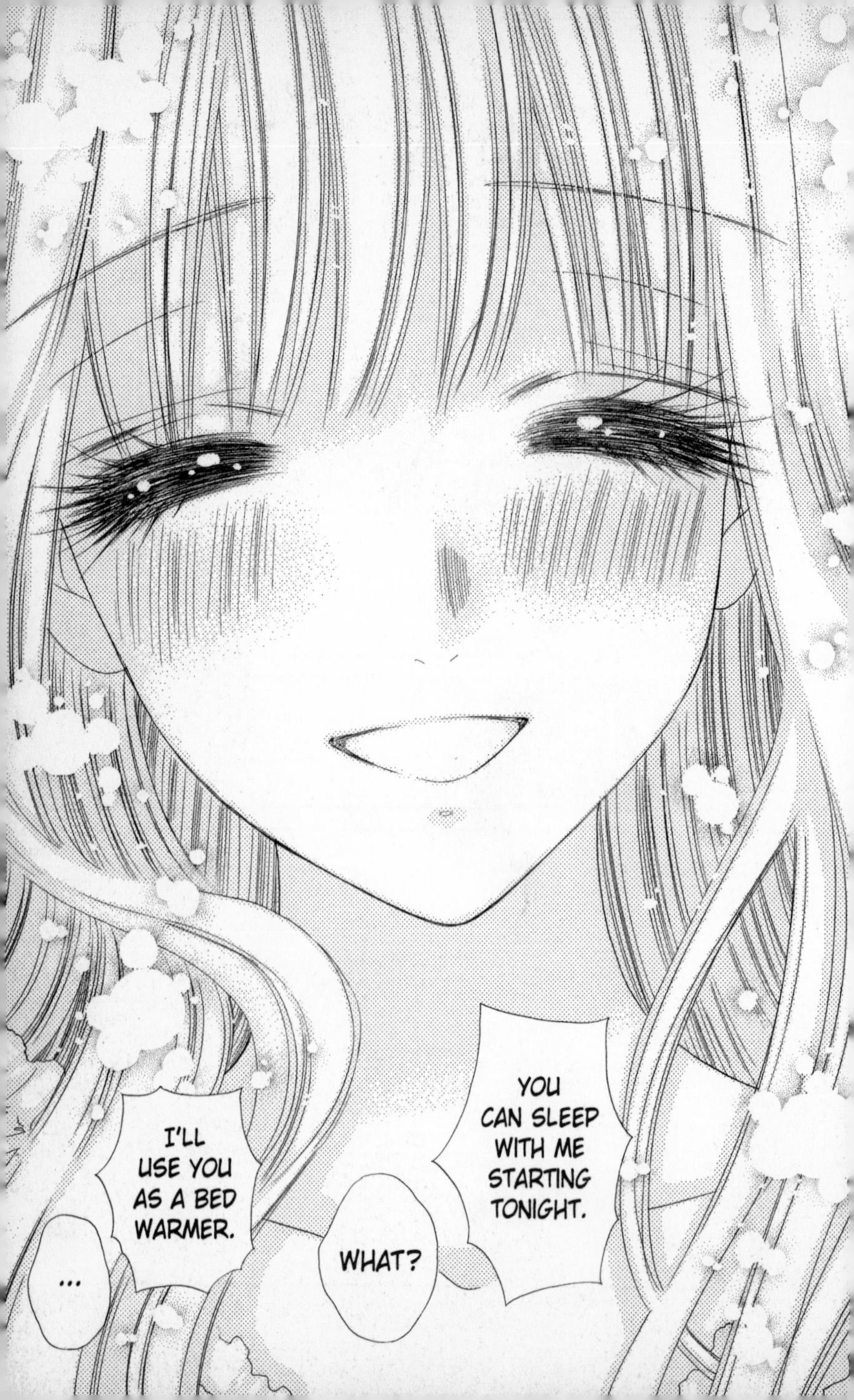
YOU CAN SLEEP WITH ME STARTING TONIGHT.
WHAT?
I'LL USE YOU AS A BED WARMER.
...

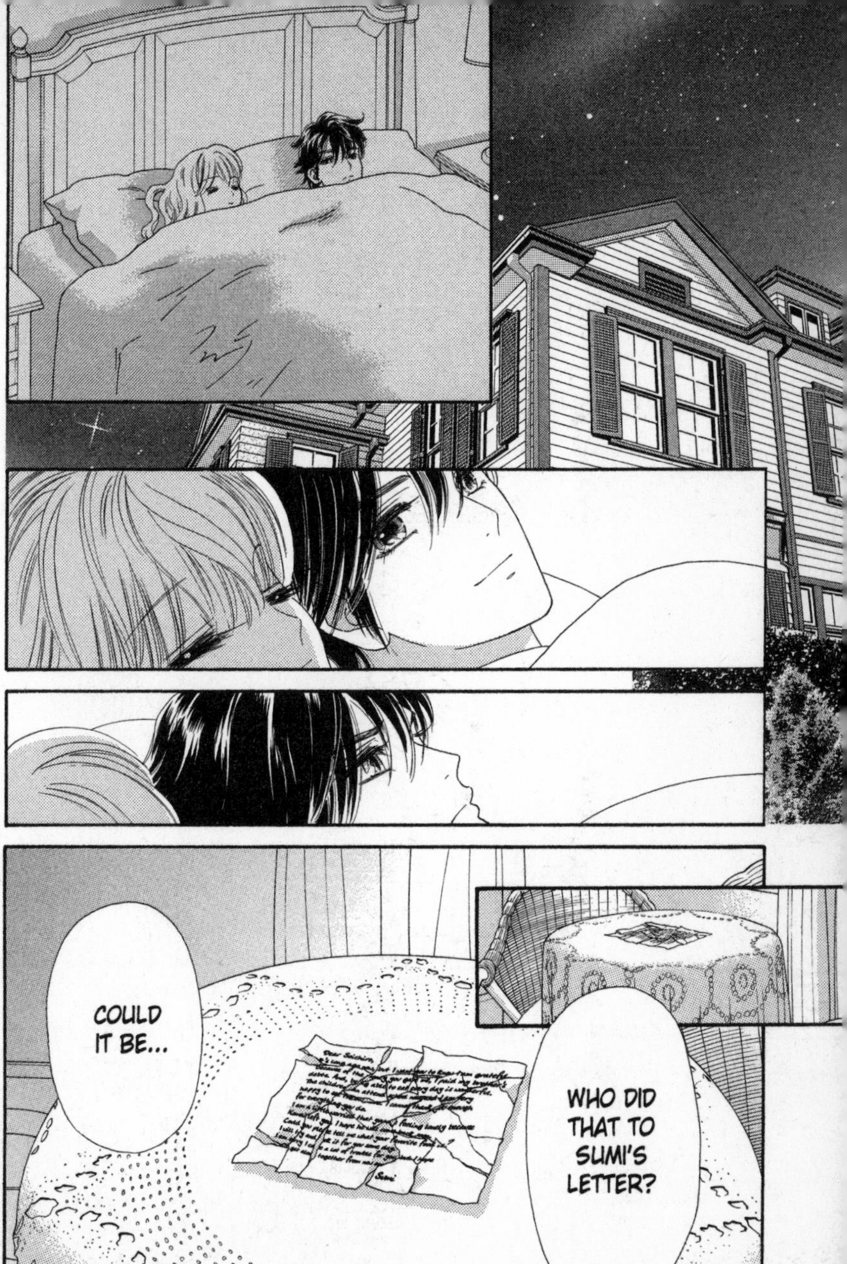
WHO DID THAT TO SUMI'S LETTER?
COULD IT BE...

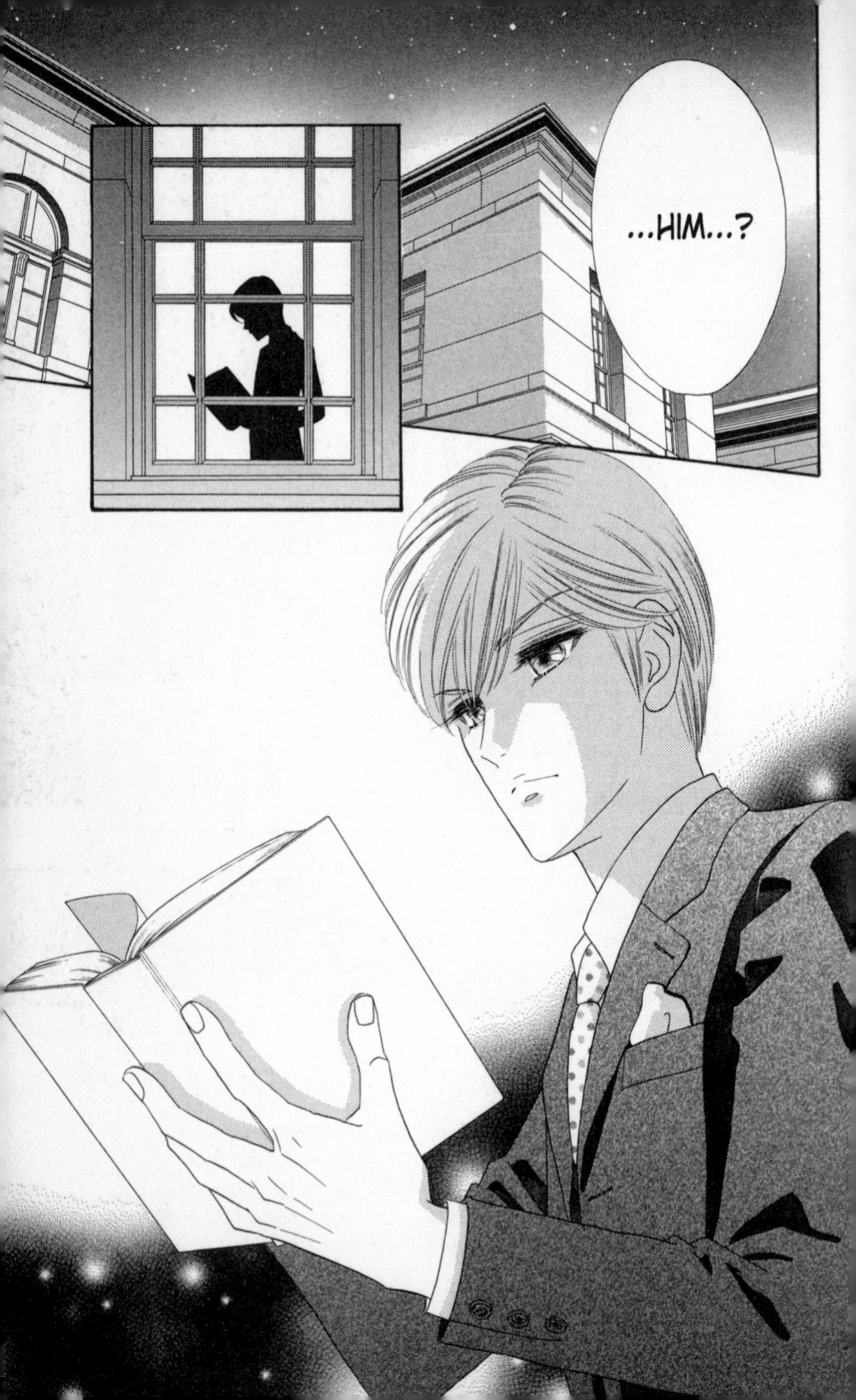
...HIM...?

ASHIDA FAMILY HOUSE → YAMATE, YOKOHAMA - DIPLOMAT'S HOUSE

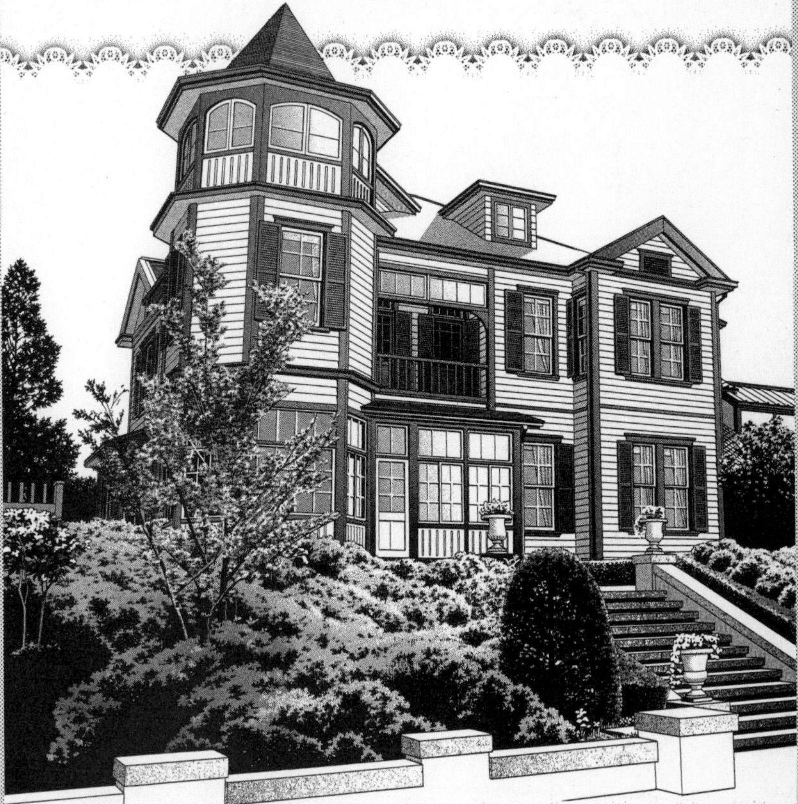

This is the old, relocated Uchida house originally built in Shibuya's Nanpeidai district in 1910. At the time, it was considered a thoroughly Western-style house for a Japanese person to live in. The owner of this house, Sadatsuchi Uchida, was a diplomat for the Meiji government.

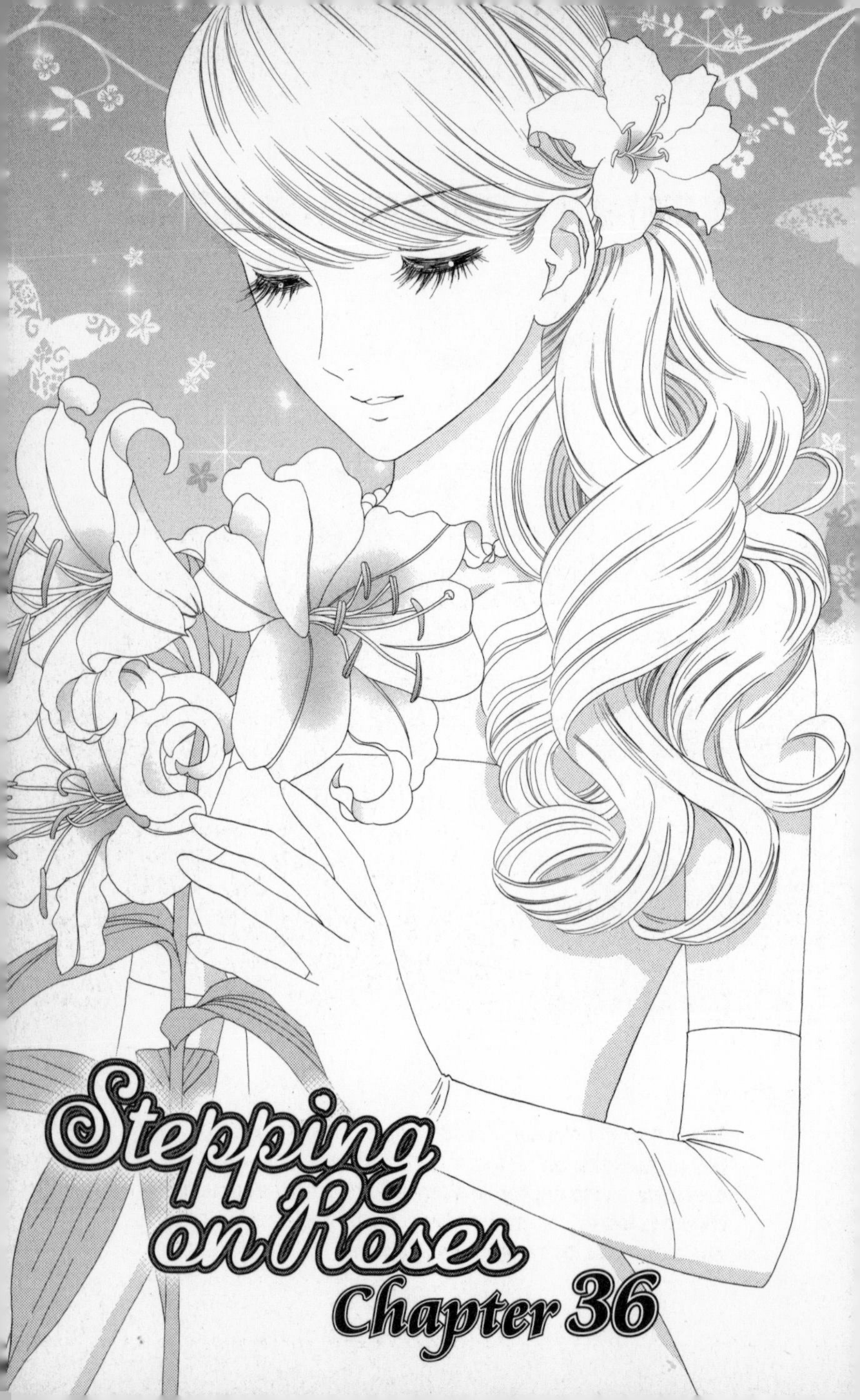
Stepping on Roses
Chapter 36

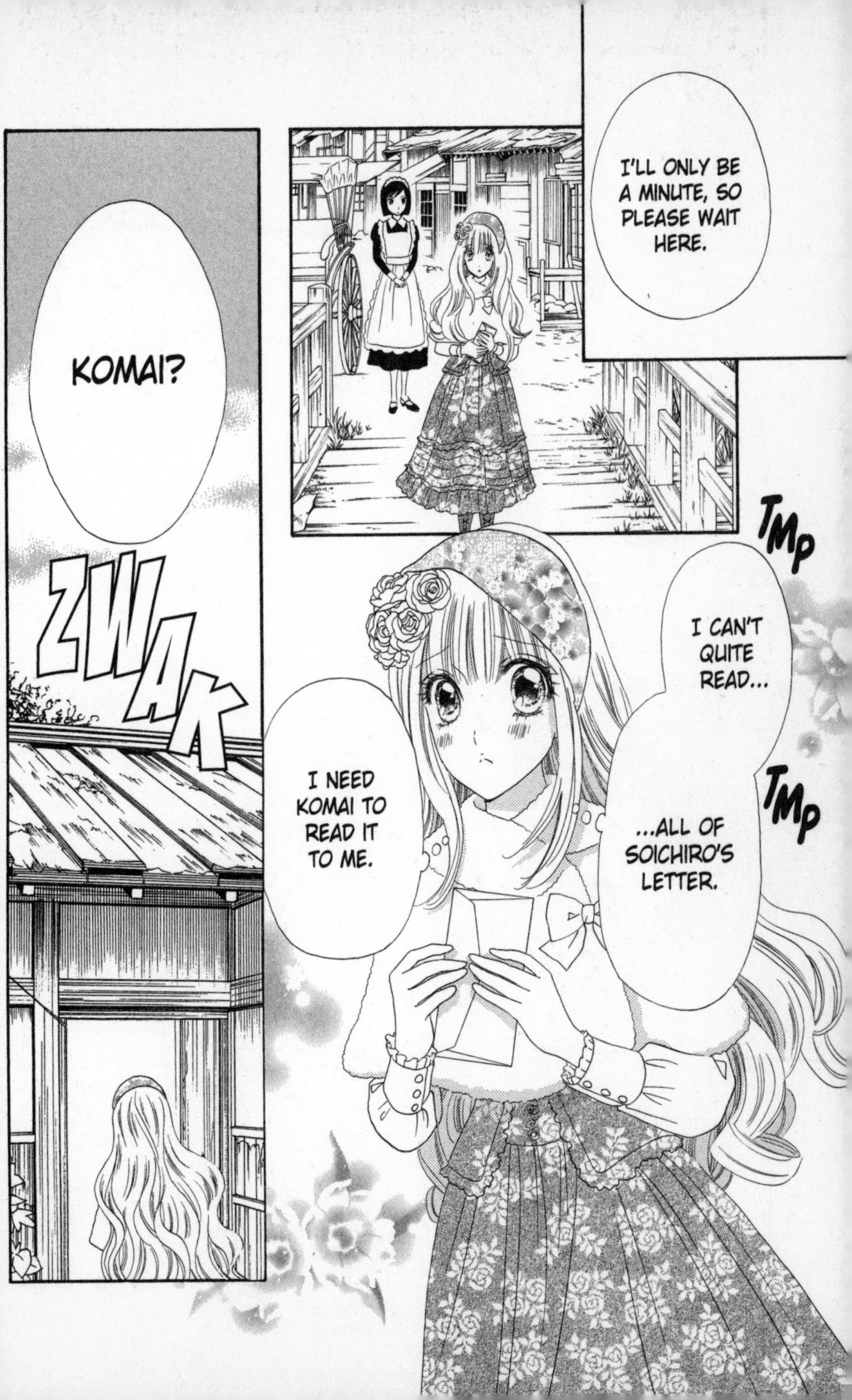
I'LL ONLY BE A MINUTE, SO PLEASE WAIT HERE.
TMP
I CAN'T QUITE READ...
TMP
...ALL OF SOICHIRO'S LETTER.
I NEED KOMAI TO READ IT TO ME.
KOMAI?
ZWAK

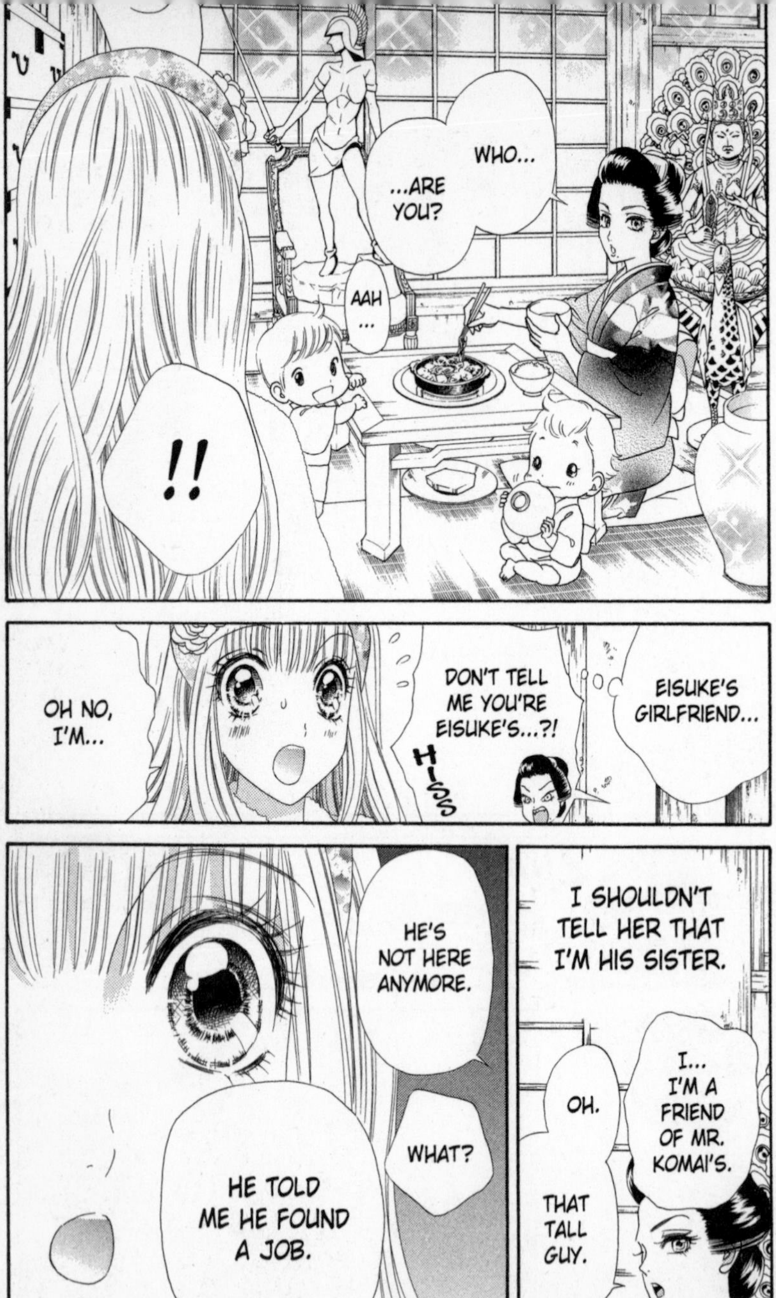
WHO... ...ARE YOU?
AAH ...
!!
EISUKE'S GIRLFRIEND...
DON'T TELL ME YOU'RE EISUKE'S...?!
HISS
OH NO, I'M...
I SHOULDN'T TELL HER THAT I'M HIS SISTER.
I... I'M A FRIEND OF MR. KOMAI'S.
OH.
THAT TALL GUY.
HE'S NOT HERE ANYMORE.
WHAT?
HE TOLD ME HE FOUND A JOB.

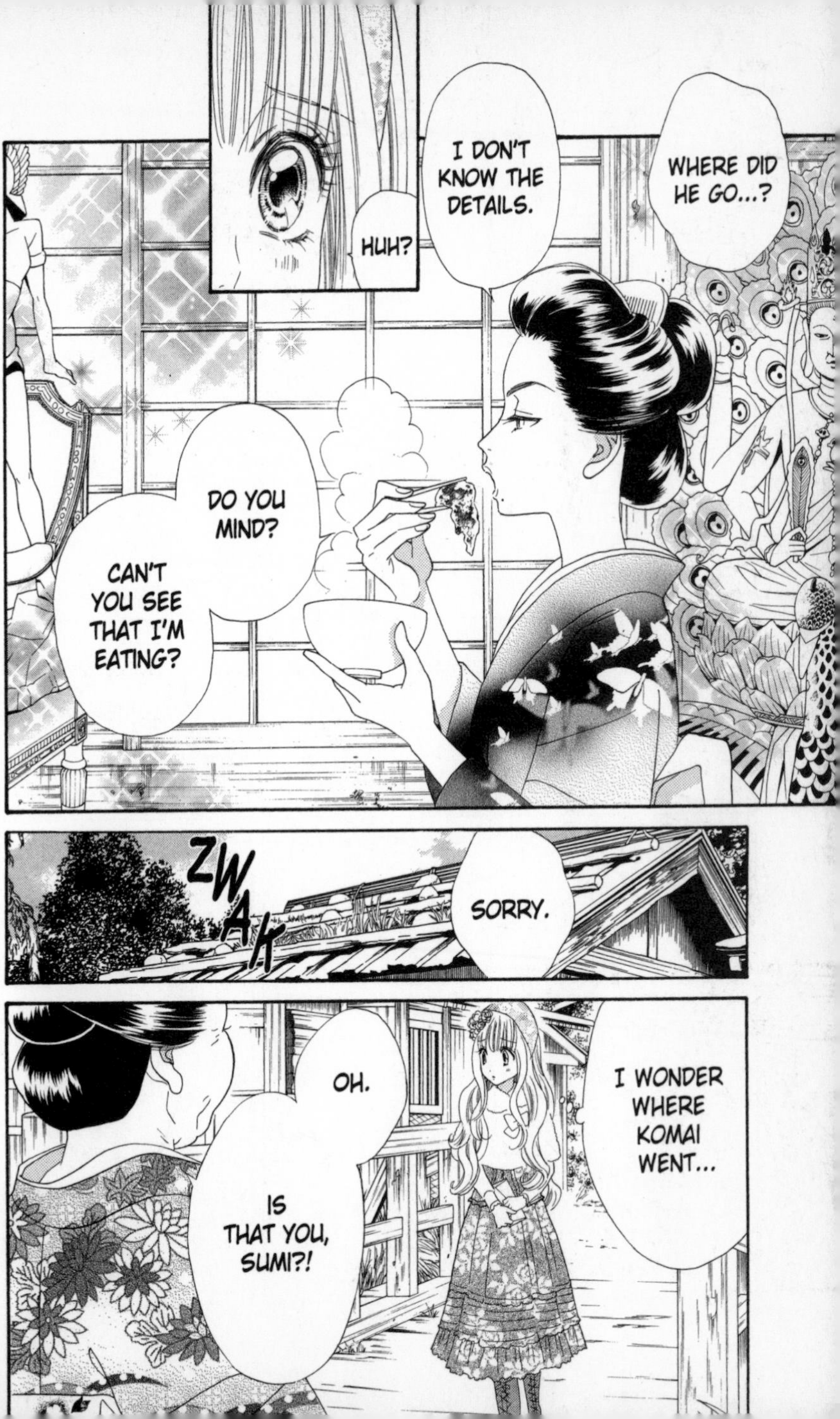
WHERE DID HE GO...?
I DON'T KNOW THE DETAILS.
HUH?
DO YOU MIND?
CAN'T YOU SEE THAT I'M EATING?
SORRY.
ZWAK
I WONDER WHERE KOMAI WENT...
OH.
IS THAT YOU, SUMI?!

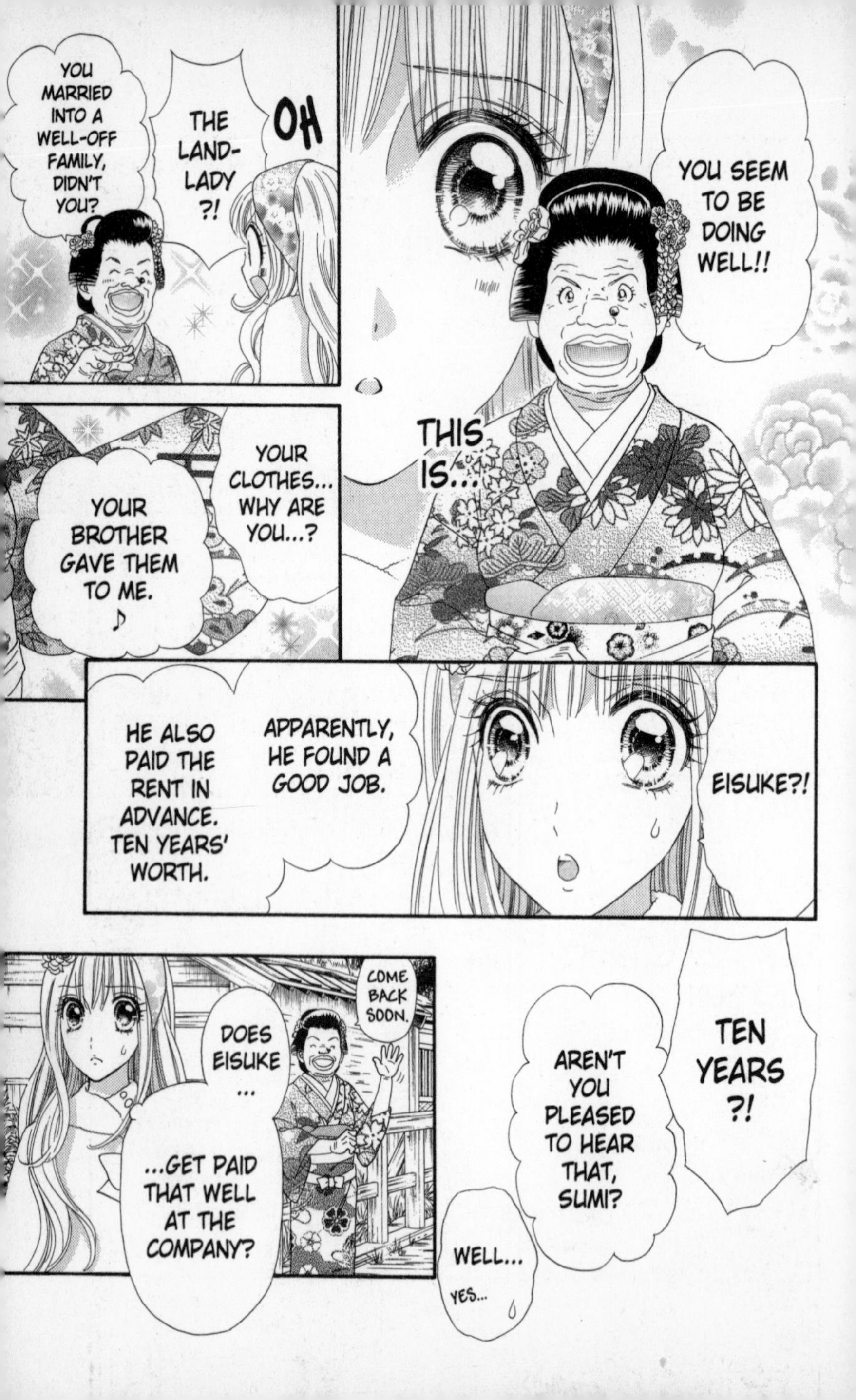

YOU SEEM TO BE DOING WELL!!
THIS IS...
OH
THE LAND-LADY?!
YOU MARRIED INTO A WELL-OFF FAMILY, DIDN'T YOU?
YOUR CLOTHES... WHY ARE YOU...?
YOUR BROTHER GAVE THEM TO ME. ♪
EISUKE?!
APPARENTLY, HE FOUND A GOOD JOB.
HE ALSO PAID THE RENT IN ADVANCE. TEN YEARS' WORTH.
TEN YEARS?!
AREN'T YOU PLEASED TO HEAR THAT, SUMI?
WELL...
YES...
COME BACK SOON.
DOES EISUKE...
...GET PAID THAT WELL AT THE COMPANY?

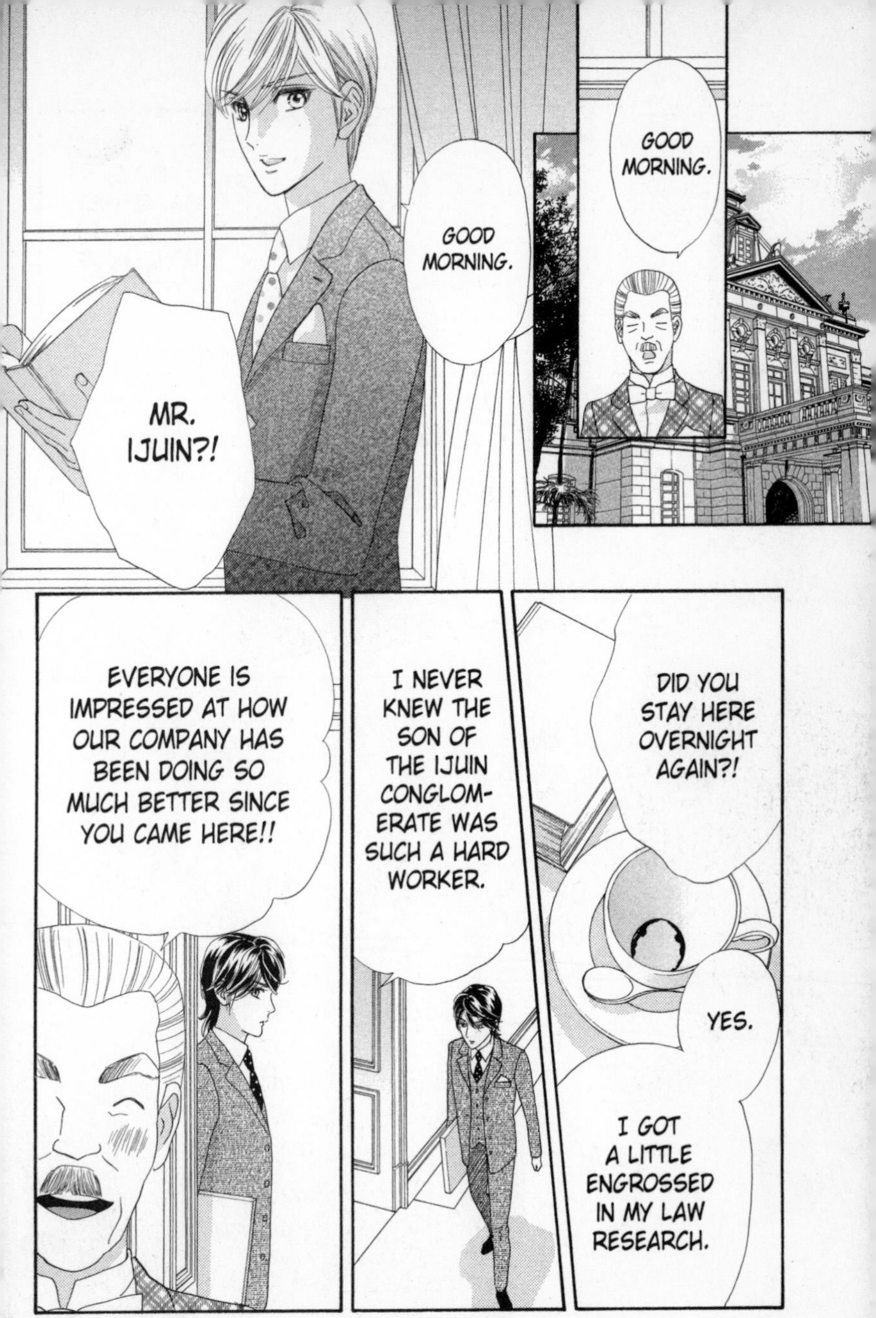
GOOD MORNING.
GOOD MORNING.
MR. IJUIN?!
DID YOU STAY HERE OVERNIGHT AGAIN?!
YES.
I GOT A LITTLE ENGROSSED IN MY LAW RESEARCH.
I NEVER KNEW THE SON OF THE IJUIN CONGLOM-ERATE WAS SUCH A HARD WORKER.
EVERYONE IS IMPRESSED AT HOW OUR COMPANY HAS BEEN DOING SO MUCH BETTER SINCE YOU CAME HERE!!

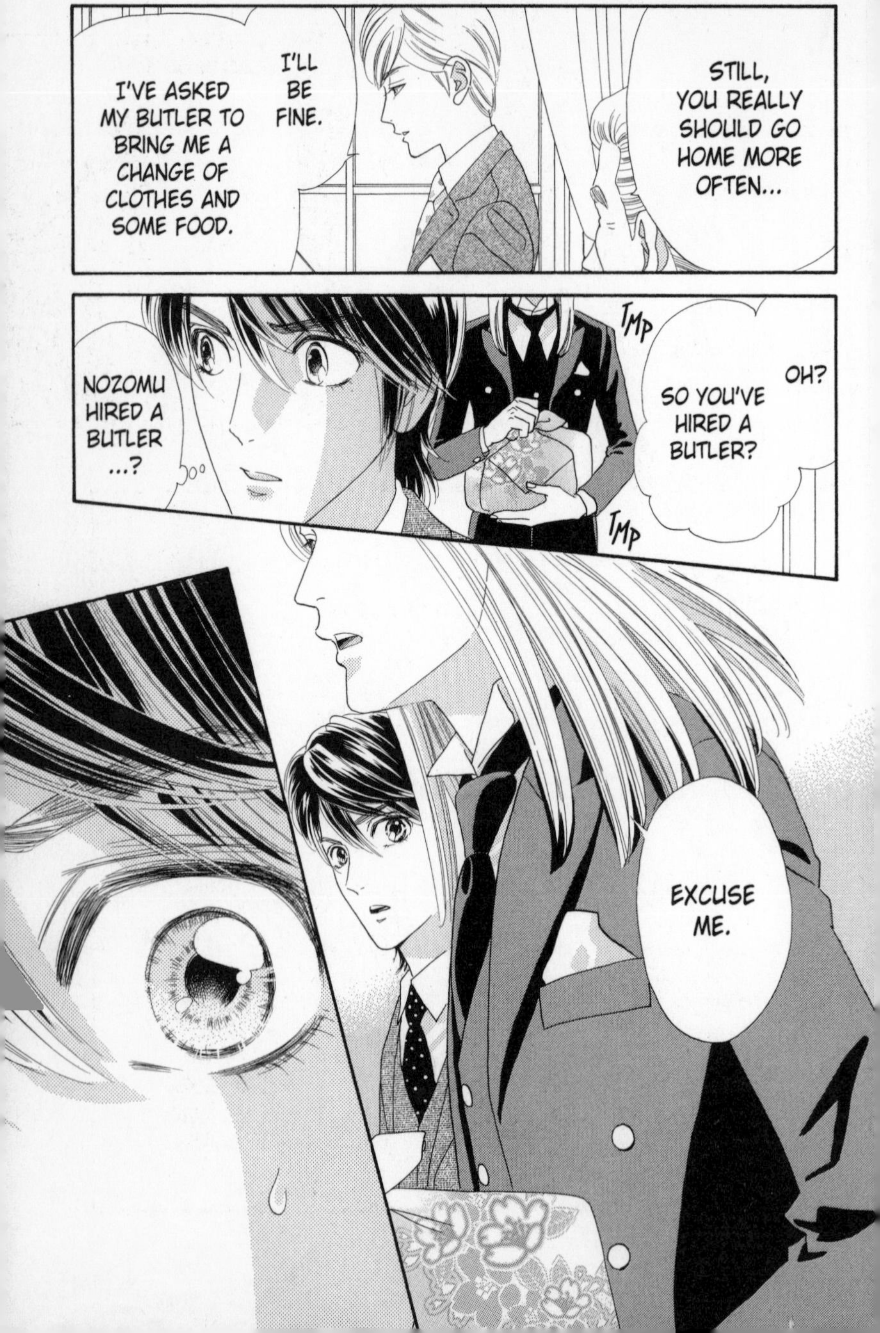
STILL, YOU REALLY SHOULD GO HOME MORE OFTEN...
I'LL BE FINE.
I'VE ASKED MY BUTLER TO BRING ME A CHANGE OF CLOTHES AND SOME FOOD.
TMP
OH?
SO YOU'VE HIRED A BUTLER?
TMP
NOZOMU HIRED A BUTLER ...?
EXCUSE ME.

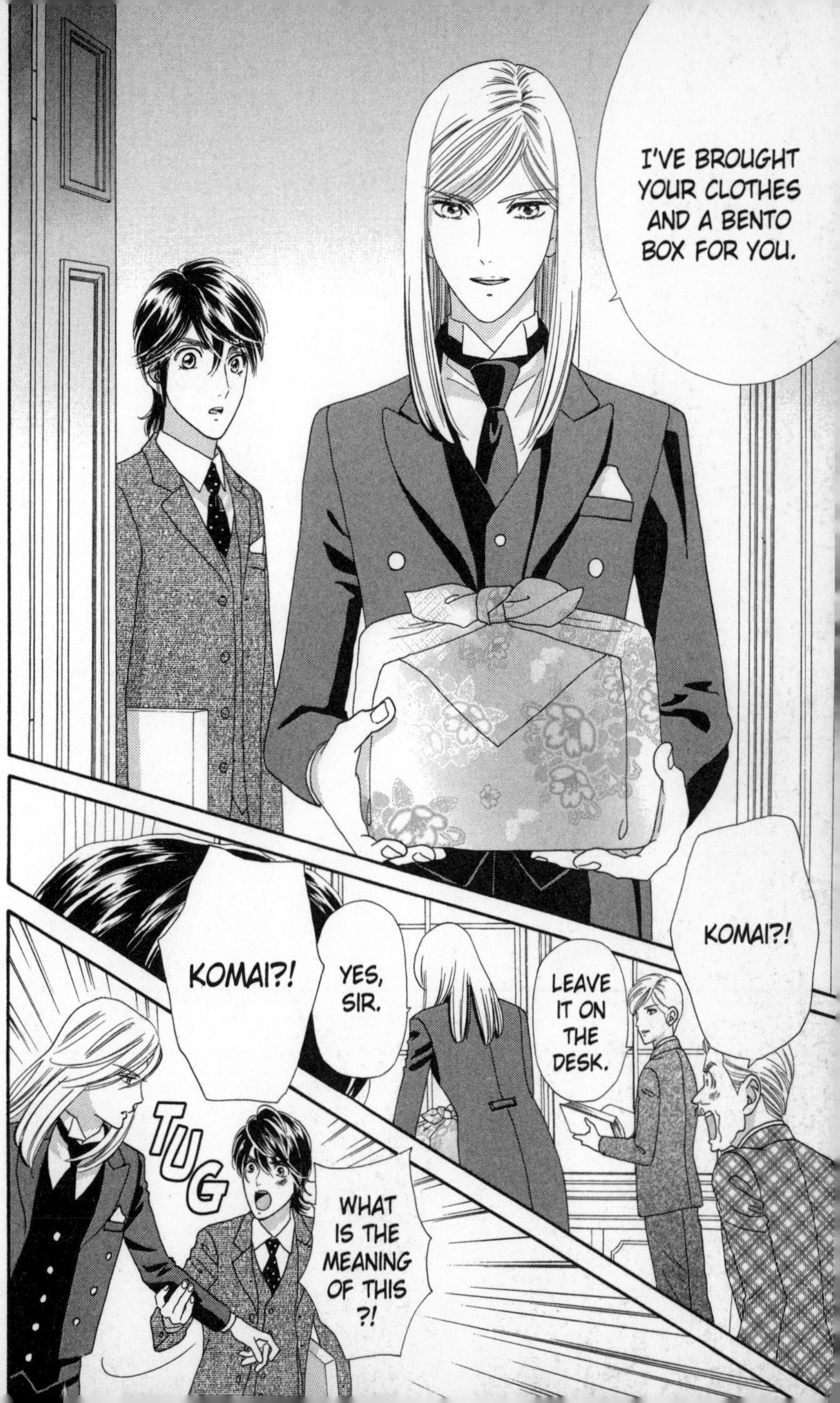
I'VE BROUGHT YOUR CLOTHES AND A BENTO BOX FOR YOU.
KOMAI?!
LEAVE IT ON THE DESK.
YES, SIR.
KOMAI?!
TUG
WHAT IS THE MEANING OF THIS ?!

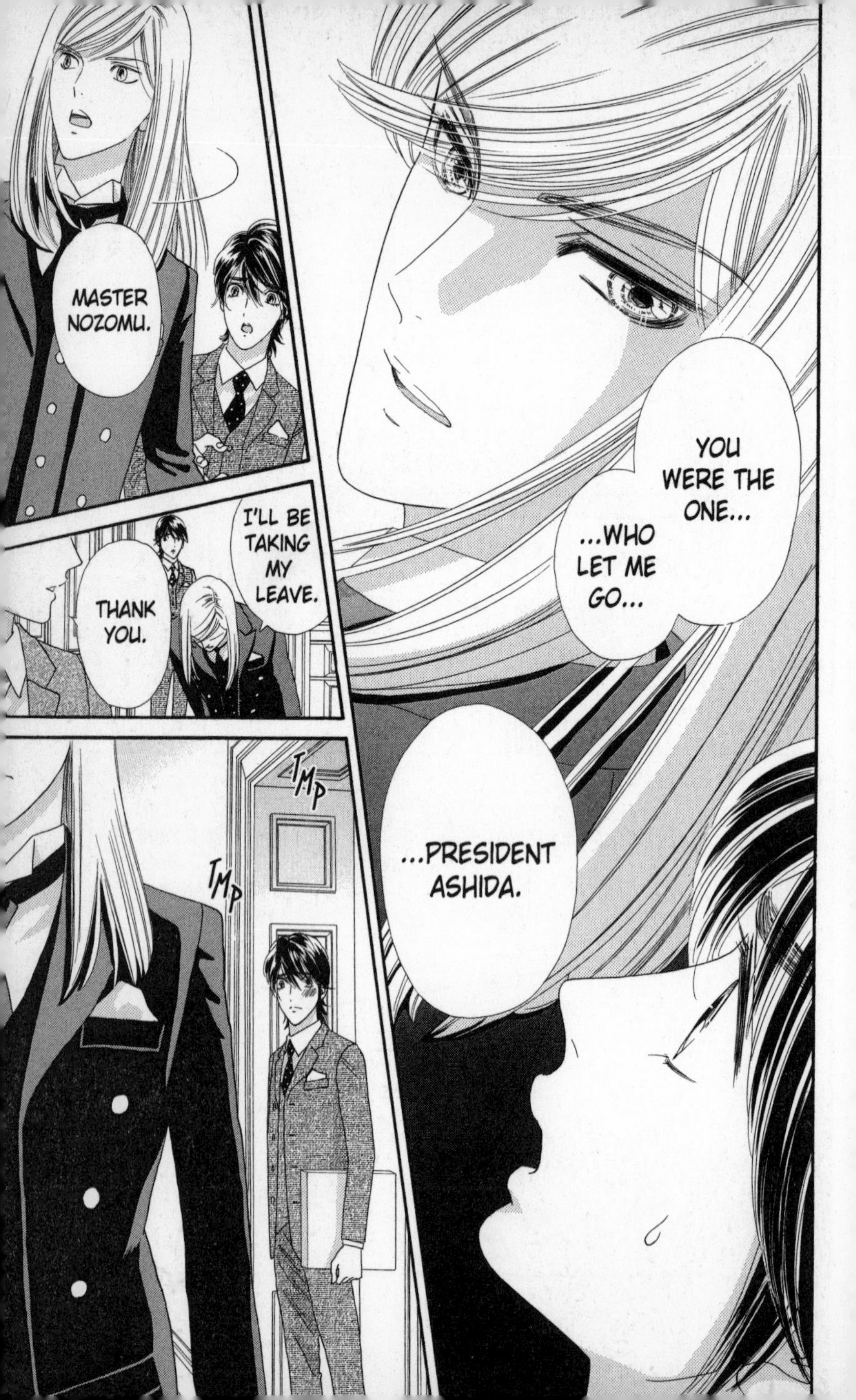
YOU WERE THE ONE...
...WHO LET ME GO...
...PRESIDENT ASHIDA.
MASTER NOZOMU.
I'LL BE TAKING MY LEAVE.
THANK YOU.
TMP
TMP

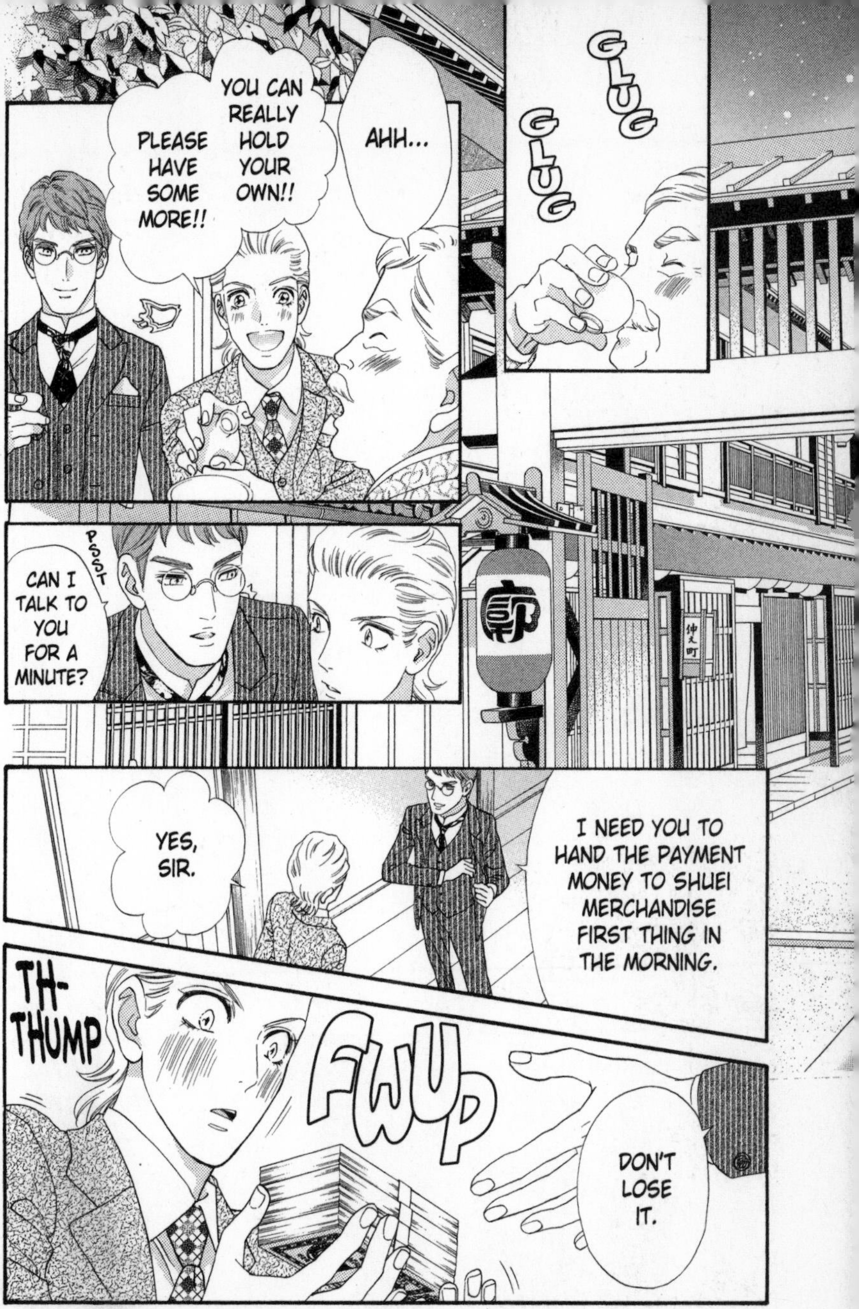
GLUG
GLUG
AHH...
YOU CAN REALLY HOLD YOUR OWN!!
PLEASE HAVE SOME MORE!!
PSSST
CAN I TALK TO YOU FOR A MINUTE?
I NEED YOU TO HAND THE PAYMENT MONEY TO SHUEI MERCHANDISE FIRST THING IN THE MORNING.
YES, SIR.
DON'T LOSE IT.
FWUP
TH-THUMP

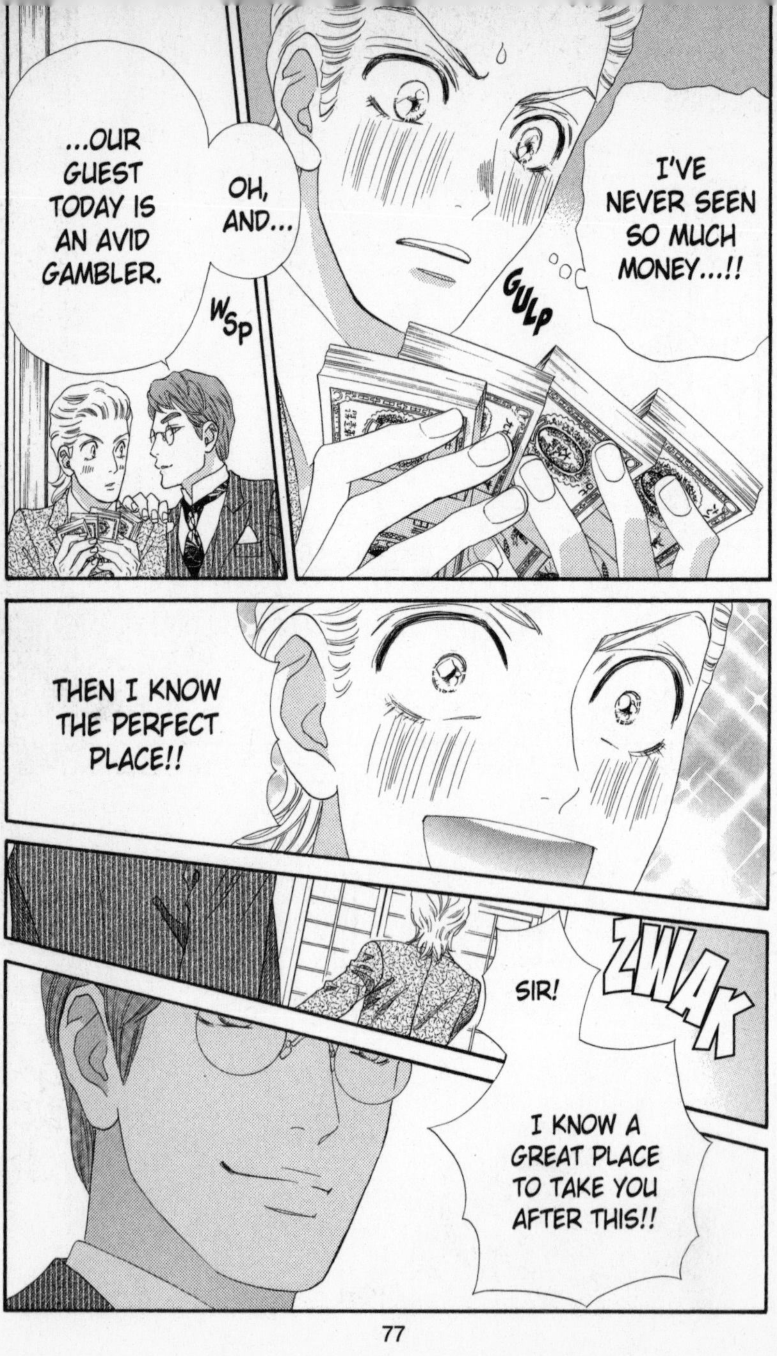
I'VE NEVER SEEN SO MUCH MONEY...!!
GULP
OH, AND...
...OUR GUEST TODAY IS AN AVID GAMBLER.
WSP
THEN I KNOW THE PERFECT PLACE!!
ZWAK
SIR!
I KNOW A GREAT PLACE TO TAKE YOU AFTER THIS!!

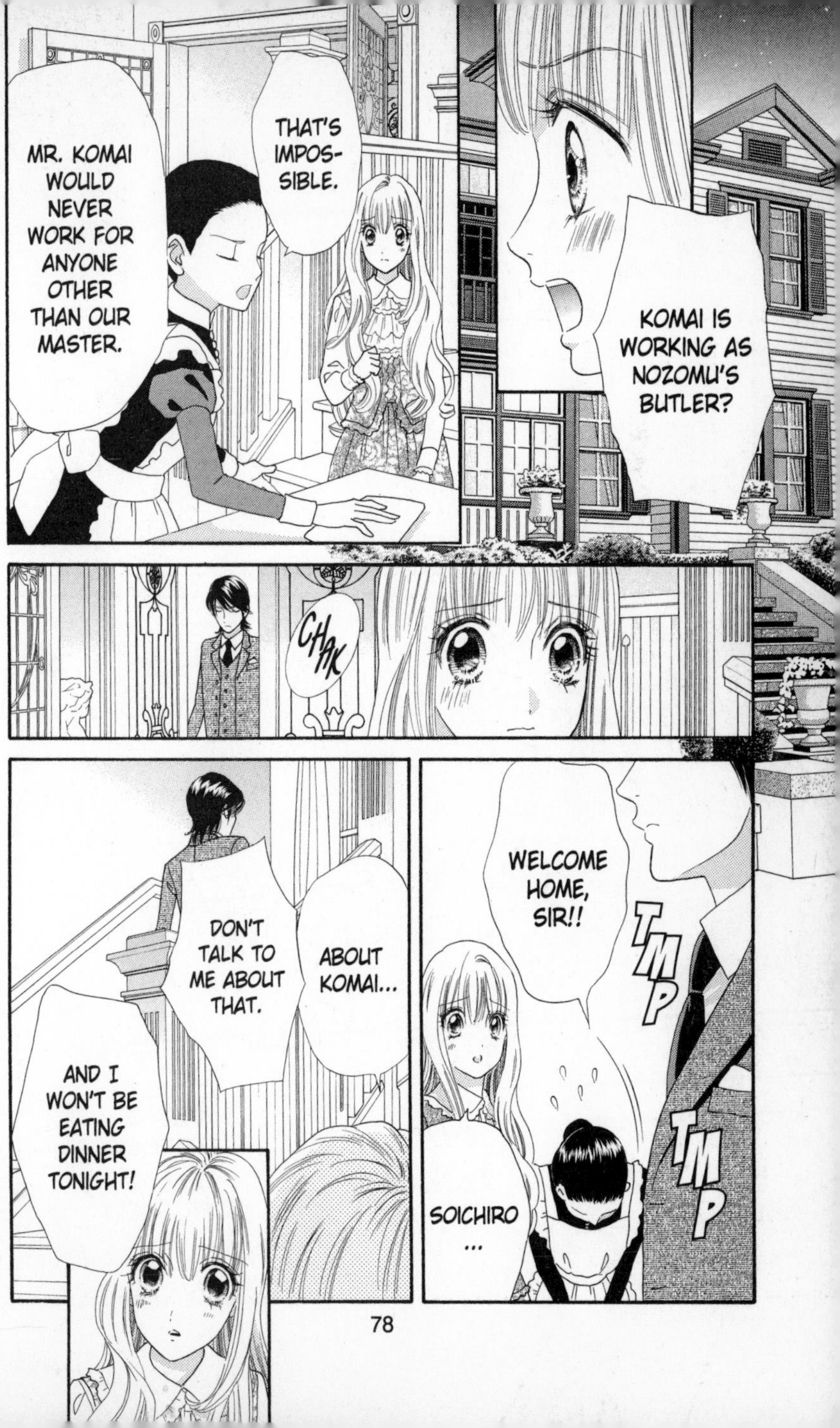
KOMAI IS WORKING AS NOZOMU'S BUTLER?
THAT'S IMPOS-SIBLE.
MR. KOMAI WOULD NEVER WORK FOR ANYONE OTHER THAN OUR MASTER.
CHAK
WELCOME HOME, SIR!!
TMP
TMP
TMP
SOICHIRO ...
ABOUT KOMAI...
DON'T TALK TO ME ABOUT THAT.
AND I WON'T BE EATING DINNER TONIGHT!

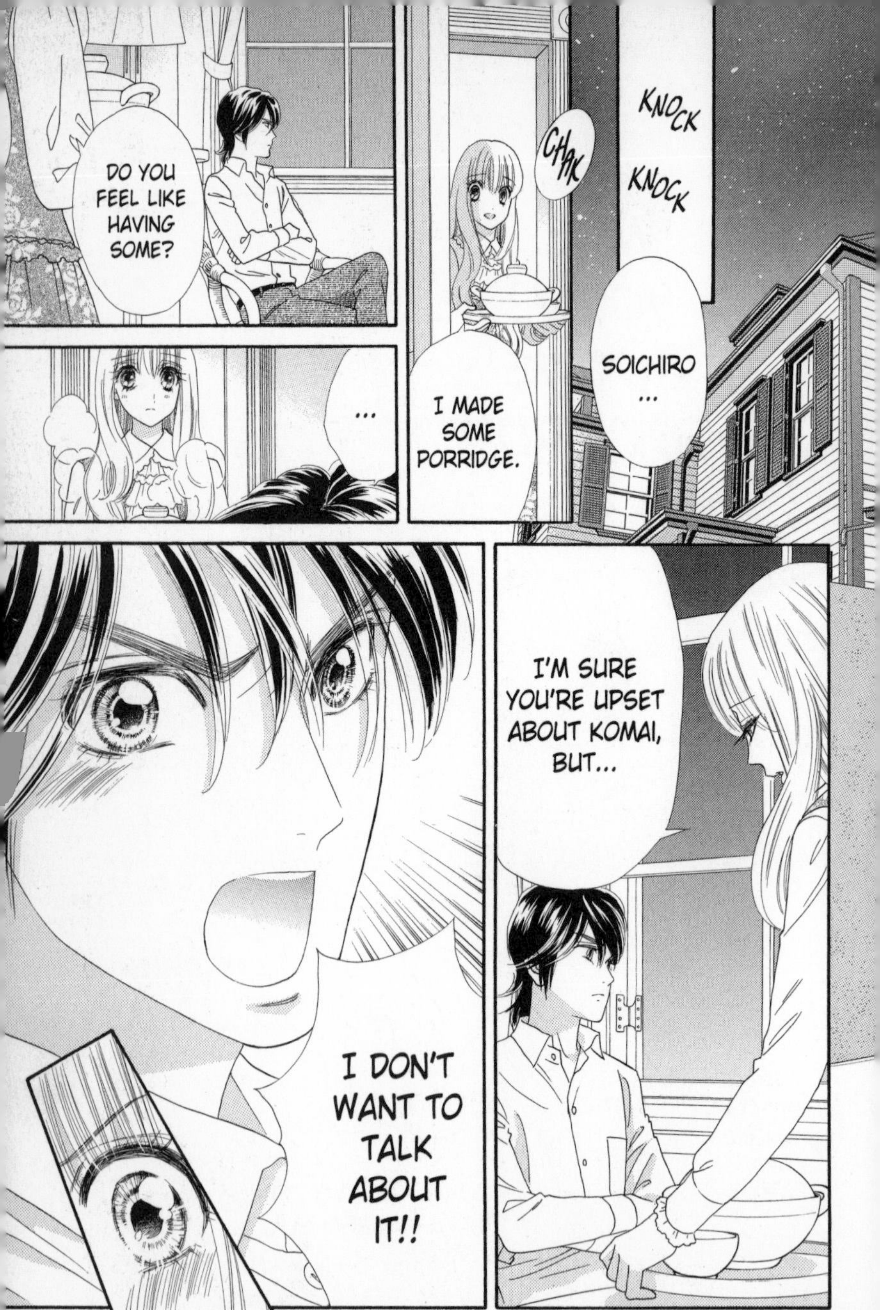
KNOCK
KNOCK
SOICHIRO...
CHAK
I MADE SOME PORRIDGE.
DO YOU FEEL LIKE HAVING SOME?
...
I'M SURE YOU'RE UPSET ABOUT KOMAI, BUT...
I DON'T WANT TO TALK ABOUT IT!!

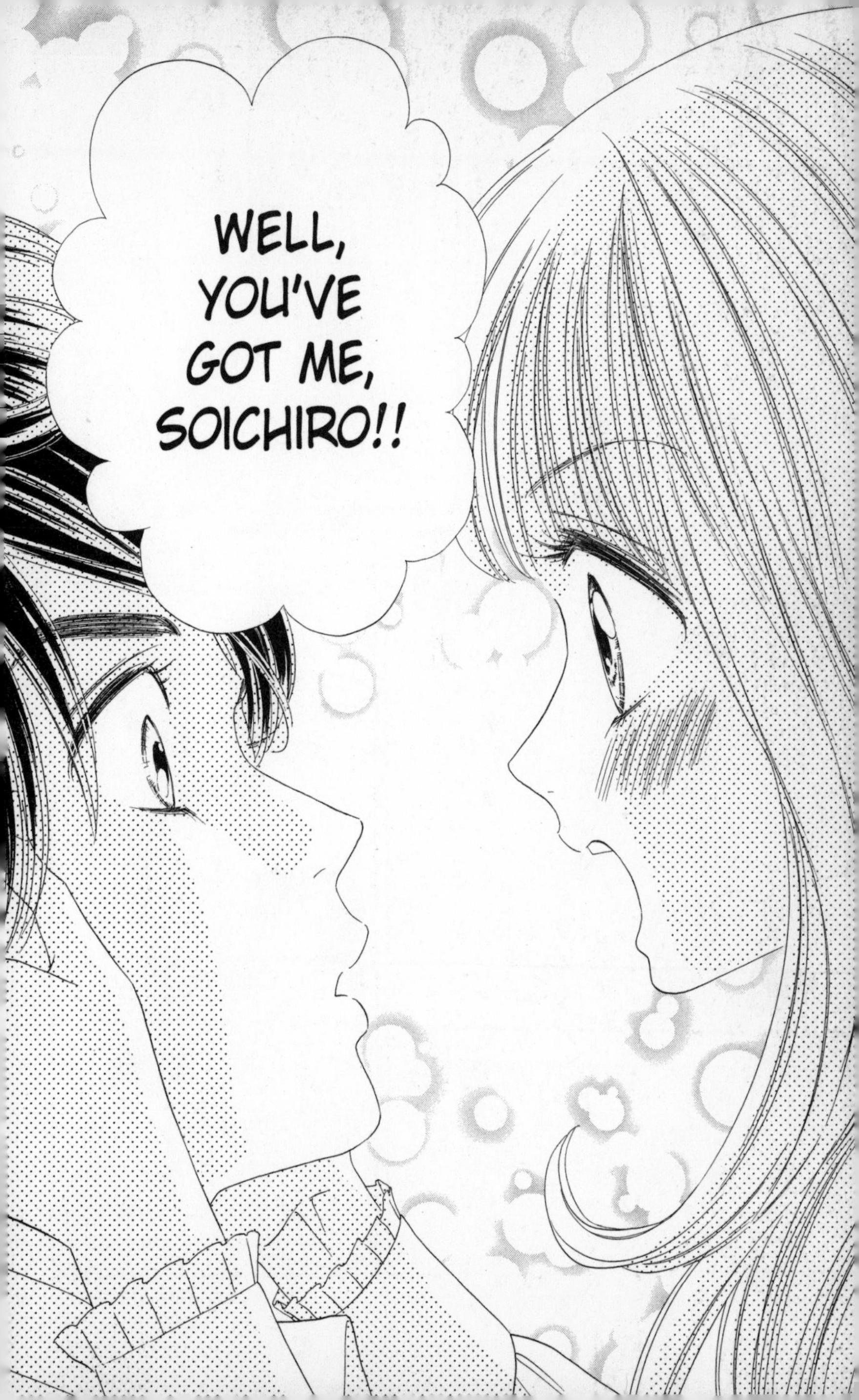
WELL, YOU'VE GOT ME, SOICHIRO!!

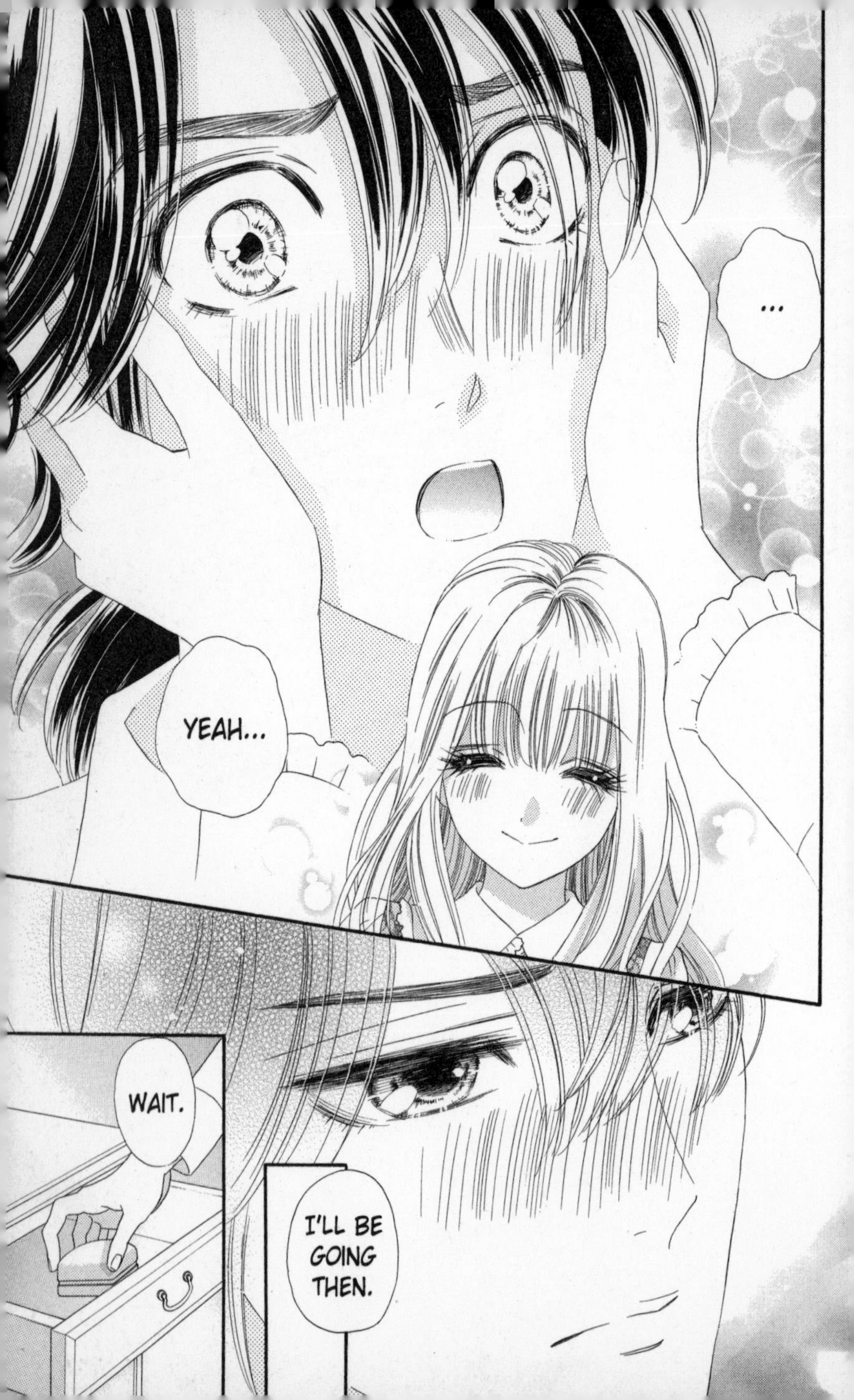
...
YEAH...
I'LL BE GOING THEN.
WAIT.

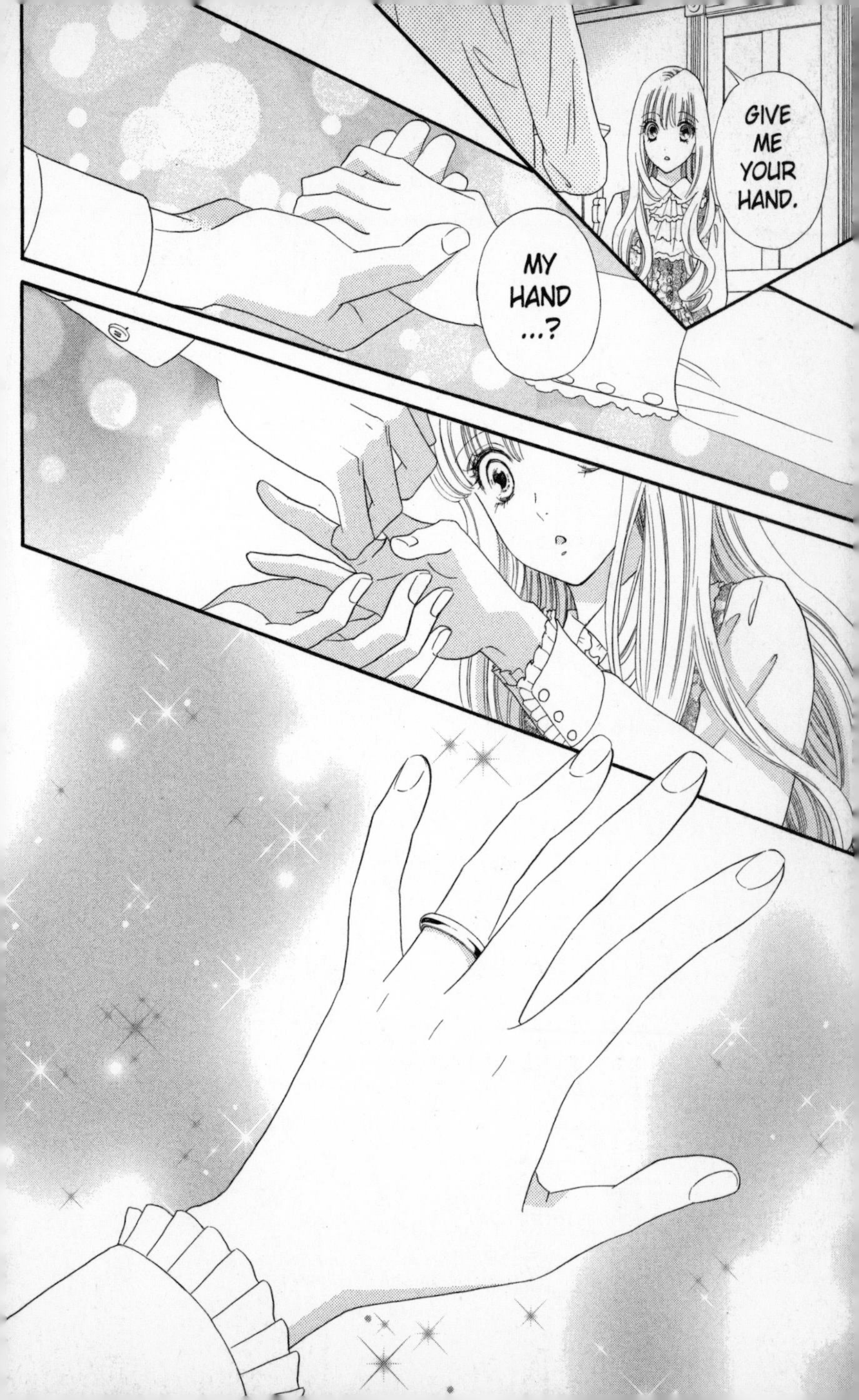
GIVE ME YOUR HAND.
MY HAND ...?

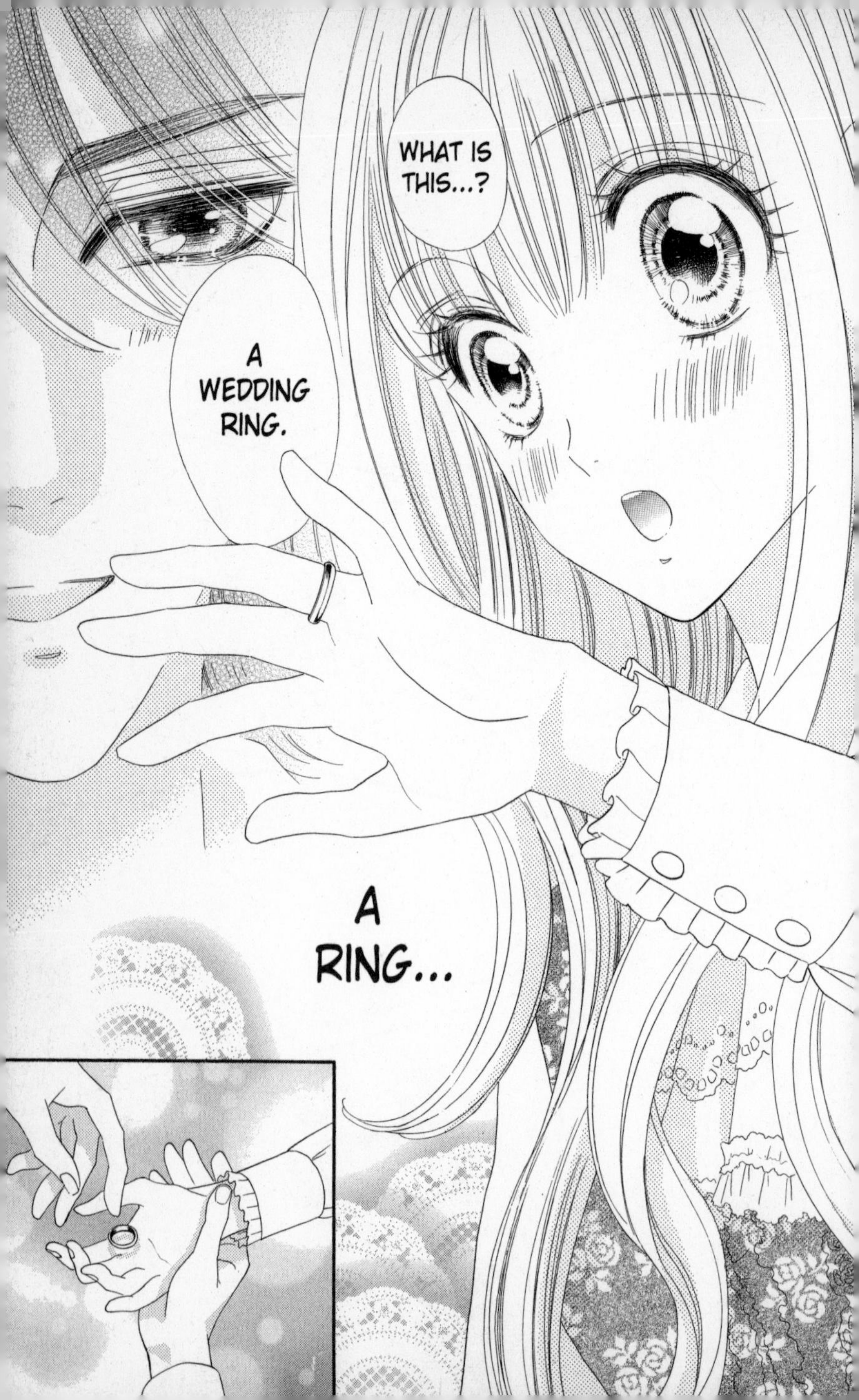
WHAT IS THIS...?
A WEDDING RING.
A RING...

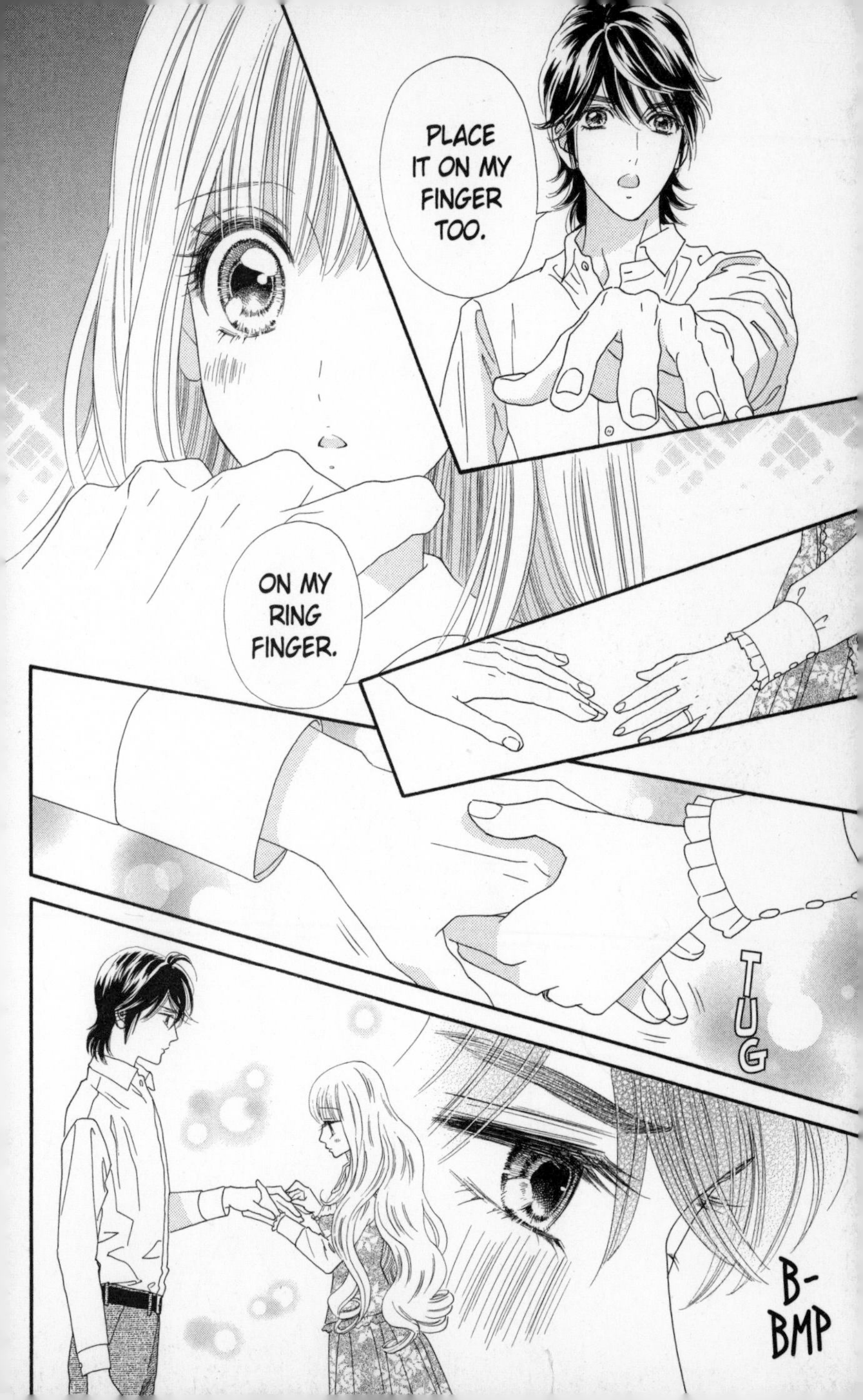
PLACE IT ON MY FINGER TOO.
ON MY RING FINGER.
TUG
B-BMP

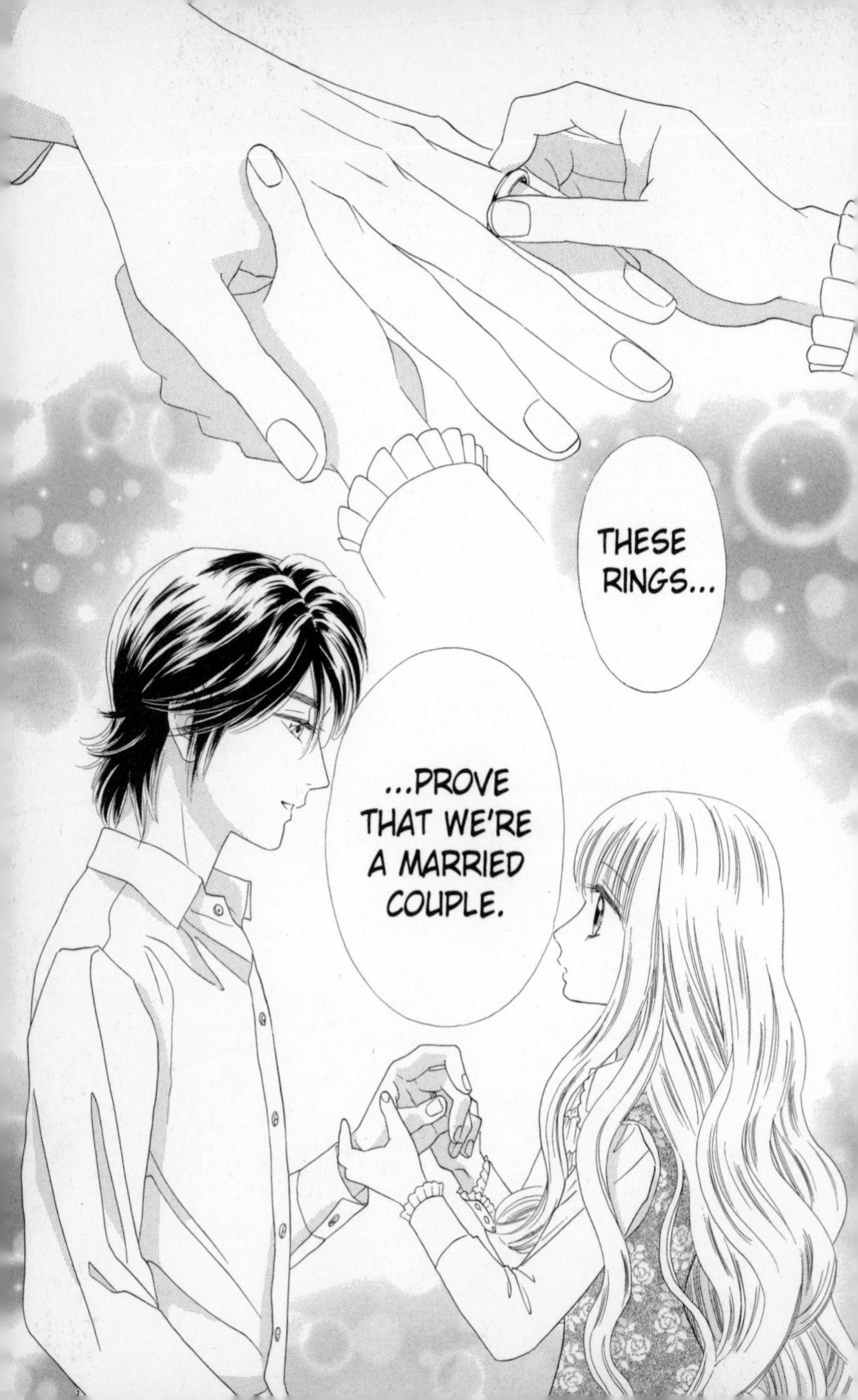
THESE RINGS...
...PROVE THAT WE'RE A MARRIED COUPLE.

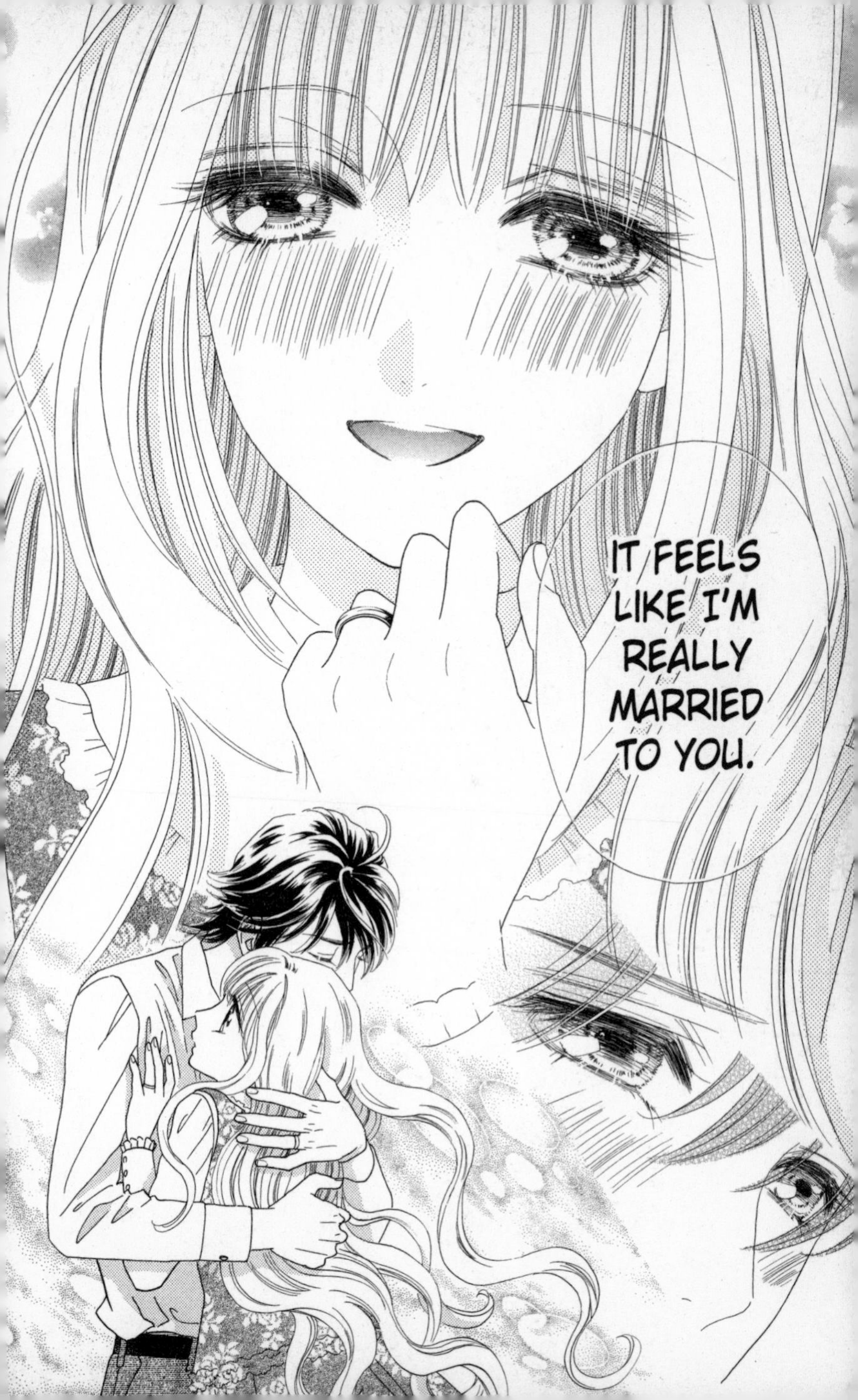
IT FEELS LIKE I'M REALLY MARRIED TO YOU.

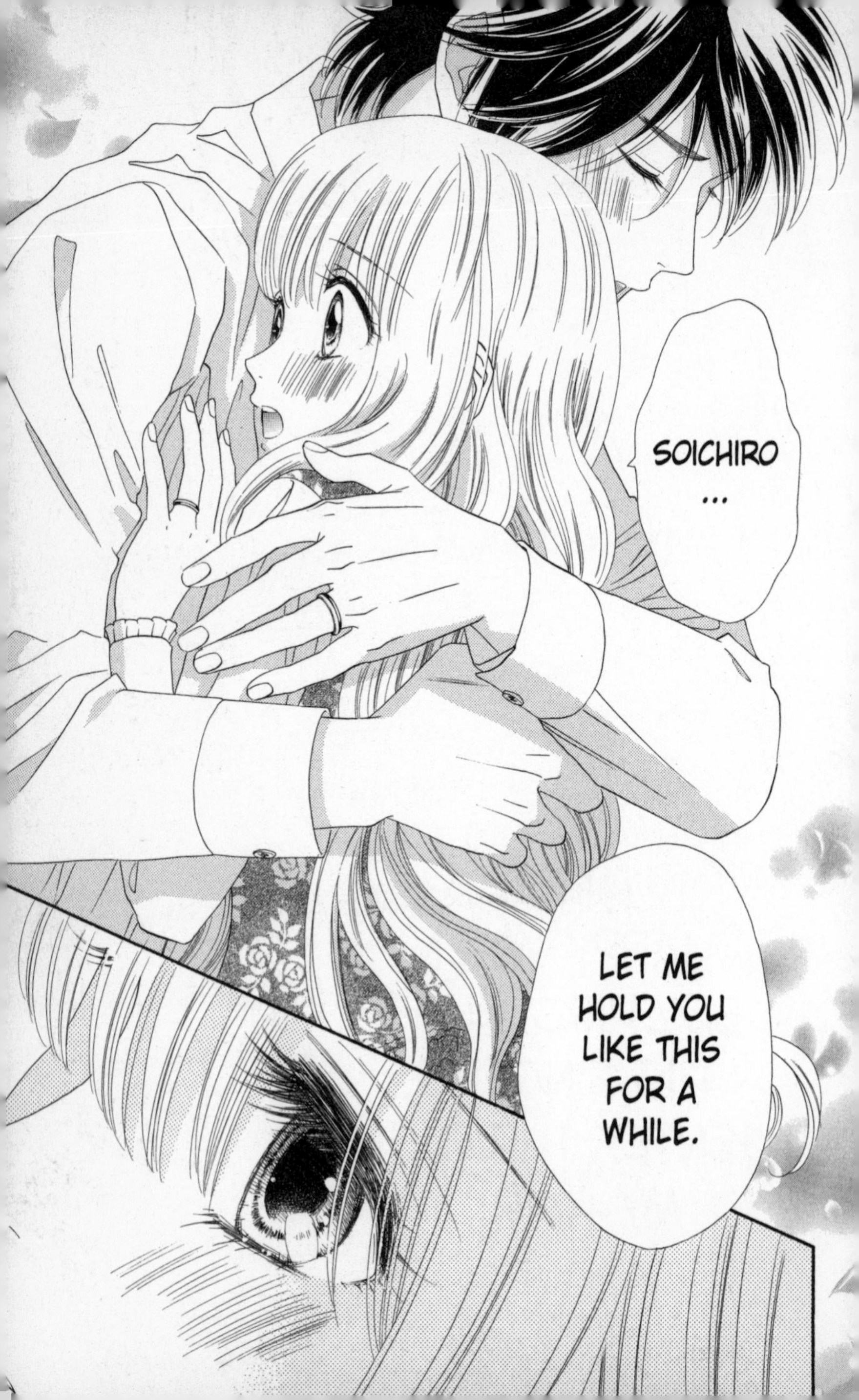
SOICHIRO ...
LET ME HOLD YOU LIKE THIS FOR A WHILE.

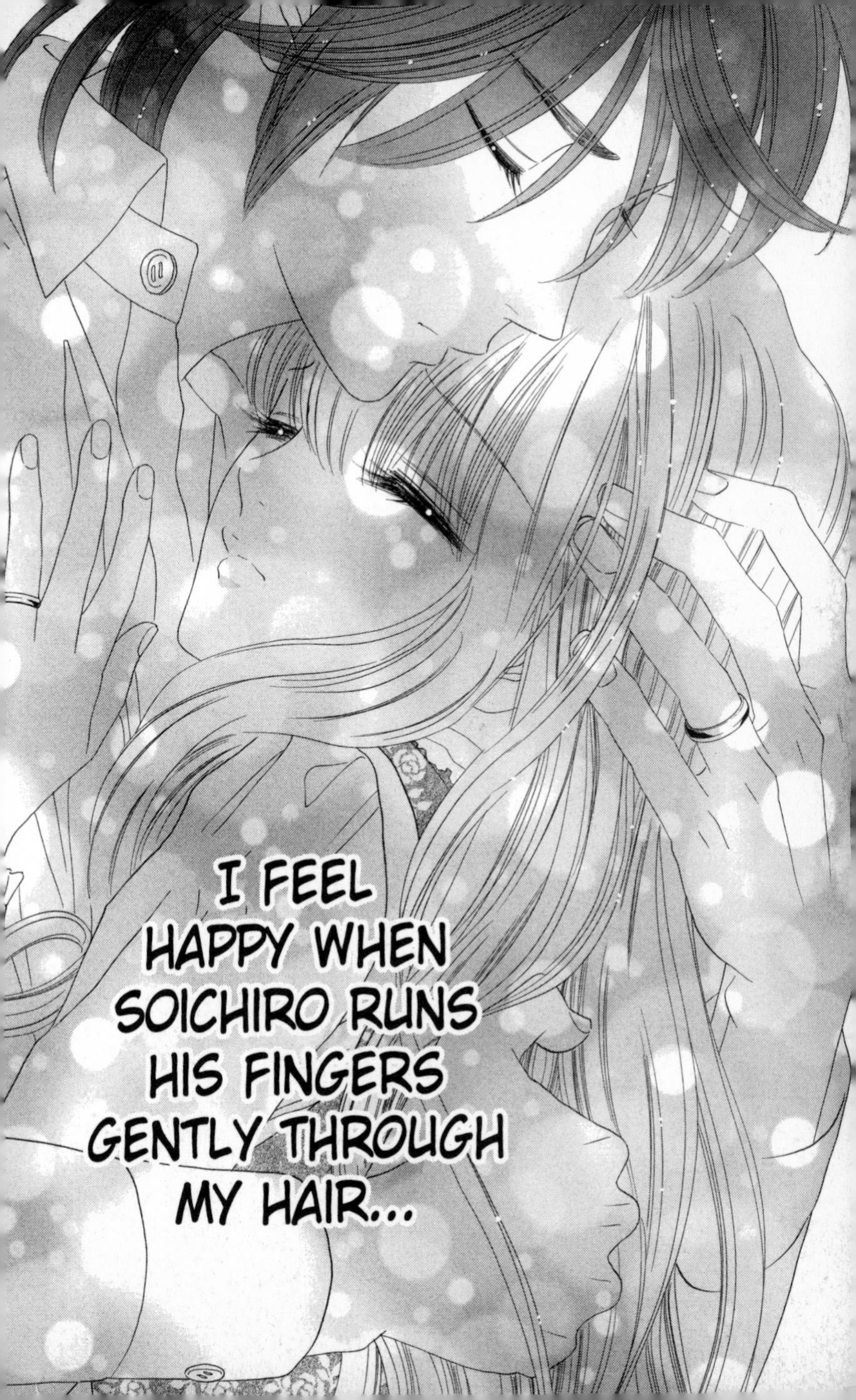
I FEEL HAPPY WHEN SOICHIRO RUNS HIS FINGERS GENTLY THROUGH MY HAIR...

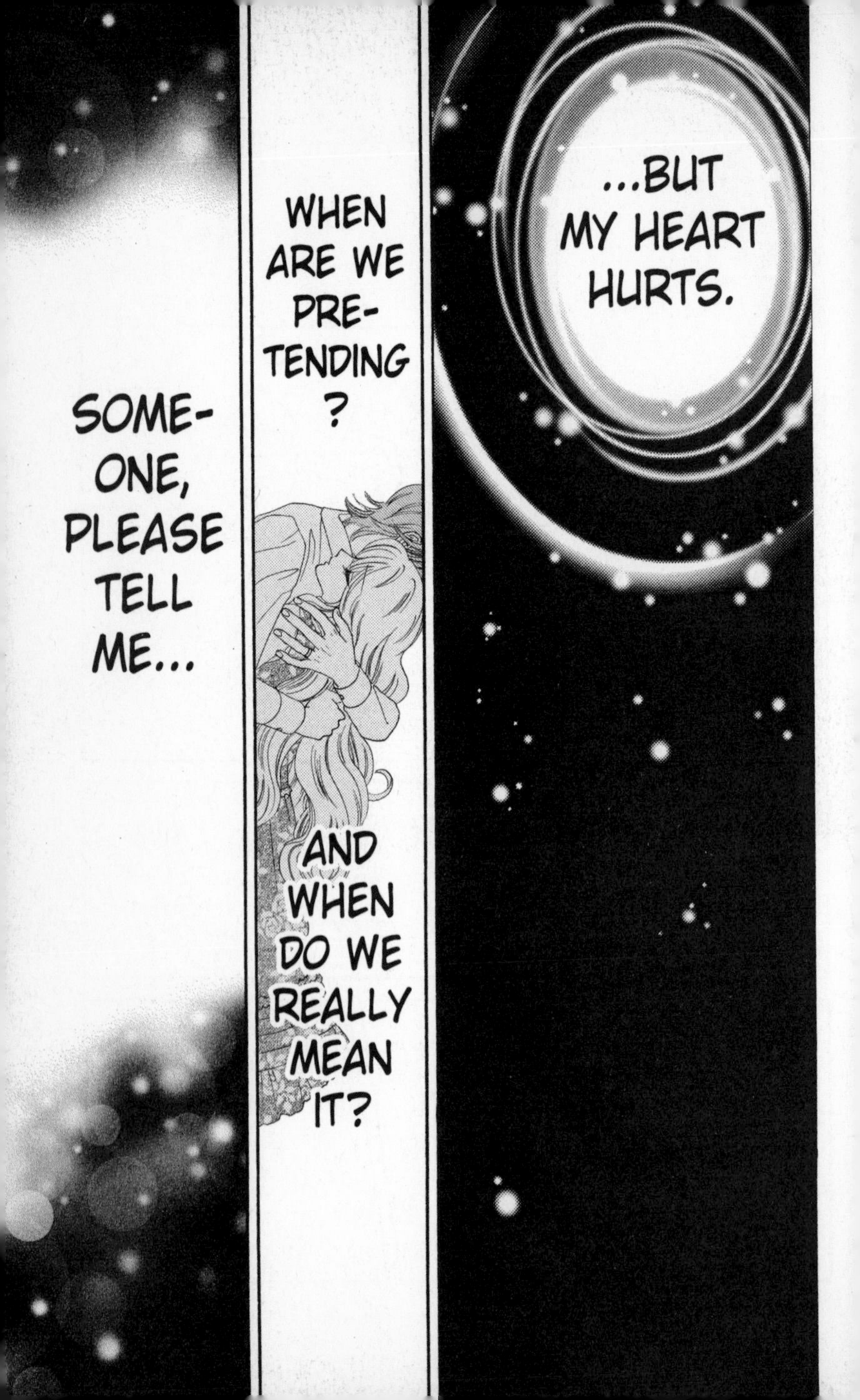
...BUT MY HEART HURTS.
WHEN ARE WE PRETENDING?
AND WHEN DO WE REALLY MEAN IT?
SOMEONE, PLEASE TELL ME...

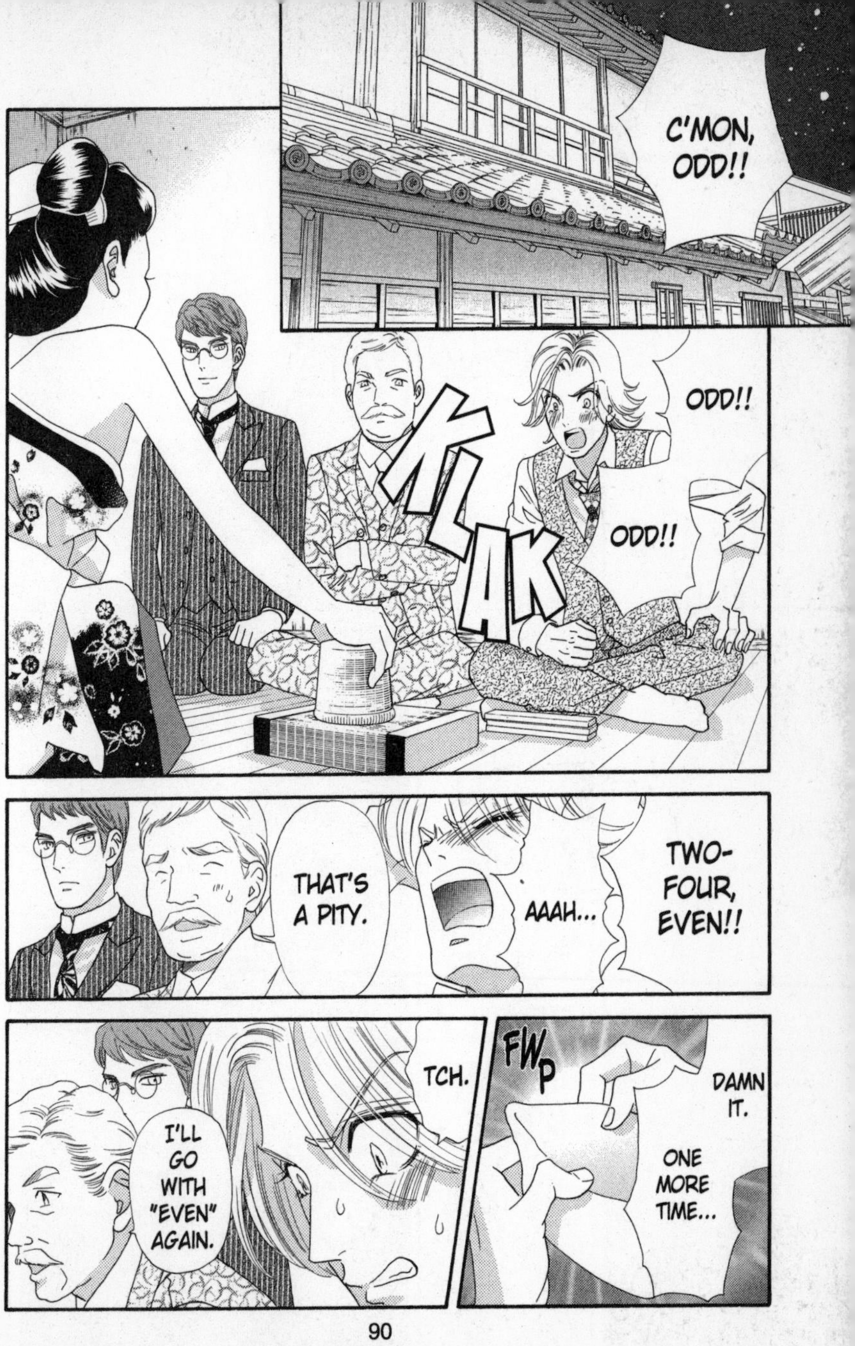

C'MON, ODD!!
ODD!!
ODD!!
KLAK
TWO-FOUR, EVEN!!
AAAH...
THAT'S A PITY.
FWP
DAMN IT.
ONE MORE TIME...
TCH.
I'LL GO WITH "EVEN" AGAIN.

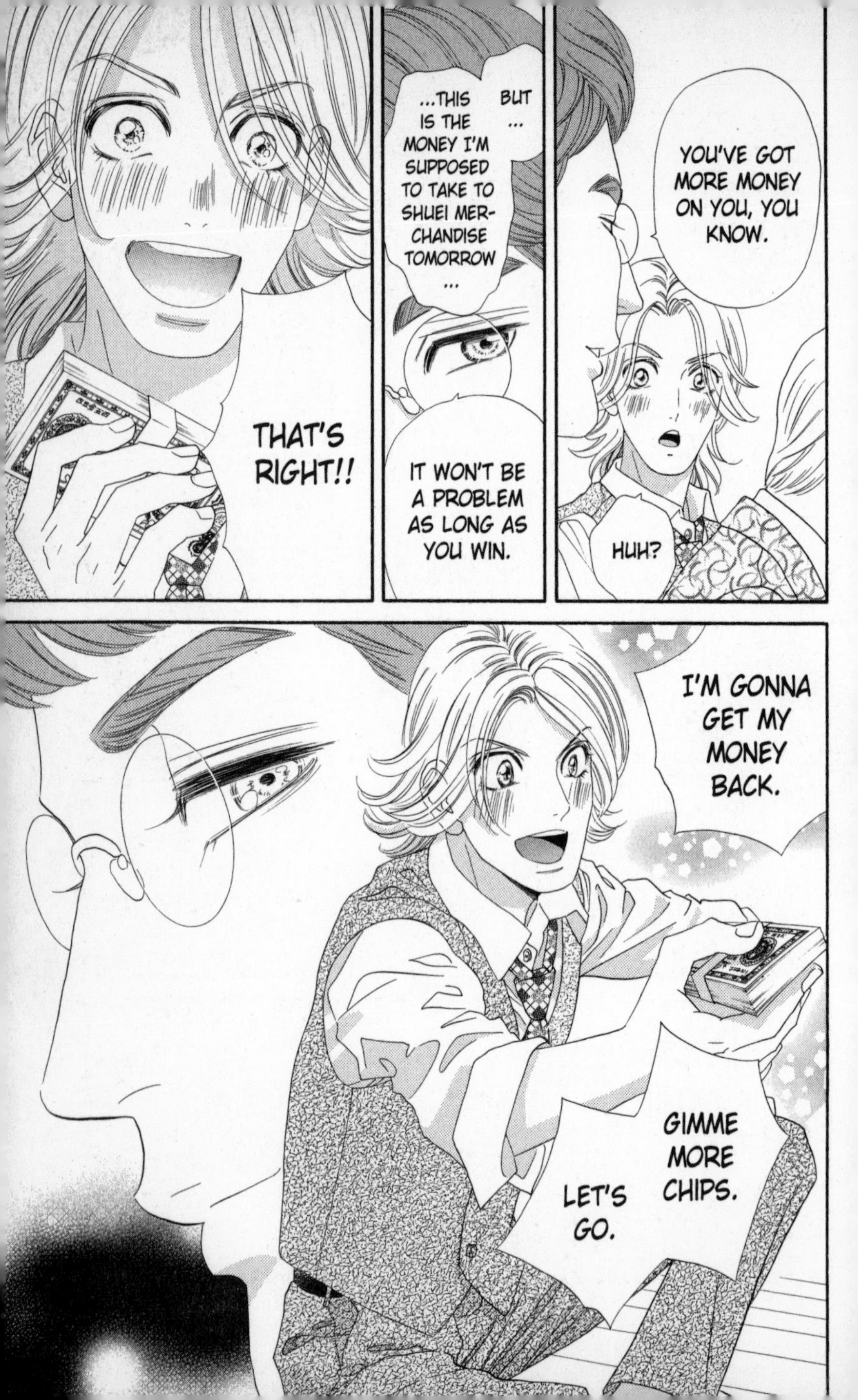
YOU'VE GOT MORE MONEY ON YOU, YOU KNOW.
HUH?
BUT ... ...THIS IS THE MONEY I'M SUPPOSED TO TAKE TO SHUEI MERCHANDISE TOMORROW ...
IT WON'T BE A PROBLEM AS LONG AS YOU WIN.
THAT'S RIGHT!!
I'M GONNA GET MY MONEY BACK.
GIMME MORE CHIPS.
LET'S GO.

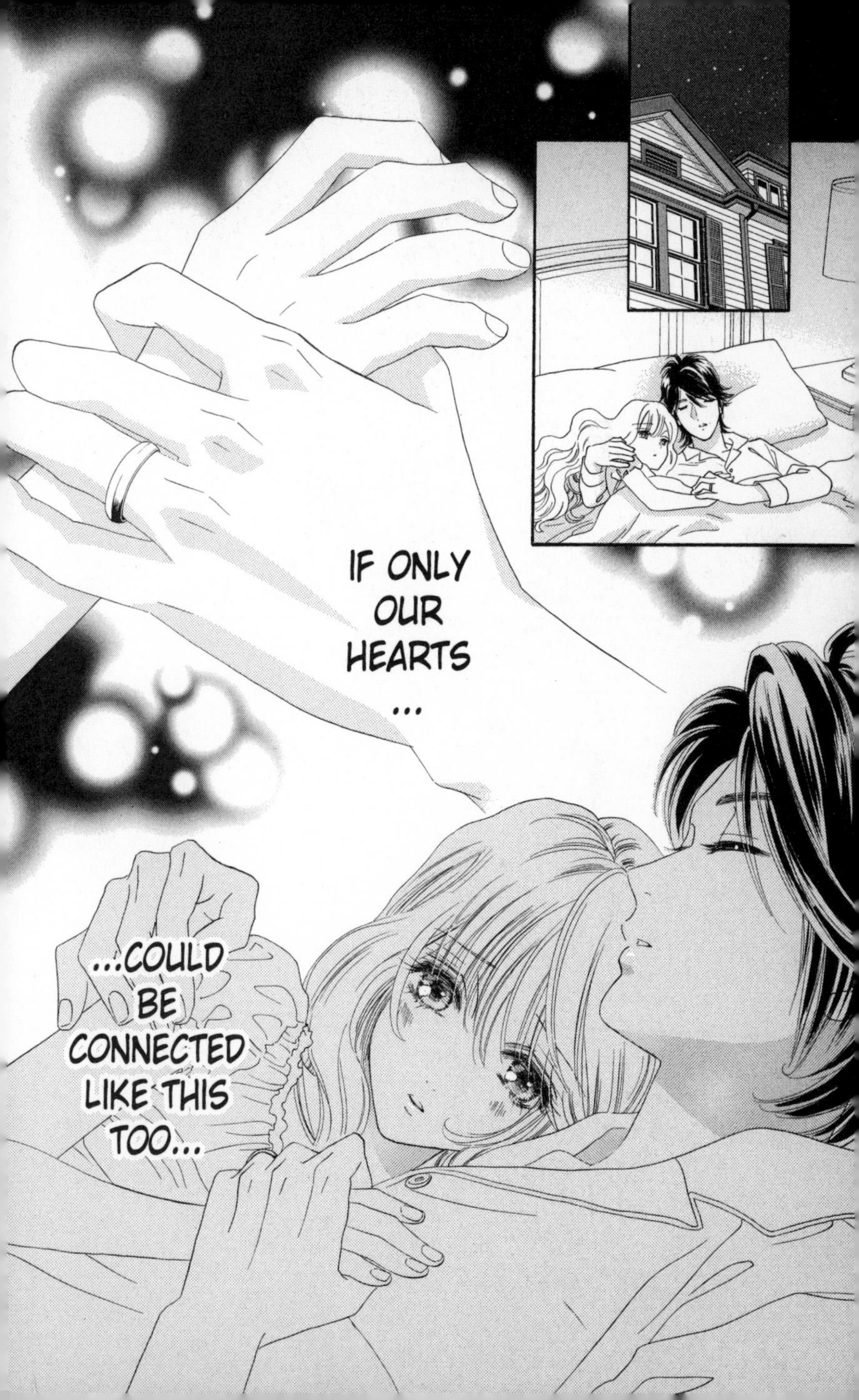
IF ONLY OUR HEARTS...
...COULD BE CONNECTED LIKE THIS TOO...

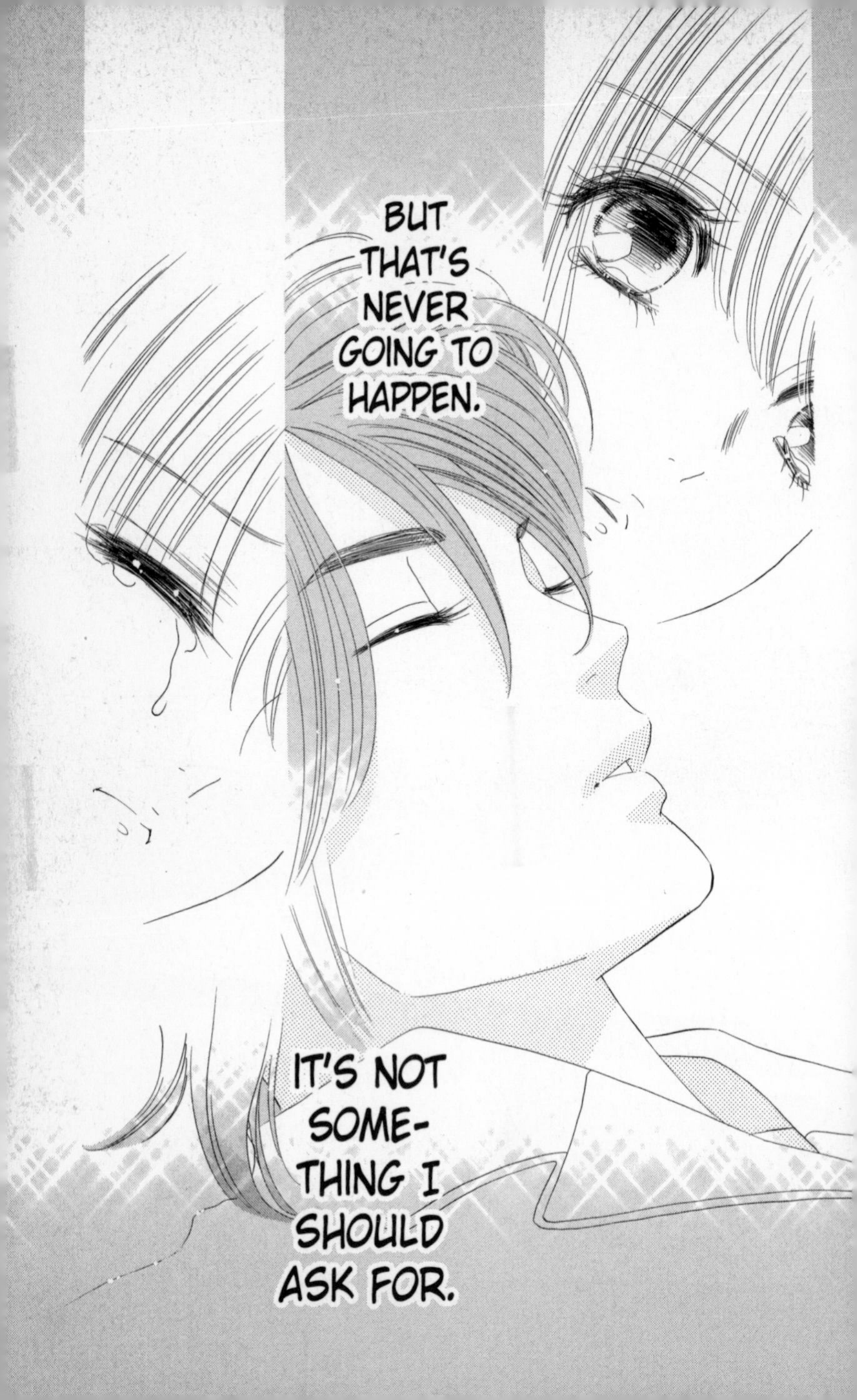
BUT THAT'S NEVER GOING TO HAPPEN.
IT'S NOT SOME-THING I SHOULD ASK FOR.

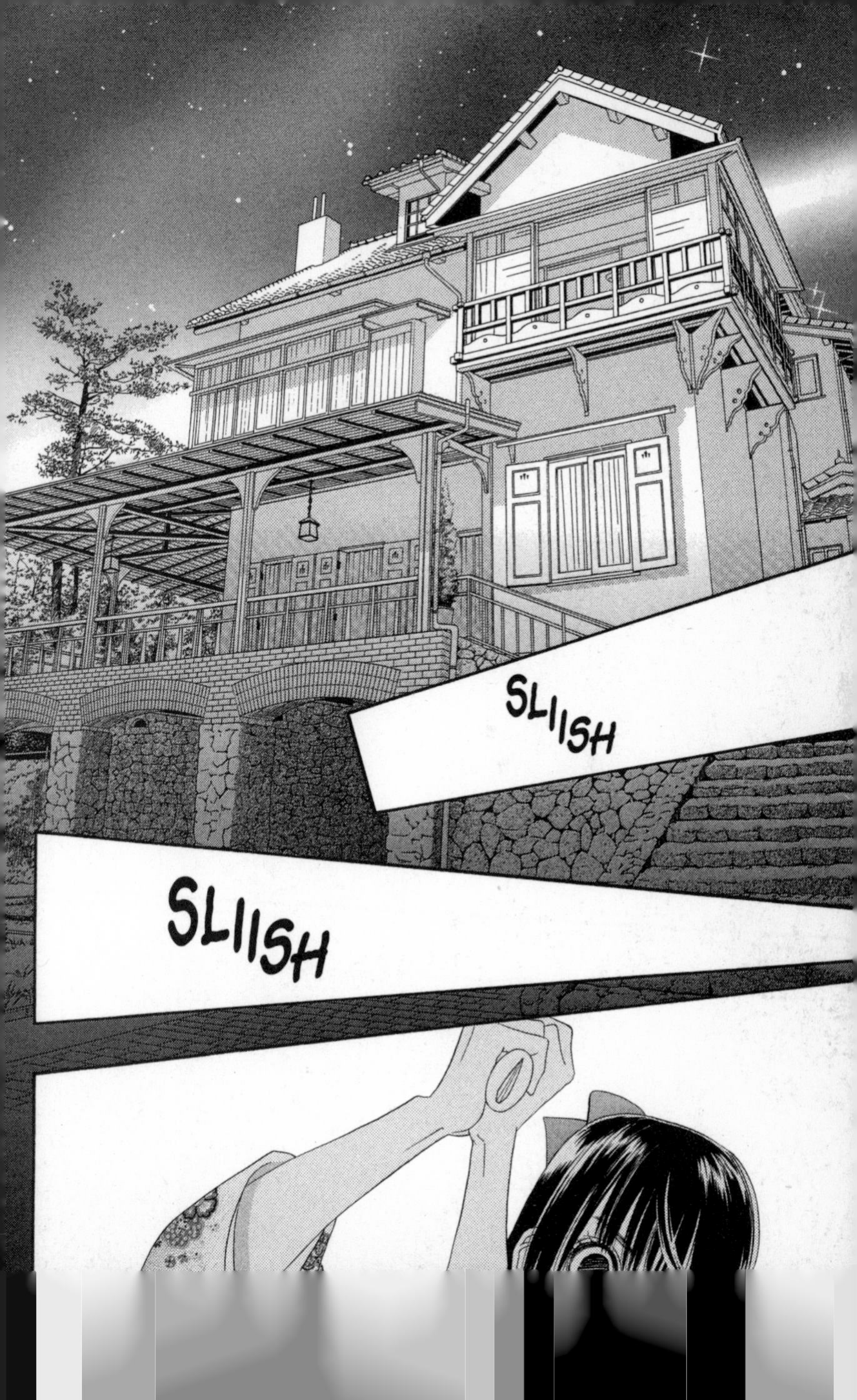
SLIISH
SLIISH

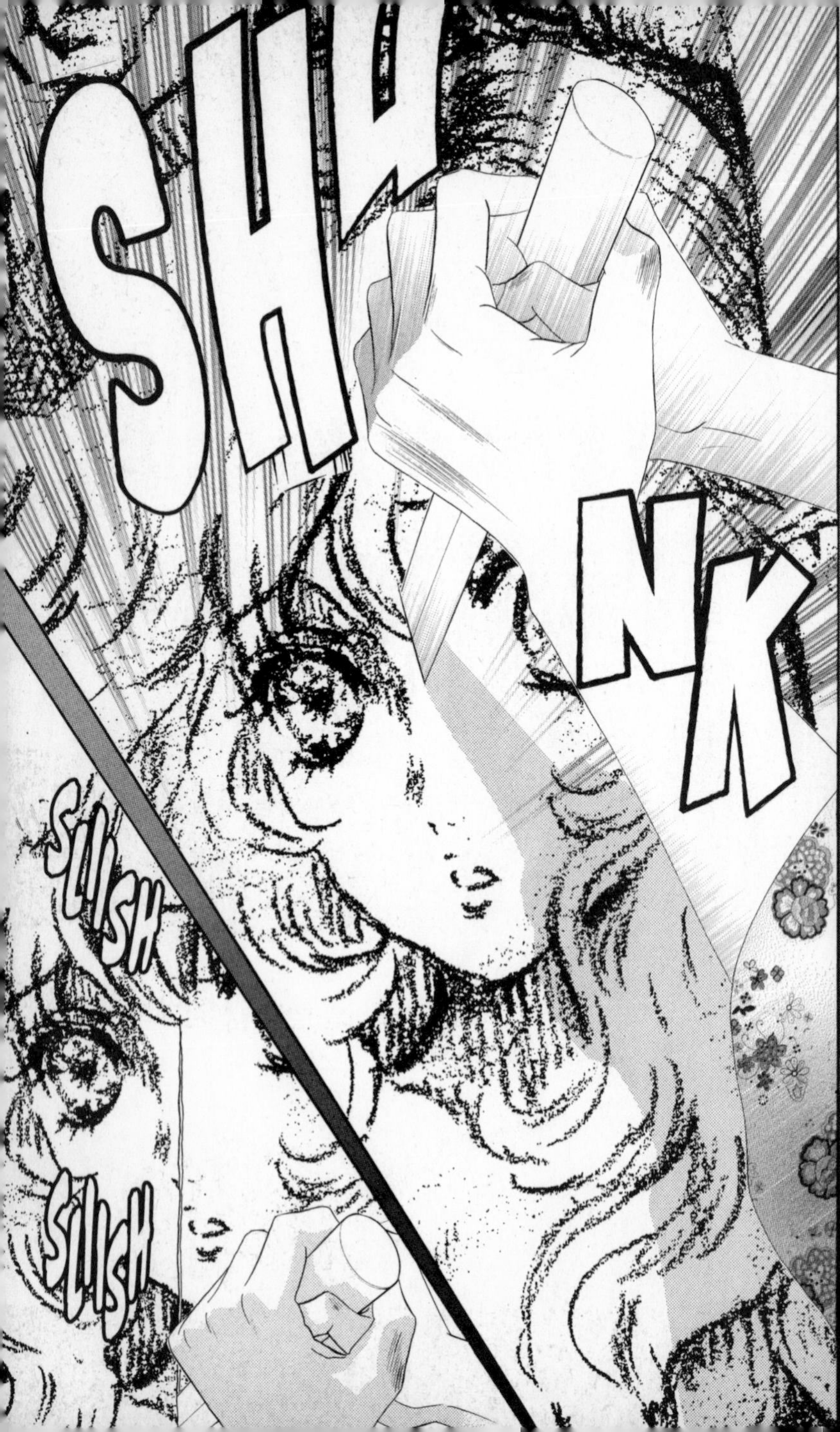
SHHNK
SLISH
SLISH

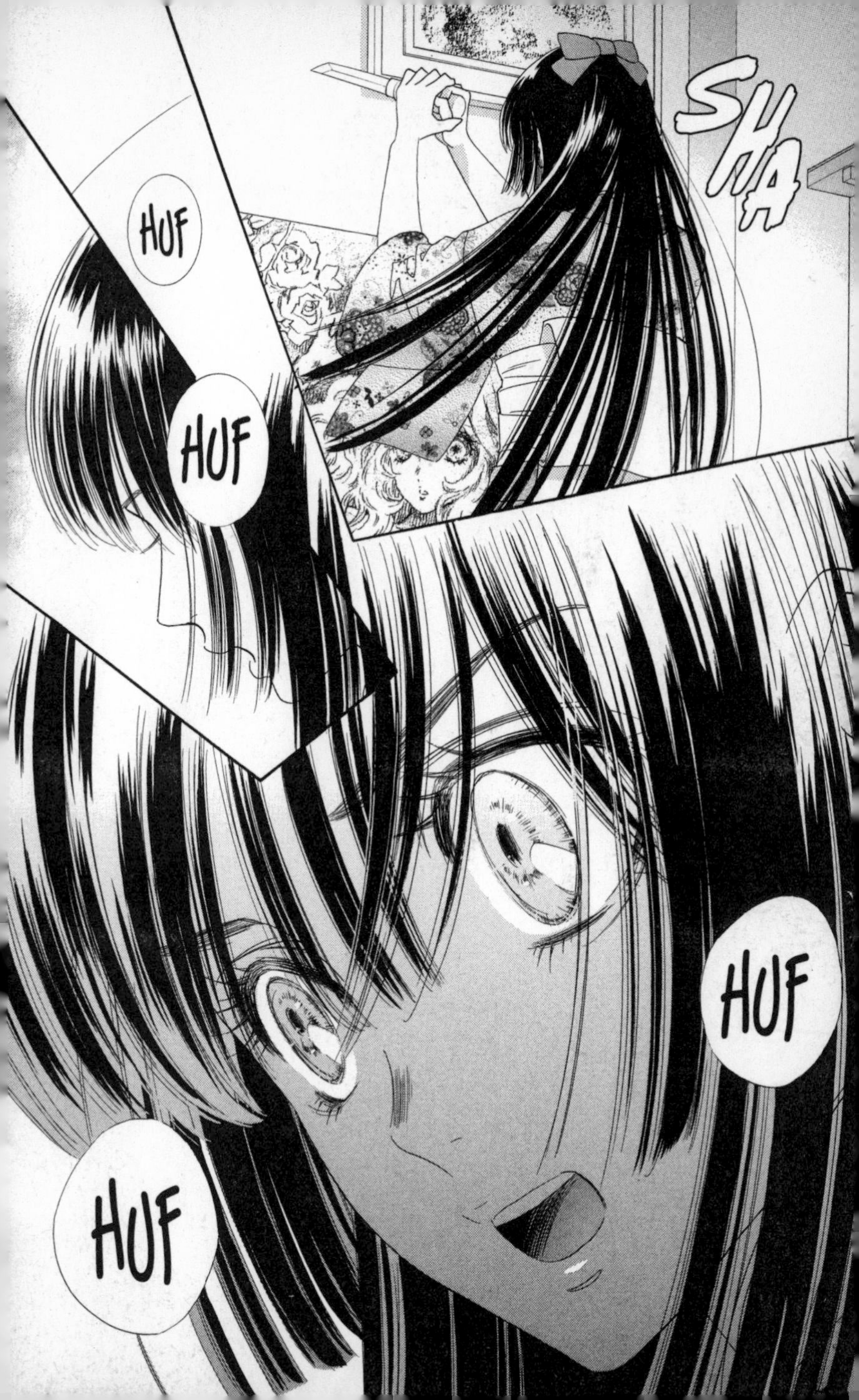
SHA
HUF
HUF
HUF
HUF

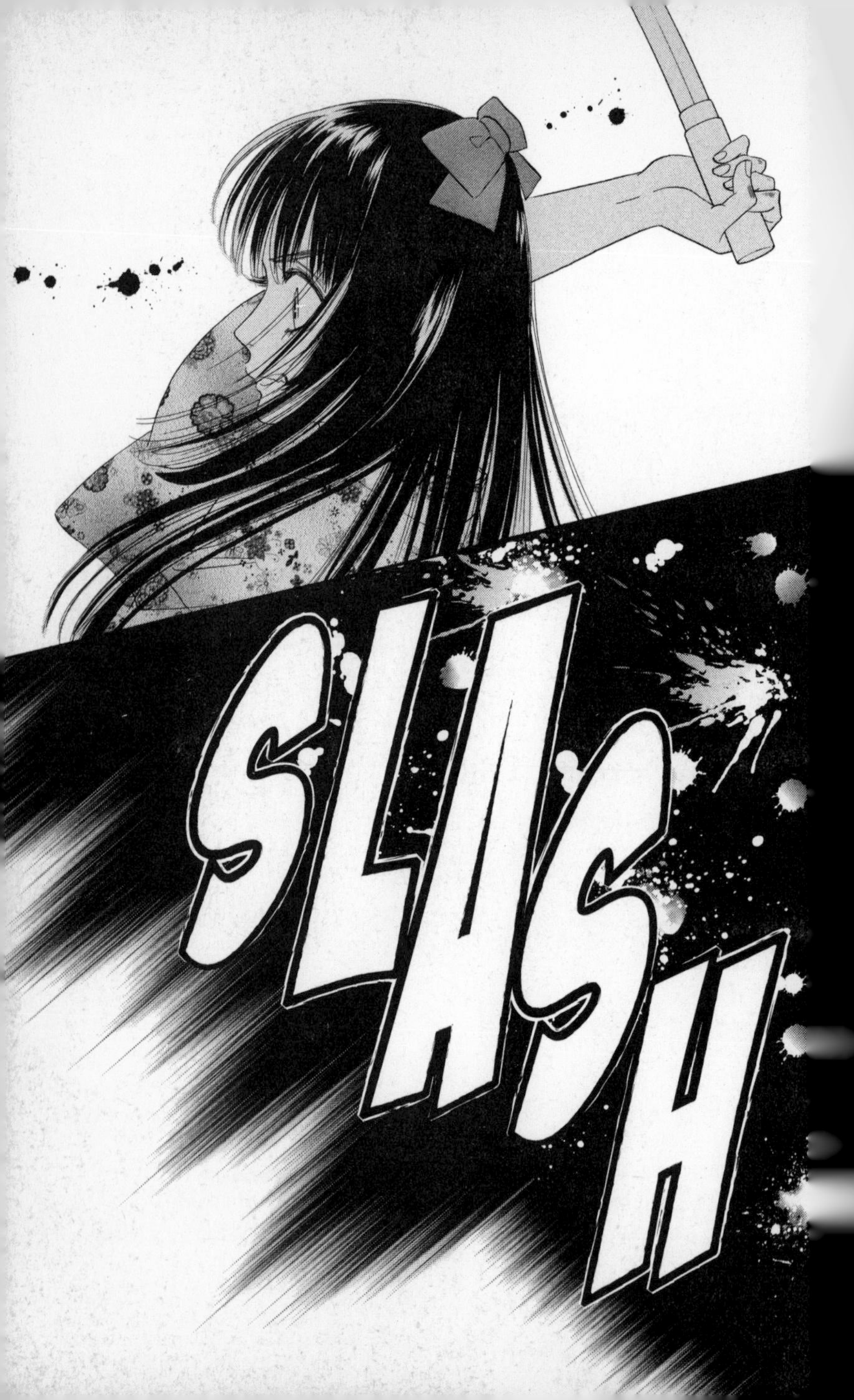
SLASH

IJUIN FAMILY HOUSE → MEIJI MURA (TSUGUMICHI SAIGO HOUSE)

Meiji Mura is an open-air museum with buildings that were relocated from Aichi Prefecture, Inuyama City. If you go there, you can learn about the history and culture of the Meiji Era.

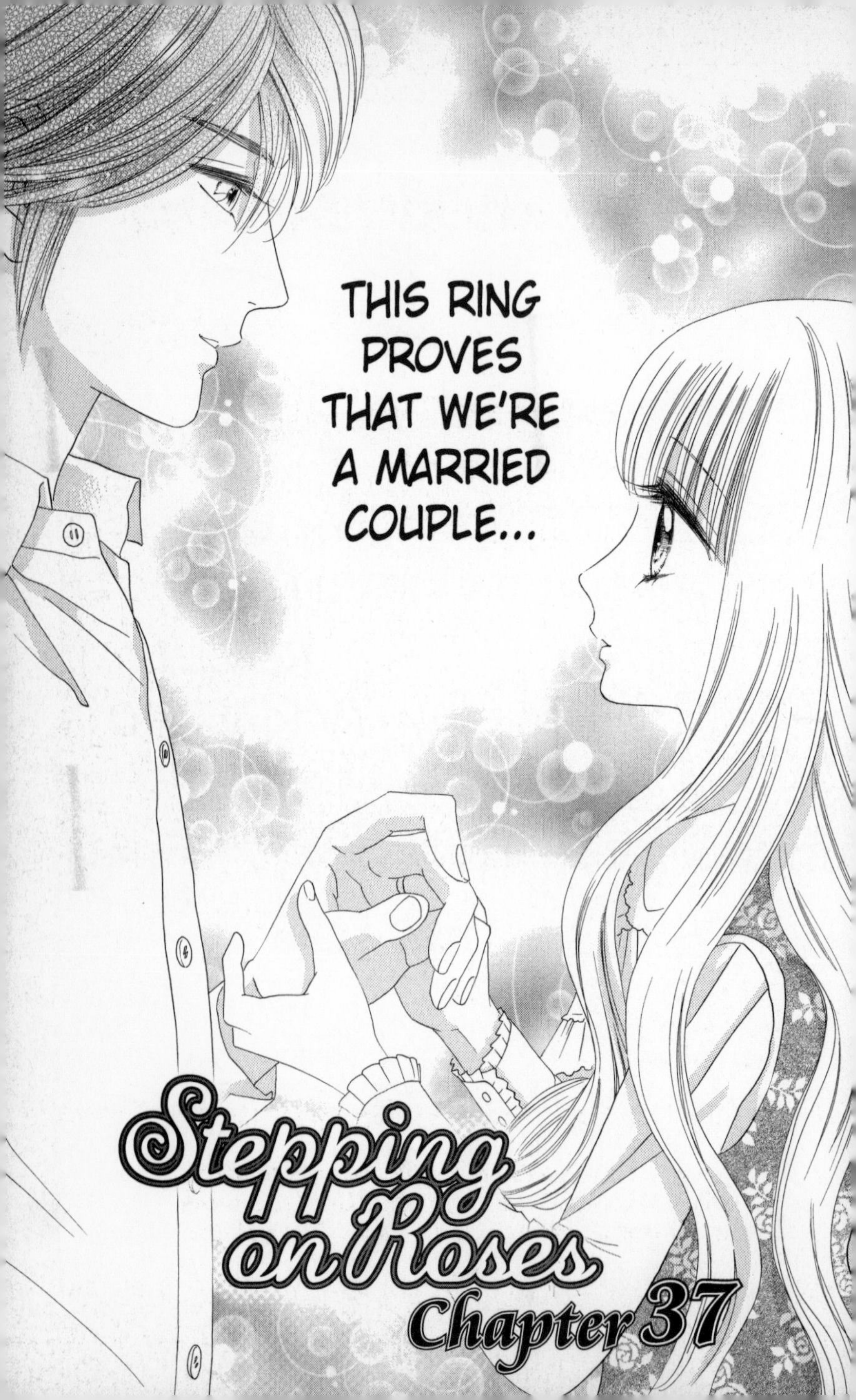
THIS RING PROVES THAT WE'RE A MARRIED COUPLE...
Stepping on Roses
Chapter 37

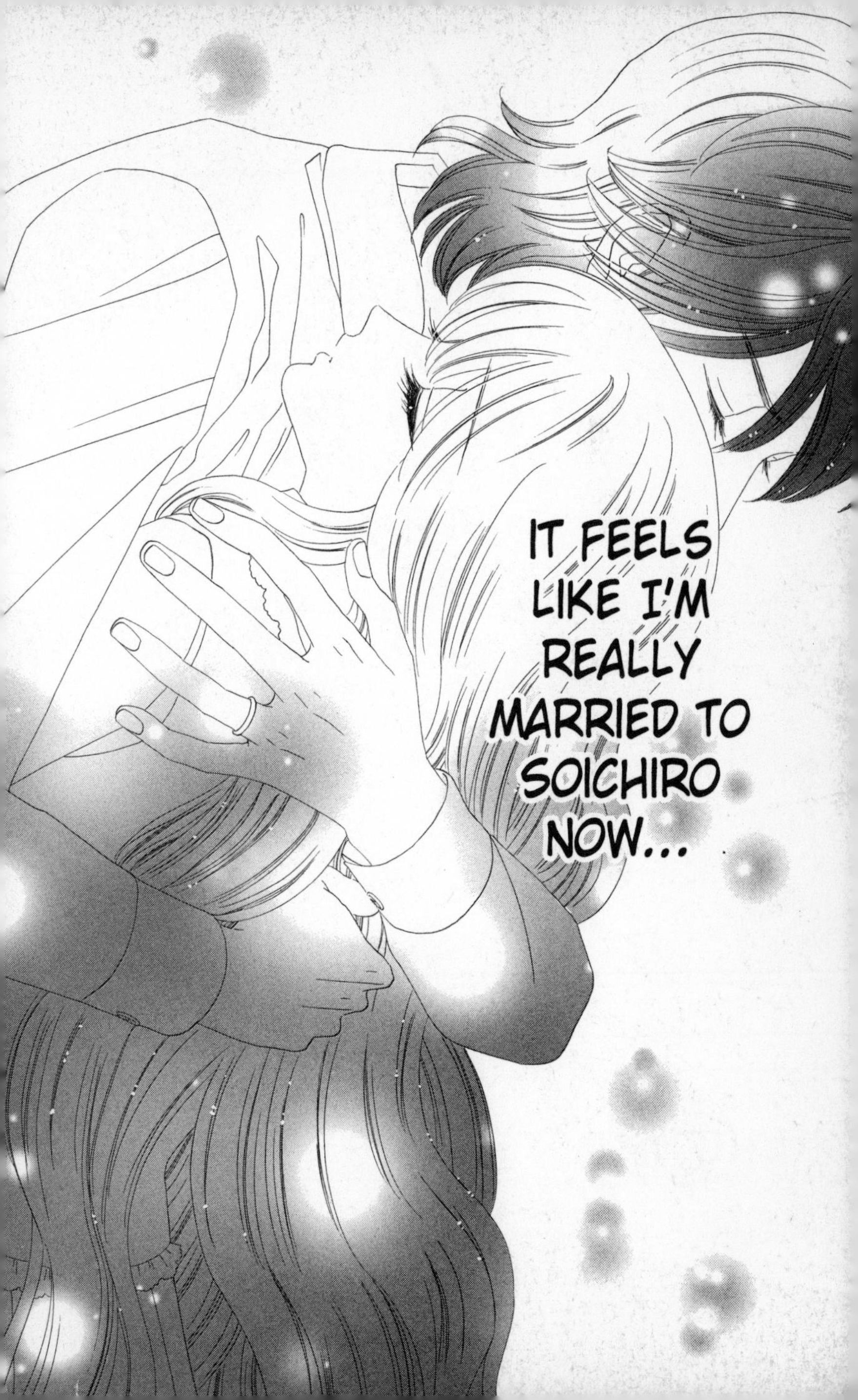
IT FEELS LIKE I'M REALLY MARRIED TO SOICHIRO NOW...

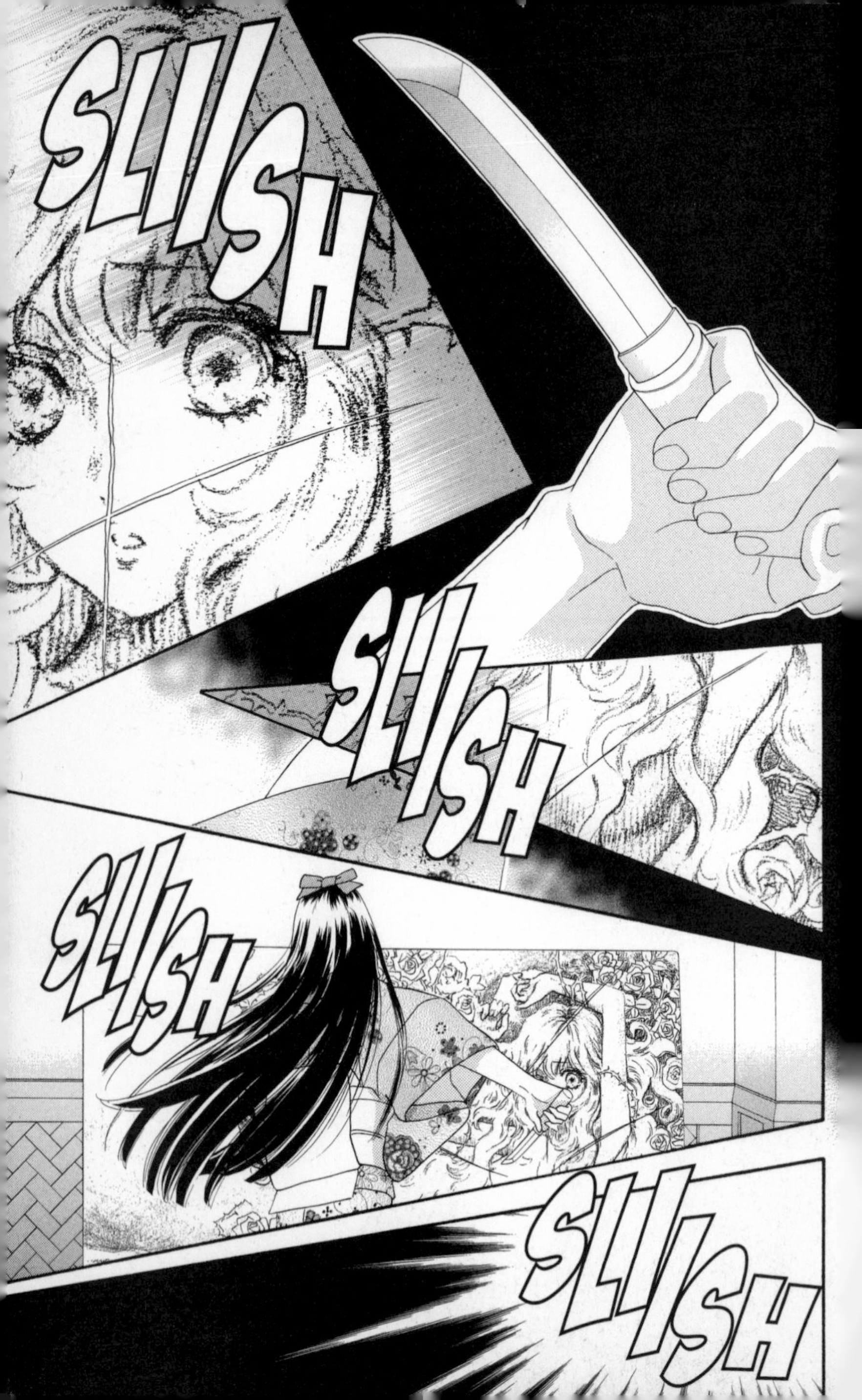
SLIISH
SLIISH
SLIISH
SLIISH

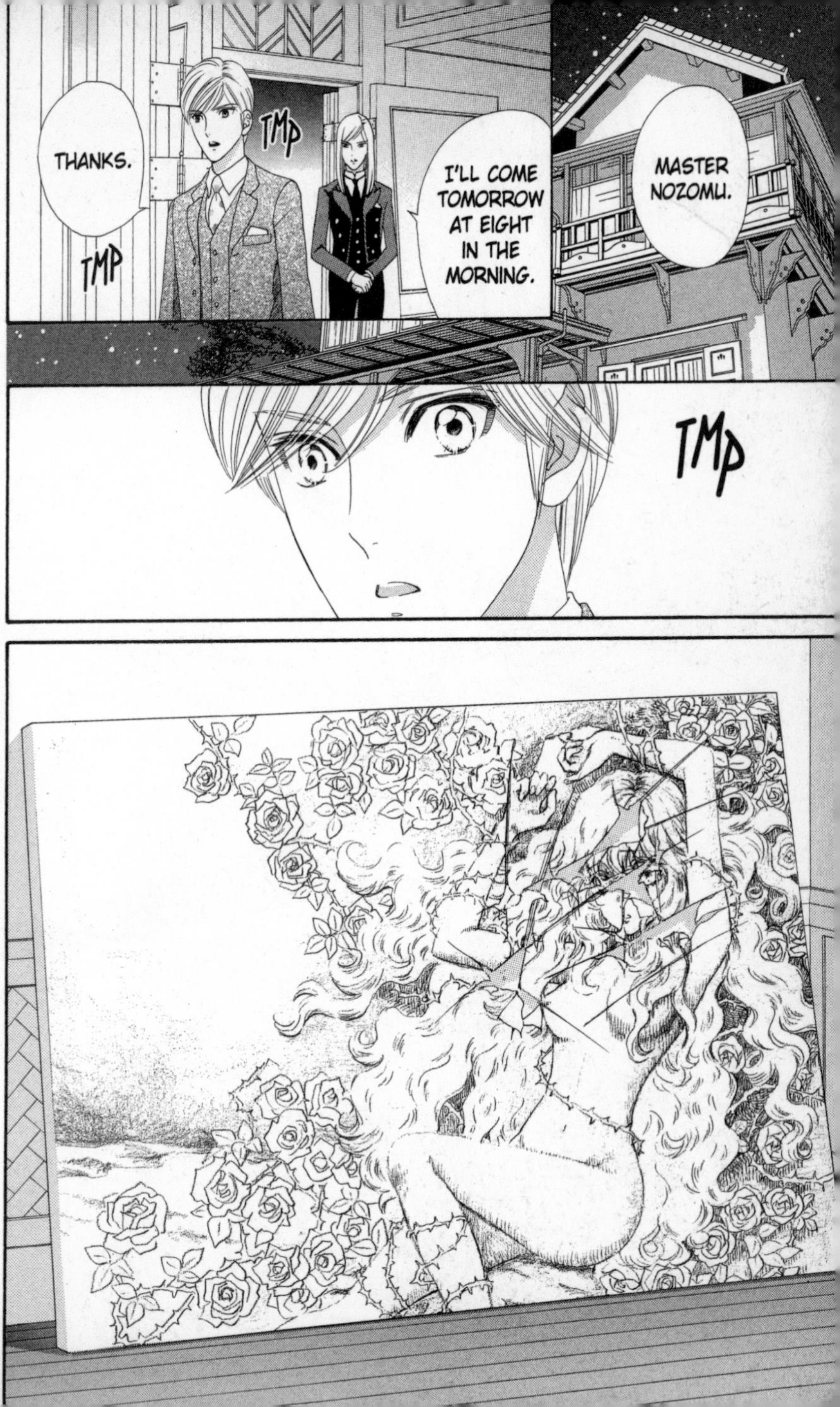
MASTER NOZOMU.
I'LL COME TOMORROW AT EIGHT IN THE MORNING.
TMP
THANKS.
TMP
TMP

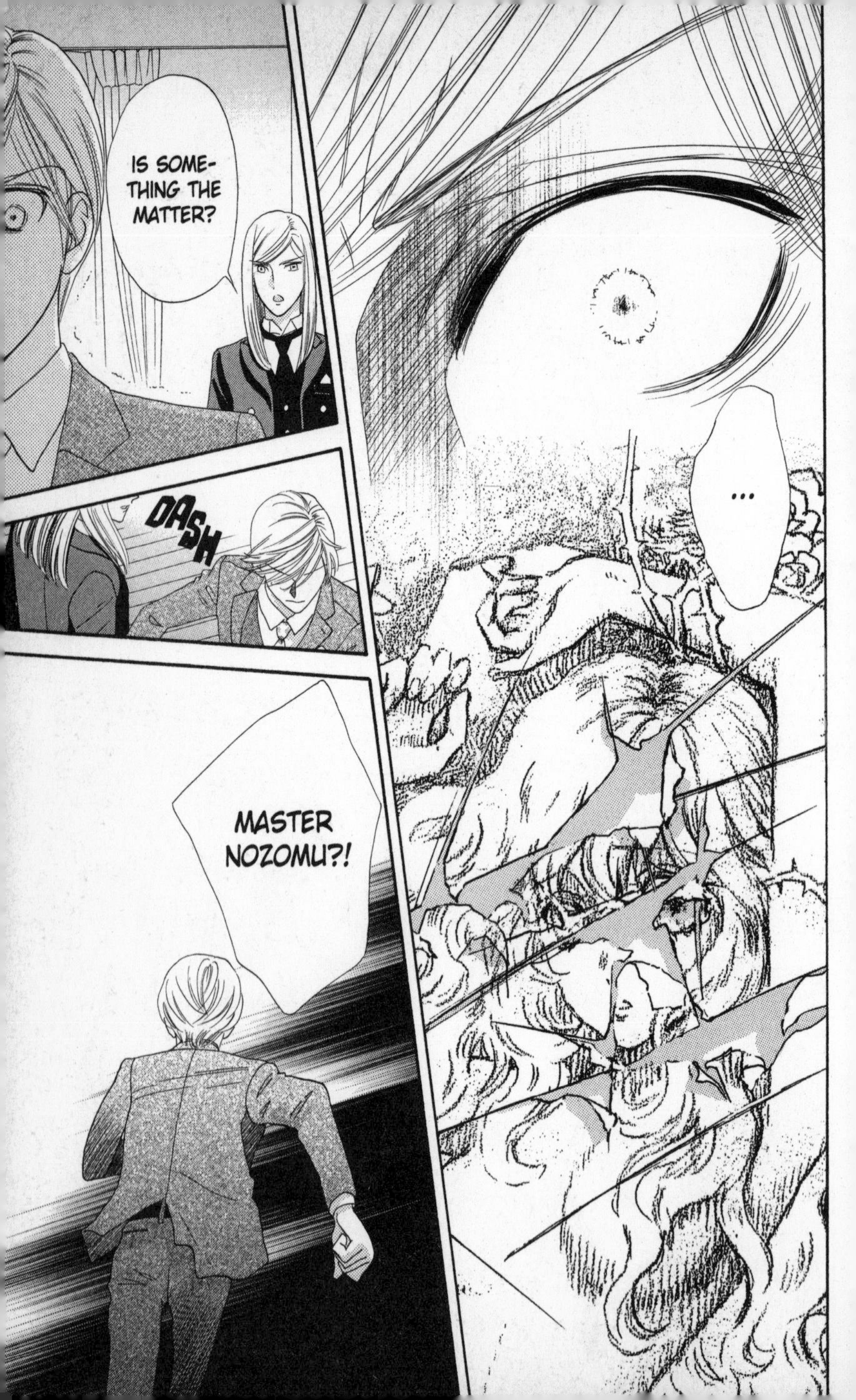
...
IS SOME-THING THE MATTER?
DASH
MASTER NOZOMU?!

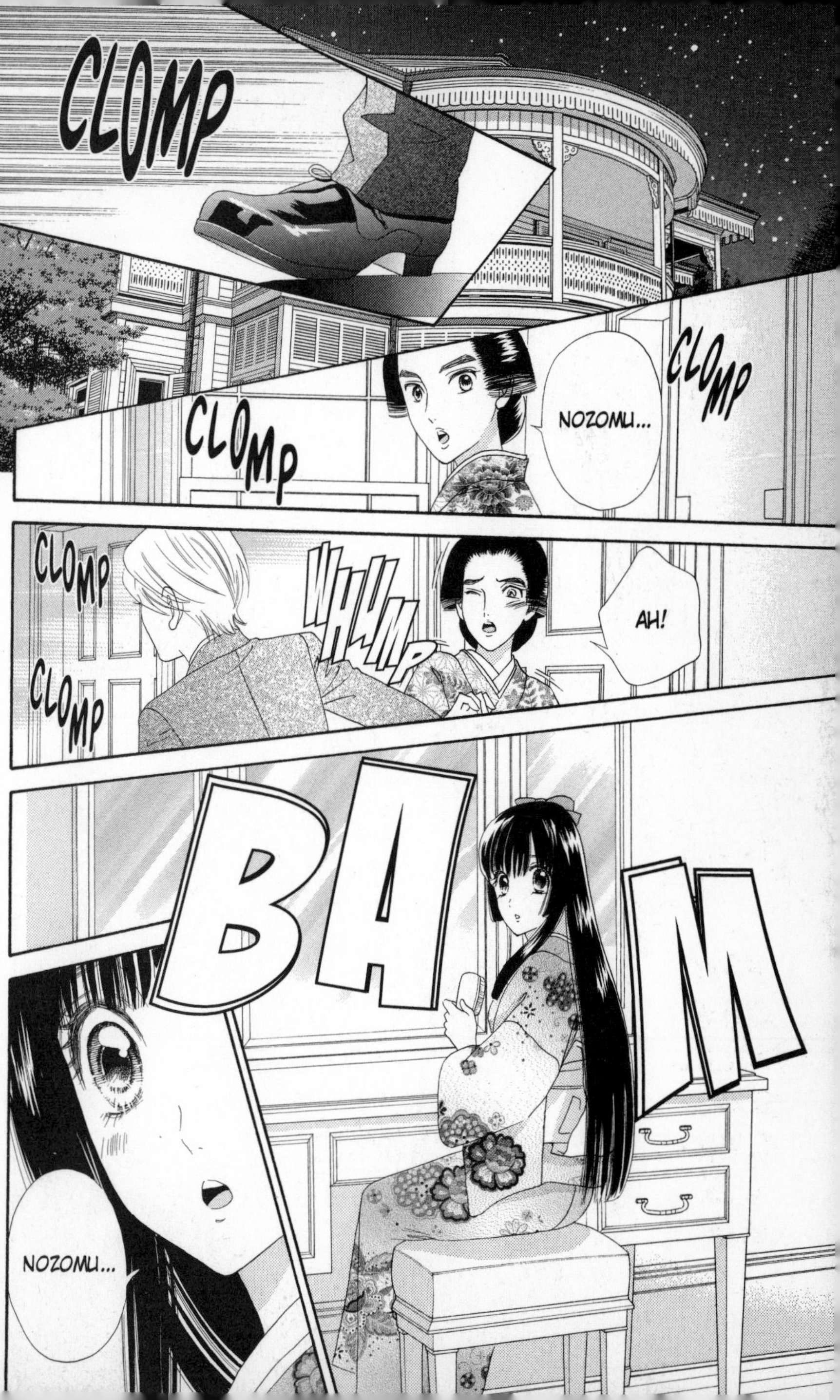
CLOMP
CLOMP
NOZOMU...
CLOMP
AH!
WHUMP
CLOMP
CLOMP
BAM
NOZOMU...

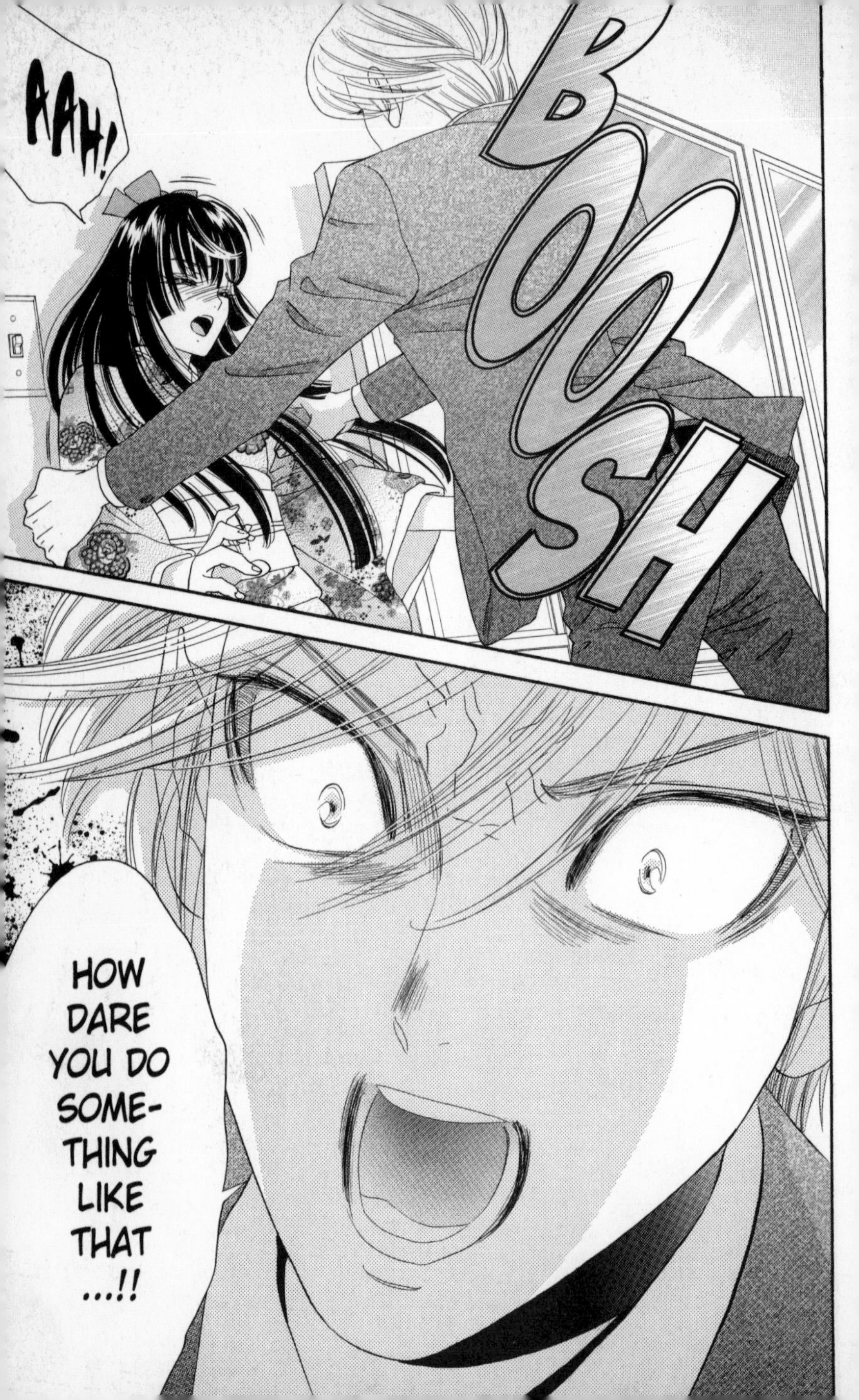
BOOOSH
AAH!
HOW DARE YOU DO SOME-THING LIKE THAT ...!!

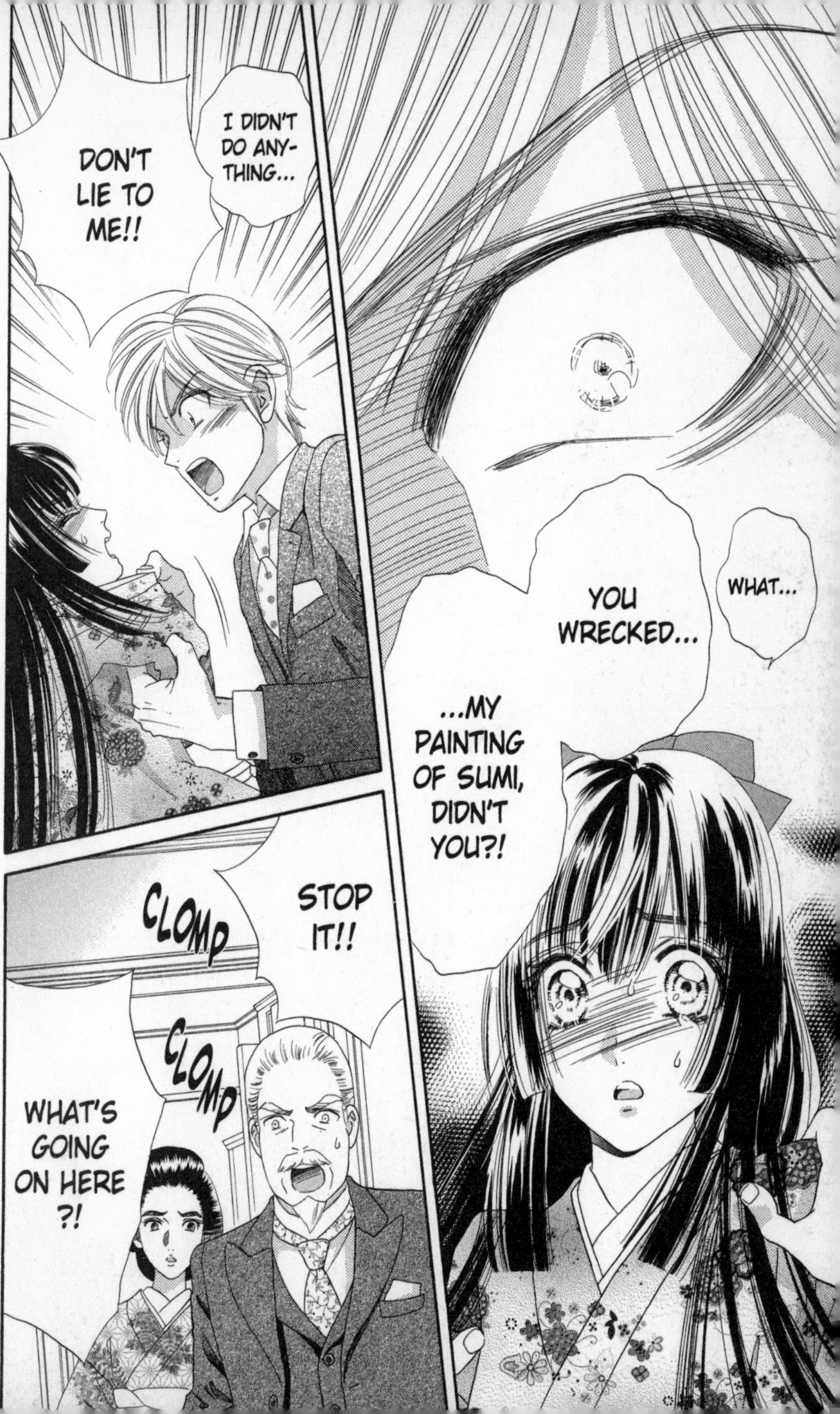
WHAT...
YOU WRECKED...
...MY PAINTING OF SUMI, DIDN'T YOU?!
I DIDN'T DO ANY-THING...
DON'T LIE TO ME!!
STOP IT!!
CLOMP
CLOMP
WHAT'S GOING ON HERE?!

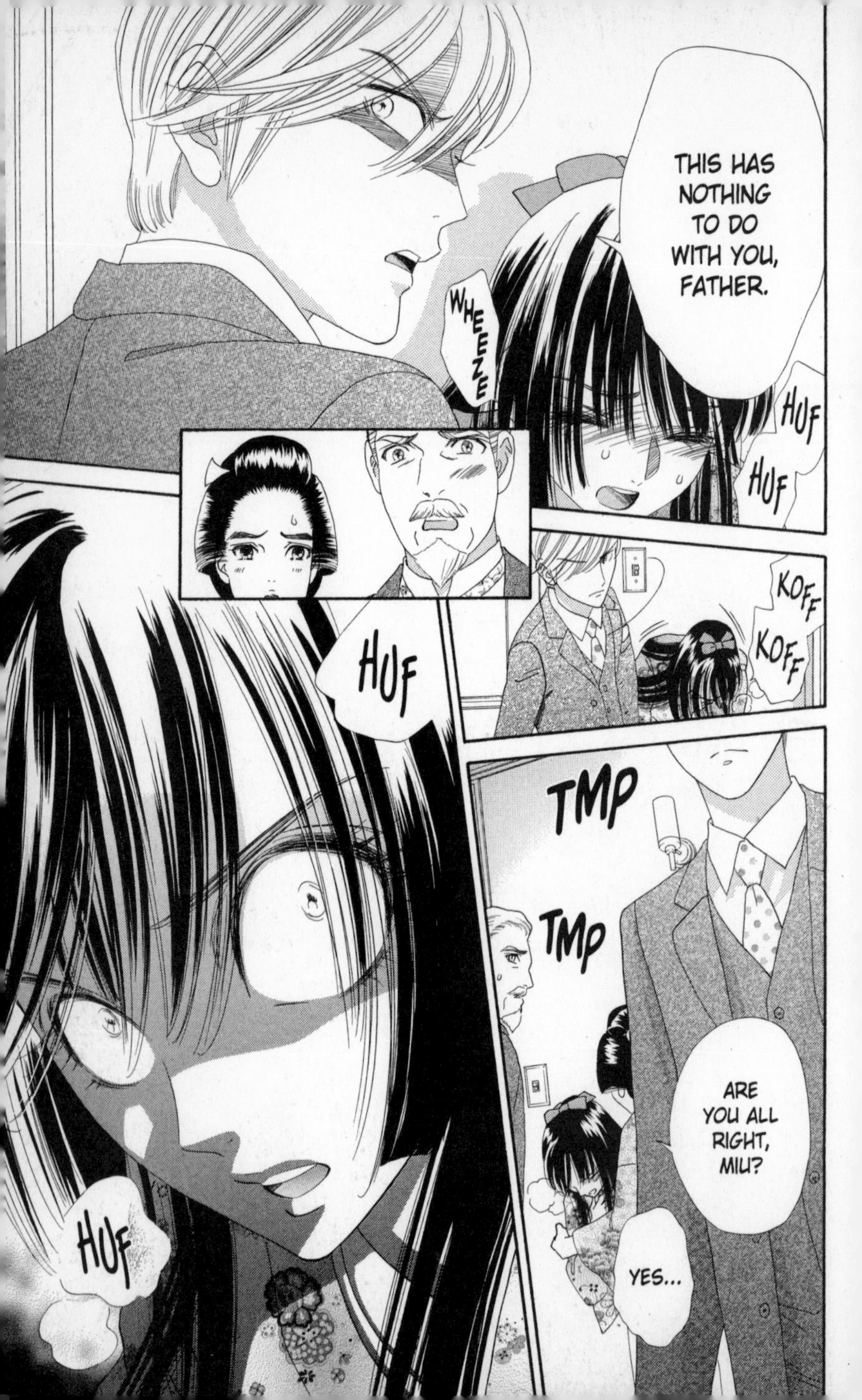
THIS HAS NOTHING TO DO WITH YOU, FATHER.
HUF
HUF
WHEEZE
KOFF
KOFF
TMP
TMP
ARE YOU ALL RIGHT, MIU?
YES...
HUF
HUF

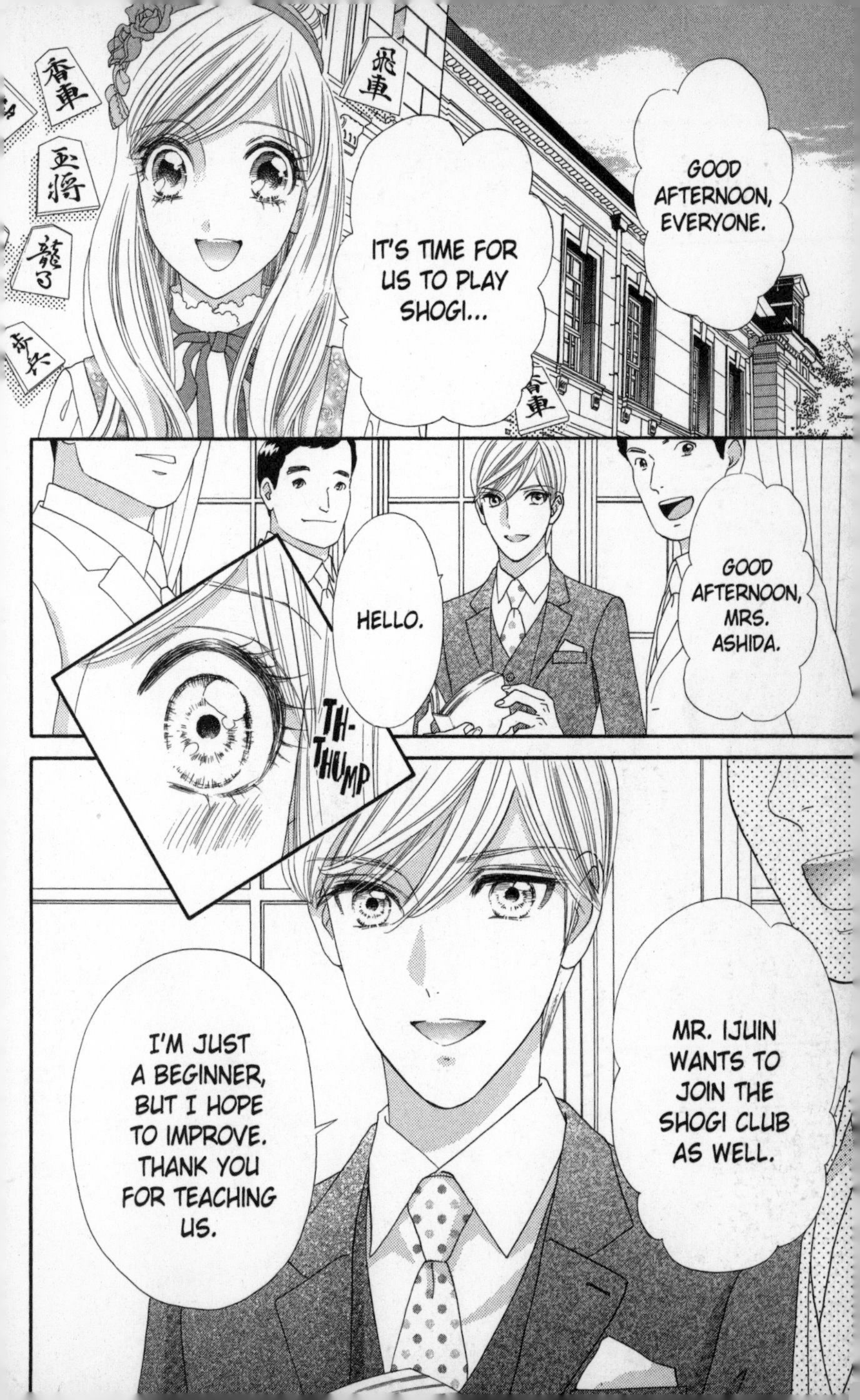
飛車
GOOD AFTERNOON, EVERYONE.
IT'S TIME FOR US TO PLAY SHOGI...
香車
玉将
歩兵
香車
GOOD AFTERNOON, MRS. ASHIDA.
HELLO.
TH-THUMP
MR. IJUIN WANTS TO JOIN THE SHOGI CLUB AS WELL.
I'M JUST A BEGINNER, BUT I HOPE TO IMPROVE. THANK YOU FOR TEACHING US.

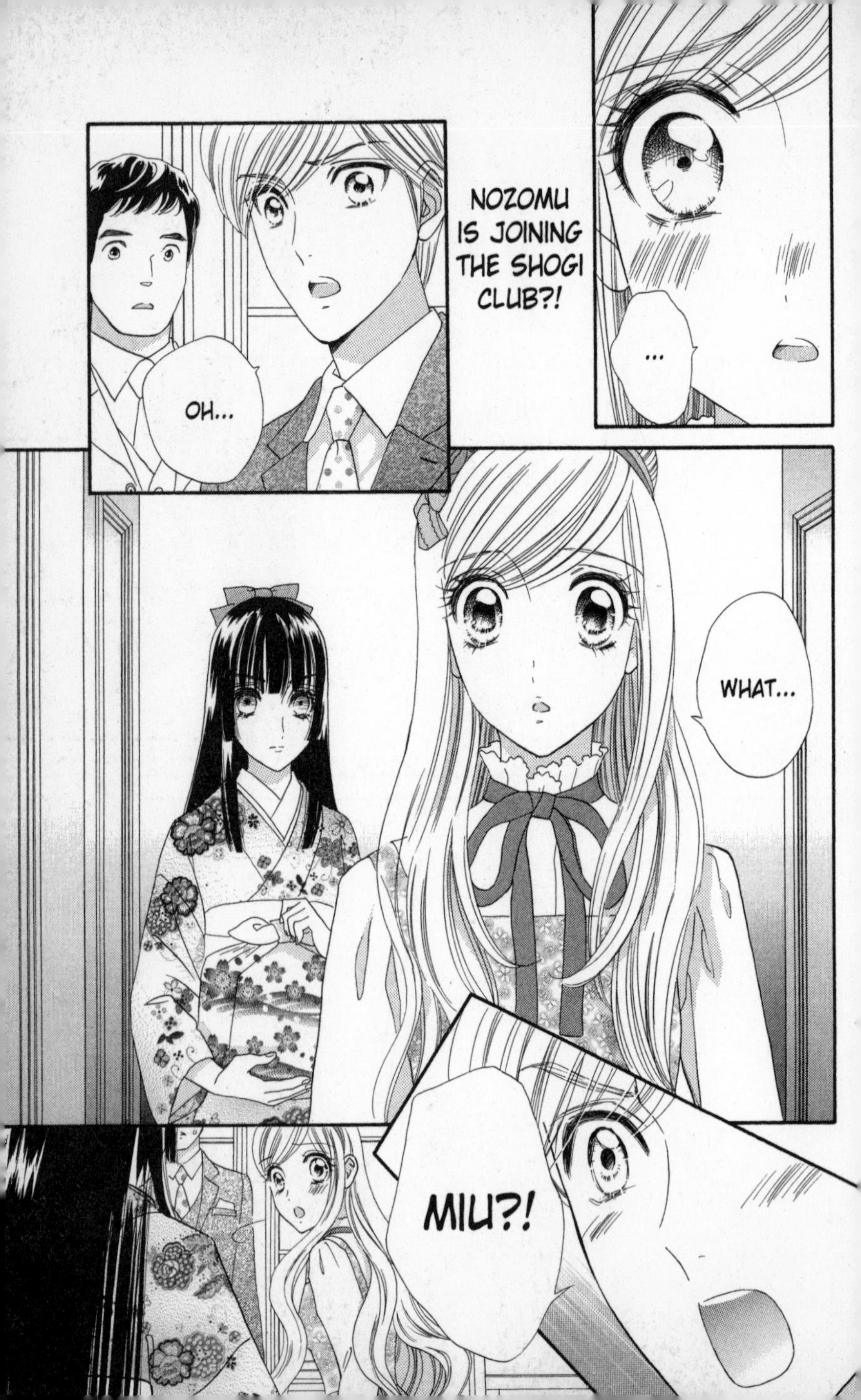
...
NOZOMU IS JOINING THE SHOGI CLUB?!
OH...
WHAT...
MIU?!

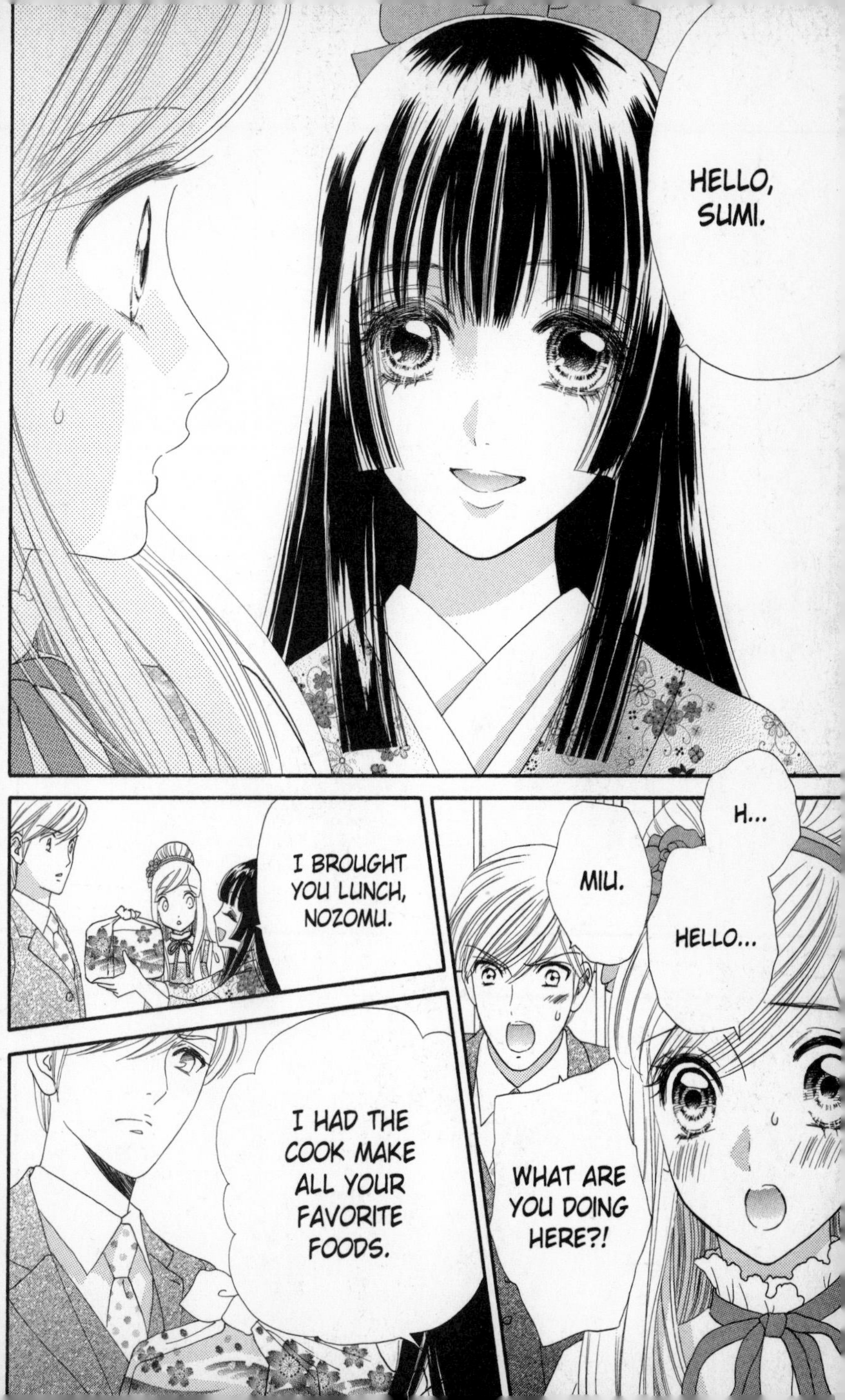
HELLO, SUMI.
H...
HELLO...
MIU.
WHAT ARE YOU DOING HERE?!
I BROUGHT YOU LUNCH, NOZOMU.
I HAD THE COOK MAKE ALL YOUR FAVORITE FOODS.

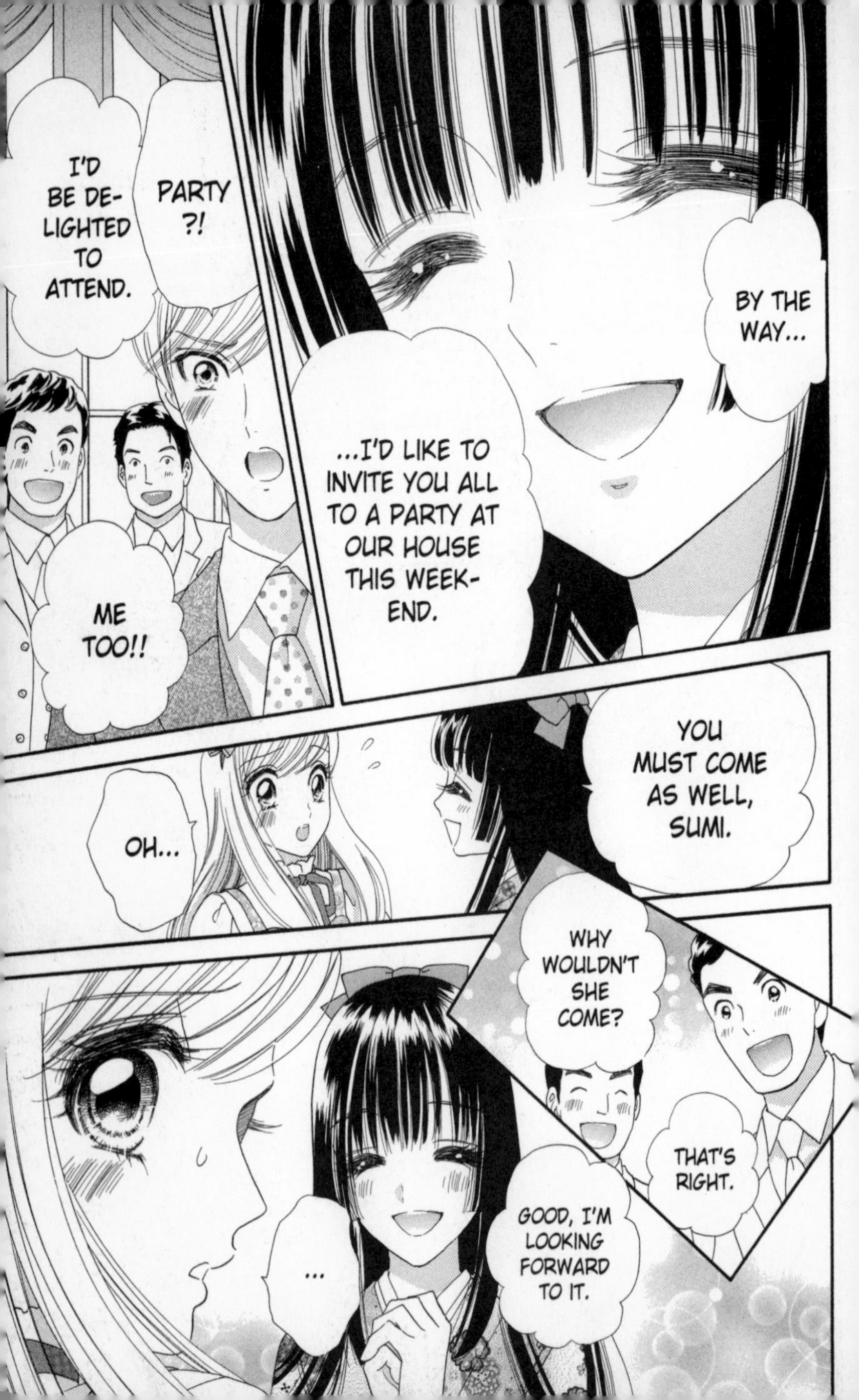
BY THE WAY...
...I'D LIKE TO INVITE YOU ALL TO A PARTY AT OUR HOUSE THIS WEEK-END.
PARTY ?!
I'D BE DE-LIGHTED TO ATTEND.
ME TOO!!
YOU MUST COME AS WELL, SUMI.
OH...
WHY WOULDN'T SHE COME?
THAT'S RIGHT.
GOOD, I'M LOOKING FORWARD TO IT.
...

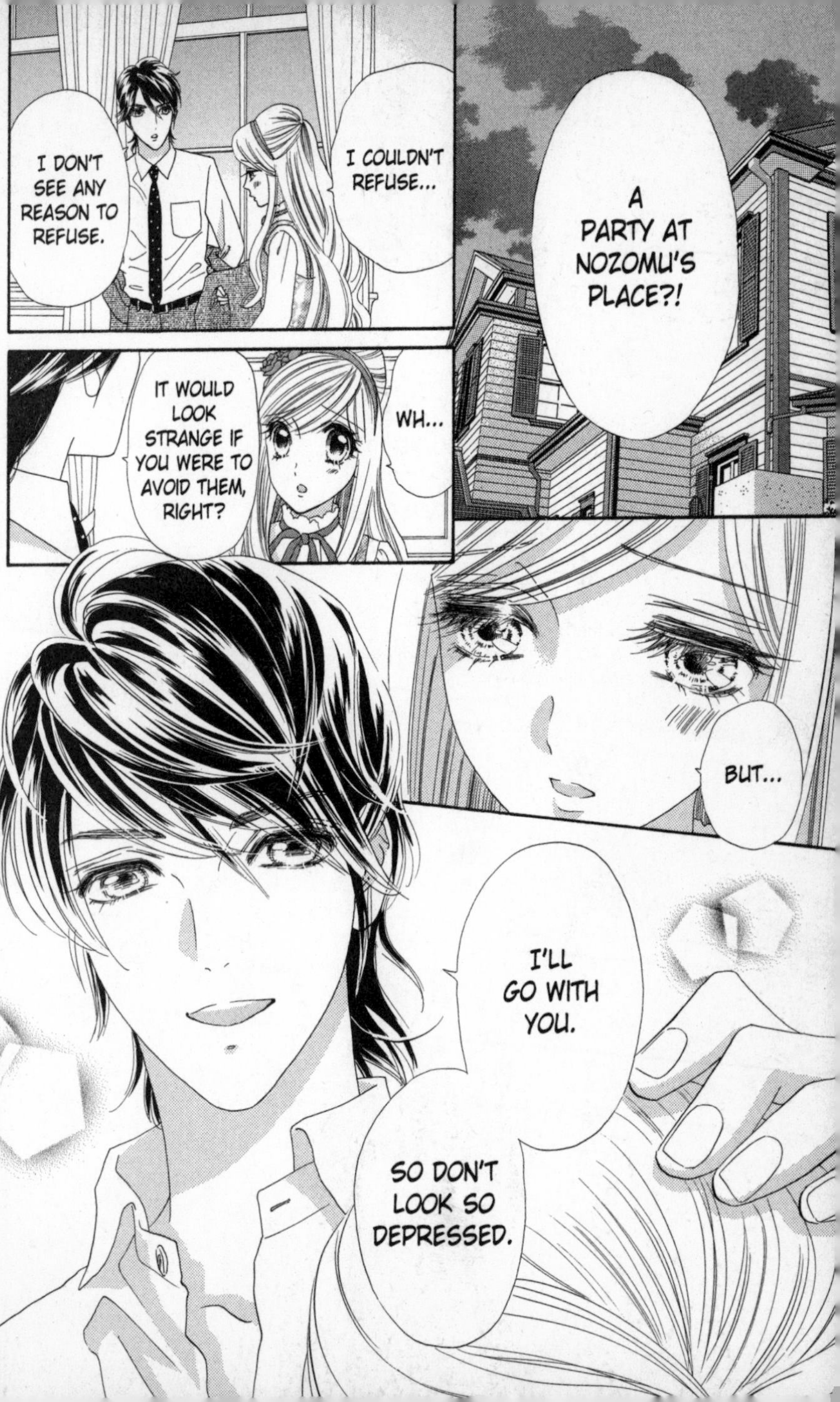
A PARTY AT NOZOMU'S PLACE?!
I COULDN'T REFUSE...
I DON'T SEE ANY REASON TO REFUSE.
WH...
IT WOULD LOOK STRANGE IF YOU WERE TO AVOID THEM, RIGHT?
BUT...
I'LL GO WITH YOU.
SO DON'T LOOK SO DEPRESSED.

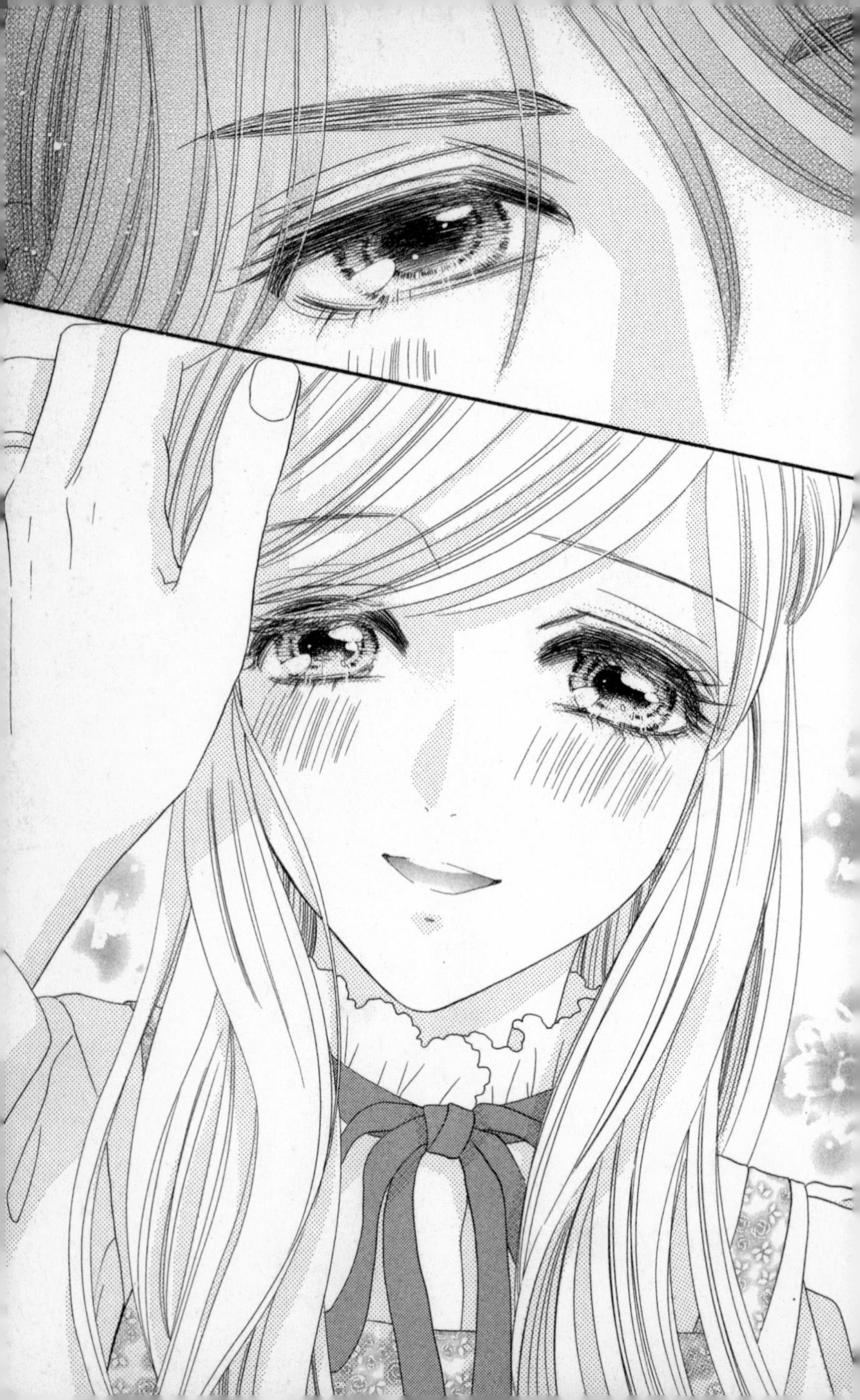

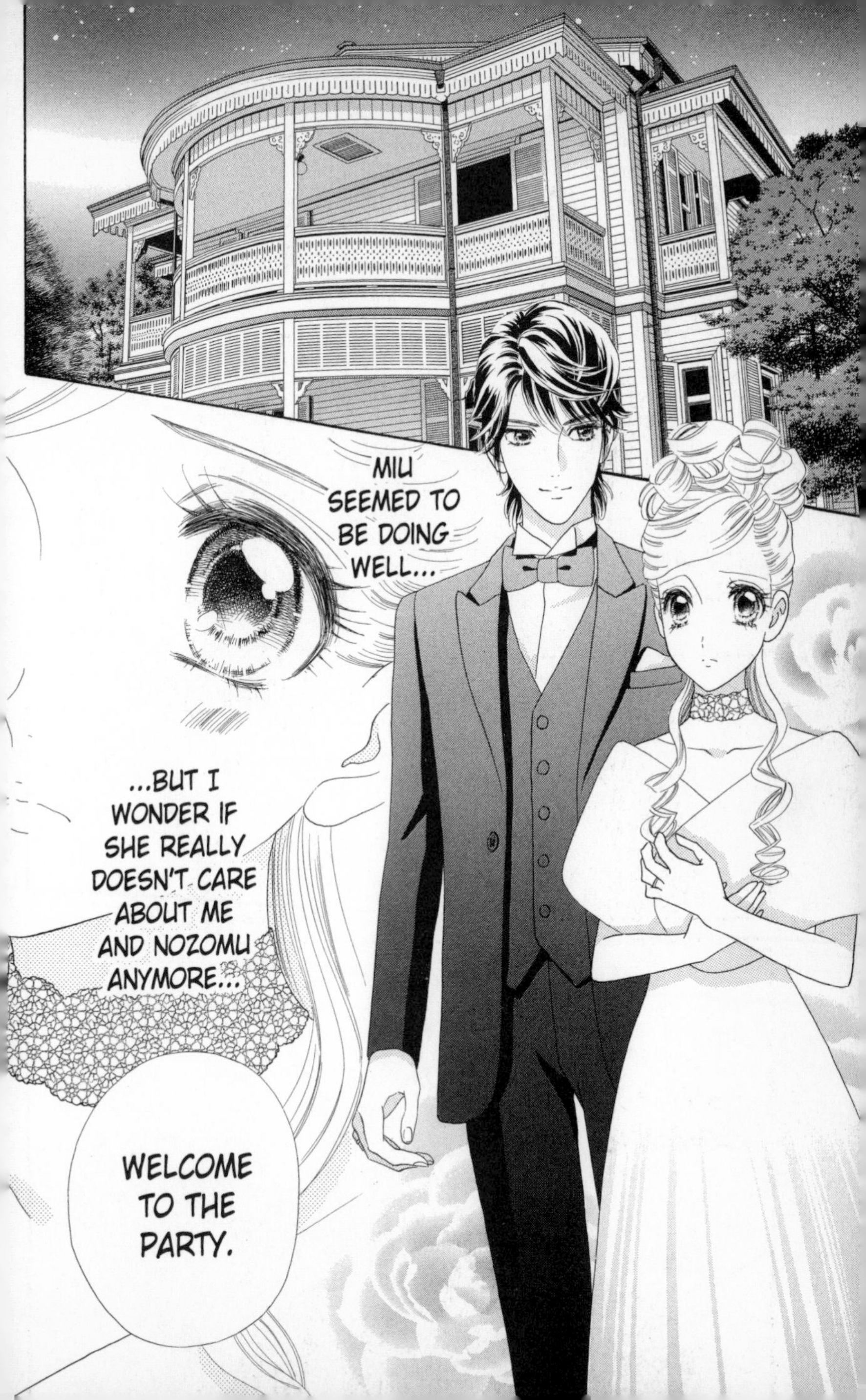
MIU SEEMED TO BE DOING WELL...
...BUT I WONDER IF SHE REALLY DOESN'T CARE ABOUT ME AND NOZOMU ANYMORE...
WELCOME TO THE PARTY.

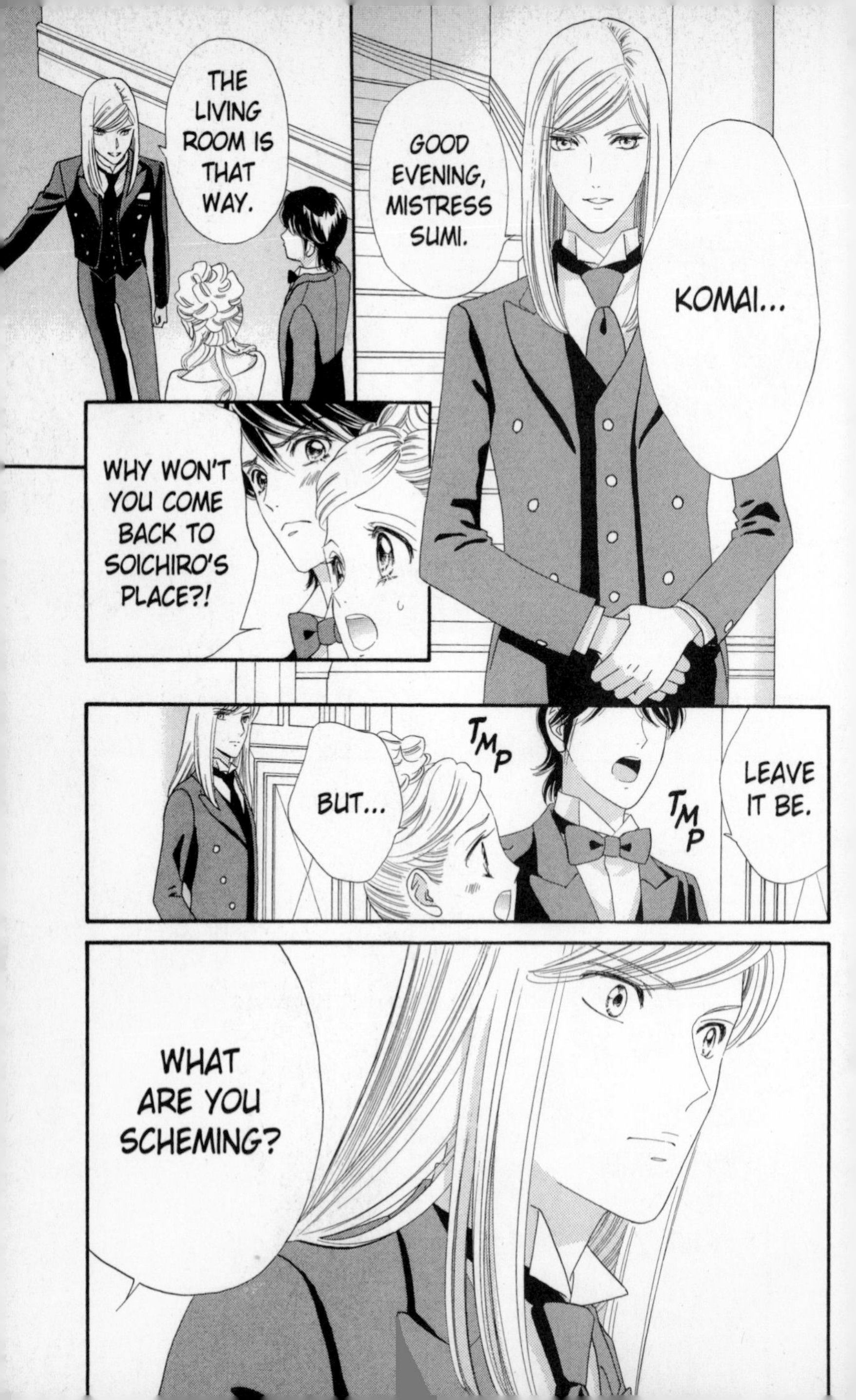
GOOD EVENING, MISTRESS SUMI.
KOMAI...
THE LIVING ROOM IS THAT WAY.
WHY WON'T YOU COME BACK TO SOICHIRO'S PLACE?!
LEAVE IT BE.
TMP
TMP
BUT...
WHAT ARE YOU SCHEMING?

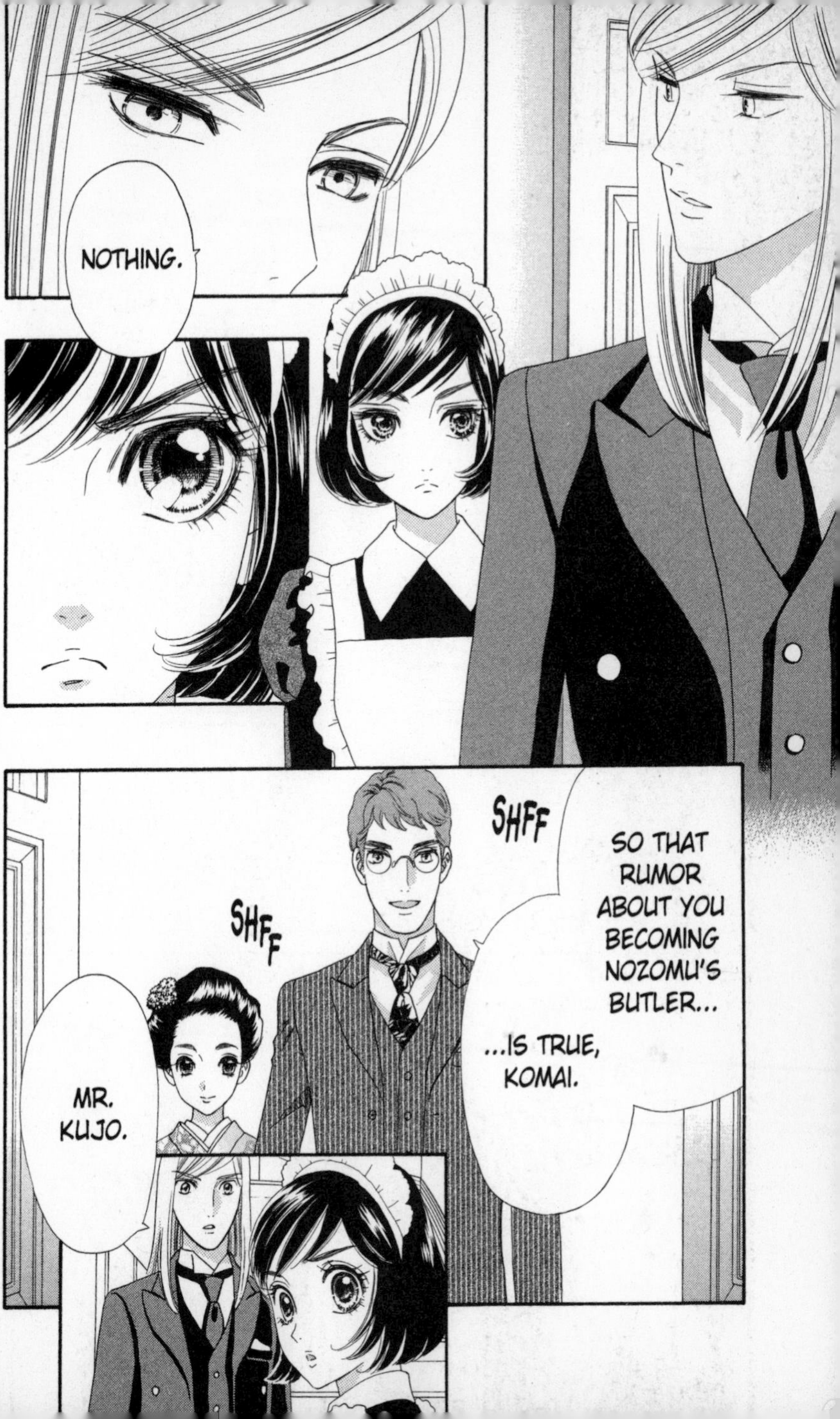
NOTHING.
SHFF
SO THAT RUMOR ABOUT YOU BECOMING NOZOMU'S BUTLER...
...IS TRUE, KOMAI.
SHFF
MR. KUJO.

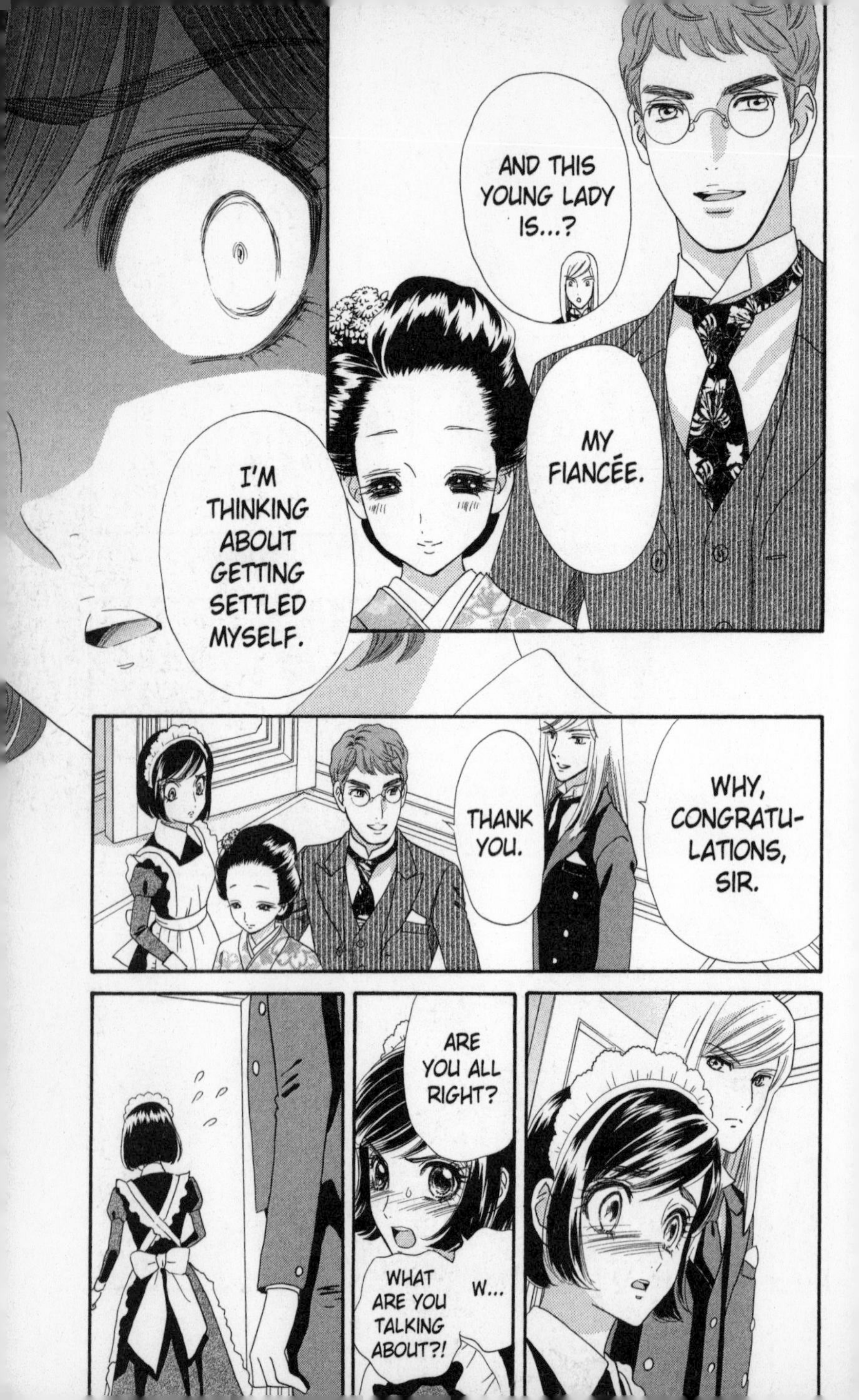
AND THIS YOUNG LADY IS...?
MY FIANCÉE.
I'M THINKING ABOUT GETTING SETTLED MYSELF.
WHY, CONGRATULATIONS, SIR.
THANK YOU.
ARE YOU ALL RIGHT?
W...
WHAT ARE YOU TALKING ABOUT?!

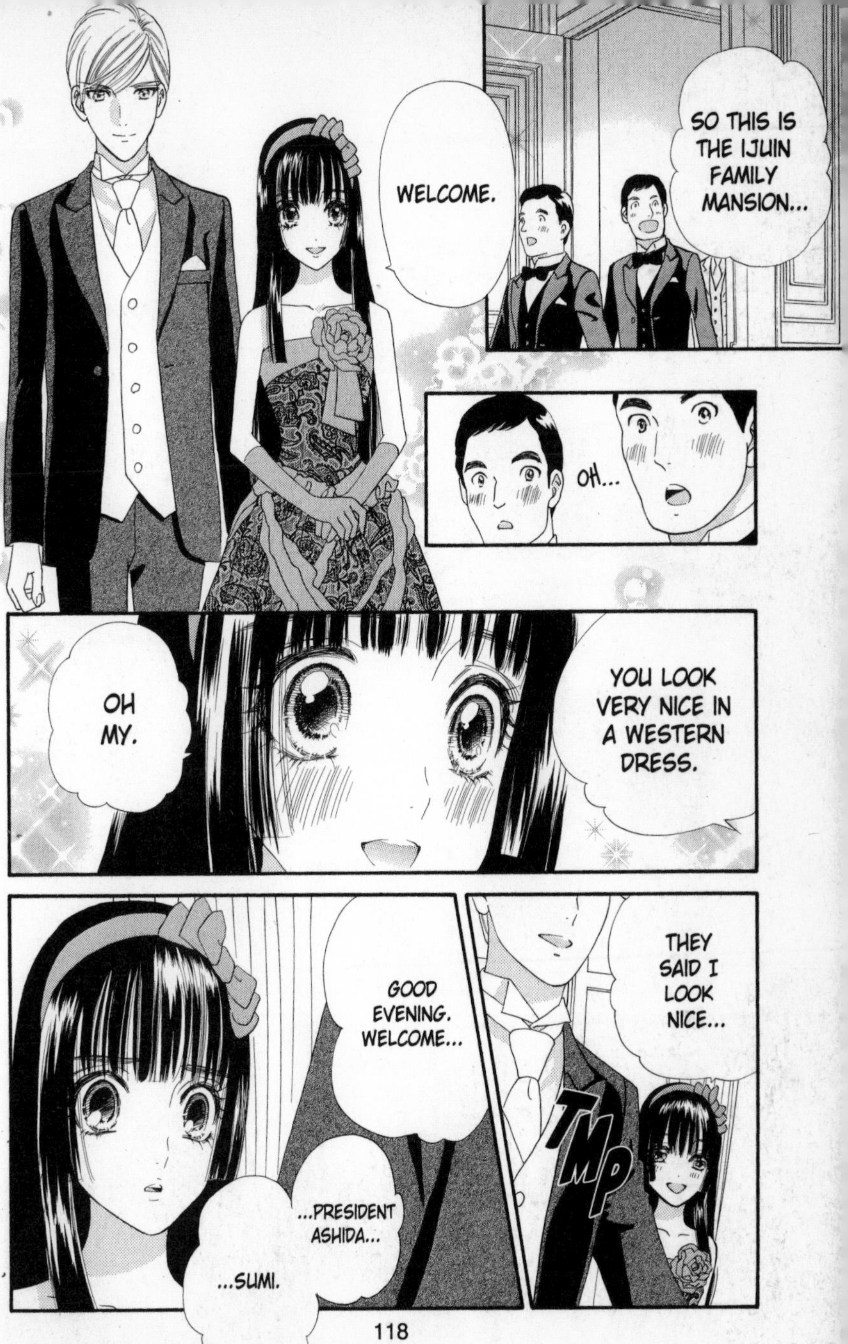
SO THIS IS THE IJUIN FAMILY MANSION...
OH...
WELCOME.
YOU LOOK VERY NICE IN A WESTERN DRESS.
OH MY.
THEY SAID I LOOK NICE...
TMP
GOOD EVENING. WELCOME...
...PRESIDENT ASHIDA...
...SUMI.

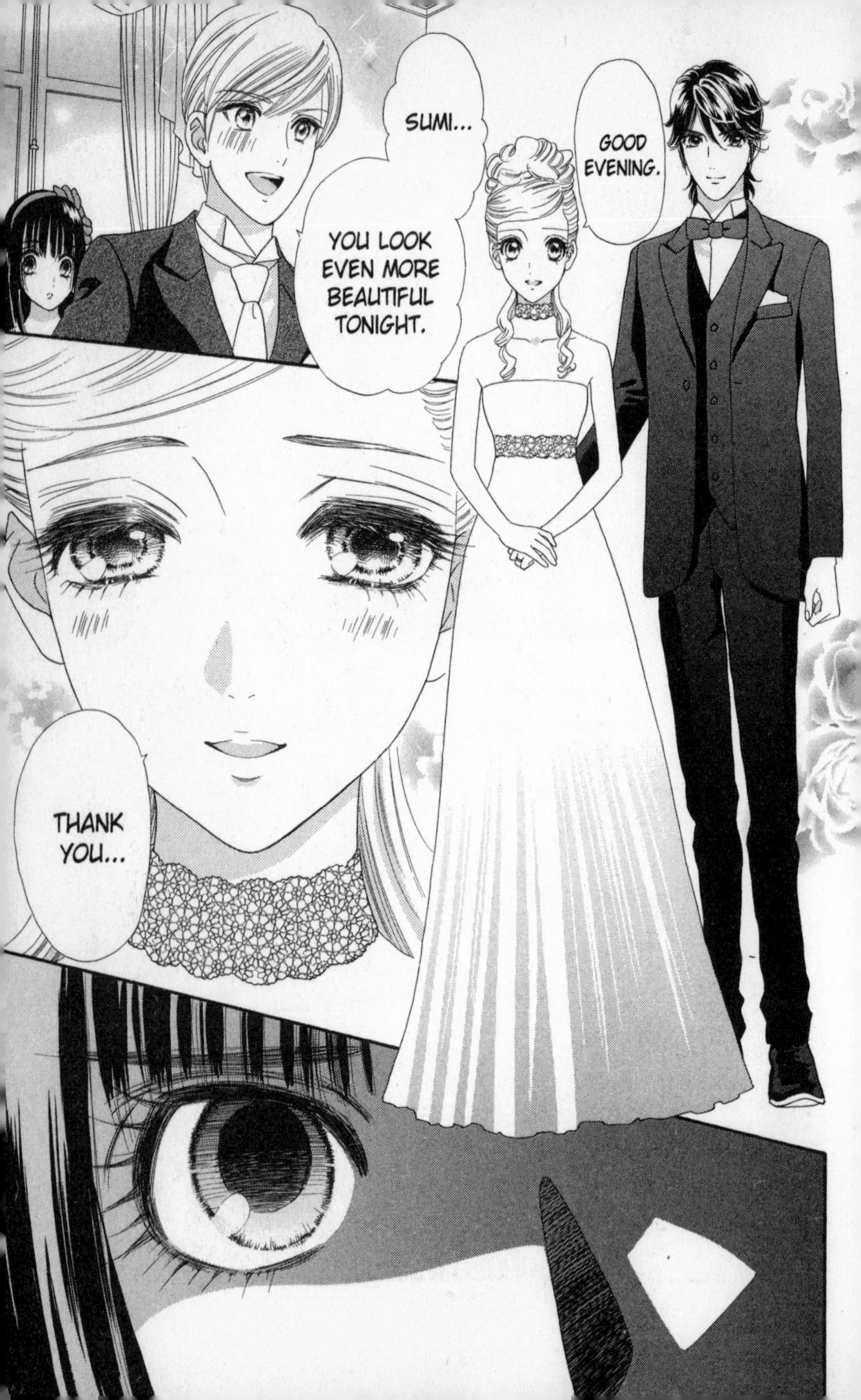
GOOD EVENING.
SUMI...
YOU LOOK EVEN MORE BEAUTIFUL TONIGHT.
THANK YOU...

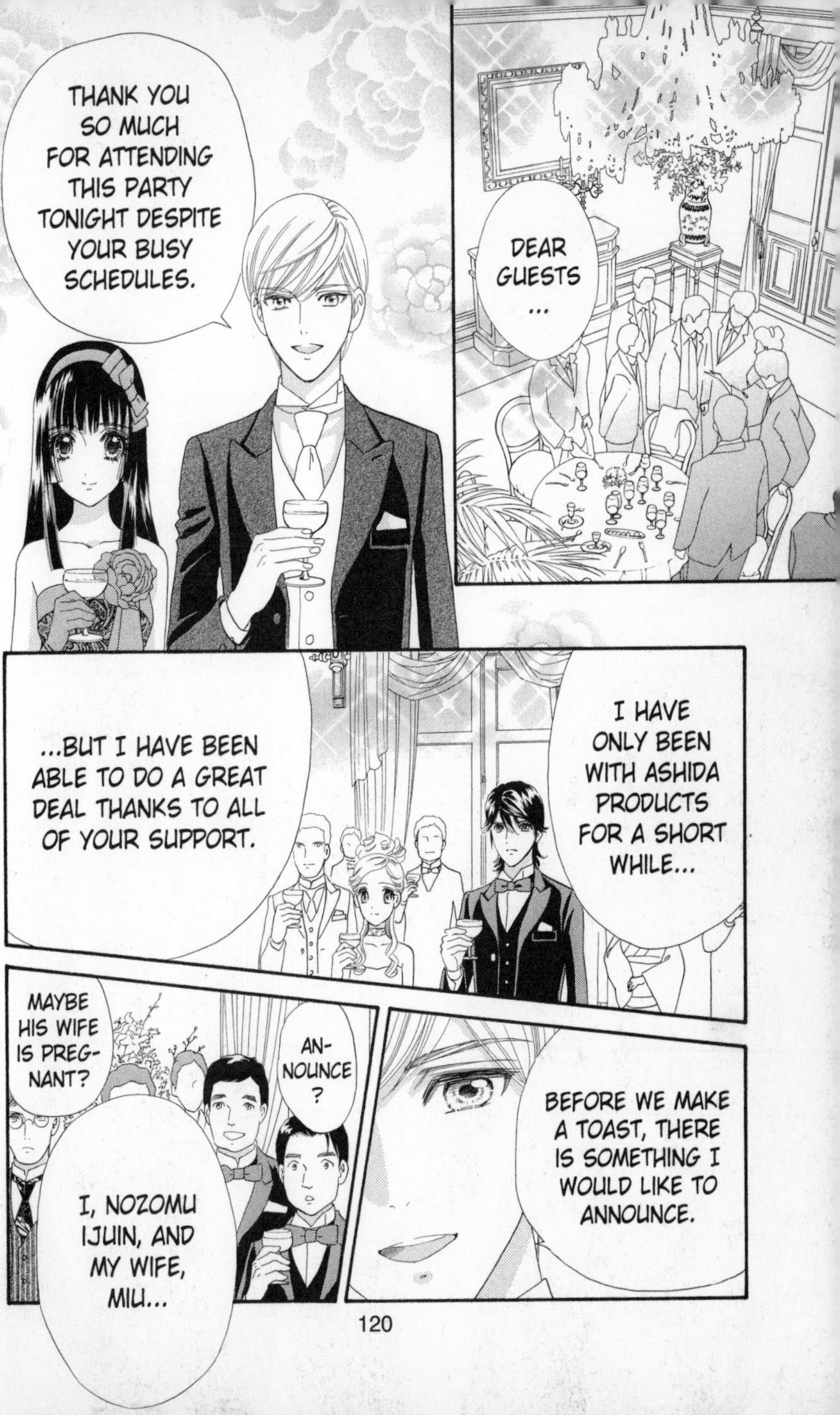
DEAR GUESTS ...
THANK YOU SO MUCH FOR ATTENDING THIS PARTY TONIGHT DESPITE YOUR BUSY SCHEDULES.
I HAVE ONLY BEEN WITH ASHIDA PRODUCTS FOR A SHORT WHILE...
...BUT I HAVE BEEN ABLE TO DO A GREAT DEAL THANKS TO ALL OF YOUR SUPPORT.
BEFORE WE MAKE A TOAST, THERE IS SOMETHING I WOULD LIKE TO ANNOUNCE.
AN-NOUNCE ?
MAYBE HIS WIFE IS PREG-NANT?
I, NOZOMU IJUIN, AND MY WIFE, MIU...

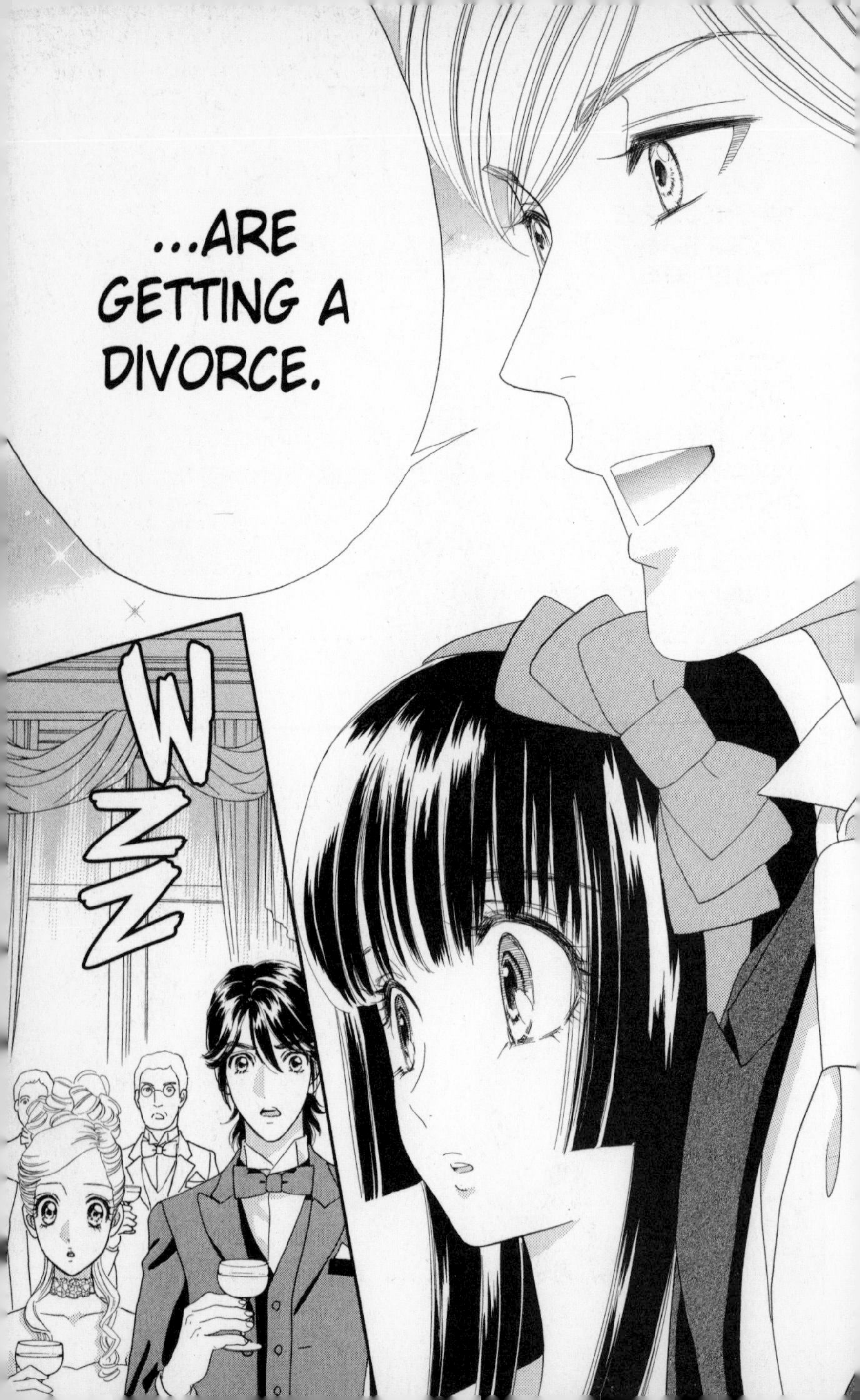
...ARE GETTING A DIVORCE.
WZZ

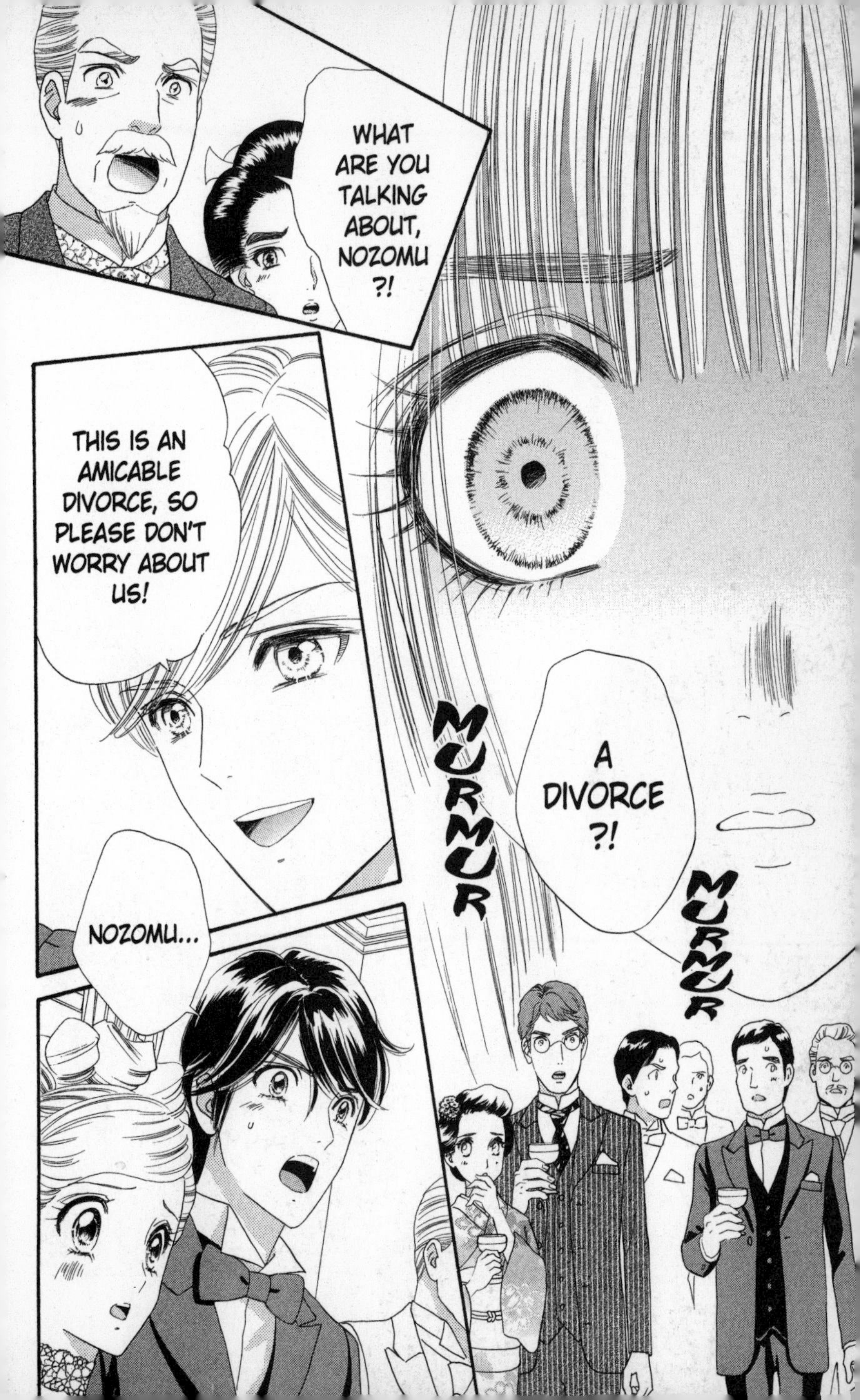

WHAT ARE YOU TALKING ABOUT, NOZOMU?!
THIS IS AN AMICABLE DIVORCE, SO PLEASE DON'T WORRY ABOUT US!
A DIVORCE?!
MURMUR
MURMUR
NOZOMU...

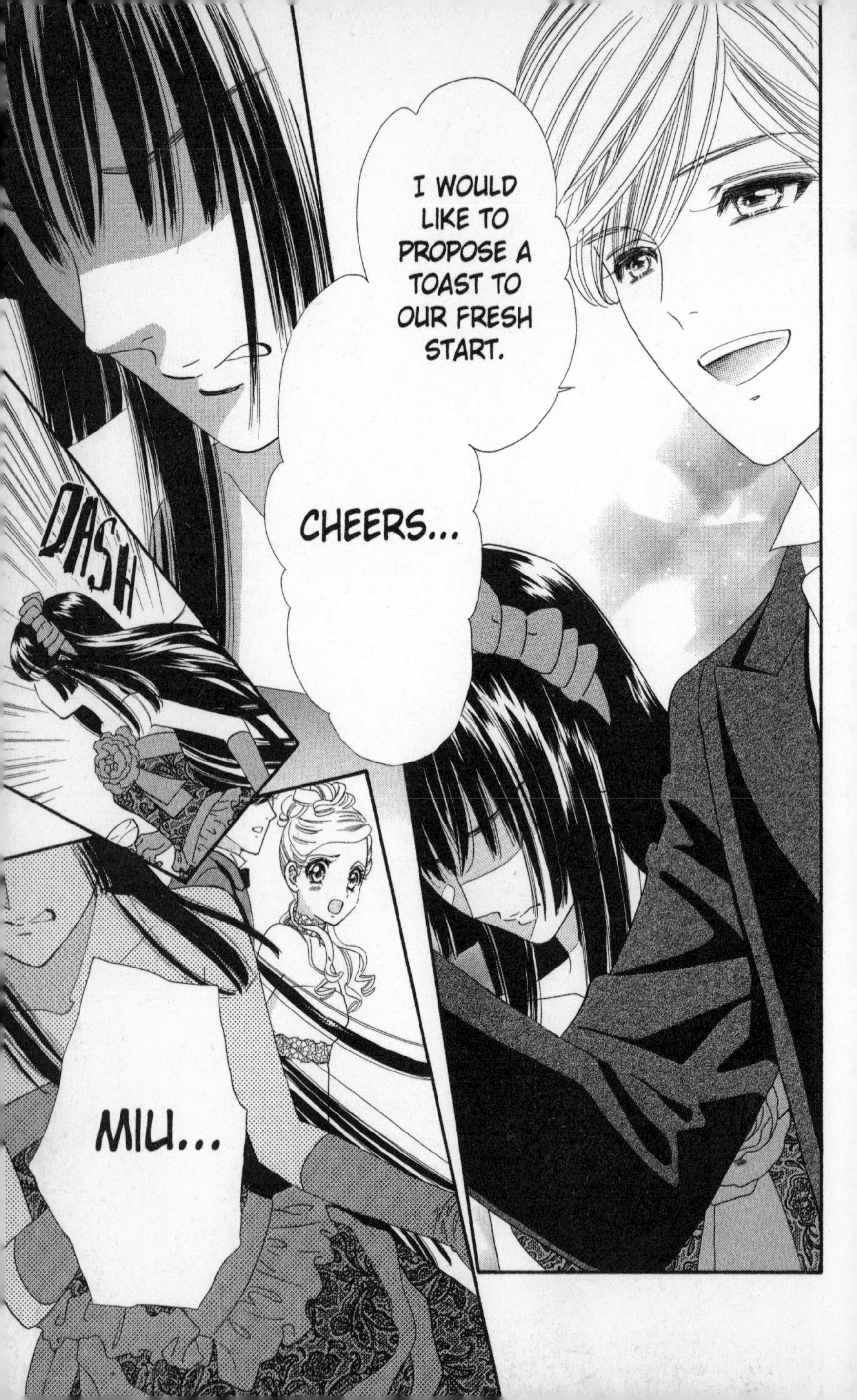
I WOULD LIKE TO PROPOSE A TOAST TO OUR FRESH START.
CHEERS...
DASH
MIU...

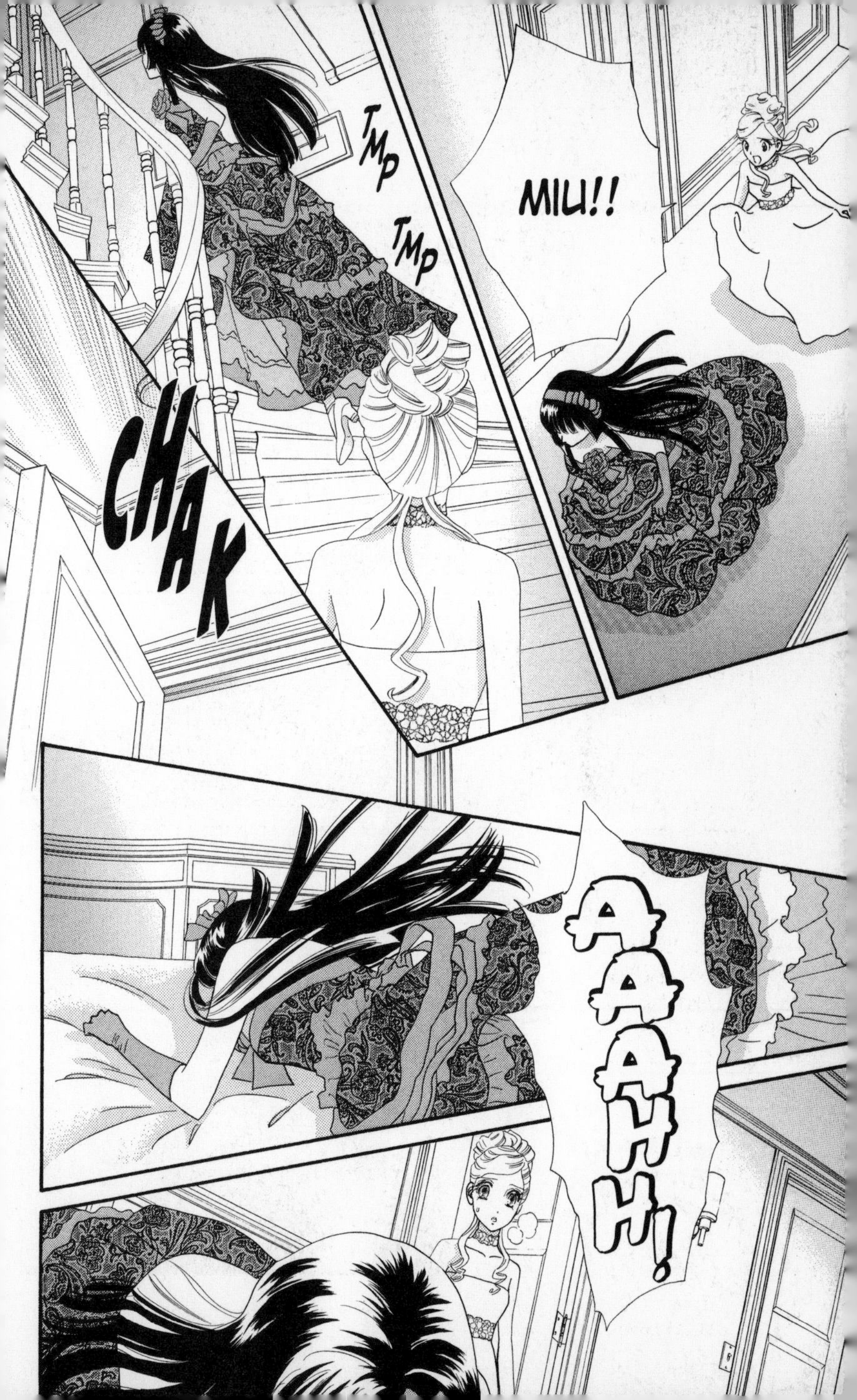
MIU!!
TMP
TMP
CHAK
AAAHH!

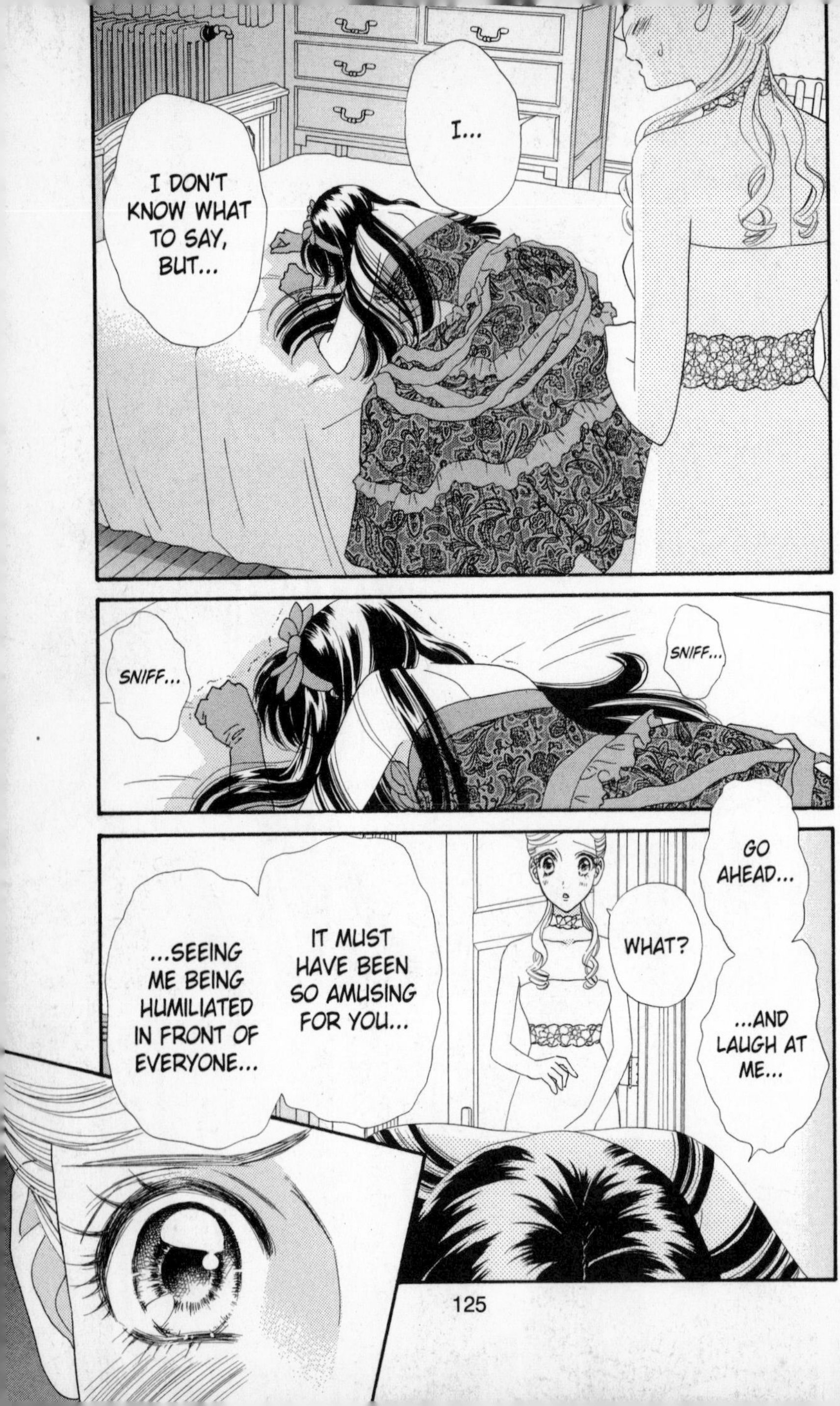
I...
I DON'T KNOW WHAT TO SAY, BUT...
SNIFF...
SNIFF...
GO AHEAD...
WHAT?
...AND LAUGH AT ME...
IT MUST HAVE BEEN SO AMUSING FOR YOU...
...SEEING ME BEING HUMILIATED IN FRONT OF EVERYONE...

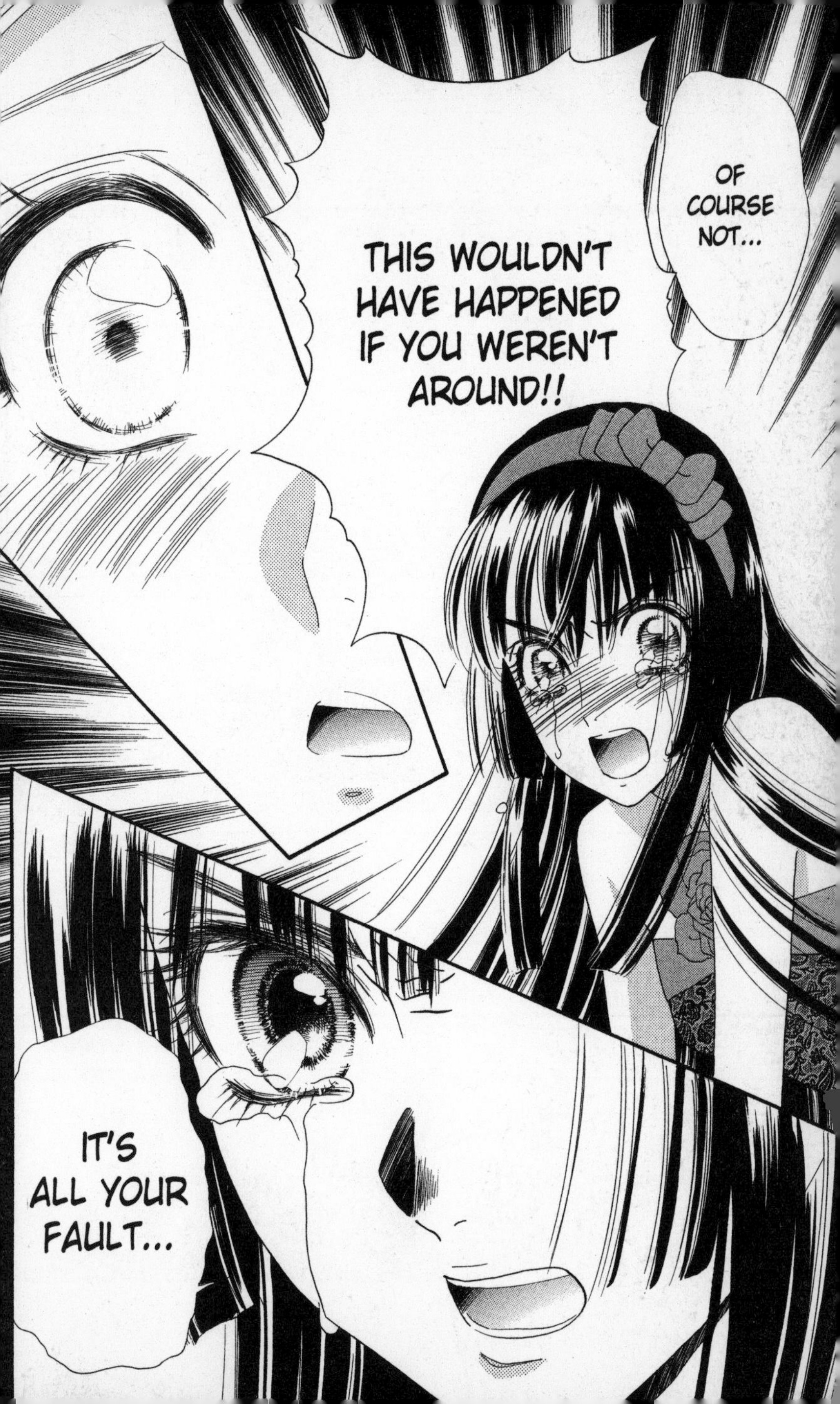
OF COURSE NOT...
THIS WOULDN'T HAVE HAPPENED IF YOU WEREN'T AROUND!!
IT'S ALL YOUR FAULT...

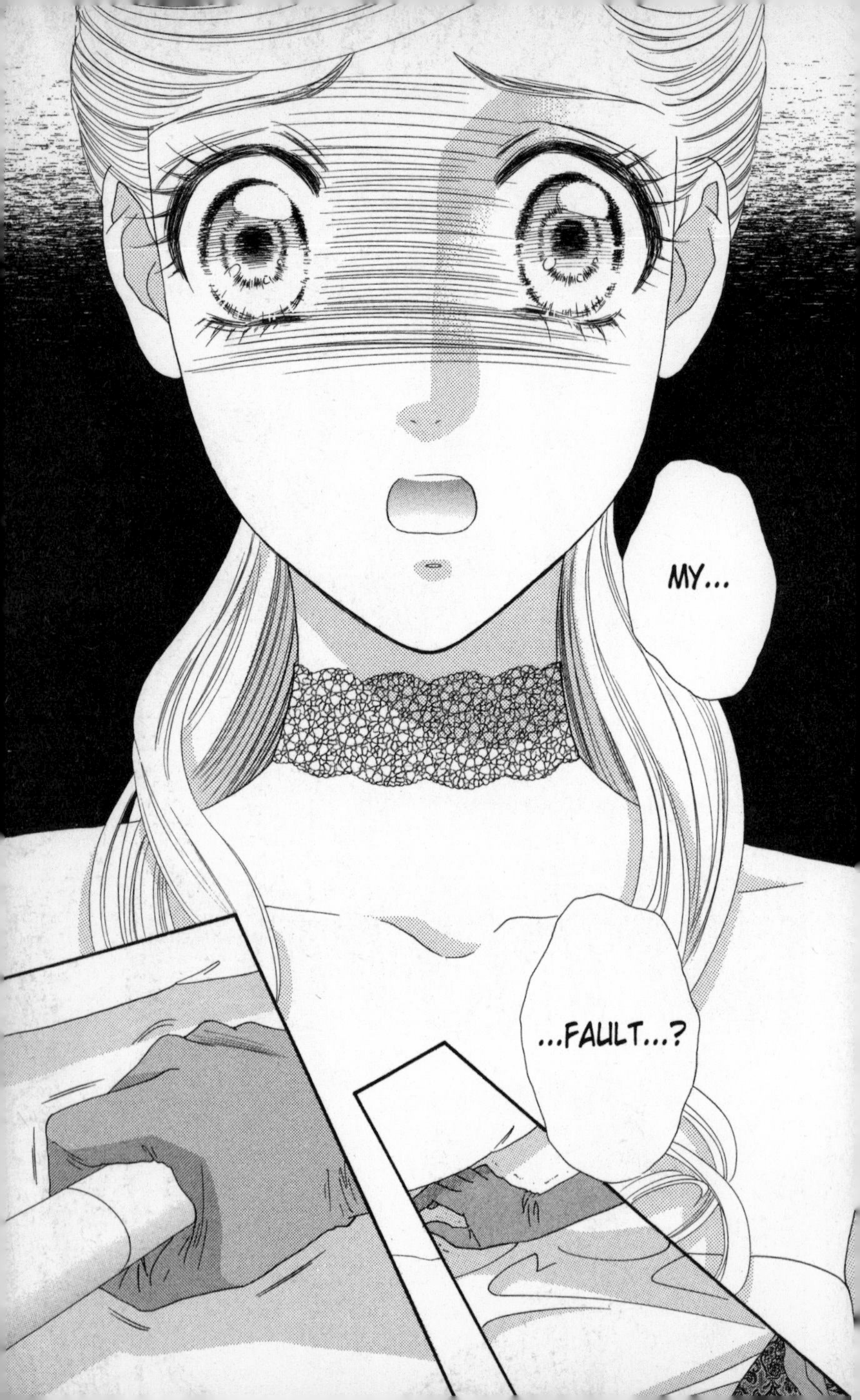
MY...
...FAULT...?

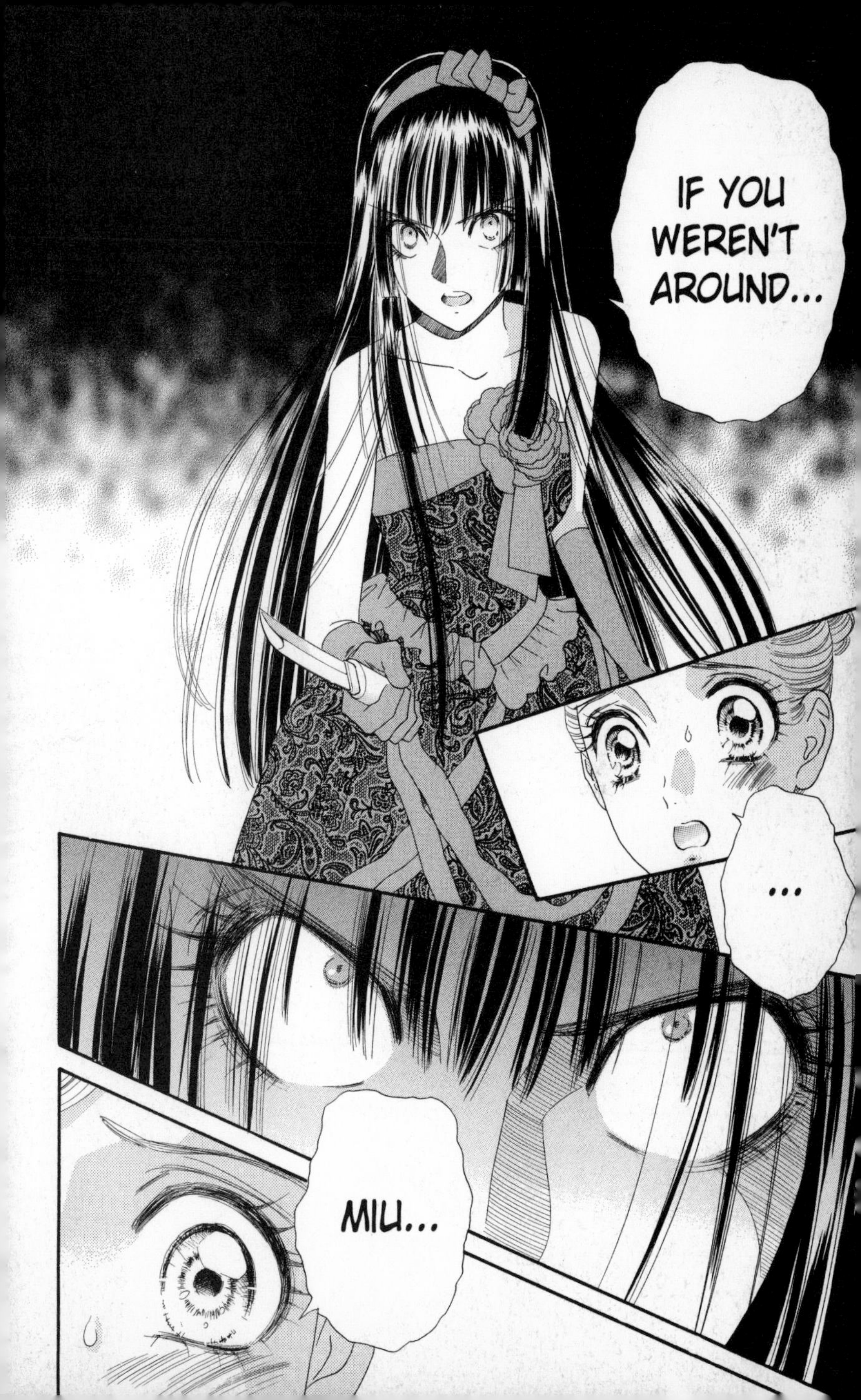
IF YOU WEREN'T AROUND...
...
MIU...

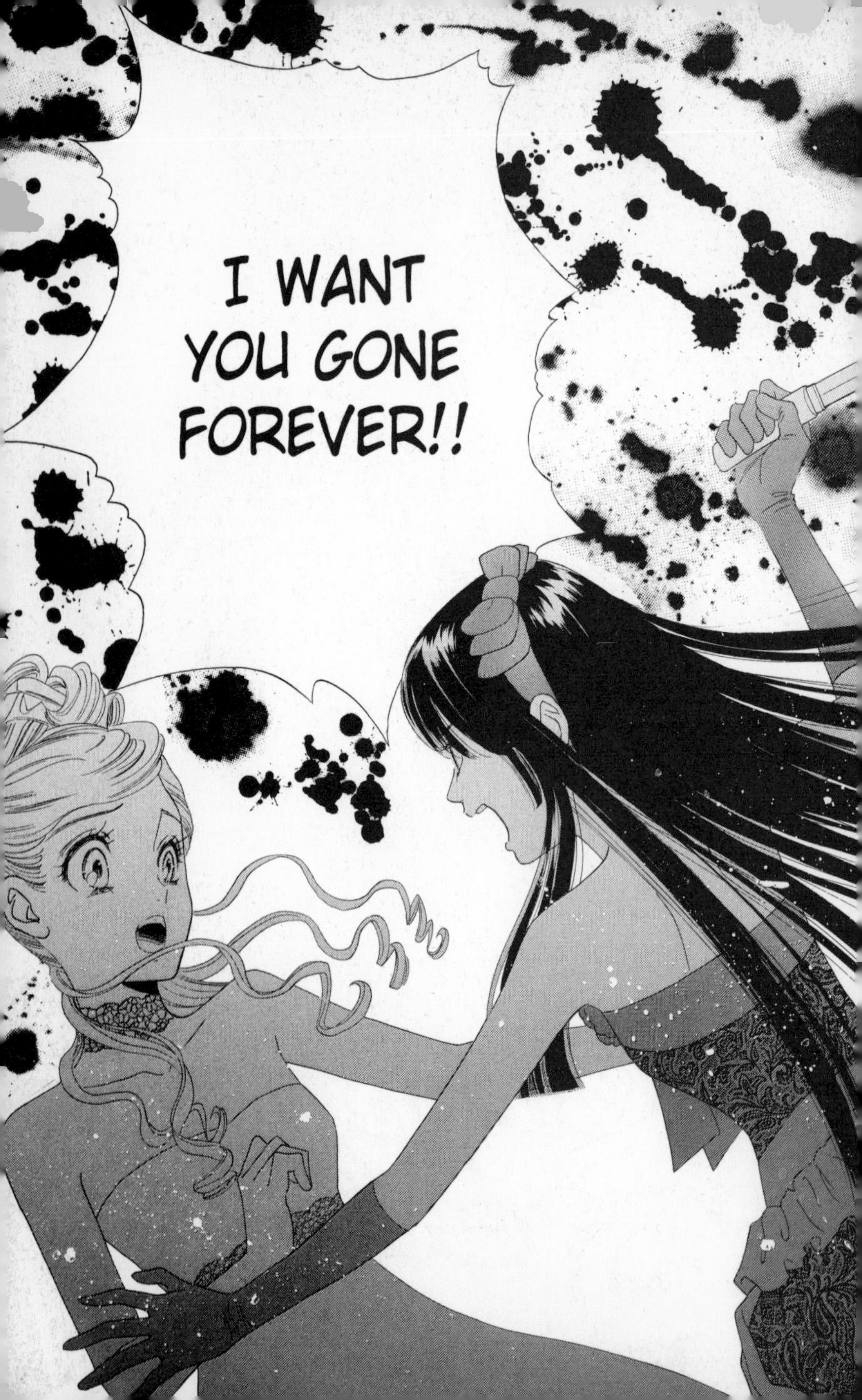
I WANT YOU GONE FOREVER!!

Stepping on Roses

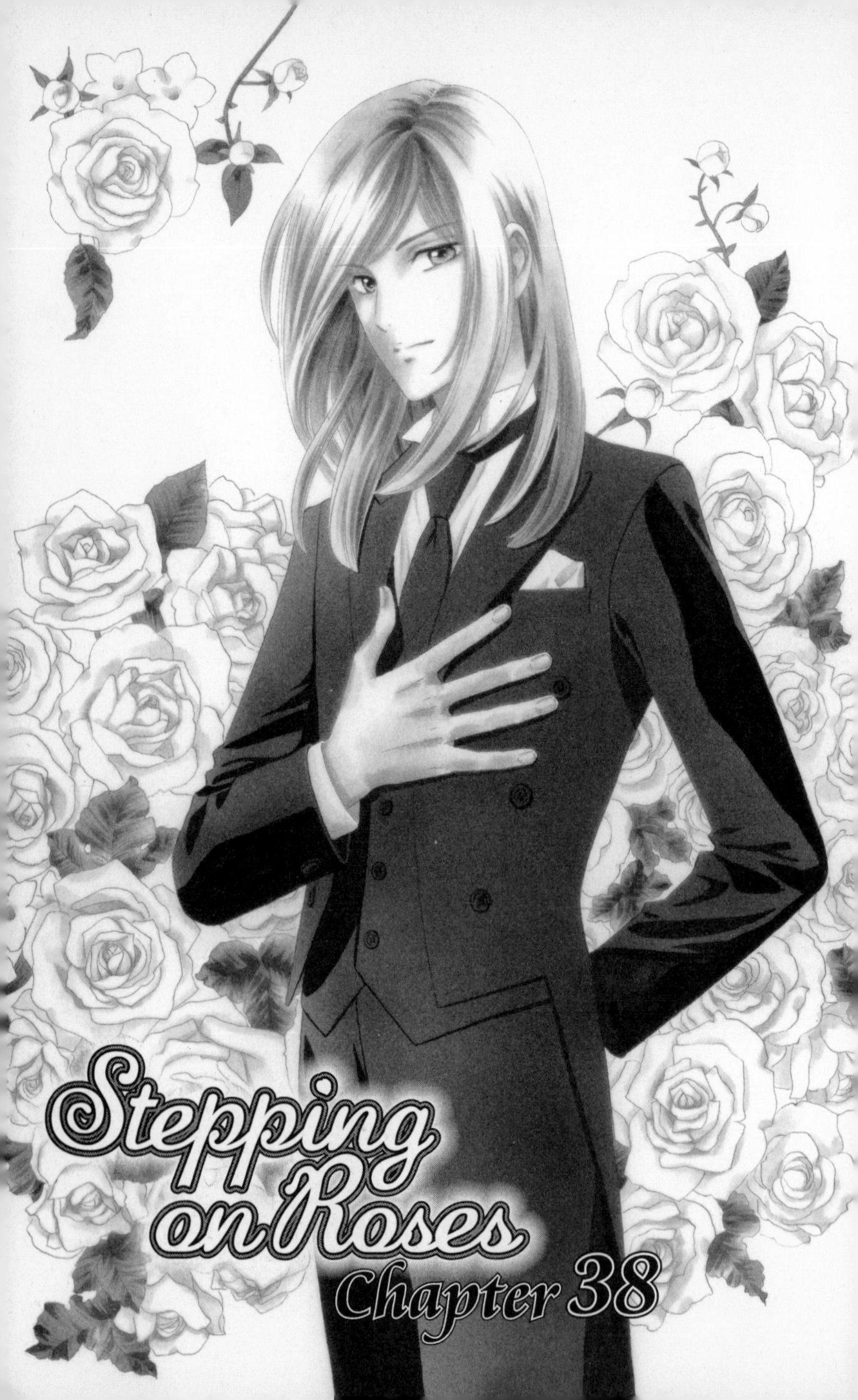
Stepping on Roses
Chapter 38

Stepping on Roses

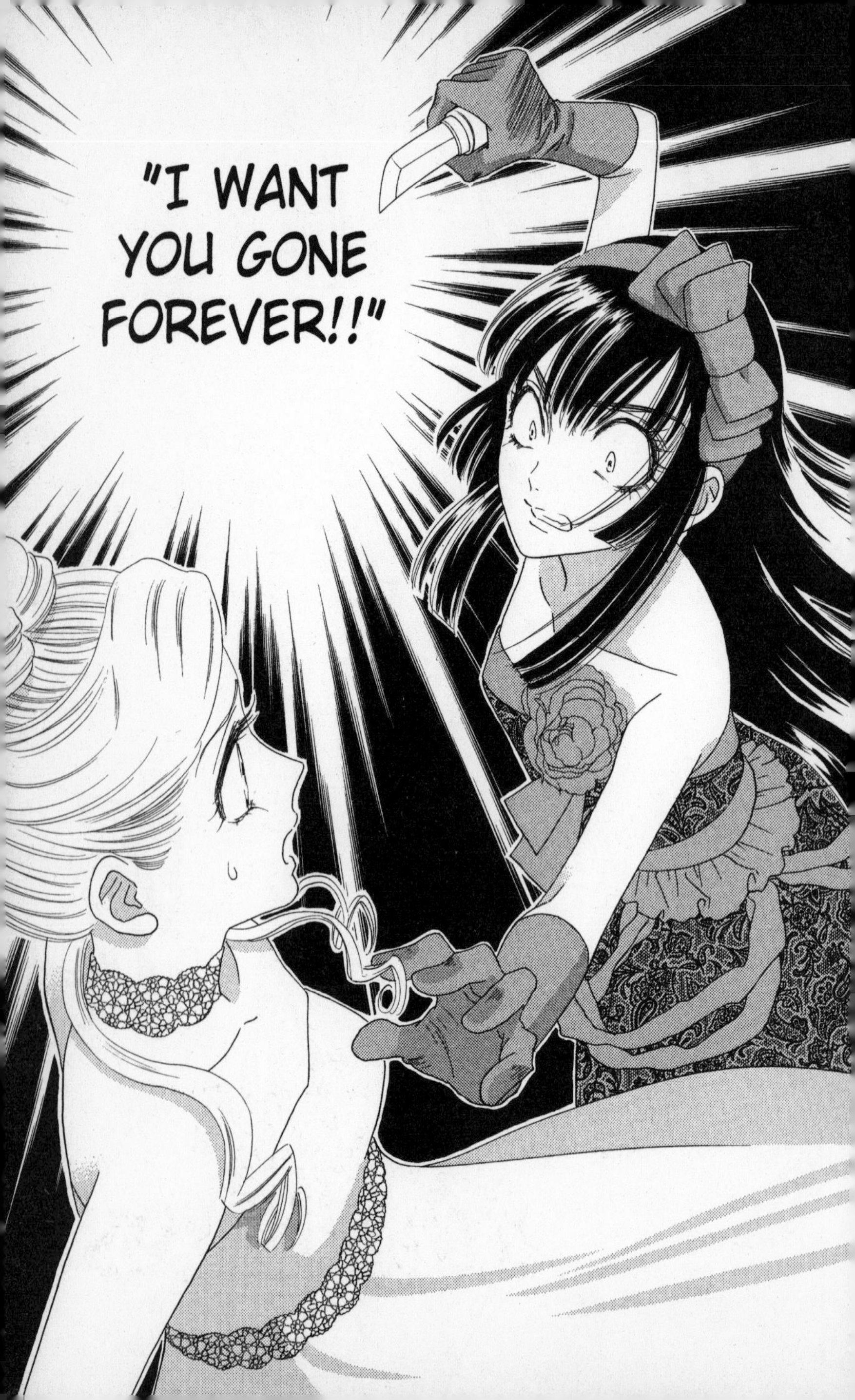
"I WANT YOU GONE FOREVER!!"

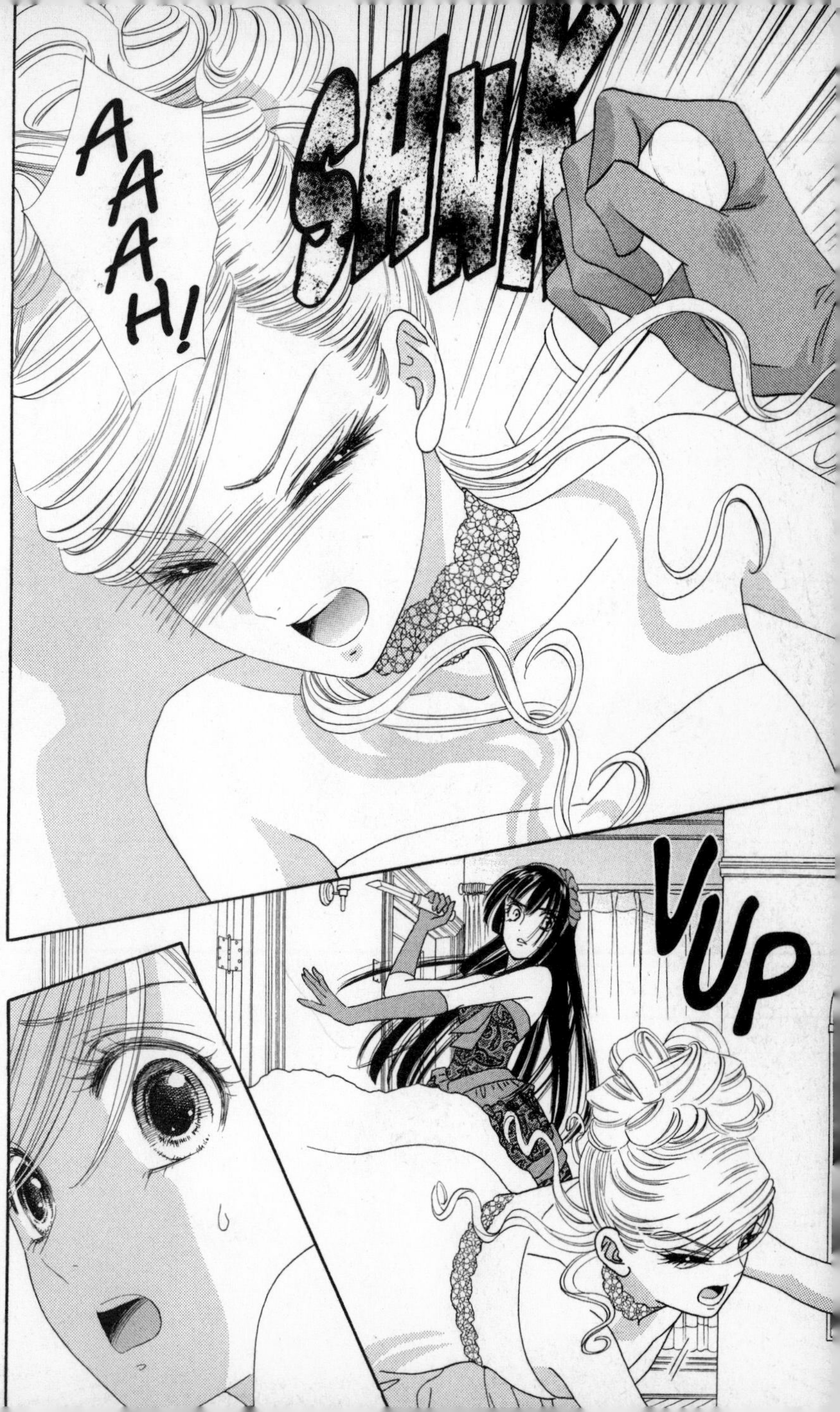
SHNK
AAAAH!
VUP

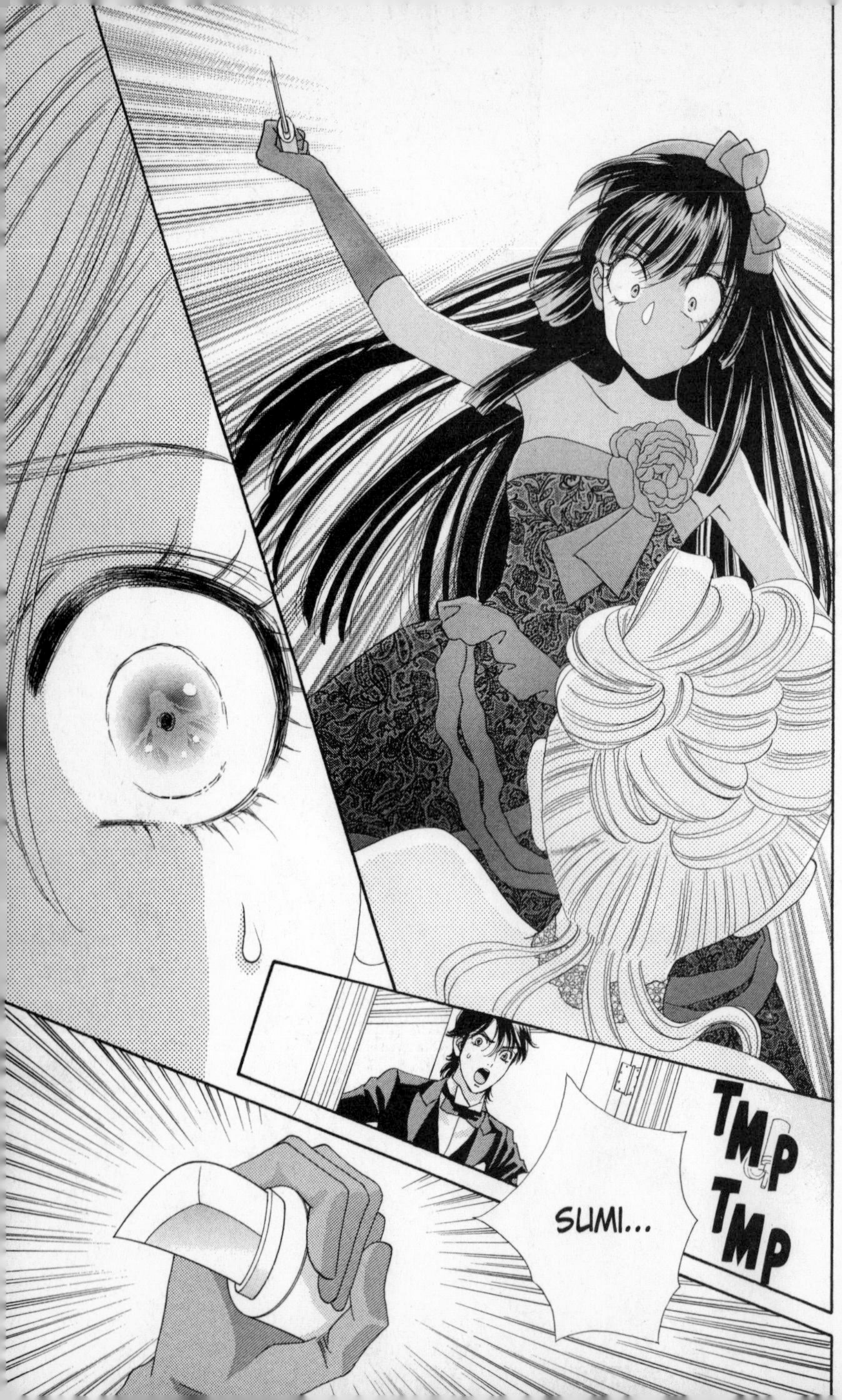
TMP TMP
SUMI...

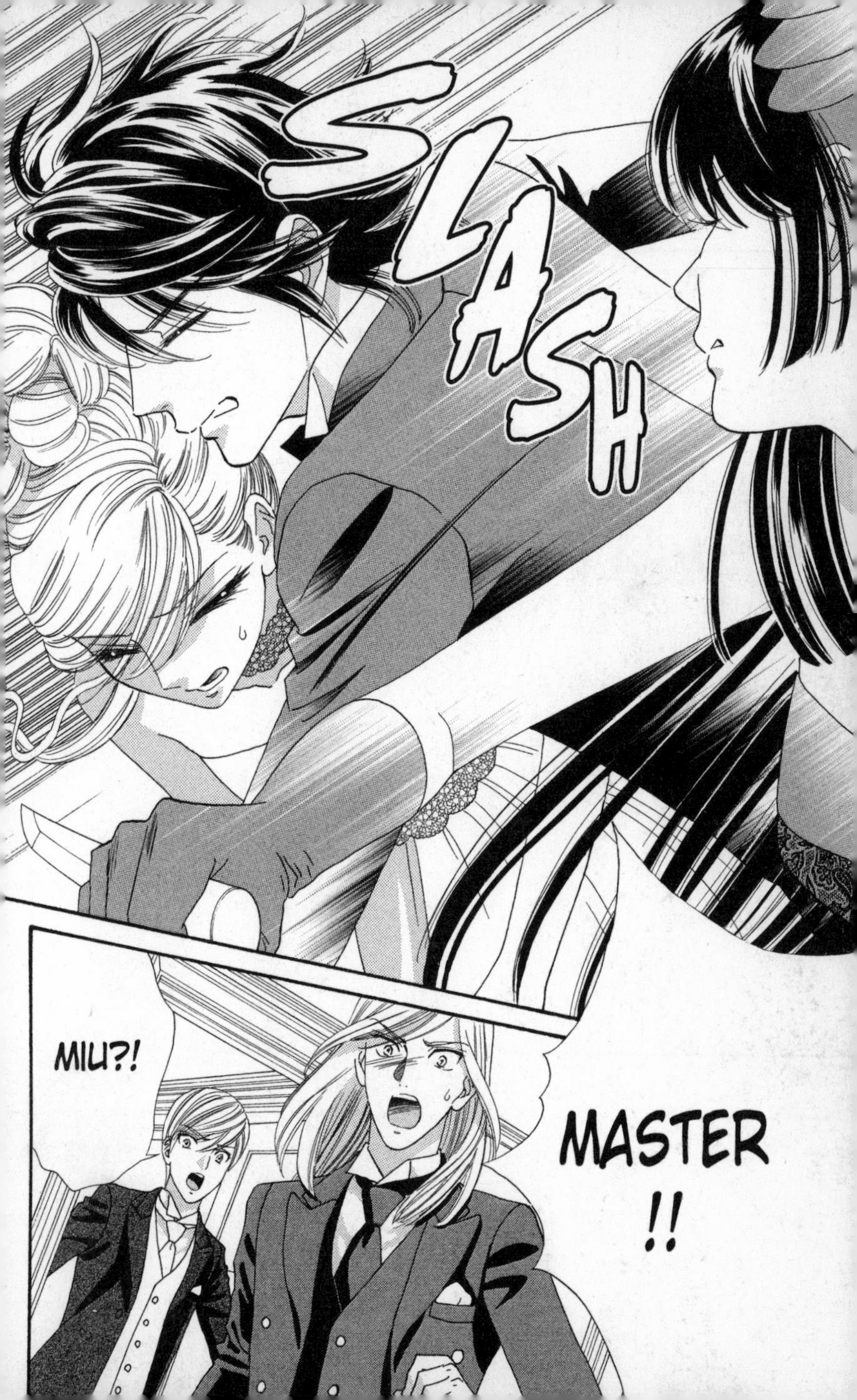
SLASH
MASTER !!
MIU?!

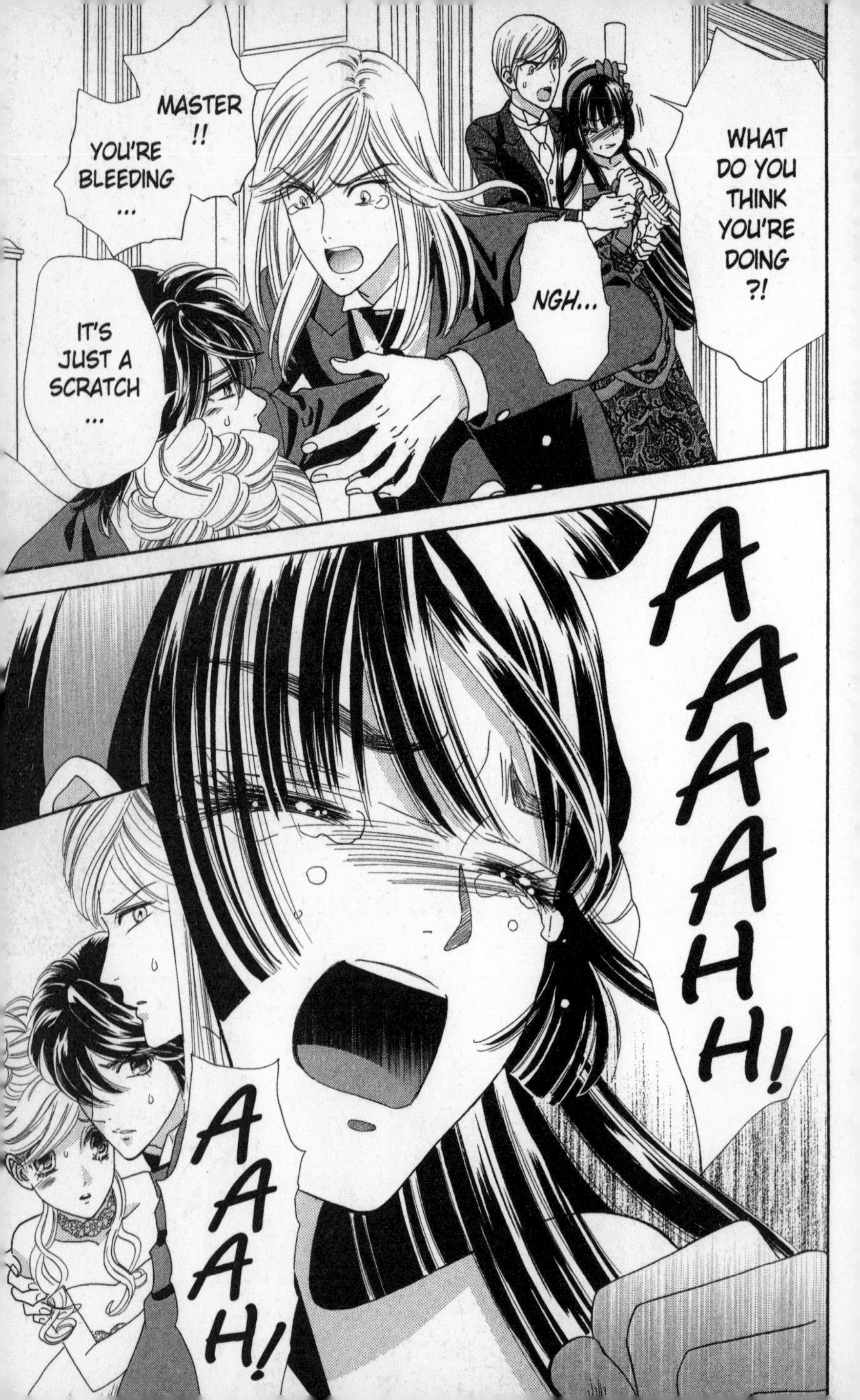
WHAT DO YOU THINK YOU'RE DOING?!
NGH...
MASTER!!
YOU'RE BLEEDING...
IT'S JUST A SCRATCH...
AAAAAH!
AAAAH!

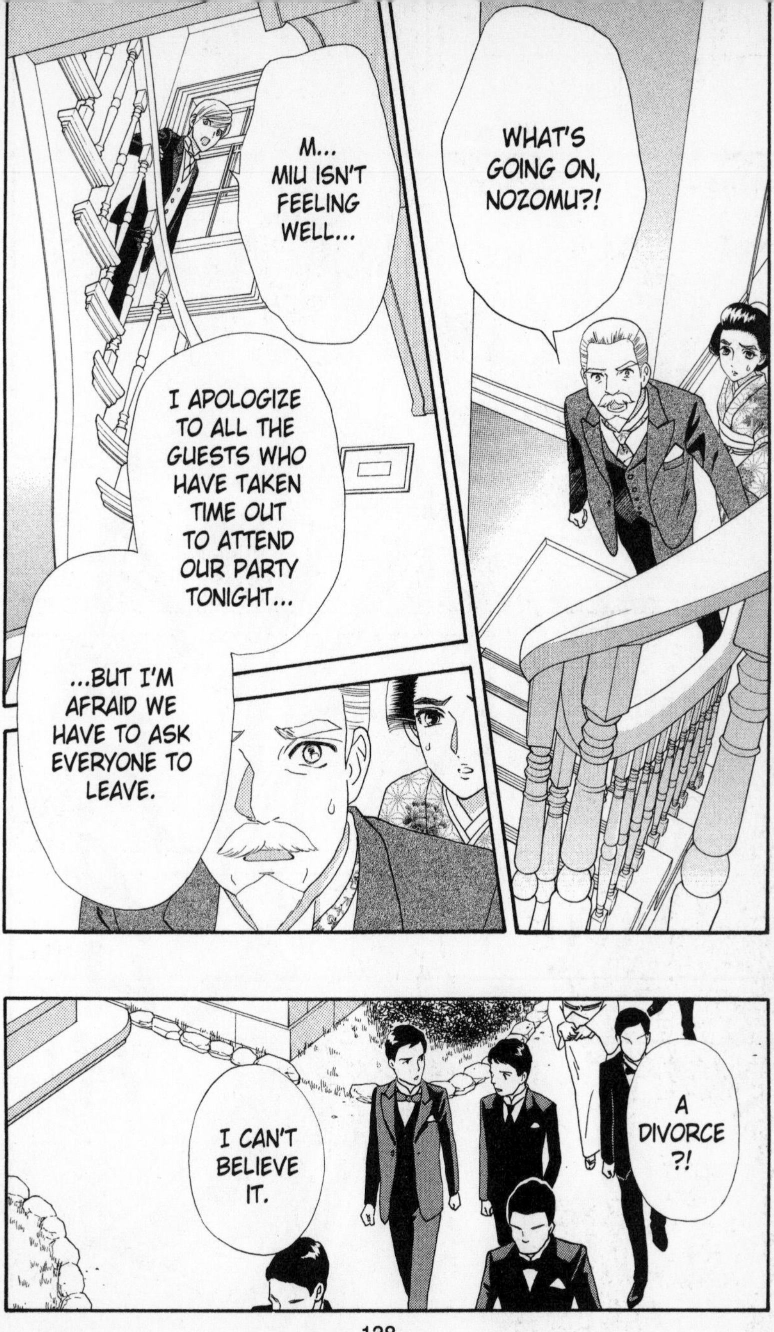
WHAT'S GOING ON, NOZOMU?!
M... MIU ISN'T FEELING WELL...
I APOLOGIZE TO ALL THE GUESTS WHO HAVE TAKEN TIME OUT TO ATTEND OUR PARTY TONIGHT...
...BUT I'M AFRAID WE HAVE TO ASK EVERYONE TO LEAVE.
A DIVORCE ?!
I CAN'T BELIEVE IT.

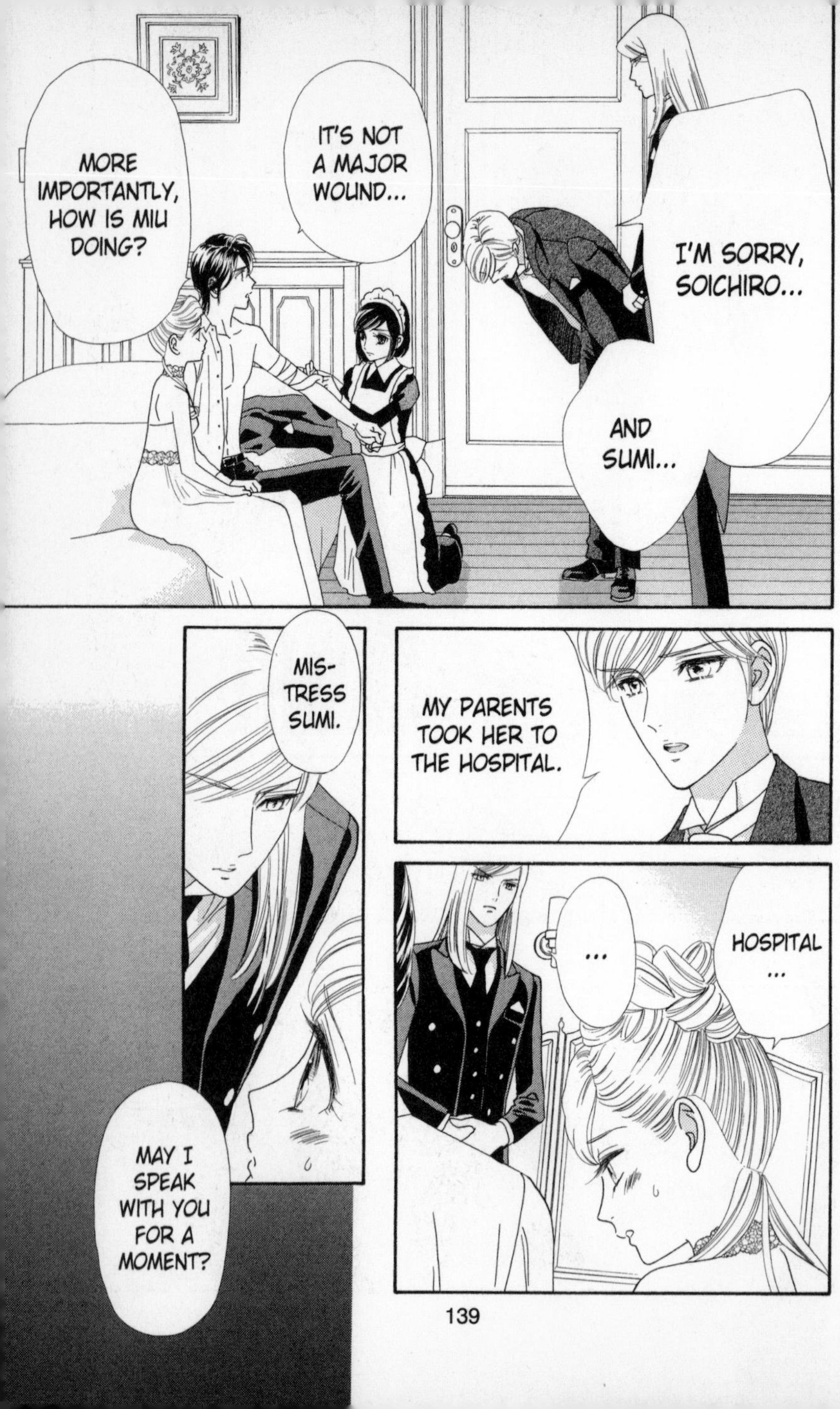
I'M SORRY, SOICHIRO...
AND SUMI...
IT'S NOT A MAJOR WOUND...
MORE IMPORTANTLY, HOW IS MIU DOING?
MY PARENTS TOOK HER TO THE HOSPITAL.
HOSPITAL...
...
MIS-TRESS SUMI.
MAY I SPEAK WITH YOU FOR A MOMENT?

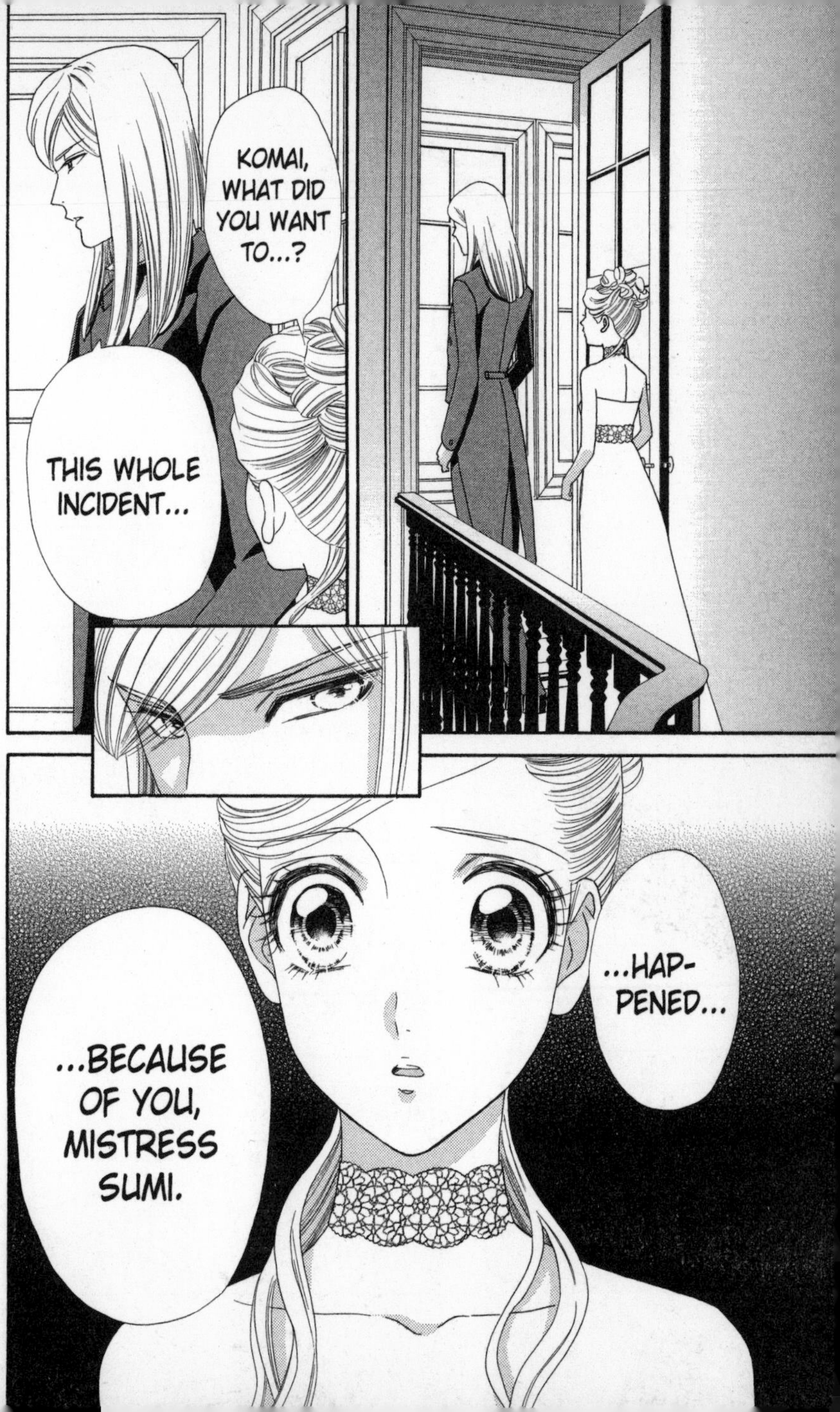
KOMAI, WHAT DID YOU WANT TO...?
THIS WHOLE INCIDENT...
...HAP-PENED...
...BECAUSE OF YOU, MISTRESS SUMI.

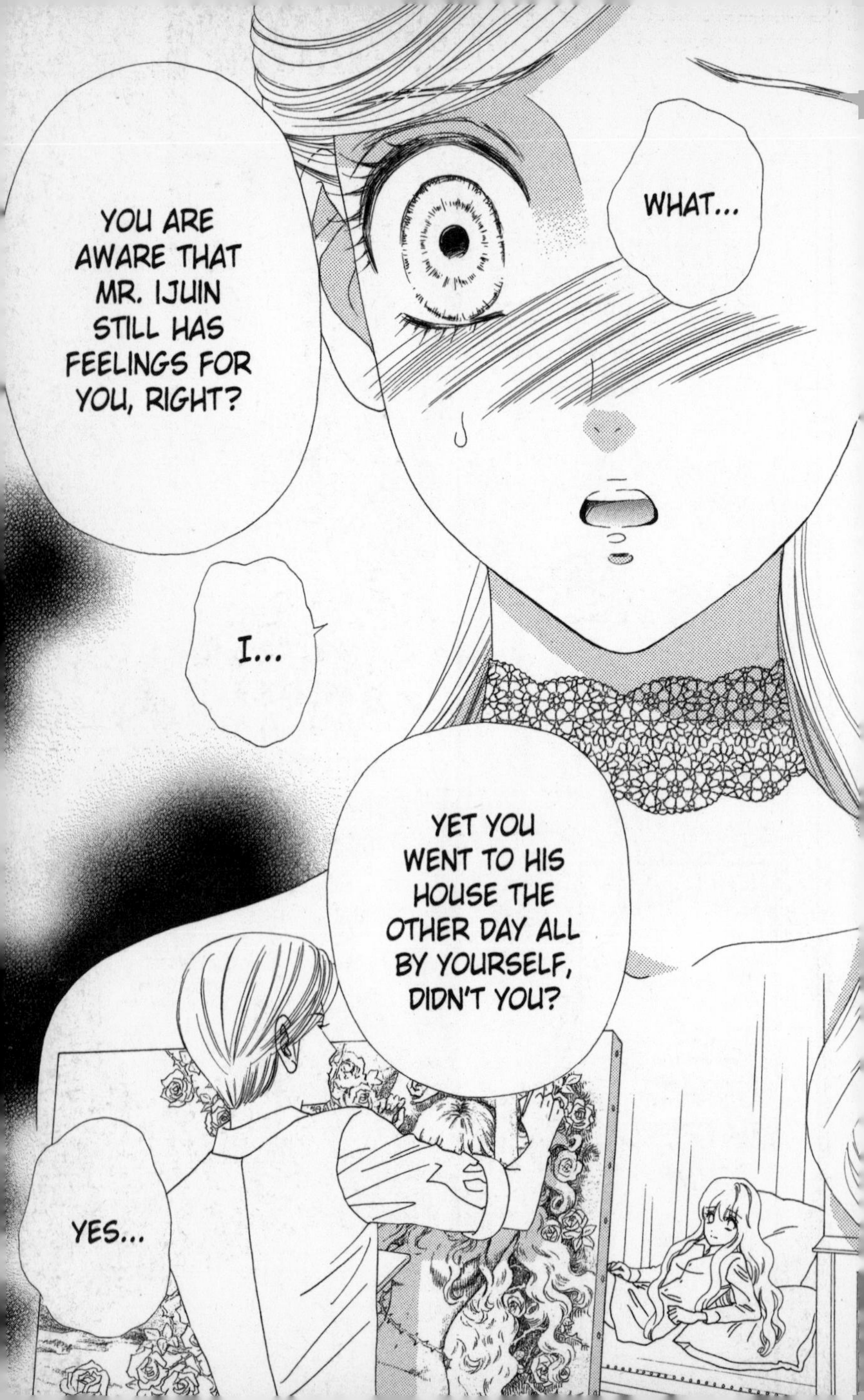
YOU ARE AWARE THAT MR. IJUIN STILL HAS FEELINGS FOR YOU, RIGHT?
WHAT...
I...
YET YOU WENT TO HIS HOUSE THE OTHER DAY ALL BY YOURSELF, DIDN'T YOU?
YES...

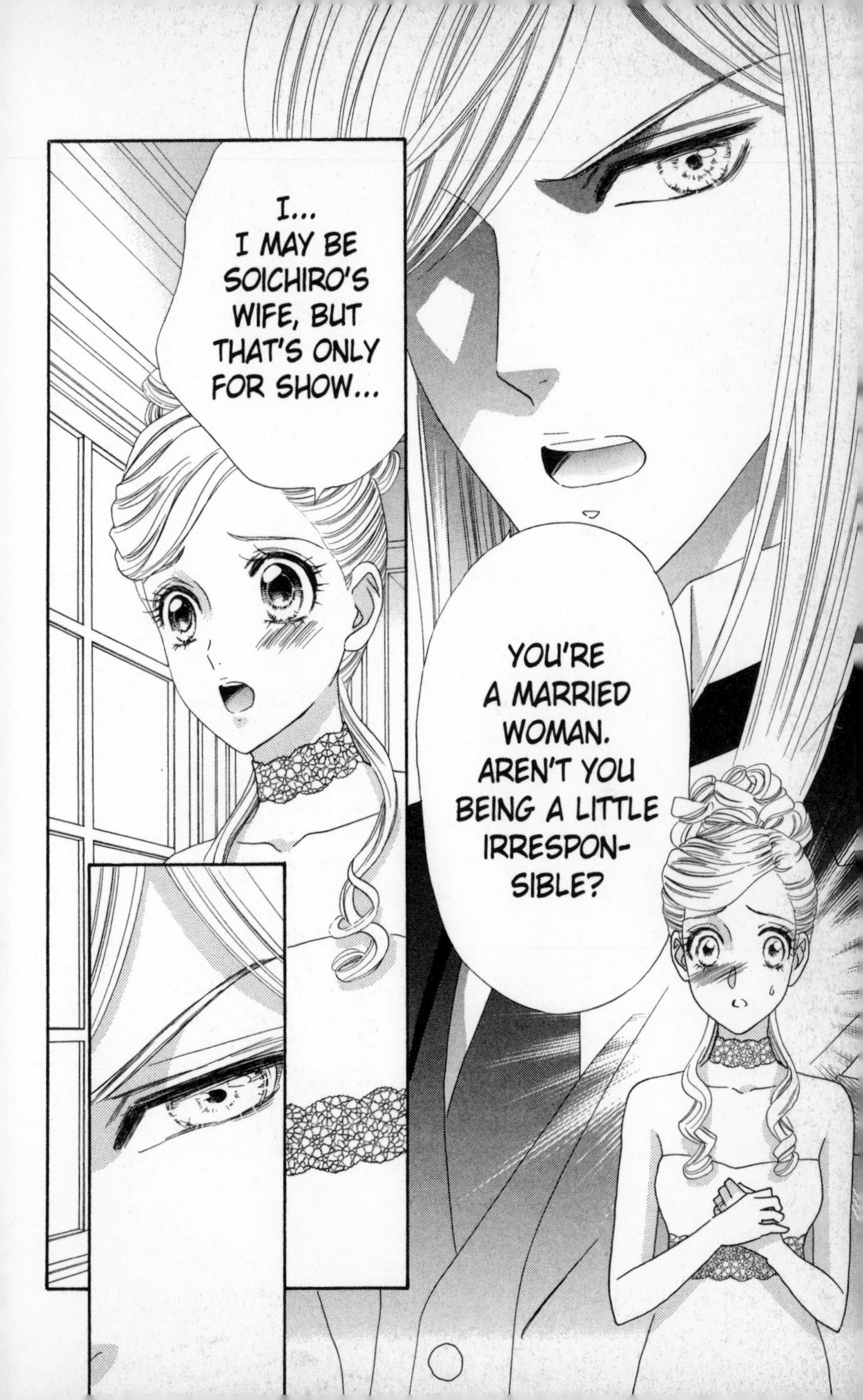
YOU'RE A MARRIED WOMAN. AREN'T YOU BEING A LITTLE IRRESPON-SIBLE?
I... I MAY BE SOICHIRO'S WIFE, BUT THAT'S ONLY FOR SHOW...

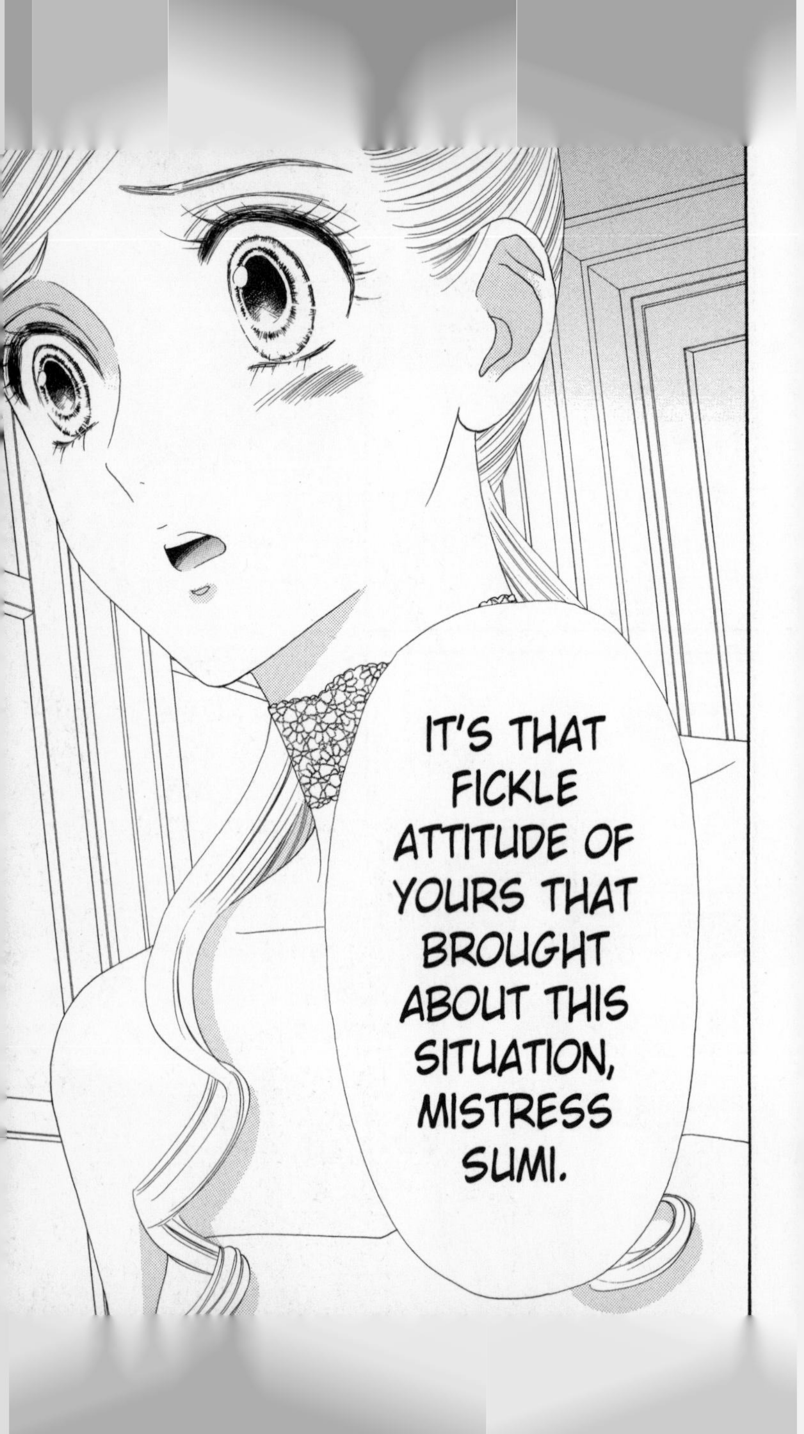
IT'S THAT FICKLE ATTITUDE OF YOURS THAT BROUGHT ABOUT THIS SITUATION, MISTRESS SUMI.

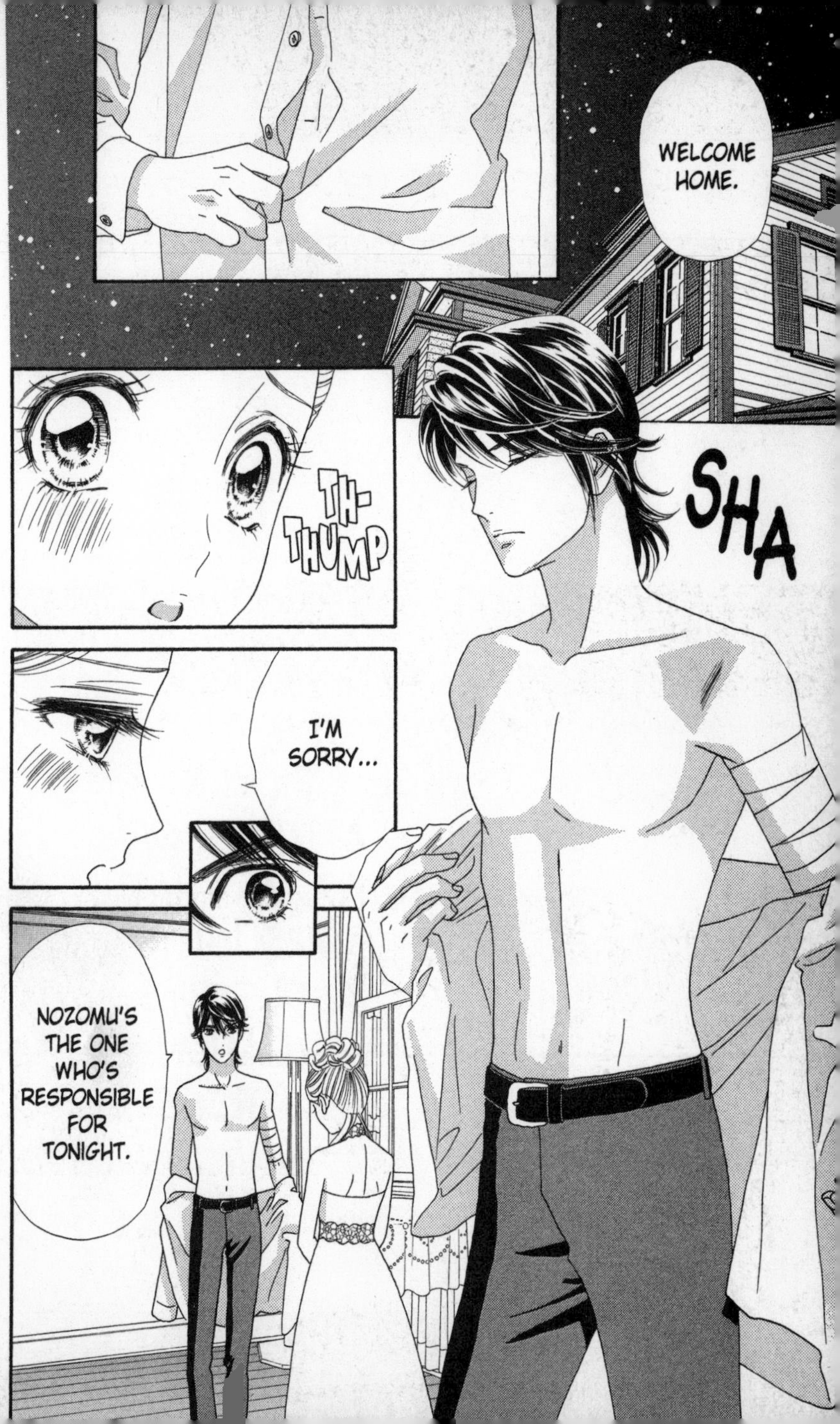
WELCOME HOME.
SHA
TH-THUMP
I'M SORRY...
NOZOMU'S THE ONE WHO'S RESPONSIBLE FOR TONIGHT.

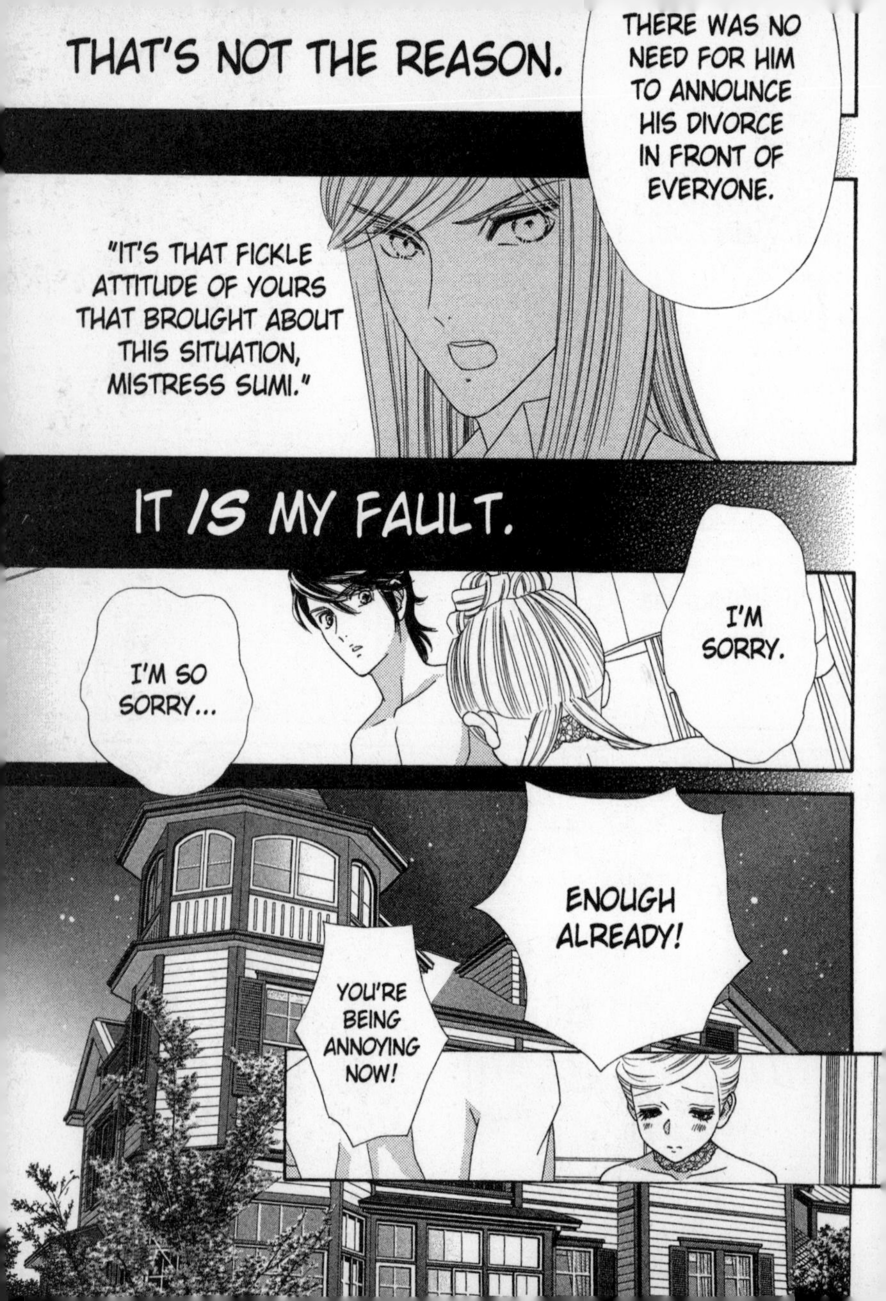
THERE WAS NO NEED FOR HIM TO ANNOUNCE HIS DIVORCE IN FRONT OF EVERYONE.
THAT'S NOT THE REASON.
"IT'S THAT FICKLE ATTITUDE OF YOURS THAT BROUGHT ABOUT THIS SITUATION, MISTRESS SUMI."
IT *IS* MY FAULT.
I'M SORRY.
I'M SO SORRY...
ENOUGH ALREADY!
YOU'RE BEING ANNOYING NOW!

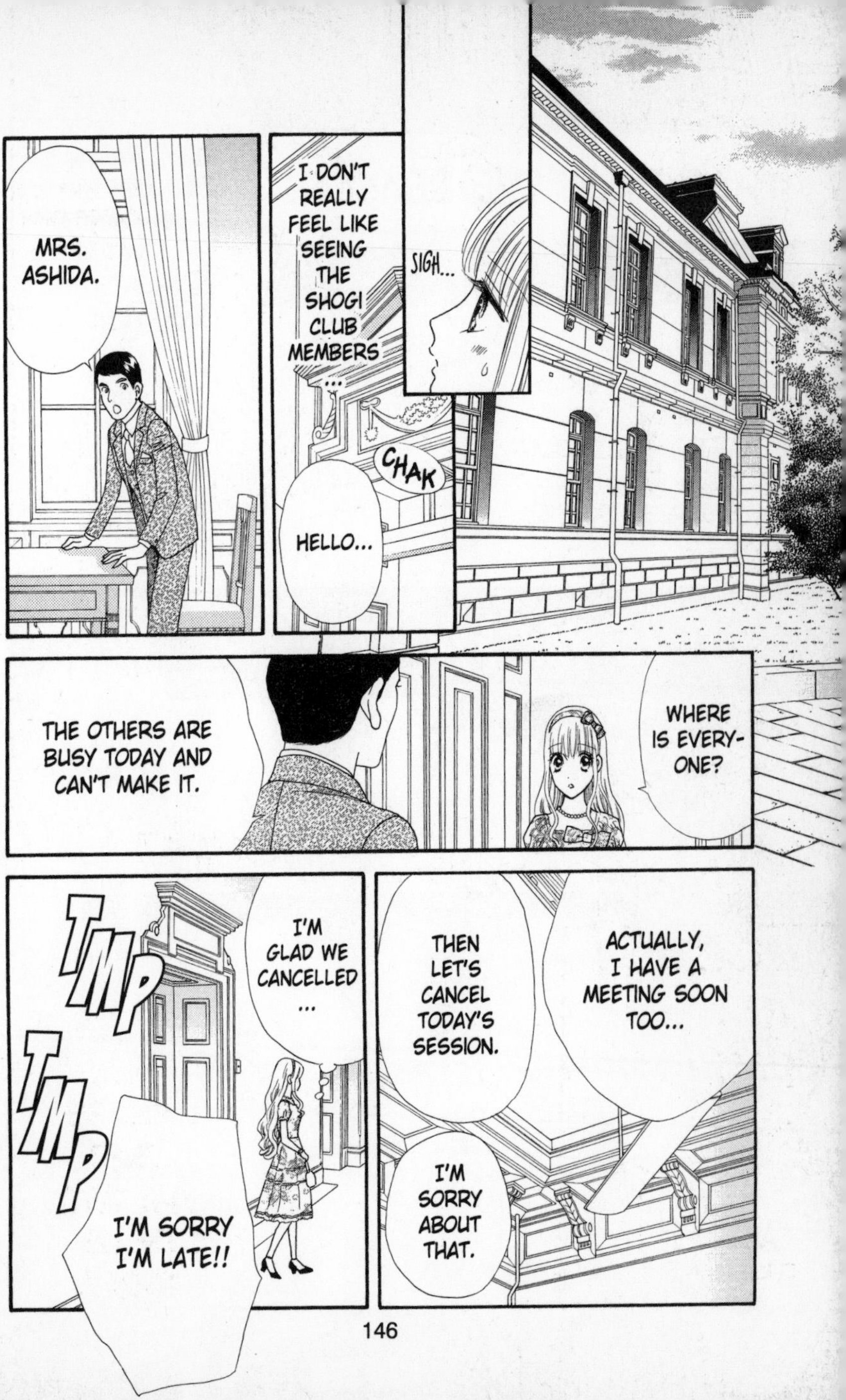
SIGH...
I DON'T REALLY FEEL LIKE SEEING THE SHOGI CLUB MEMBERS...
CHAK
HELLO...
MRS. ASHIDA.
WHERE IS EVERY-ONE?
THE OTHERS ARE BUSY TODAY AND CAN'T MAKE IT.
ACTUALLY, I HAVE A MEETING SOON TOO...
THEN LET'S CANCEL TODAY'S SESSION.
I'M SORRY ABOUT THAT.
I'M GLAD WE CANCELLED...
TMP
TMP
I'M SORRY I'M LATE!!

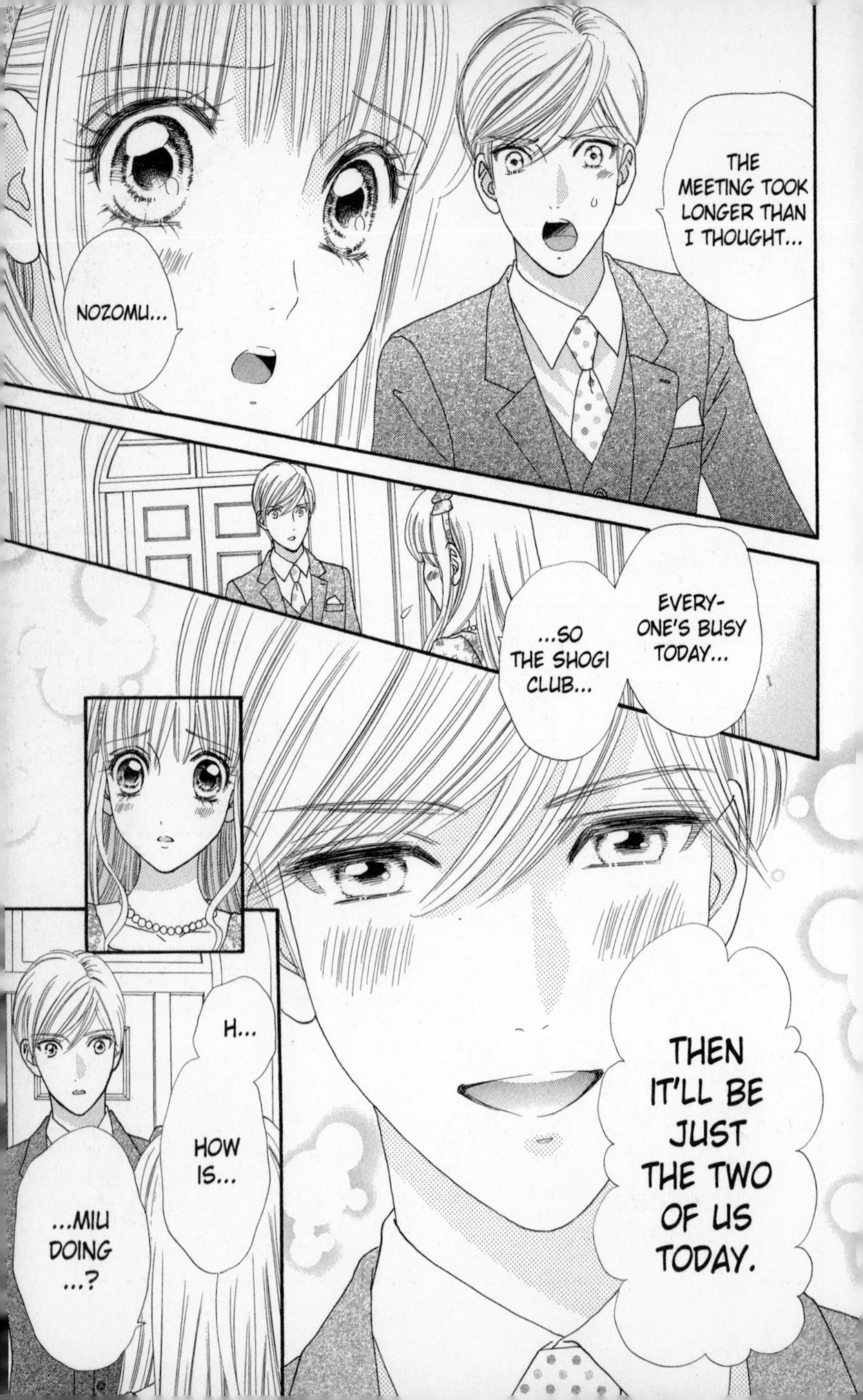
THE MEETING TOOK LONGER THAN I THOUGHT...
NOZOMU...
EVERY-ONE'S BUSY TODAY...
...SO THE SHOGI CLUB...
THEN IT'LL BE JUST THE TWO OF US TODAY.
H...
HOW IS...
...MIU DOING ...?

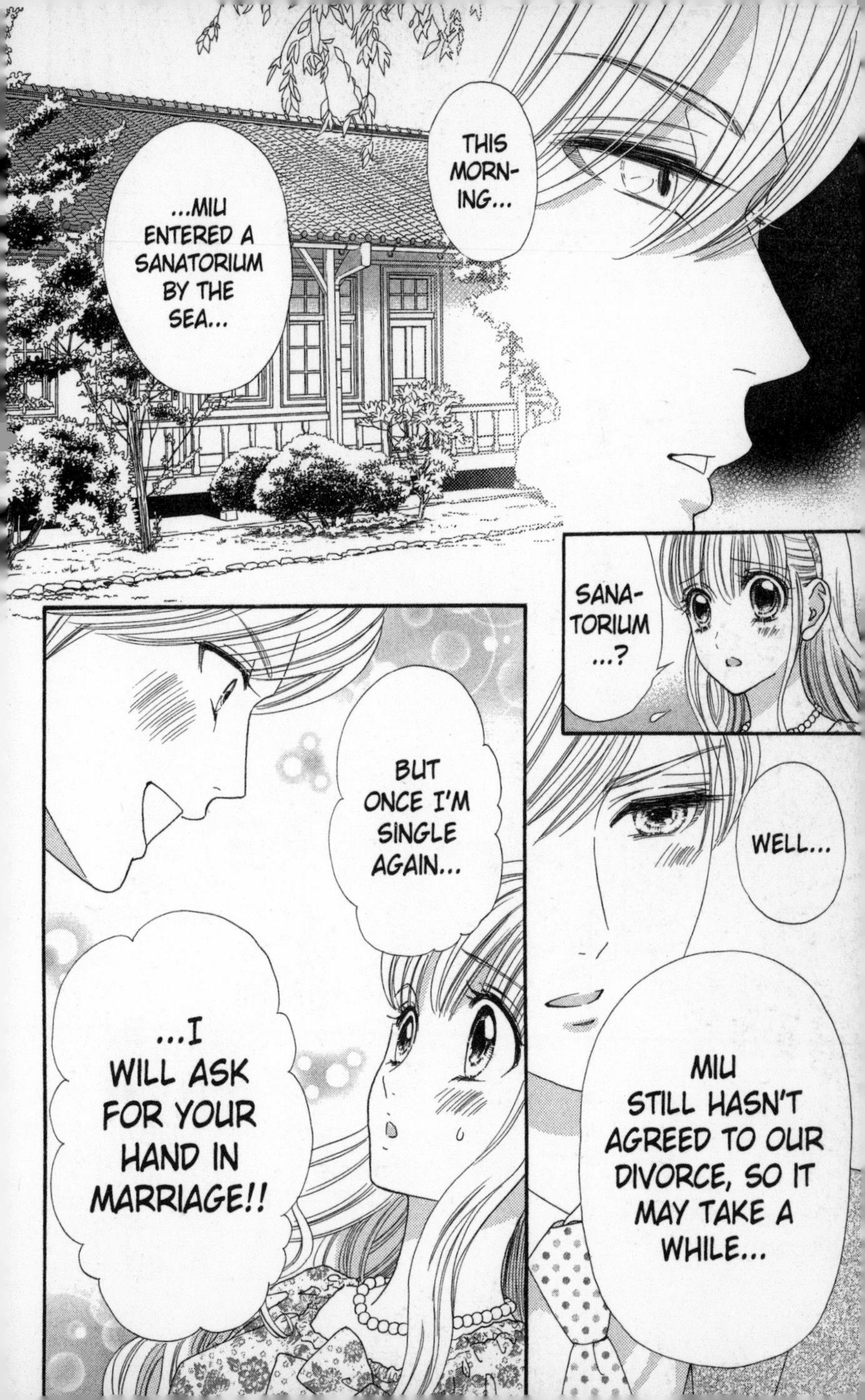
THIS MORNING...
...MIU ENTERED A SANATORIUM BY THE SEA...
SANATORIUM...?
WELL...
MIU STILL HASN'T AGREED TO OUR DIVORCE, SO IT MAY TAKE A WHILE...
BUT ONCE I'M SINGLE AGAIN...
...I WILL ASK FOR YOUR HAND IN MARRIAGE!!

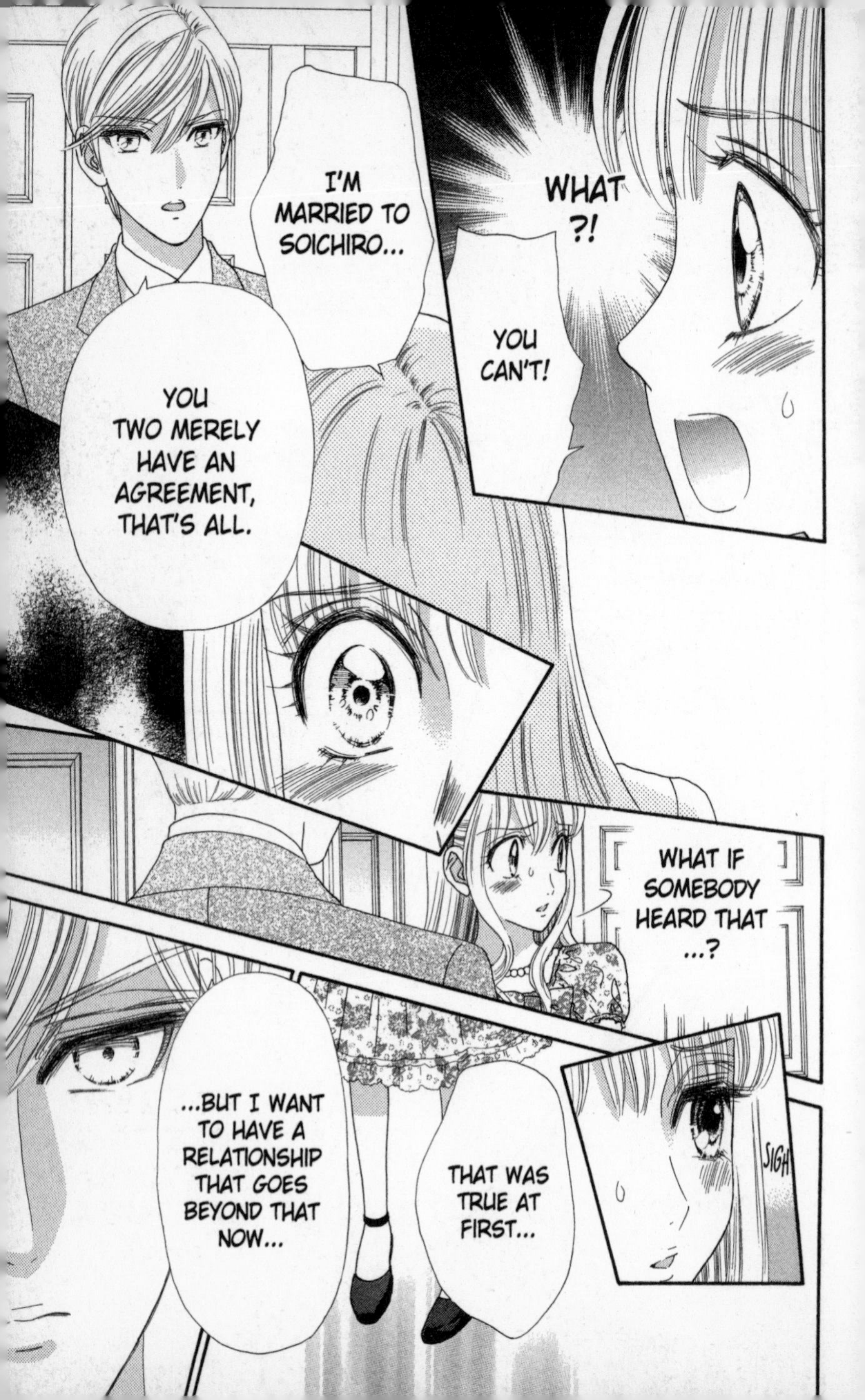
WHAT ?!
YOU CAN'T!
I'M MARRIED TO SOICHIRO...
YOU TWO MERELY HAVE AN AGREEMENT, THAT'S ALL.
WHAT IF SOMEBODY HEARD THAT ...?
SIGH
THAT WAS TRUE AT FIRST...
...BUT I WANT TO HAVE A RELATIONSHIP THAT GOES BEYOND THAT NOW...

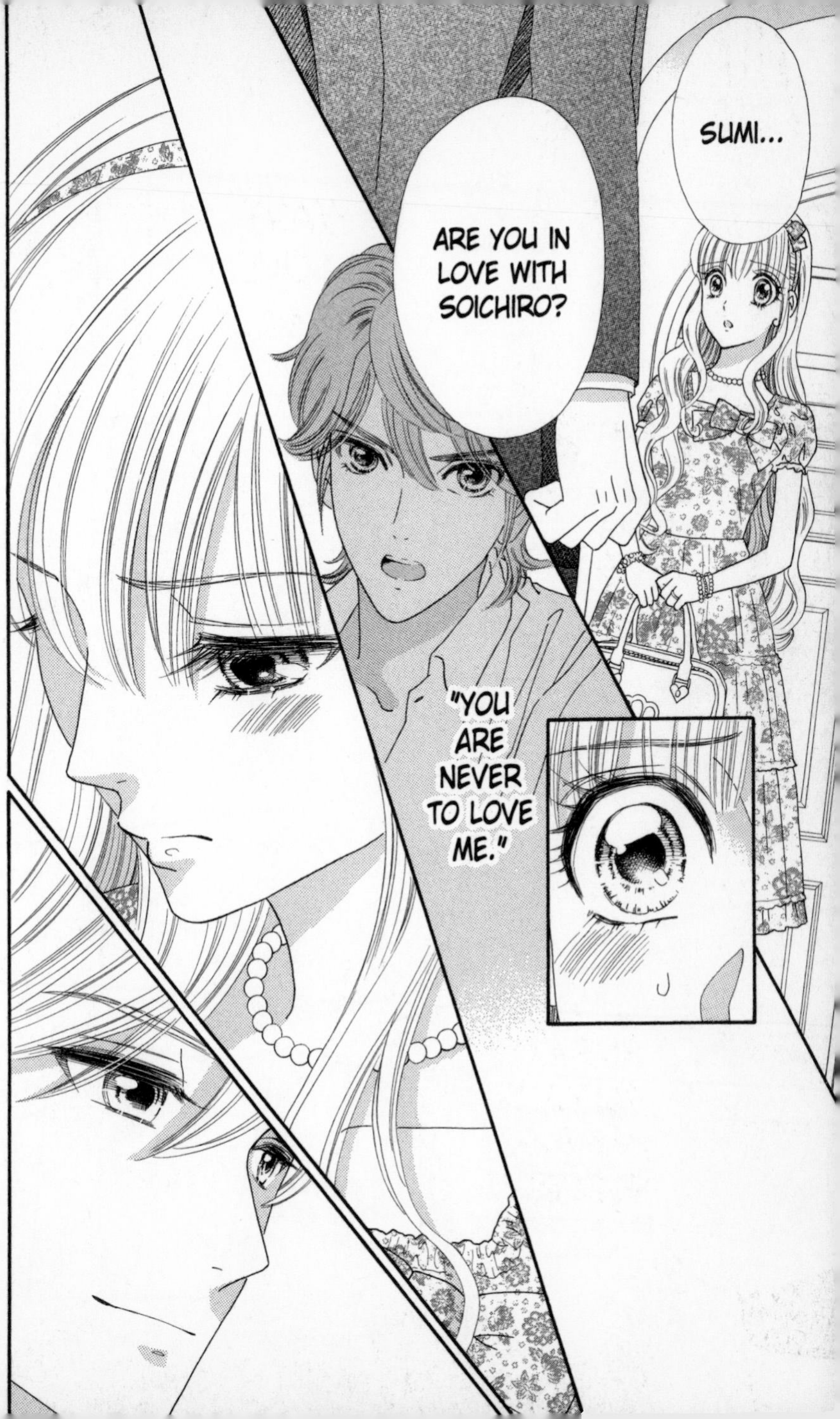
SUMI...
ARE YOU IN LOVE WITH SOICHIRO?
"YOU ARE NEVER TO LOVE ME."

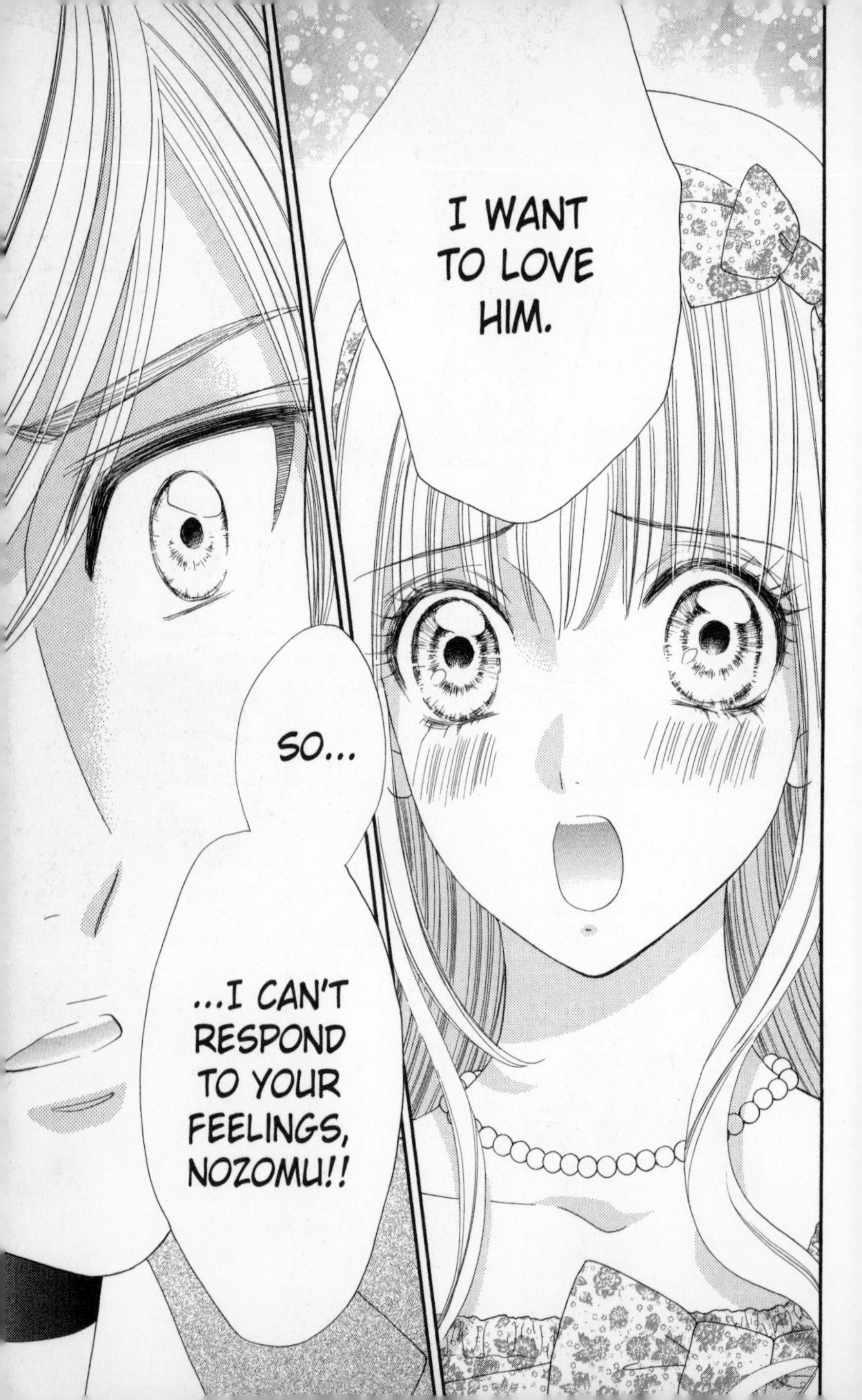
I WANT TO LOVE HIM.
SO...
...I CAN'T RESPOND TO YOUR FEELINGS, NOZOMU!!

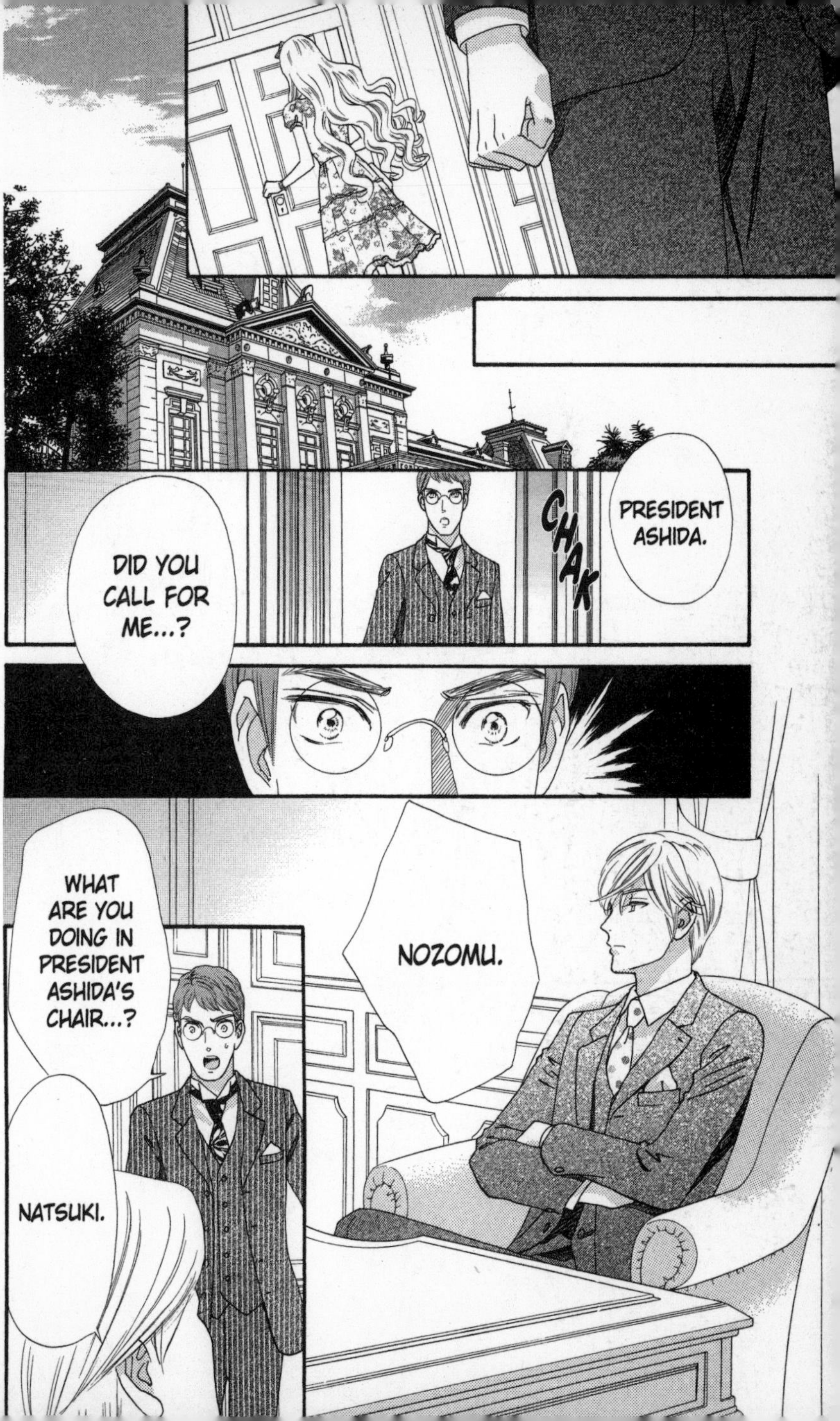
PRESIDENT ASHIDA.
CHAK
DID YOU CALL FOR ME...?
NOZOMU.
WHAT ARE YOU DOING IN PRESIDENT ASHIDA'S CHAIR...?
NATSUKI.

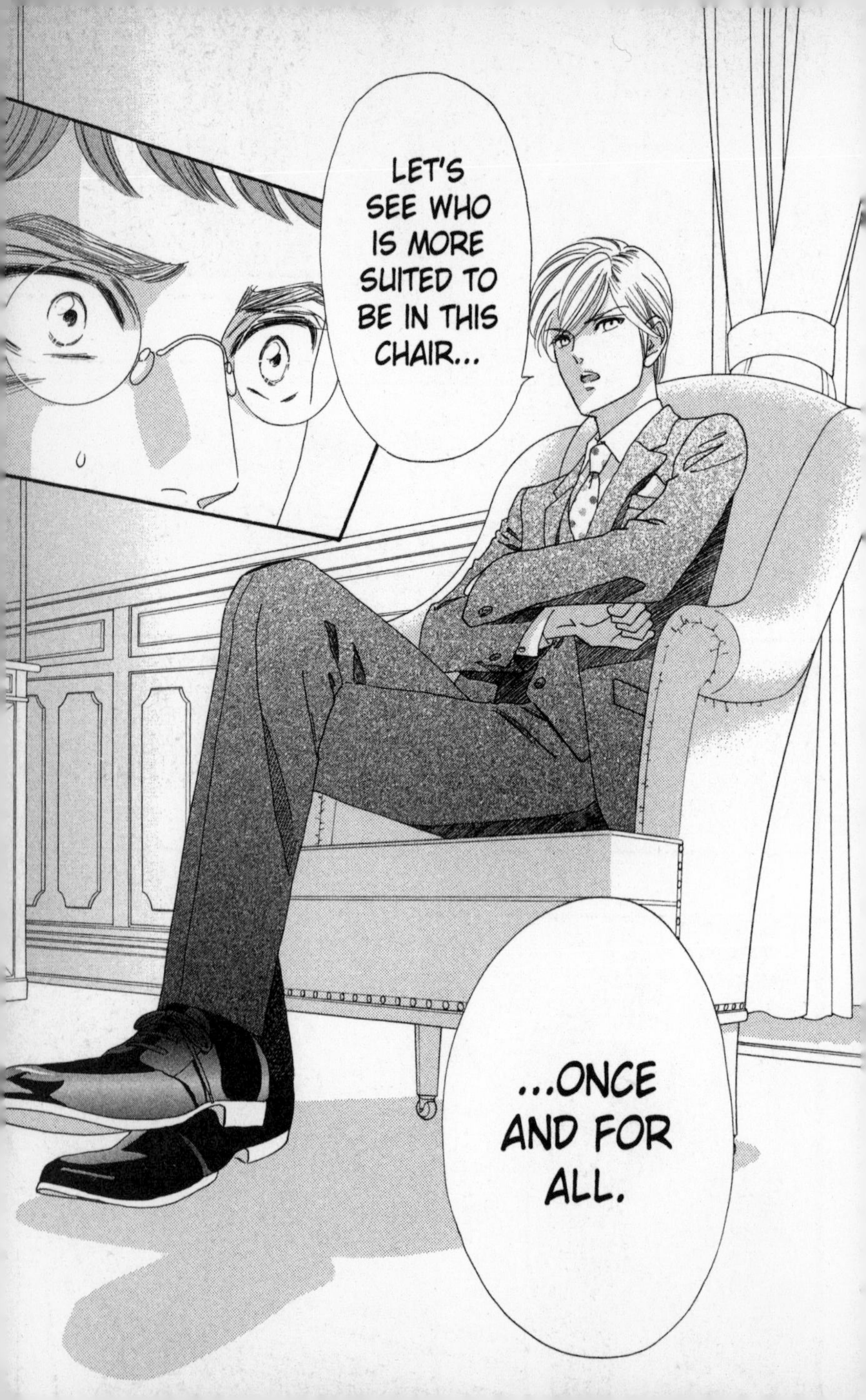
LET'S SEE WHO IS MORE SUITED TO BE IN THIS CHAIR...
...ONCE AND FOR ALL.

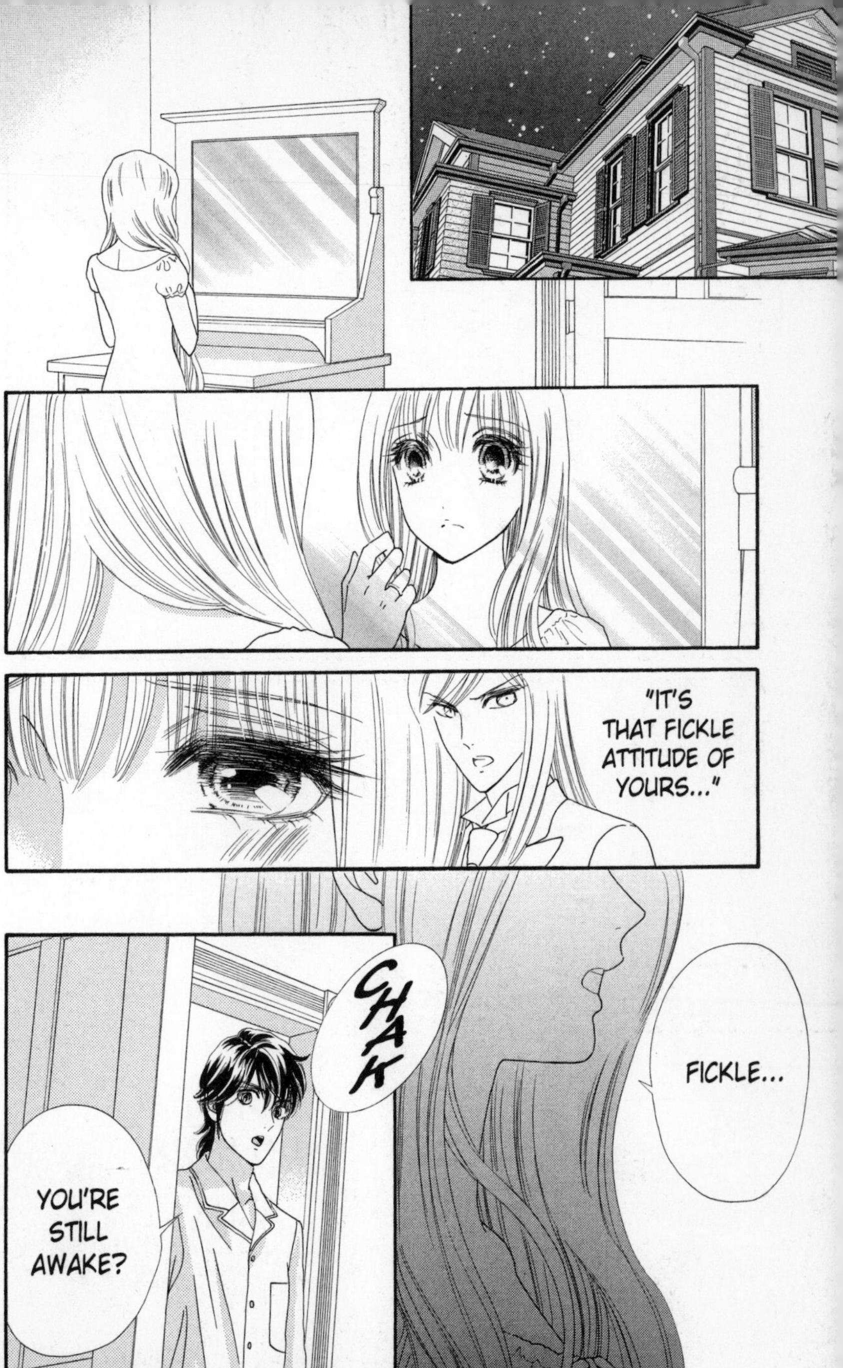
"IT'S THAT FICKLE ATTITUDE OF YOURS..."
FICKLE...
CHAK
YOU'RE STILL AWAKE?

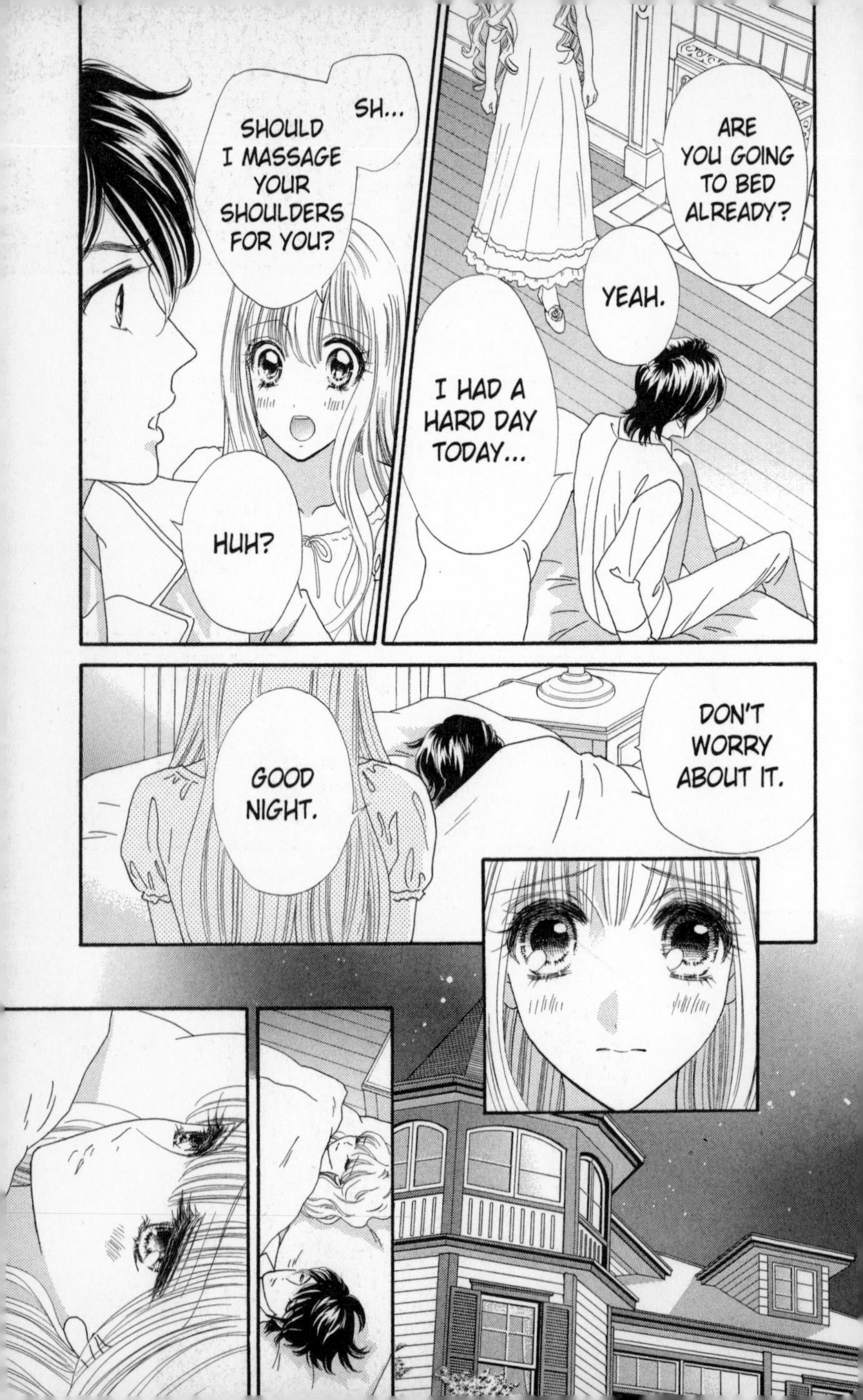
ARE YOU GOING TO BED ALREADY?
YEAH.
I HAD A HARD DAY TODAY...
SH...
SHOULD I MASSAGE YOUR SHOULDERS FOR YOU?
HUH?
DON'T WORRY ABOUT IT.
GOOD NIGHT.

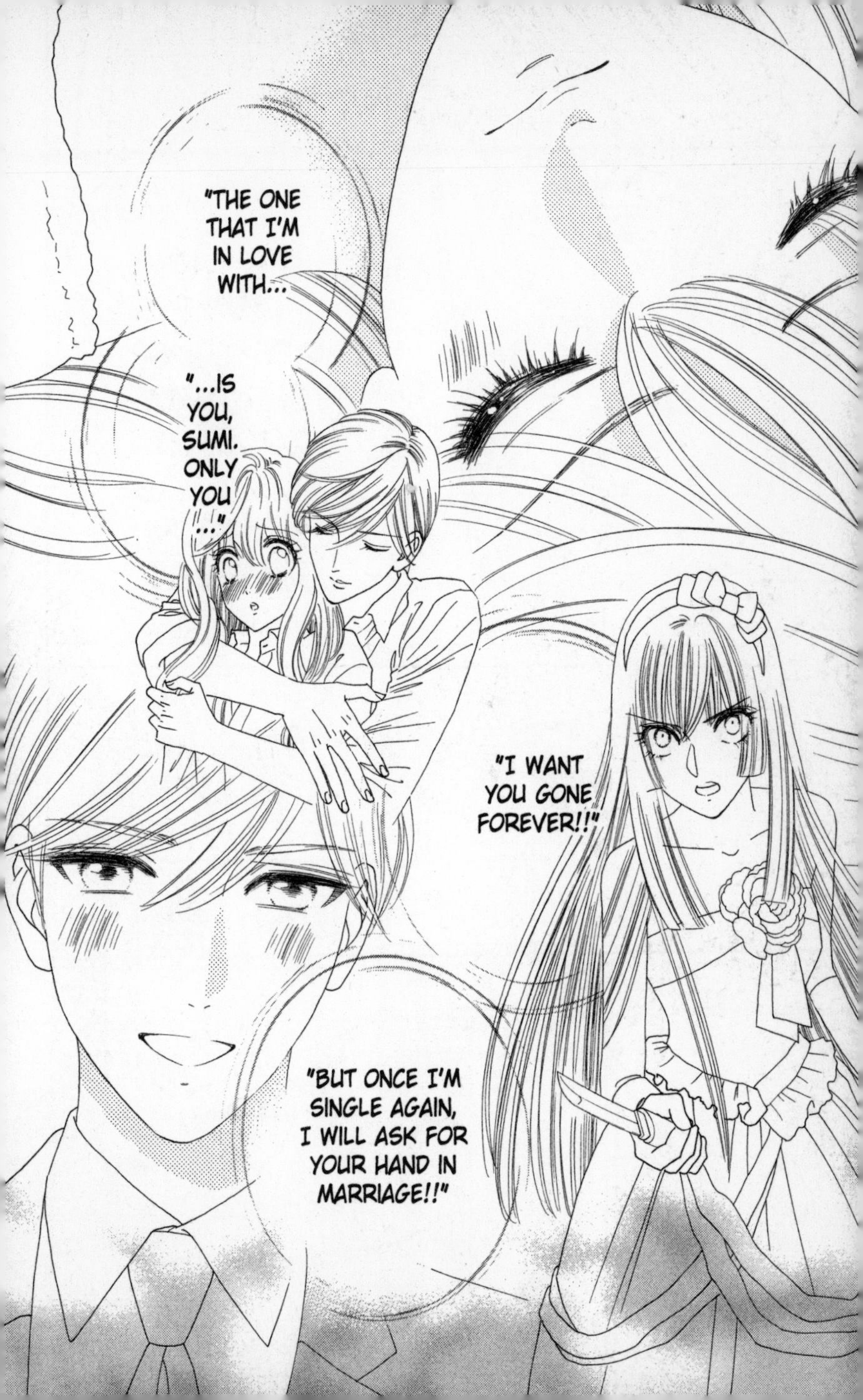
"THE ONE THAT I'M IN LOVE WITH...
"...IS YOU, SUMI. ONLY YOU...!"
"I WANT YOU GONE FOREVER!!"
"BUT ONCE I'M SINGLE AGAIN, I WILL ASK FOR YOUR HAND IN MARRIAGE!!"

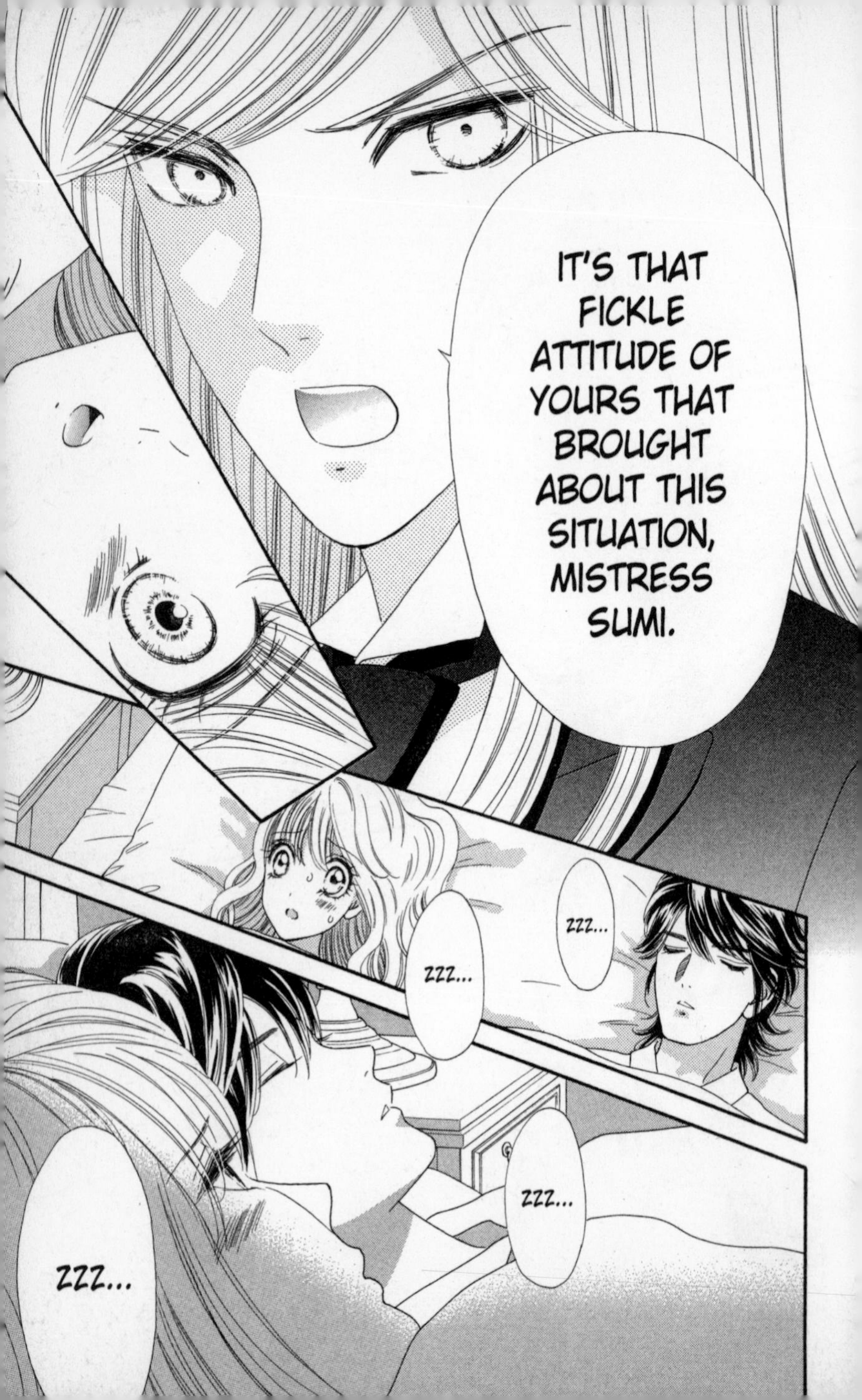
IT'S THAT FICKLE ATTITUDE OF YOURS THAT BROUGHT ABOUT THIS SITUATION, MISTRESS SUMI.
ZZZ...
ZZZ...
ZZZ...
ZZZ...

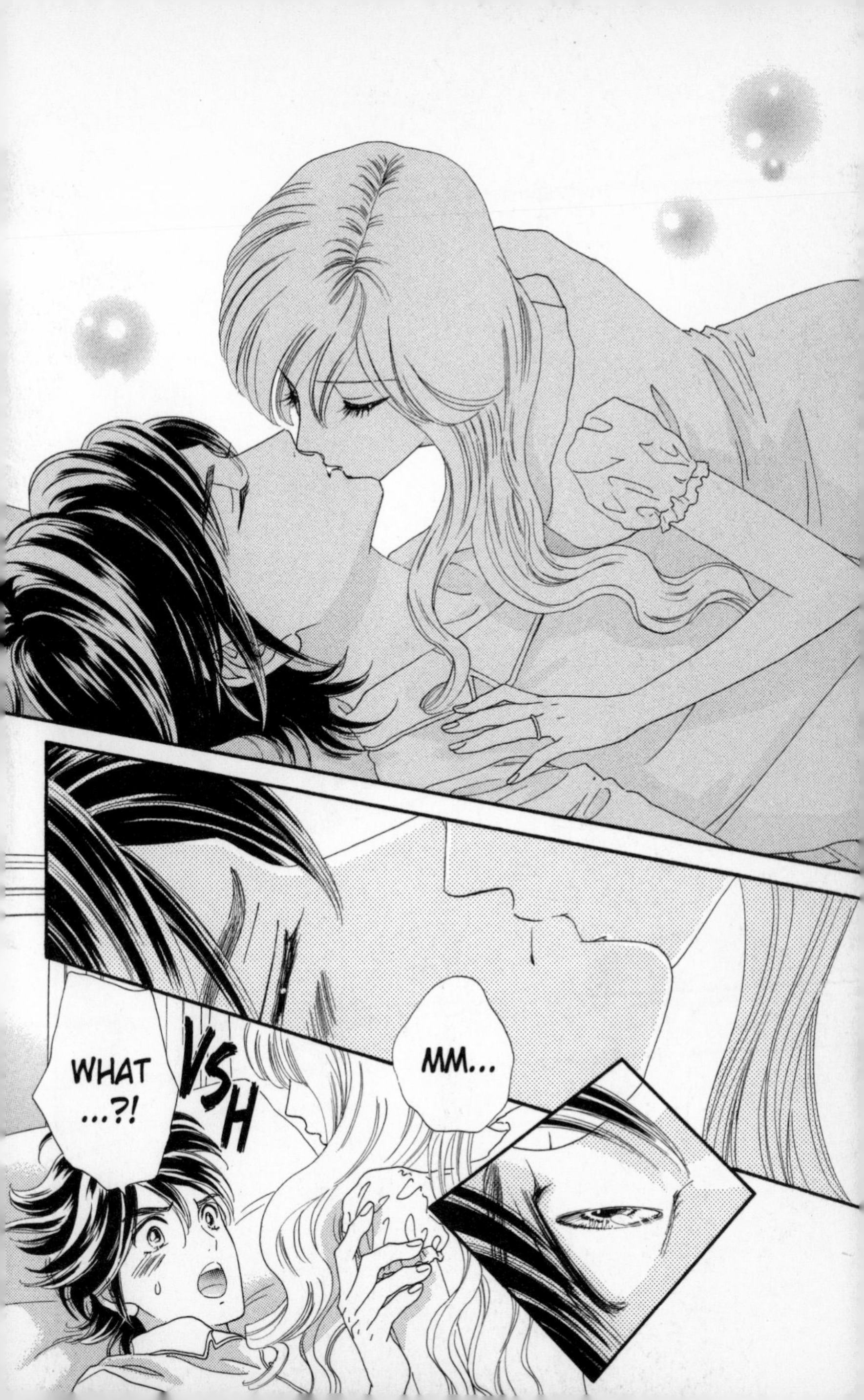
MM...
VSH
WHAT ...?!

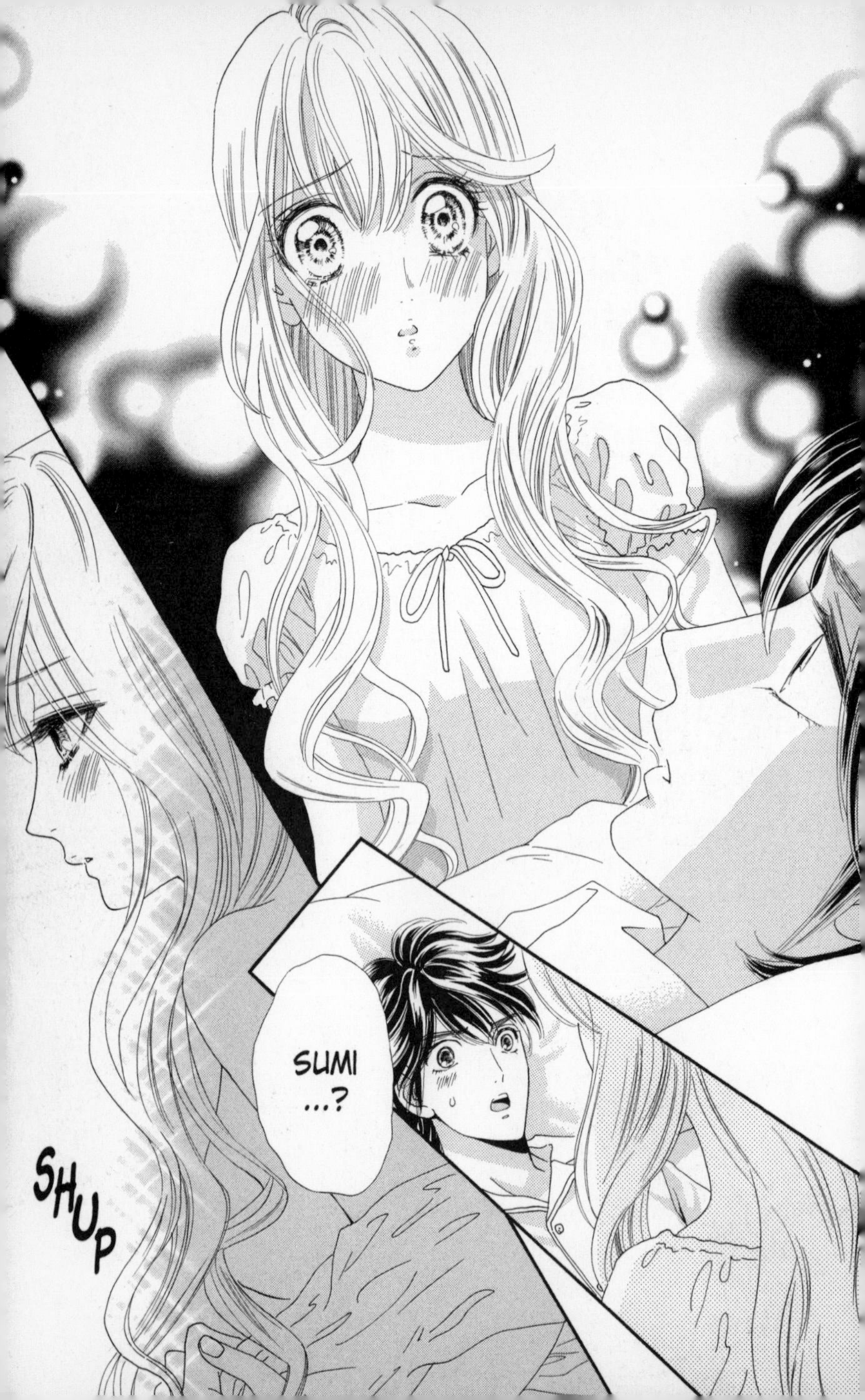
SUMI ...?
SHUP

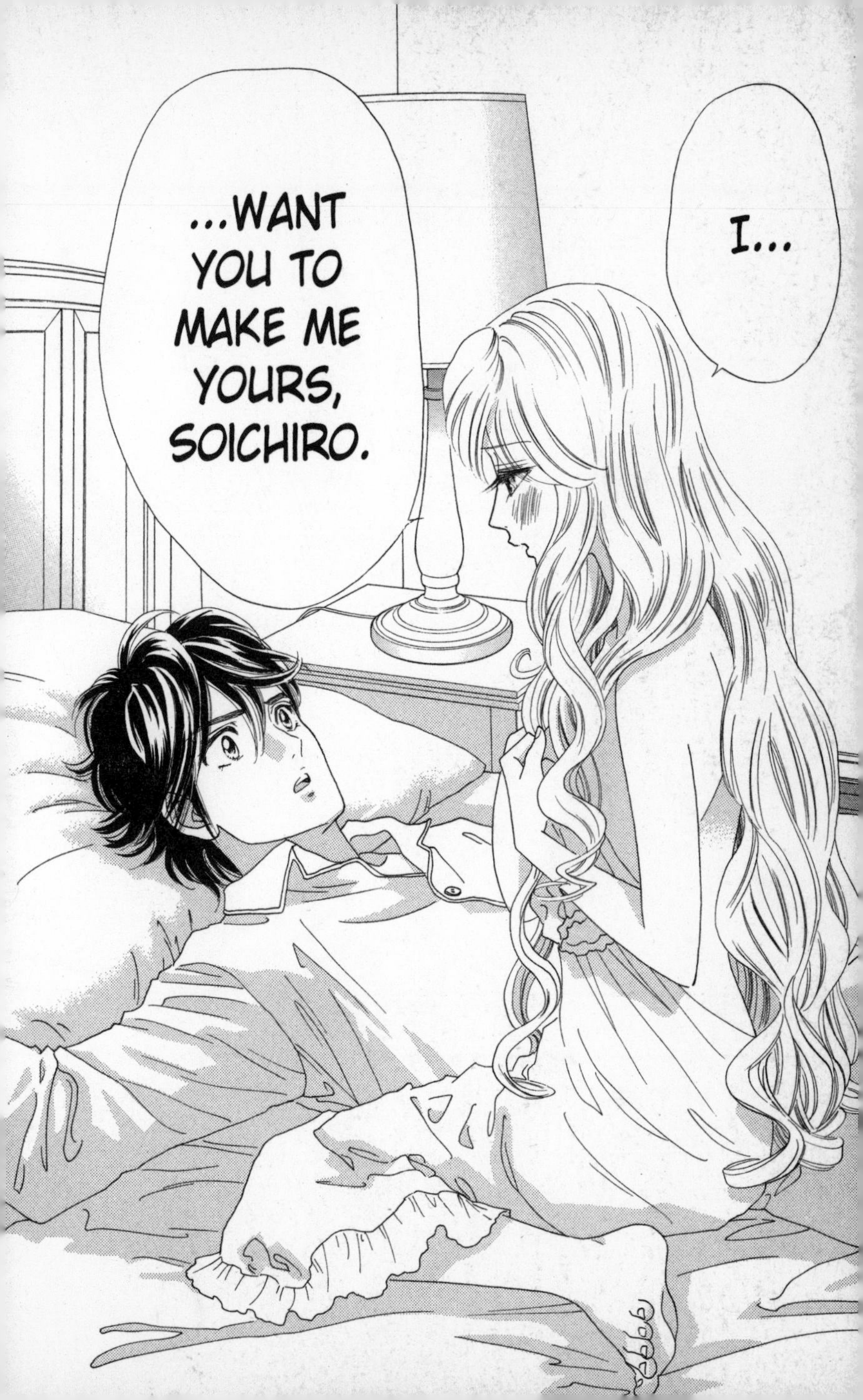
I...
...WANT YOU TO MAKE ME YOURS, SOICHIRO.

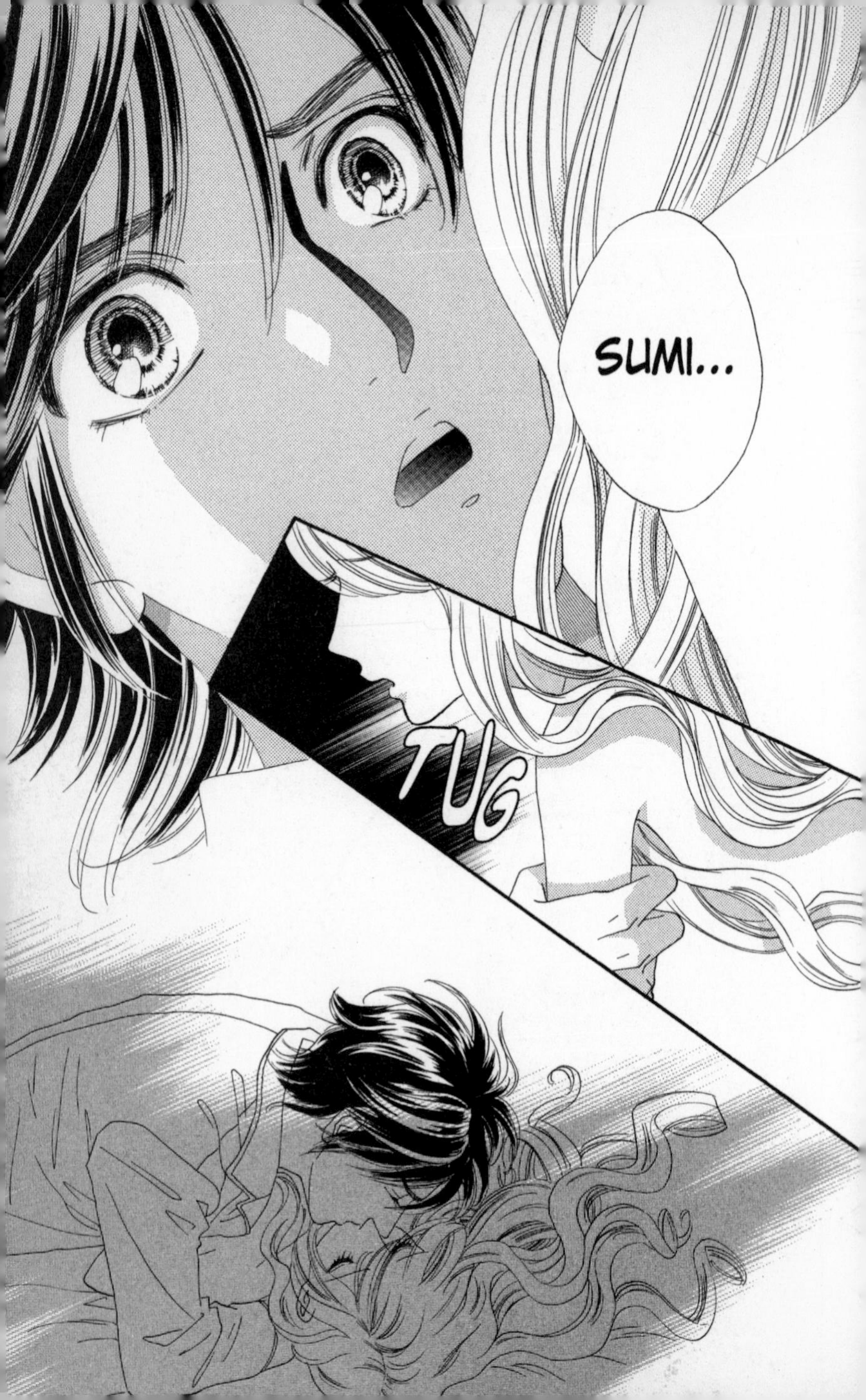
SUMI...
TUG

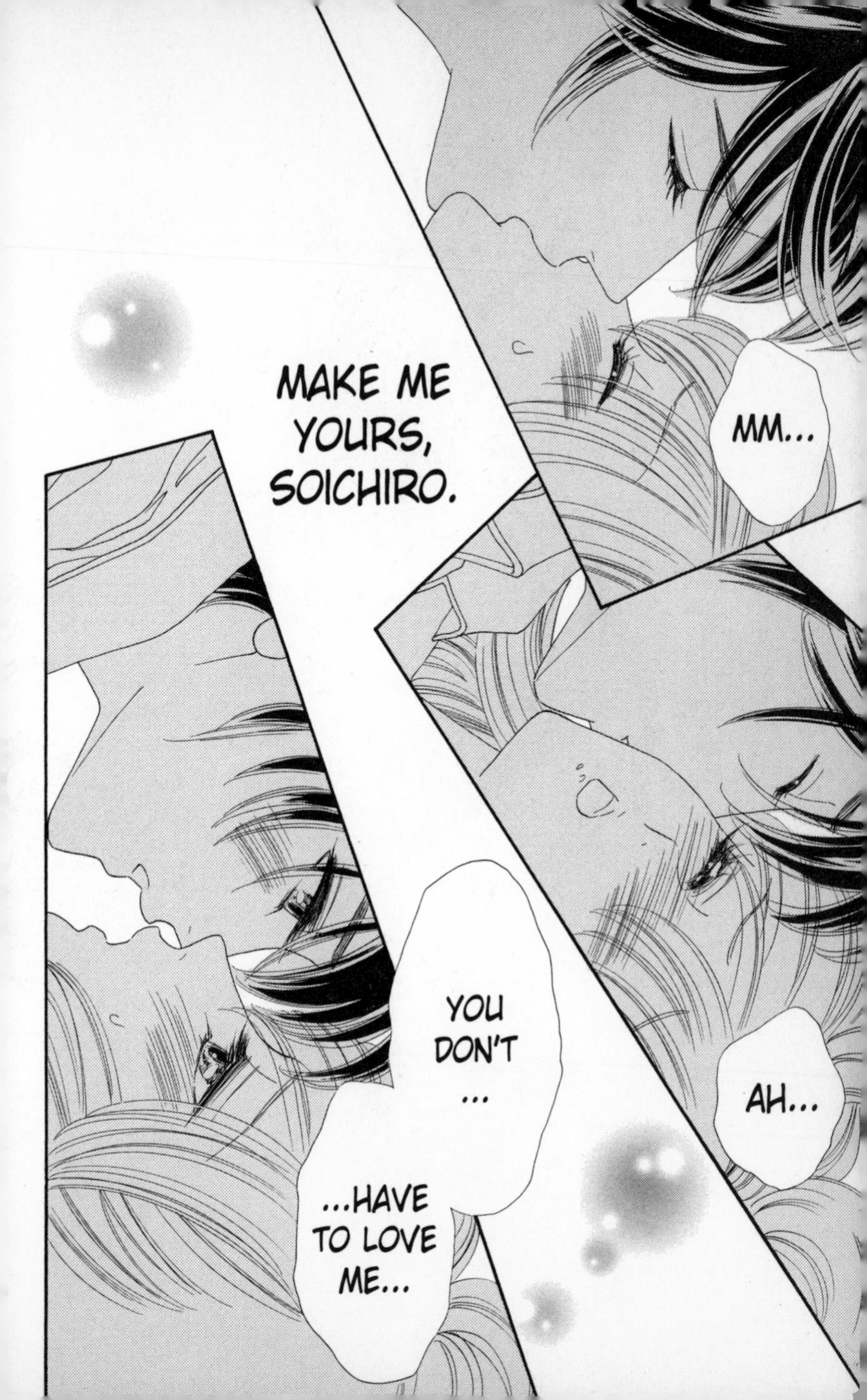
MM...
MAKE ME YOURS, SOICHIRO.
AH...
YOU DON'T ...
...HAVE TO LOVE ME...

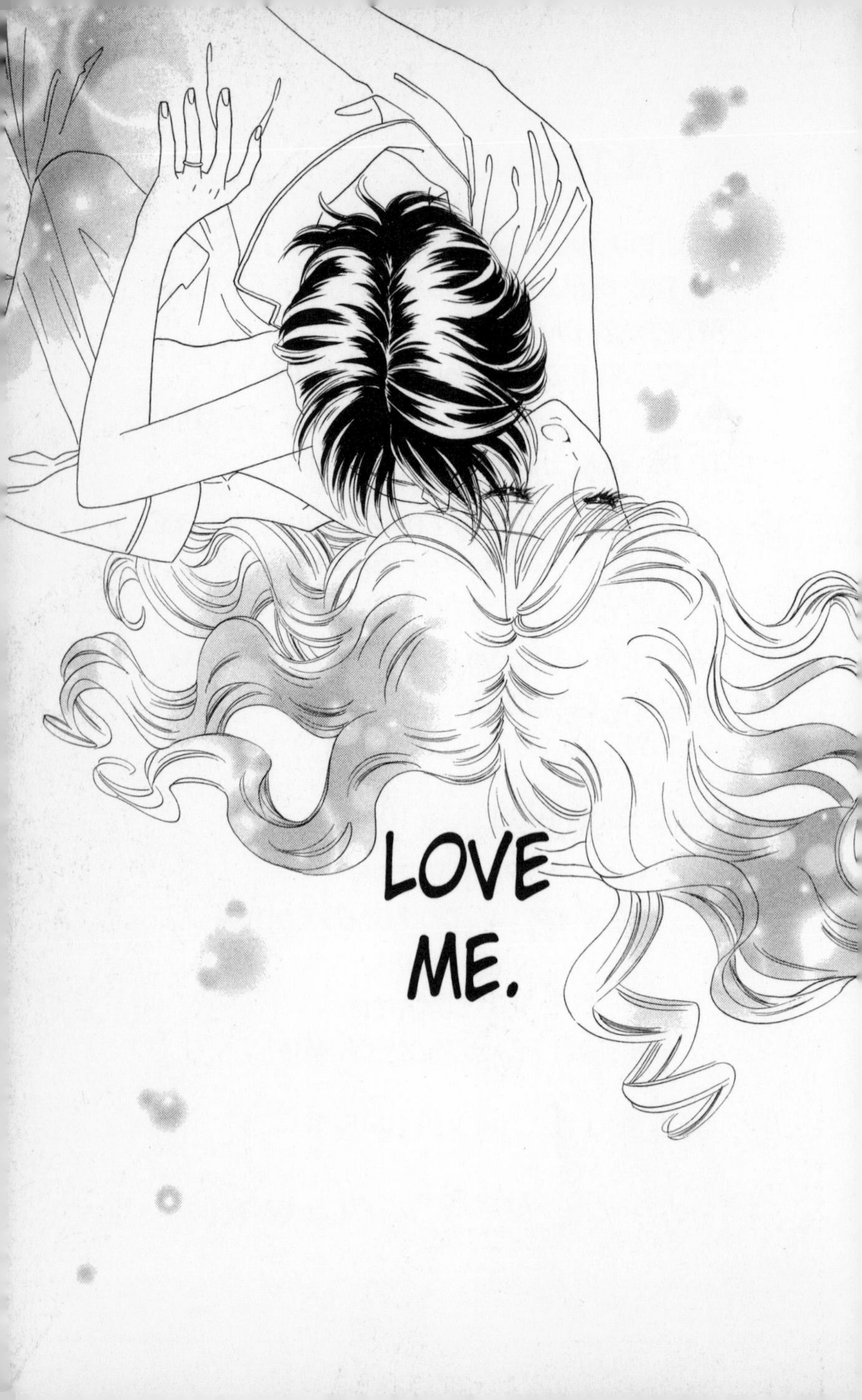
LOVE ME.

AFTERWORD ~

✿ HOW DID YOU LIKE THE INTRODUCTION TO THE BUILDING LOCATIONS I USED FOR *STEPPING ON ROSES*? THERE ARE OTHER BUILDINGS THAT I HAVEN'T MENTIONED YET, SO I'LL CONTINUE TO DO THAT IN THE NEXT VOLUME.

✿ I WAS WHINING AND COMPLAINING AT THE END OF VOLUME 5, BUT THANKS TO ALL YOUR LETTERS OF SUPPORT, I AM NOW GRADUALLY RETURNING TO MY NORMAL CONDITION. (I STILL HAVEN'T RECOVERED 100 PERCENT YET...)

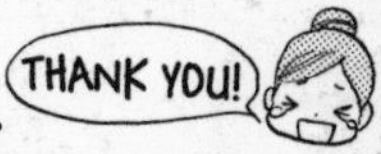
THANK YOU!

SEND YOUR THOUGHTS TO:

RINKO UEDA
C/O STEPPING ON ROSES EDITOR
VIZ MEDIA
P.O. BOX 77010
SAN FRANCISCO, CA 94107

✿ SEE YOU ALL IN VOLUME 7! — ♡

Rinko Ueda

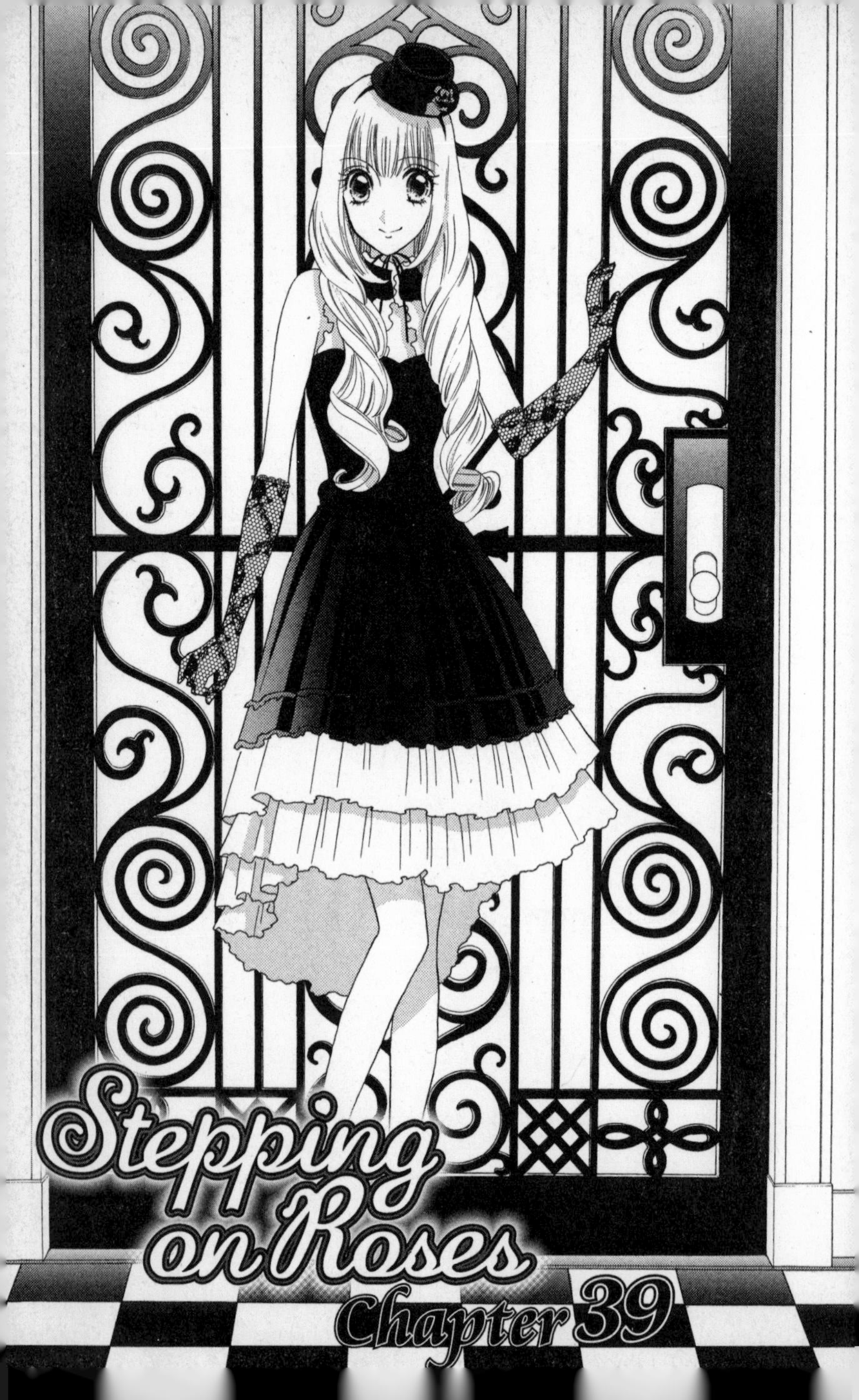
Stepping on Roses
Chapter 39

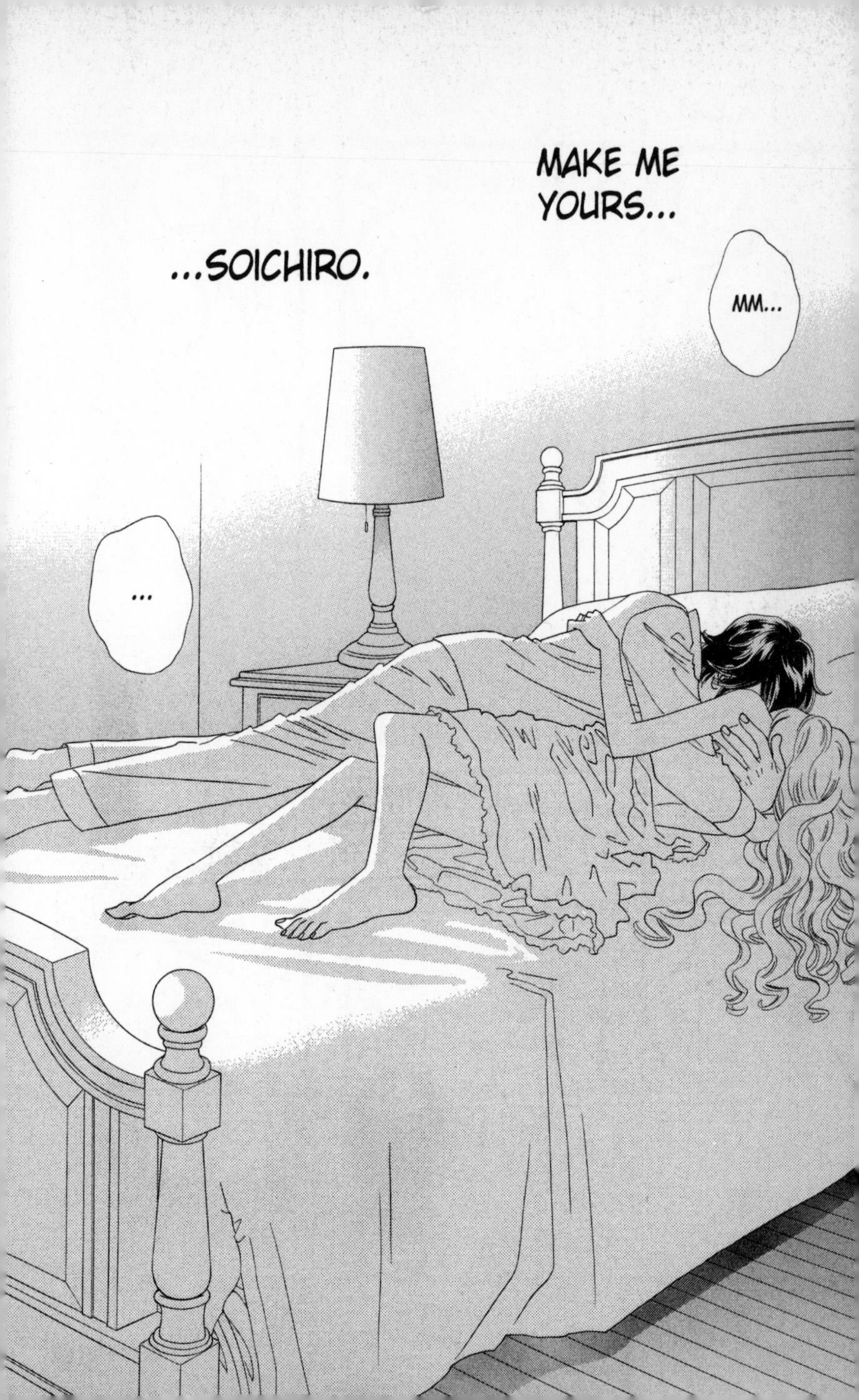
MAKE ME YOURS...
MM...
...SOICHIRO.
...

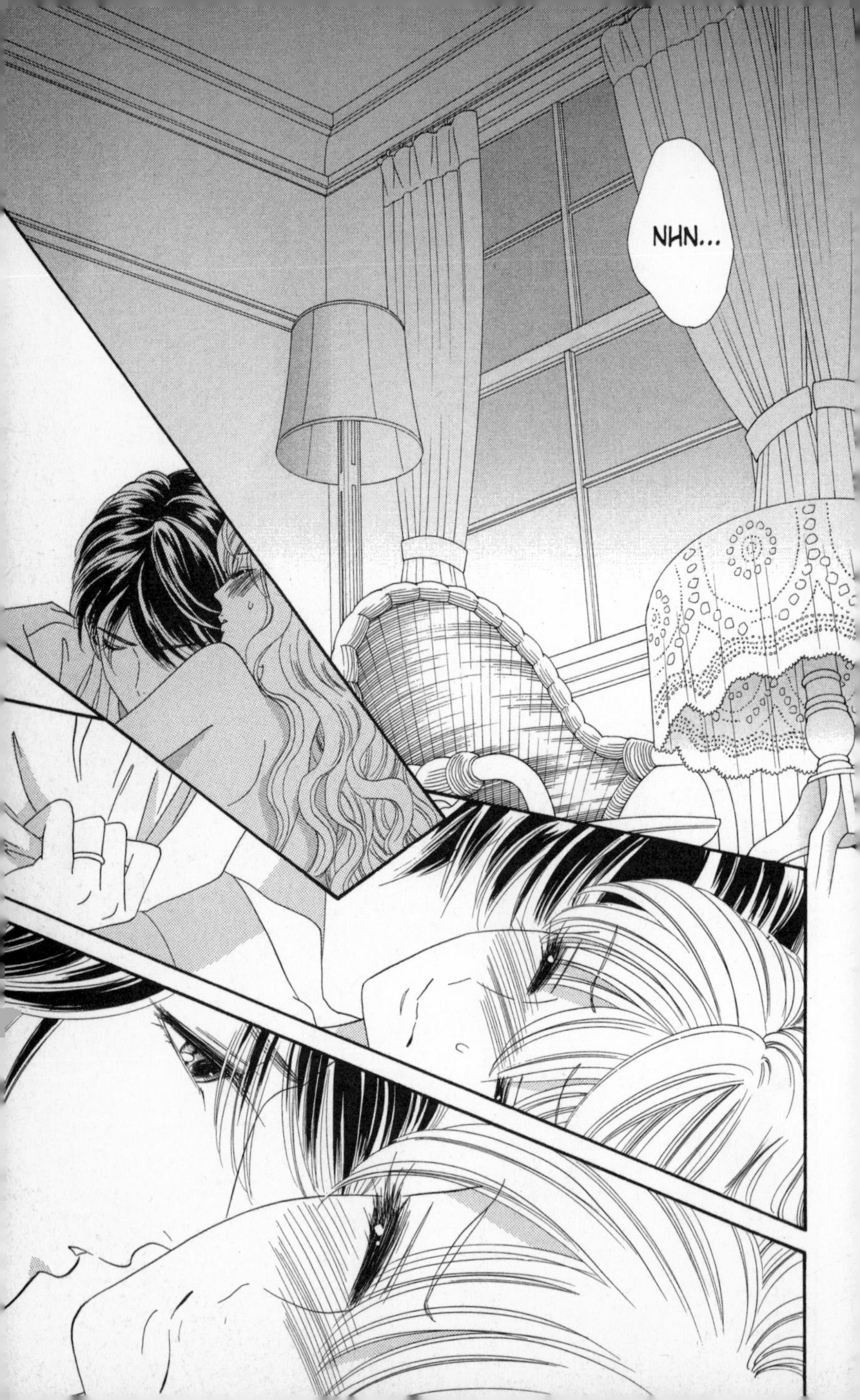
NHN...

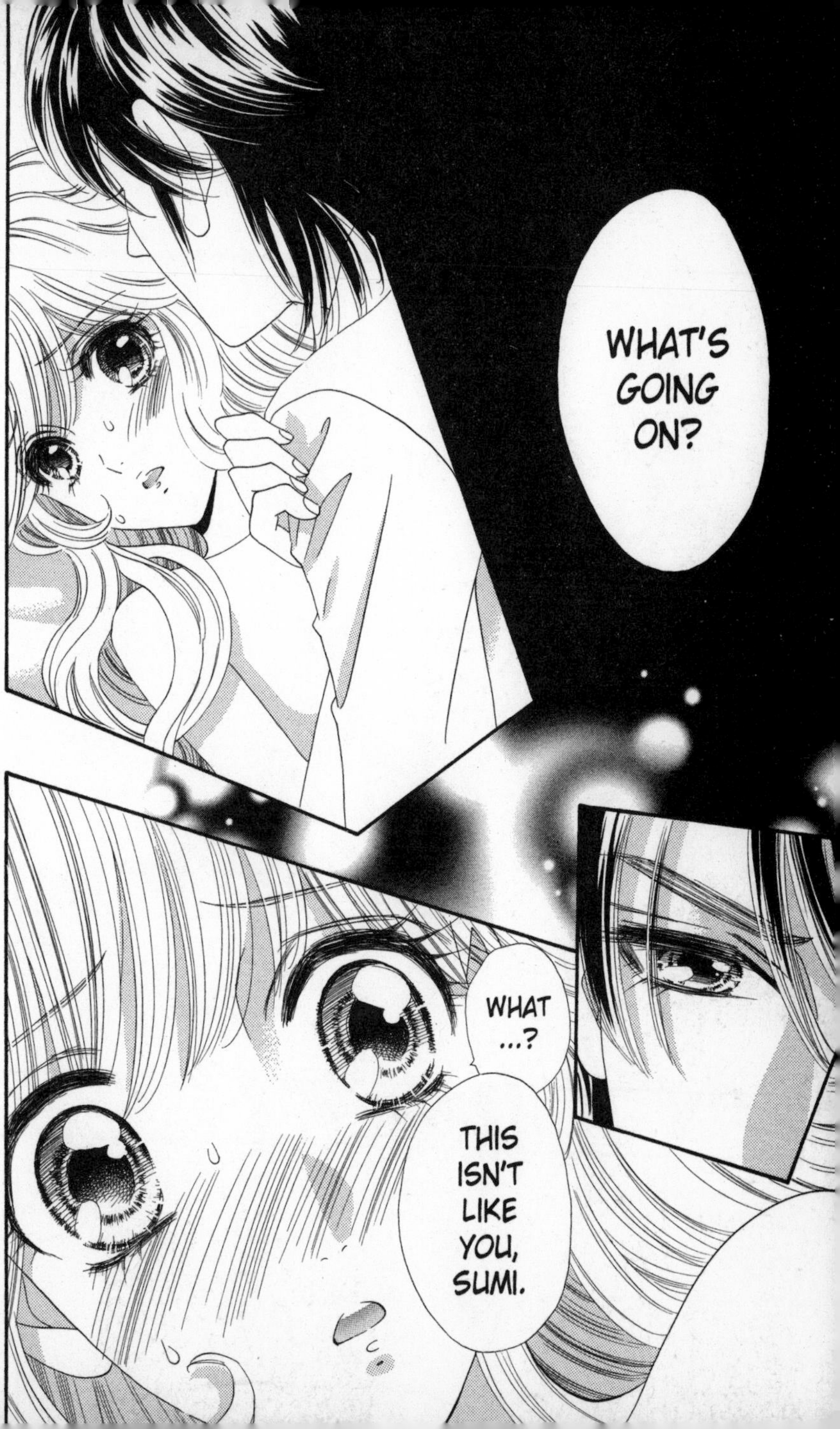
WHAT'S GOING ON?
WHAT ...?
THIS ISN'T LIKE YOU, SUMI.

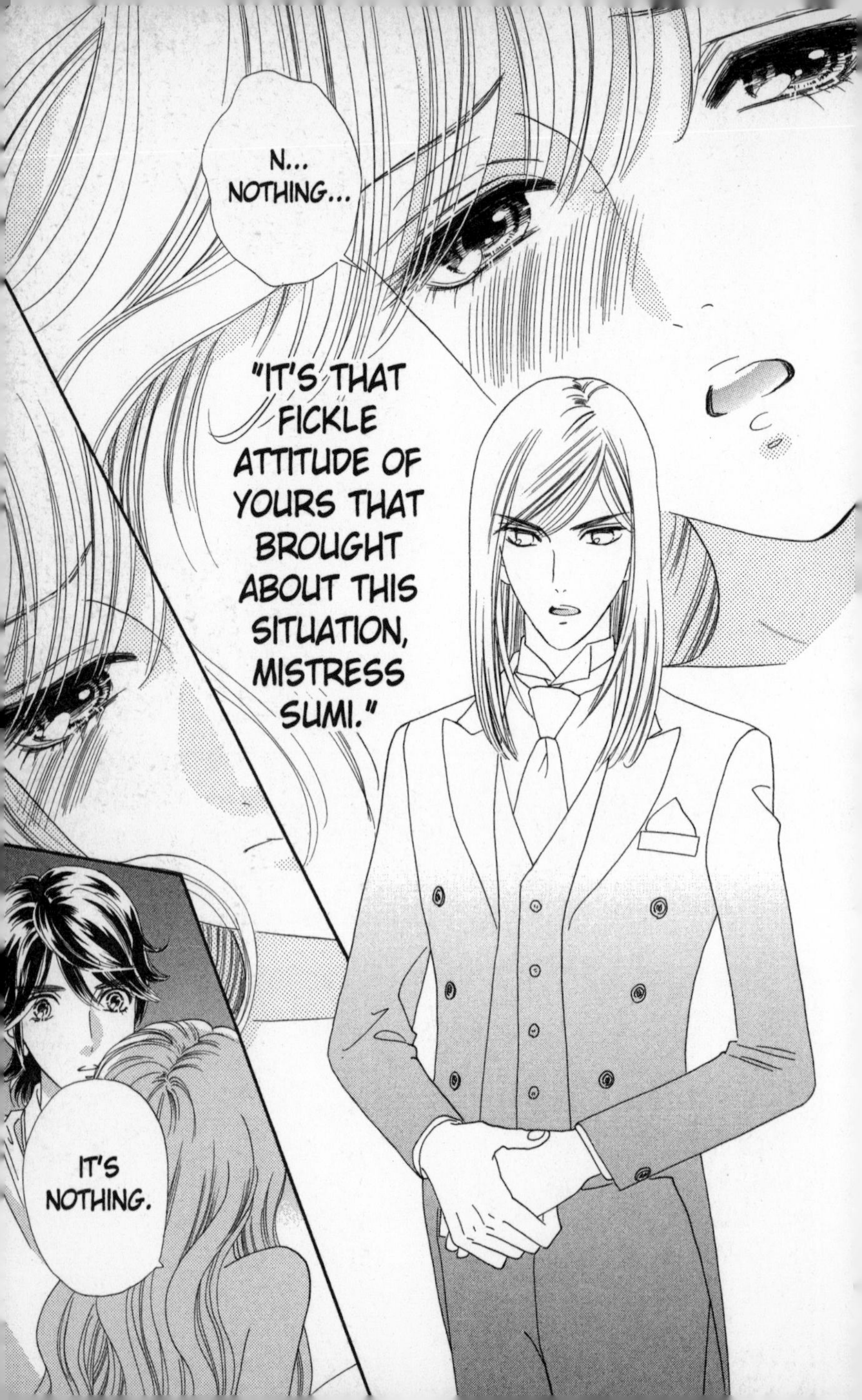
N... NOTHING...
"IT'S THAT FICKLE ATTITUDE OF YOURS THAT BROUGHT ABOUT THIS SITUATION, MISTRESS SUMI."
IT'S NOTHING.

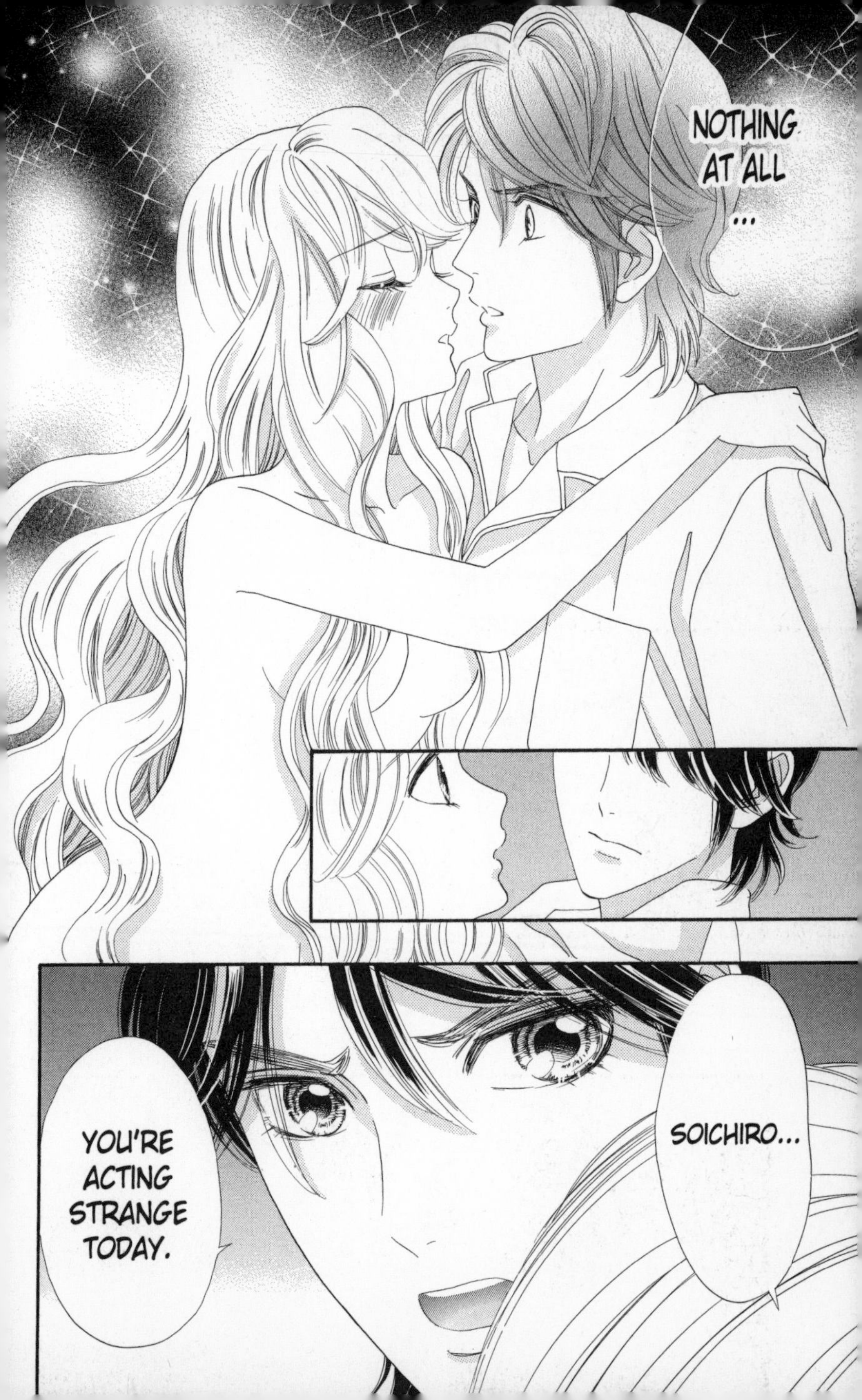
NOTHING AT ALL ...
SOICHIRO...
YOU'RE ACTING STRANGE TODAY.

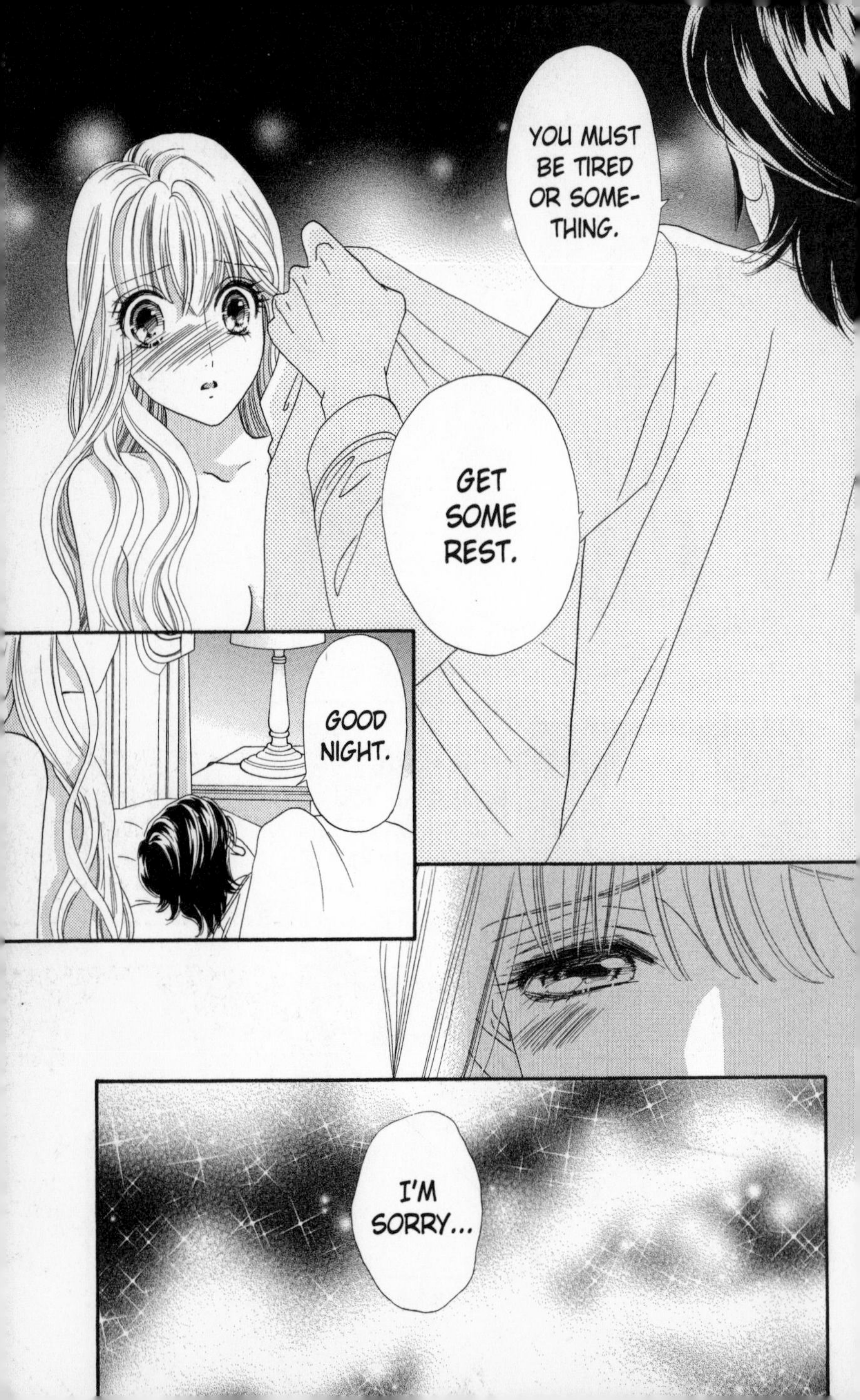
YOU MUST BE TIRED OR SOME-THING.
GET SOME REST.
GOOD NIGHT.
I'M SORRY...

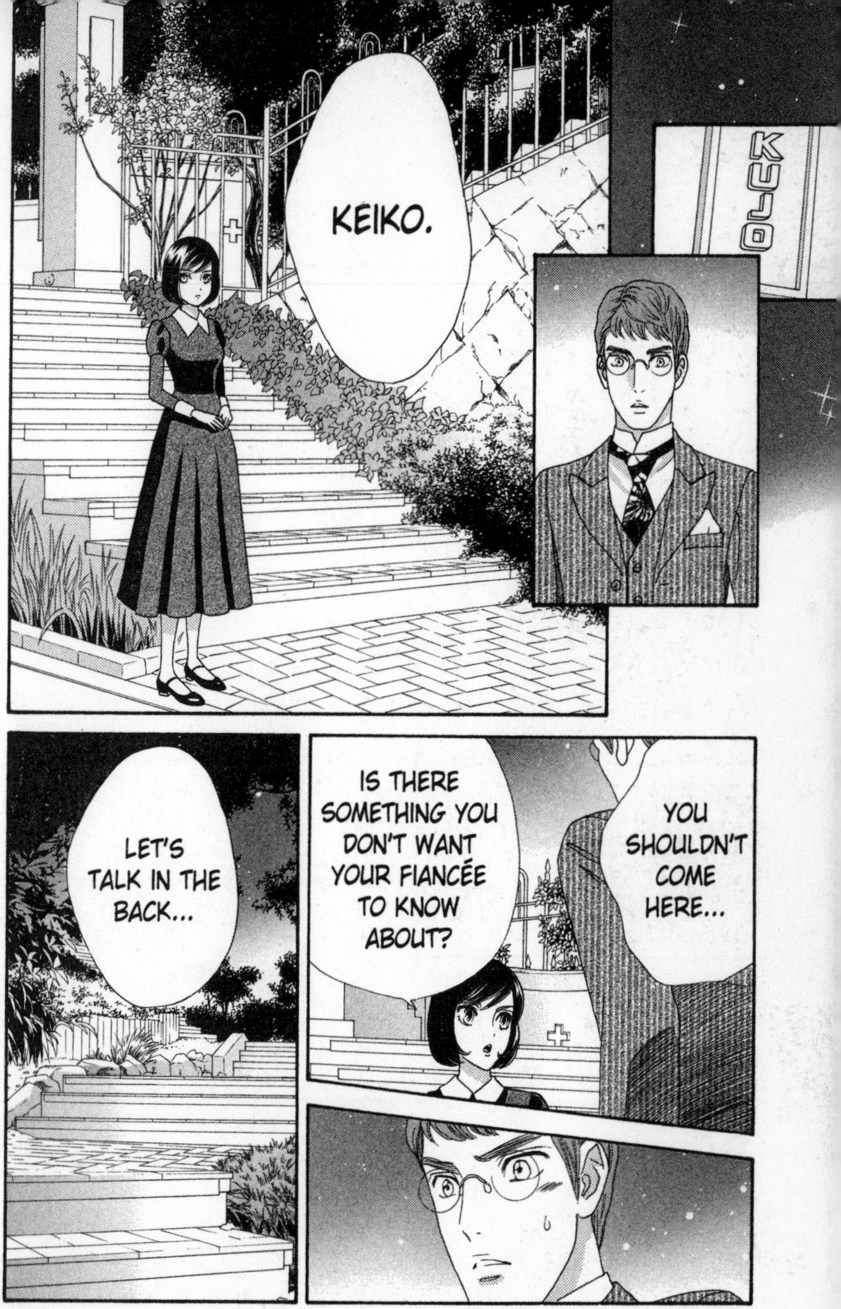
KUJO
KEIKO.
YOU SHOULDN'T COME HERE...
IS THERE SOMETHING YOU DON'T WANT YOUR FIANCÉE TO KNOW ABOUT?
LET'S TALK IN THE BACK...

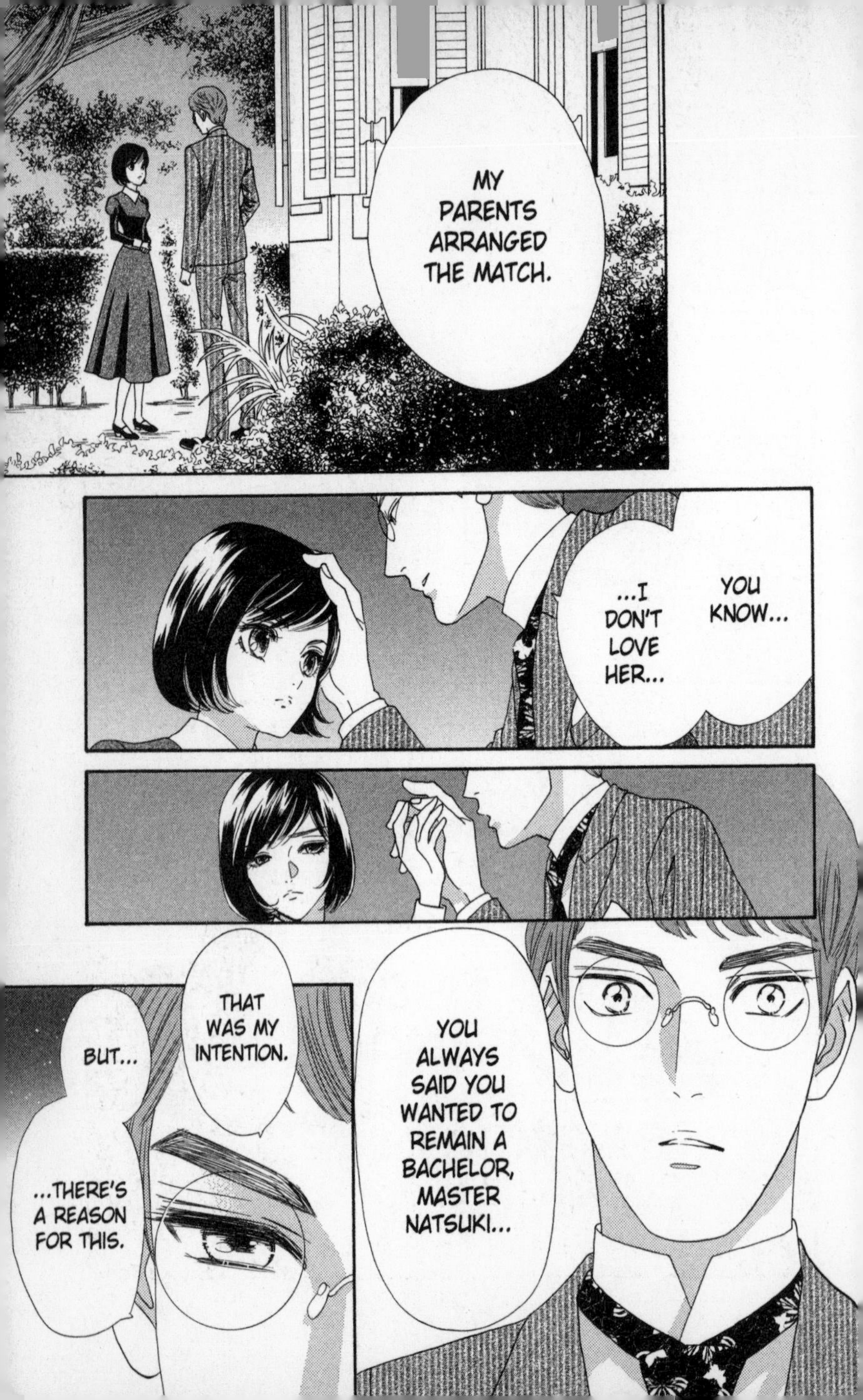
MY PARENTS ARRANGED THE MATCH.
YOU KNOW...
...I DON'T LOVE HER...
YOU ALWAYS SAID YOU WANTED TO REMAIN A BACHELOR, MASTER NATSUKI...
THAT WAS MY INTENTION.
BUT...
...THERE'S A REASON FOR THIS.

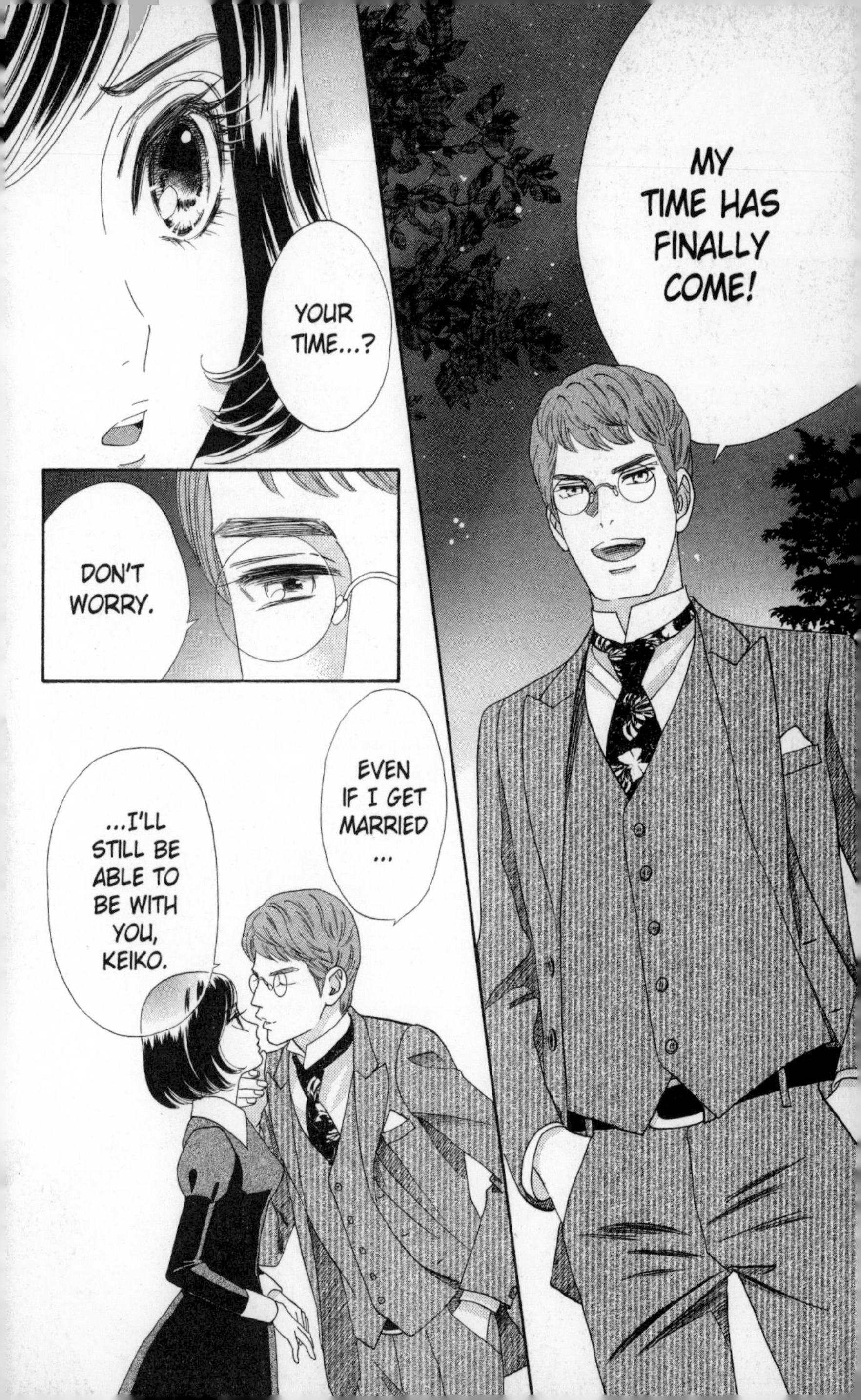
MY TIME HAS FINALLY COME!
YOUR TIME...?
DON'T WORRY.
EVEN IF I GET MARRIED ...
...I'LL STILL BE ABLE TO BE WITH YOU, KEIKO.

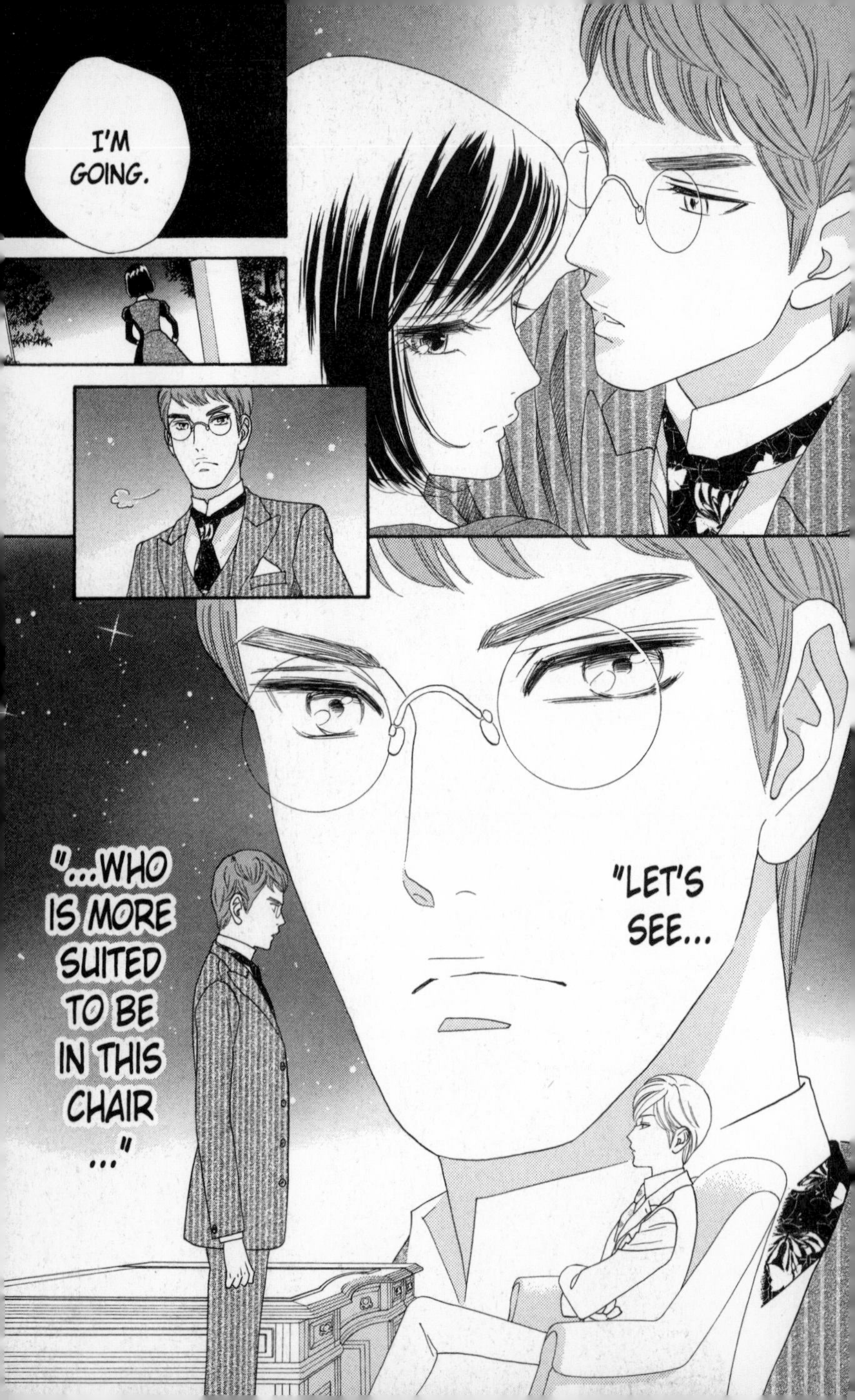
I'M GOING.
"LET'S SEE...
"...WHO IS MORE SUITED TO BE IN THIS CHAIR ..."

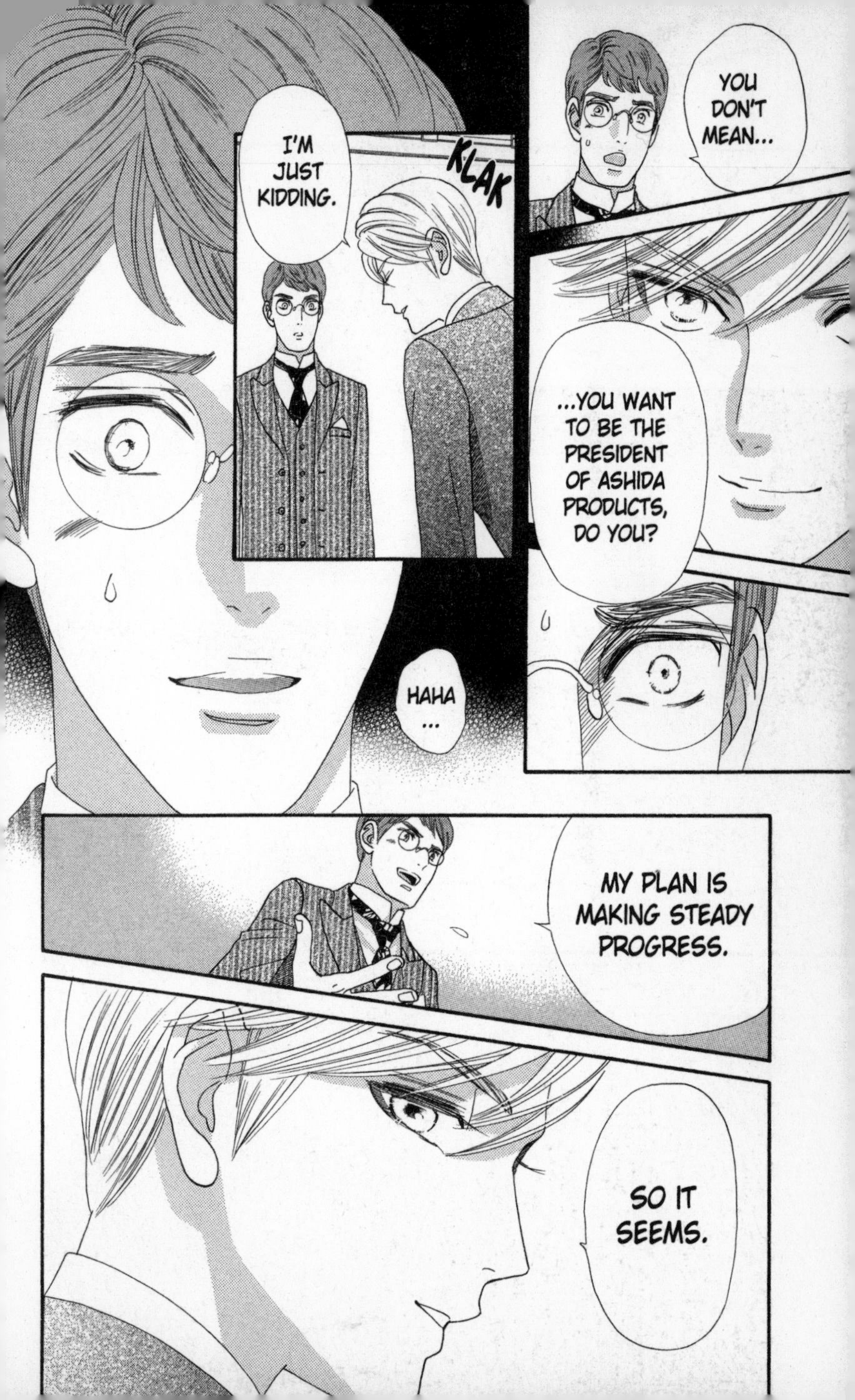
YOU DON'T MEAN...
...YOU WANT TO BE THE PRESIDENT OF ASHIDA PRODUCTS, DO YOU?
I'M JUST KIDDING.
KLAK
HAHA ...
MY PLAN IS MAKING STEADY PROGRESS.
SO IT SEEMS.

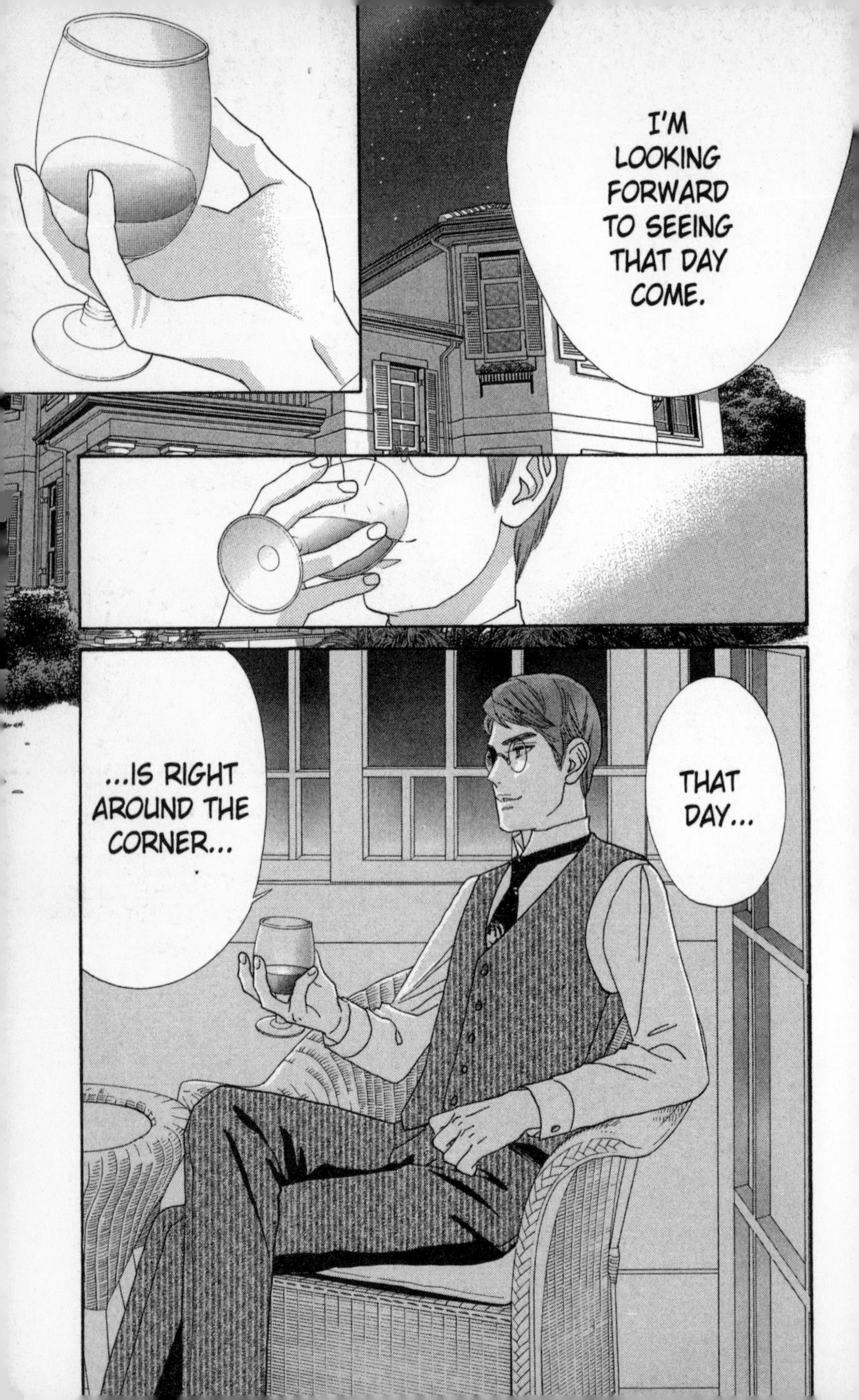
I'M LOOKING FORWARD TO SEEING THAT DAY COME.
THAT DAY...
...IS RIGHT AROUND THE CORNER...

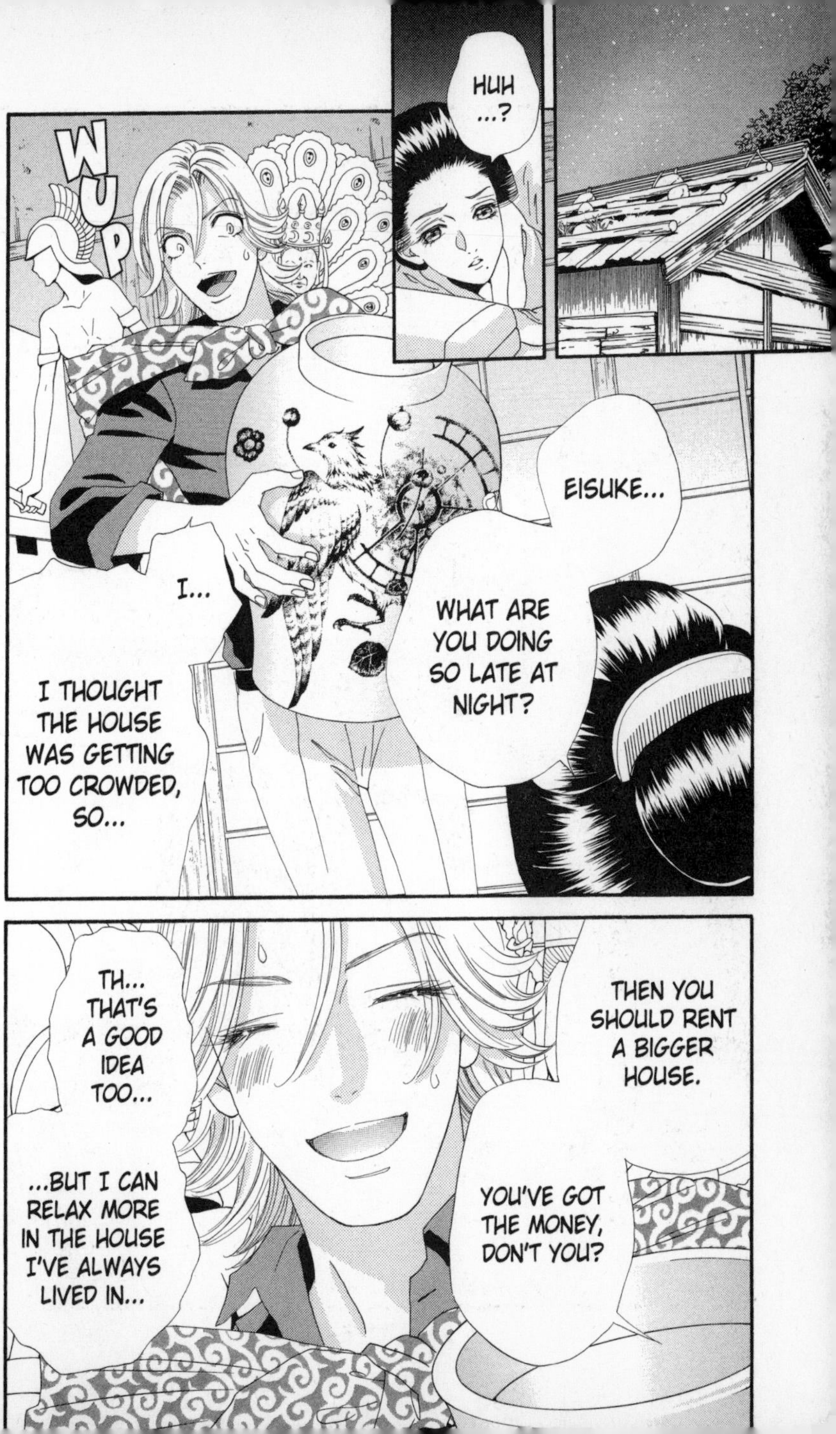
HUH ...?
WUP
EISUKE...
WHAT ARE YOU DOING SO LATE AT NIGHT?
I...
I THOUGHT THE HOUSE WAS GETTING TOO CROWDED, SO...
THEN YOU SHOULD RENT A BIGGER HOUSE.
YOU'VE GOT THE MONEY, DON'T YOU?
TH... THAT'S A GOOD IDEA TOO...
...BUT I CAN RELAX MORE IN THE HOUSE I'VE ALWAYS LIVED IN...

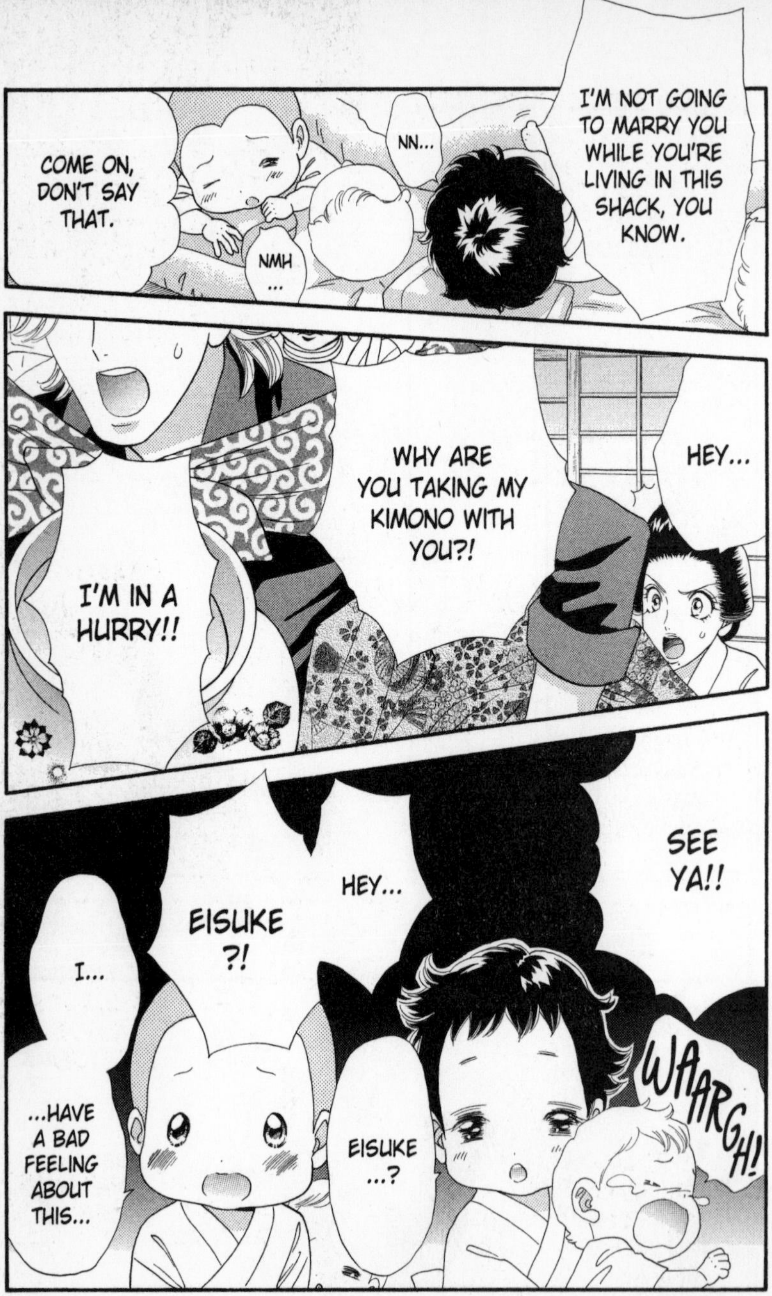
I'M NOT GOING TO MARRY YOU WHILE YOU'RE LIVING IN THIS SHACK, YOU KNOW.
NN...
NMH ...
COME ON, DON'T SAY THAT.
HEY...
WHY ARE YOU TAKING MY KIMONO WITH YOU?!
I'M IN A HURRY!!
SEE YA!!
HEY...
EISUKE ?!
WAARGH!
EISUKE ...?
I...
...HAVE A BAD FEELING ABOUT THIS...

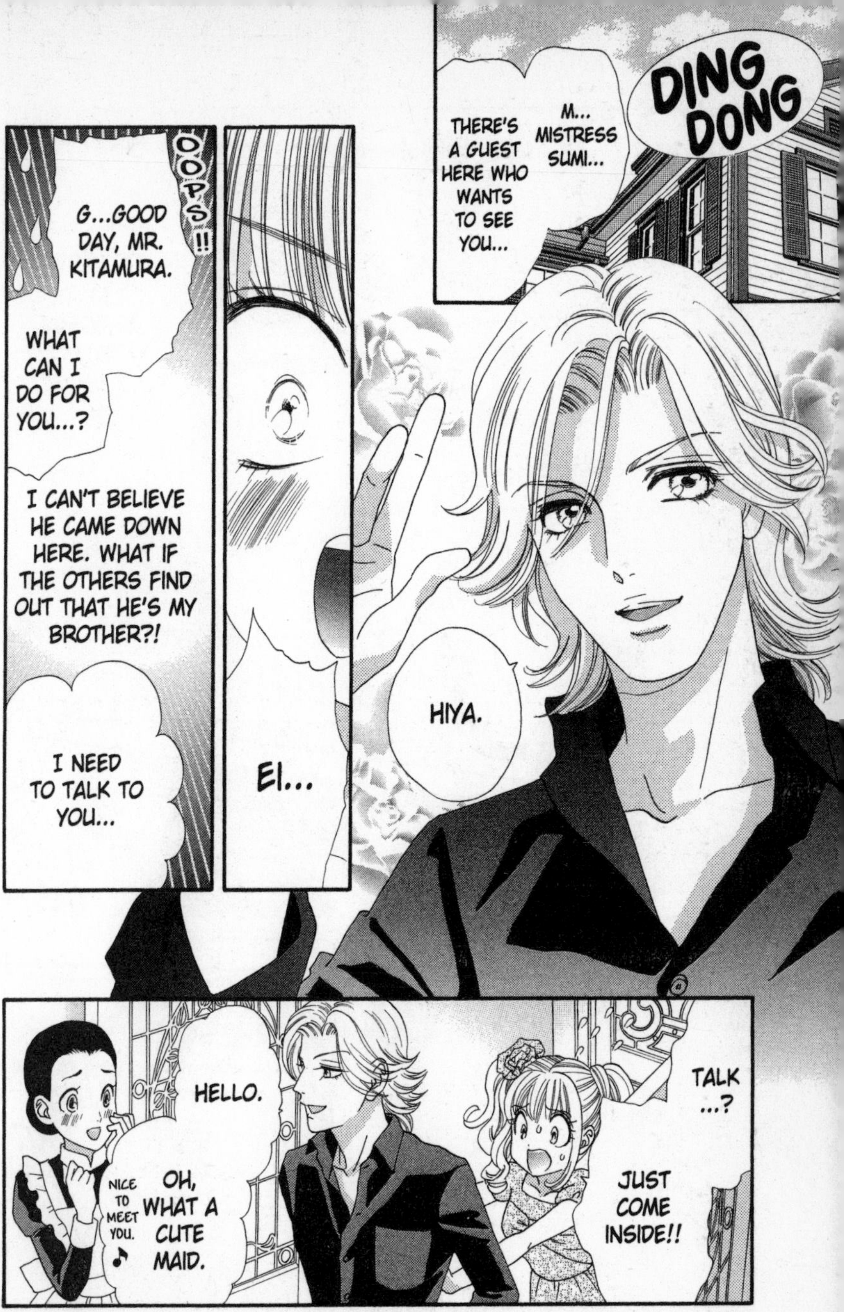
DING DONG
M... MISTRESS SUMI...
THERE'S A GUEST HERE WHO WANTS TO SEE YOU...
HIYA.
EI...
OOPS!!
G...GOOD DAY, MR. KITAMURA.
WHAT CAN I DO FOR YOU...?
I CAN'T BELIEVE HE CAME DOWN HERE. WHAT IF THE OTHERS FIND OUT THAT HE'S MY BROTHER?!
I NEED TO TALK TO YOU...
TALK ...?
JUST COME INSIDE!!
HELLO.
OH, WHAT A CUTE MAID.
NICE TO MEET YOU. ♪

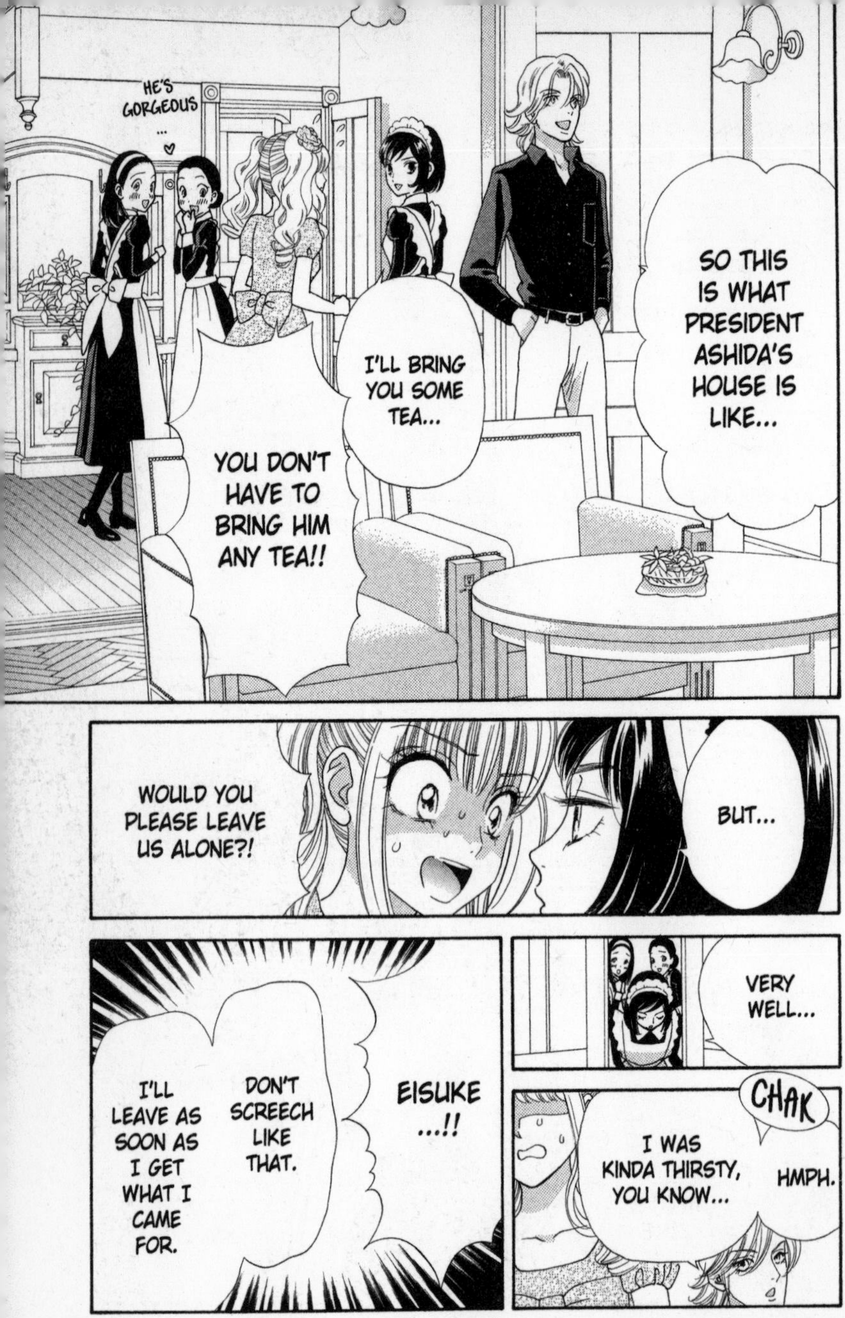
SO THIS IS WHAT PRESIDENT ASHIDA'S HOUSE IS LIKE...
I'LL BRING YOU SOME TEA...
YOU DON'T HAVE TO BRING HIM ANY TEA!!
HE'S GORGEOUS ... ♥
BUT...
WOULD YOU PLEASE LEAVE US ALONE?!
VERY WELL...
CHAK
HMPH.
I WAS KINDA THIRSTY, YOU KNOW...
EISUKE ...!!
DON'T SCREECH LIKE THAT.
I'LL LEAVE AS SOON AS I GET WHAT I CAME FOR.

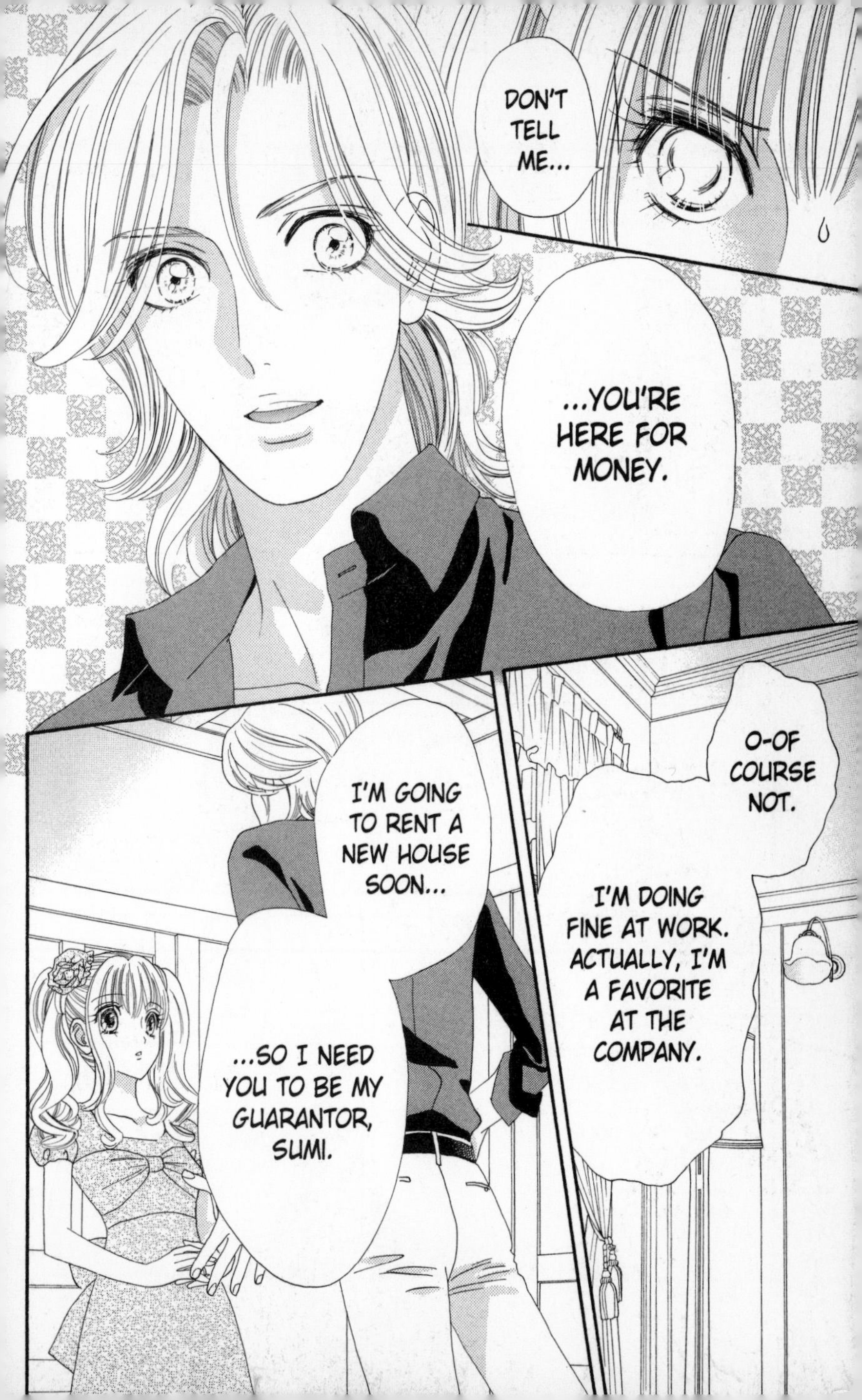
DON'T TELL ME...
...YOU'RE HERE FOR MONEY.
O-OF COURSE NOT.
I'M DOING FINE AT WORK. ACTUALLY, I'M A FAVORITE AT THE COMPANY.
I'M GOING TO RENT A NEW HOUSE SOON...
...SO I NEED YOU TO BE MY GUARANTOR, SUMI.

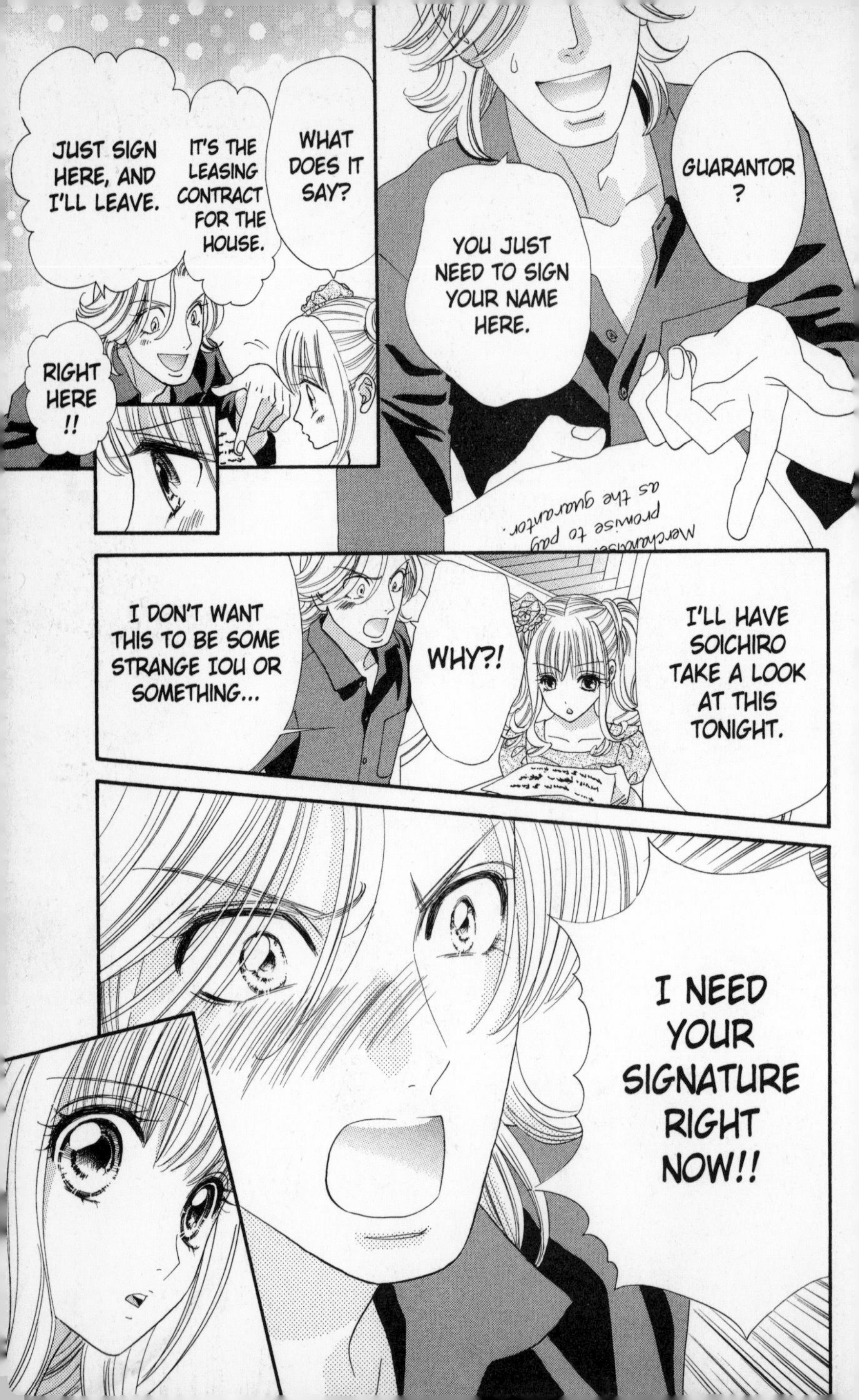

GUARANTOR?
YOU JUST NEED TO SIGN YOUR NAME HERE.
promise to pay as the guarantor.
WHAT DOES IT SAY?
IT'S THE LEASING CONTRACT FOR THE HOUSE.
JUST SIGN HERE, AND I'LL LEAVE.
RIGHT HERE!!
I'LL HAVE SOICHIRO TAKE A LOOK AT THIS TONIGHT.
WHY?!
I DON'T WANT THIS TO BE SOME STRANGE IOU OR SOMETHING...
I NEED YOUR SIGNATURE RIGHT NOW!!

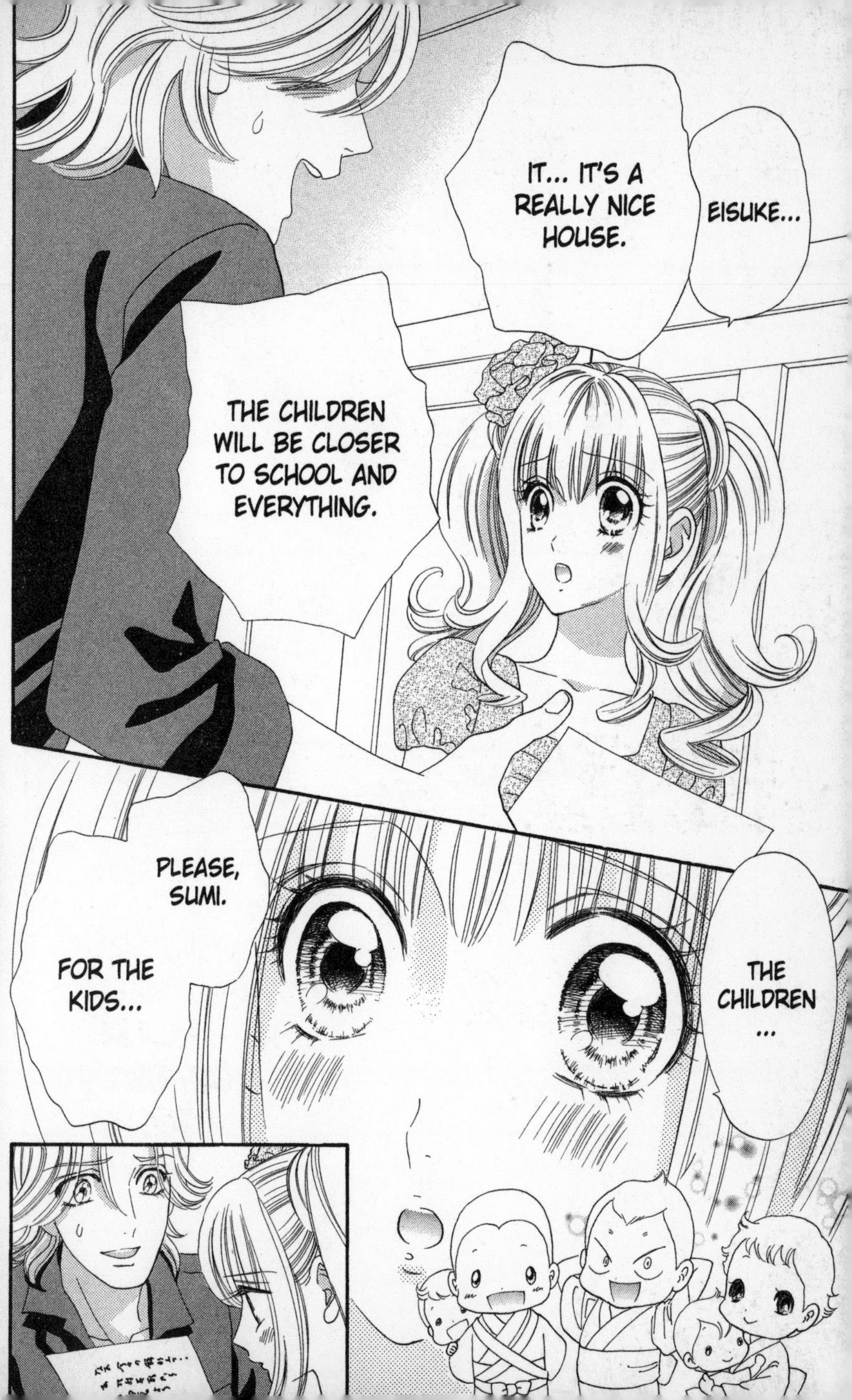
EISUKE...
IT... IT'S A REALLY NICE HOUSE.
THE CHILDREN WILL BE CLOSER TO SCHOOL AND EVERYTHING.
THE CHILDREN ...
PLEASE, SUMI.
FOR THE KIDS...

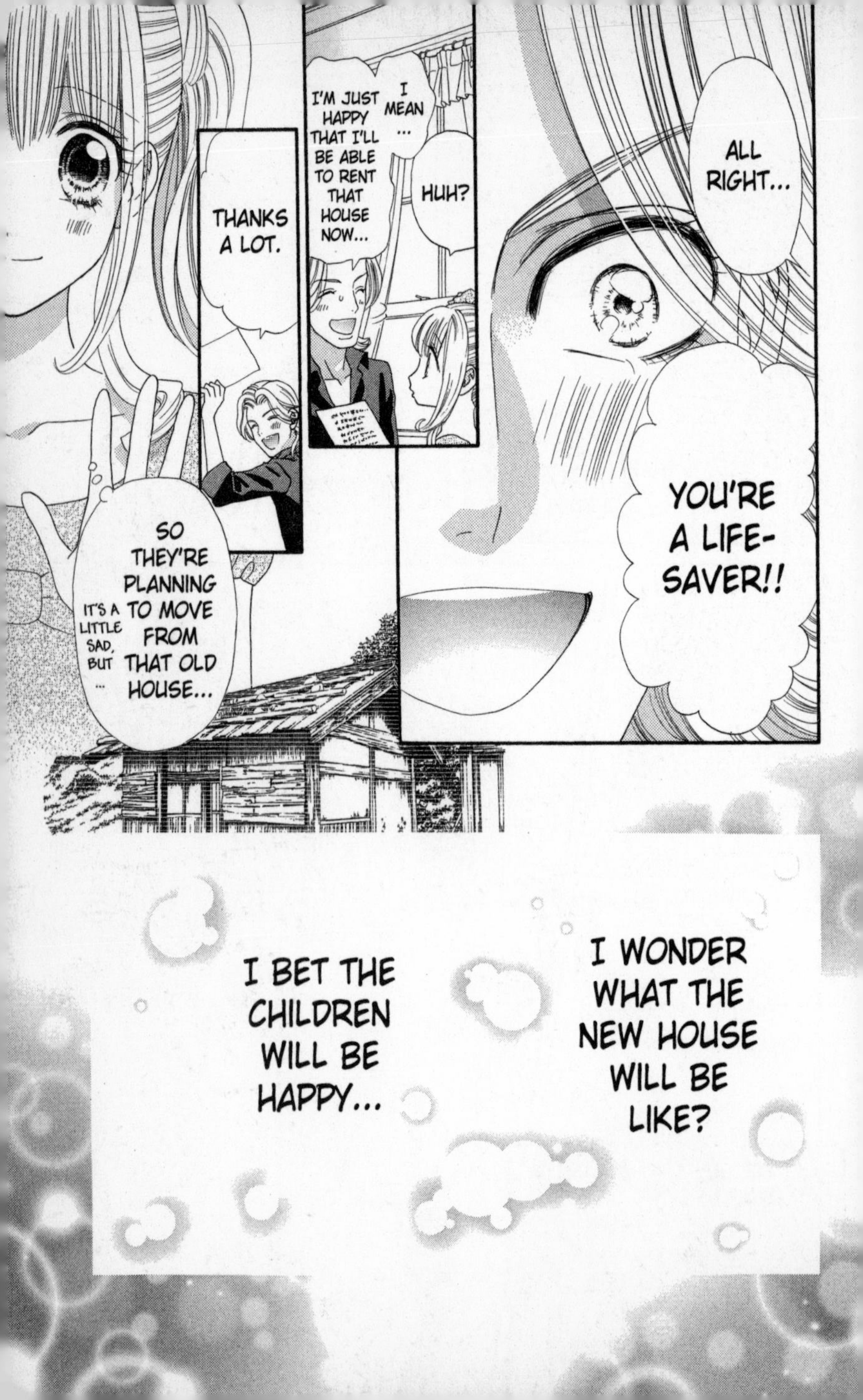
ALL RIGHT...
YOU'RE A LIFE-SAVER!!
I MEAN ...
I'M JUST HAPPY THAT I'LL BE ABLE TO RENT THAT HOUSE NOW...
HUH?
THANKS A LOT.
SO THEY'RE PLANNING TO MOVE FROM THAT OLD HOUSE...
IT'S A LITTLE SAD, BUT ...
I WONDER WHAT THE NEW HOUSE WILL BE LIKE?
I BET THE CHILDREN WILL BE HAPPY...

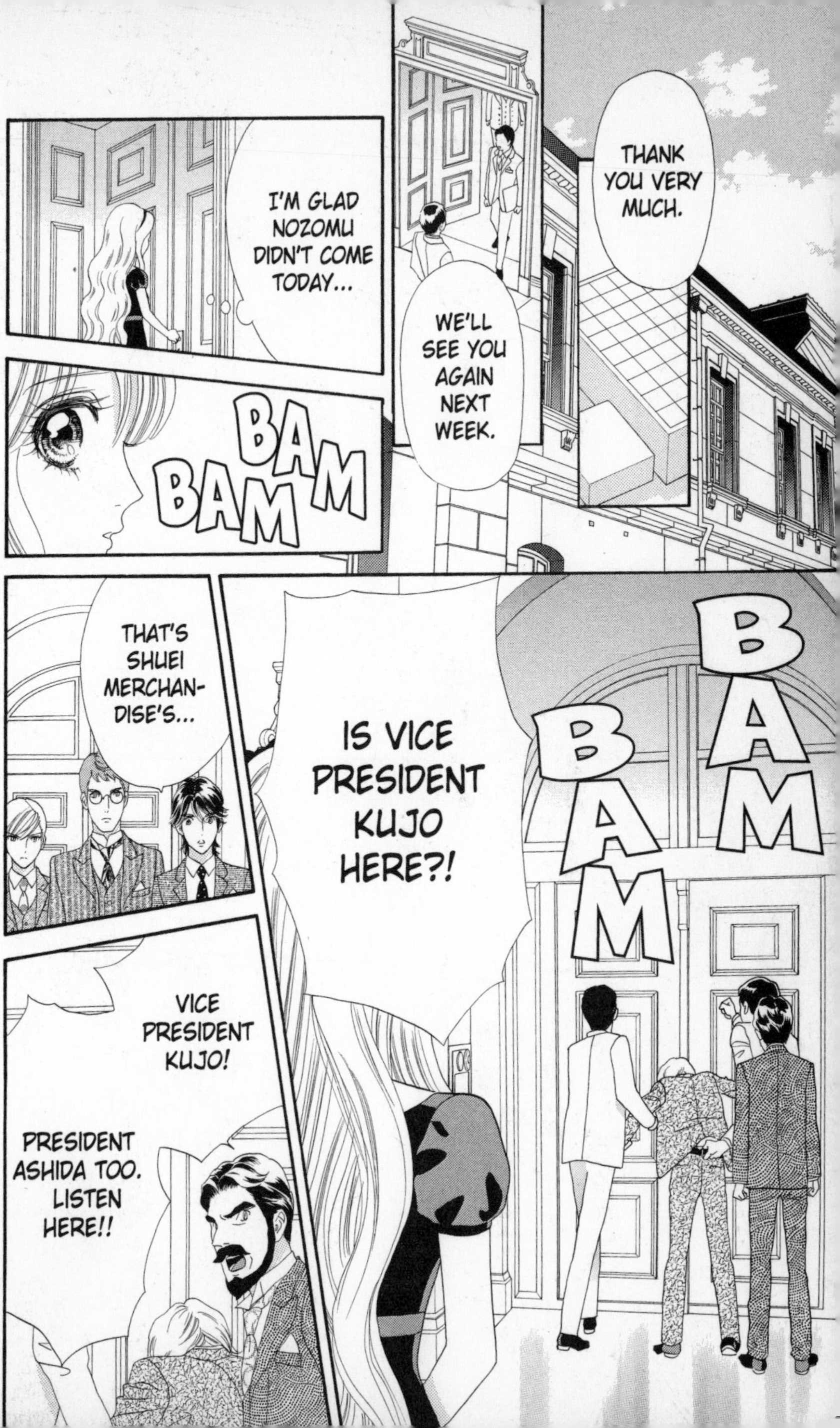
THANK YOU VERY MUCH.
WE'LL SEE YOU AGAIN NEXT WEEK.
I'M GLAD NOZOMU DIDN'T COME TODAY...
BAM BAM
BAM BAM
IS VICE PRESIDENT KUJO HERE?!
THAT'S SHUEI MERCHANDISE'S...
VICE PRESIDENT KUJO!
PRESIDENT ASHIDA TOO. LISTEN HERE!!

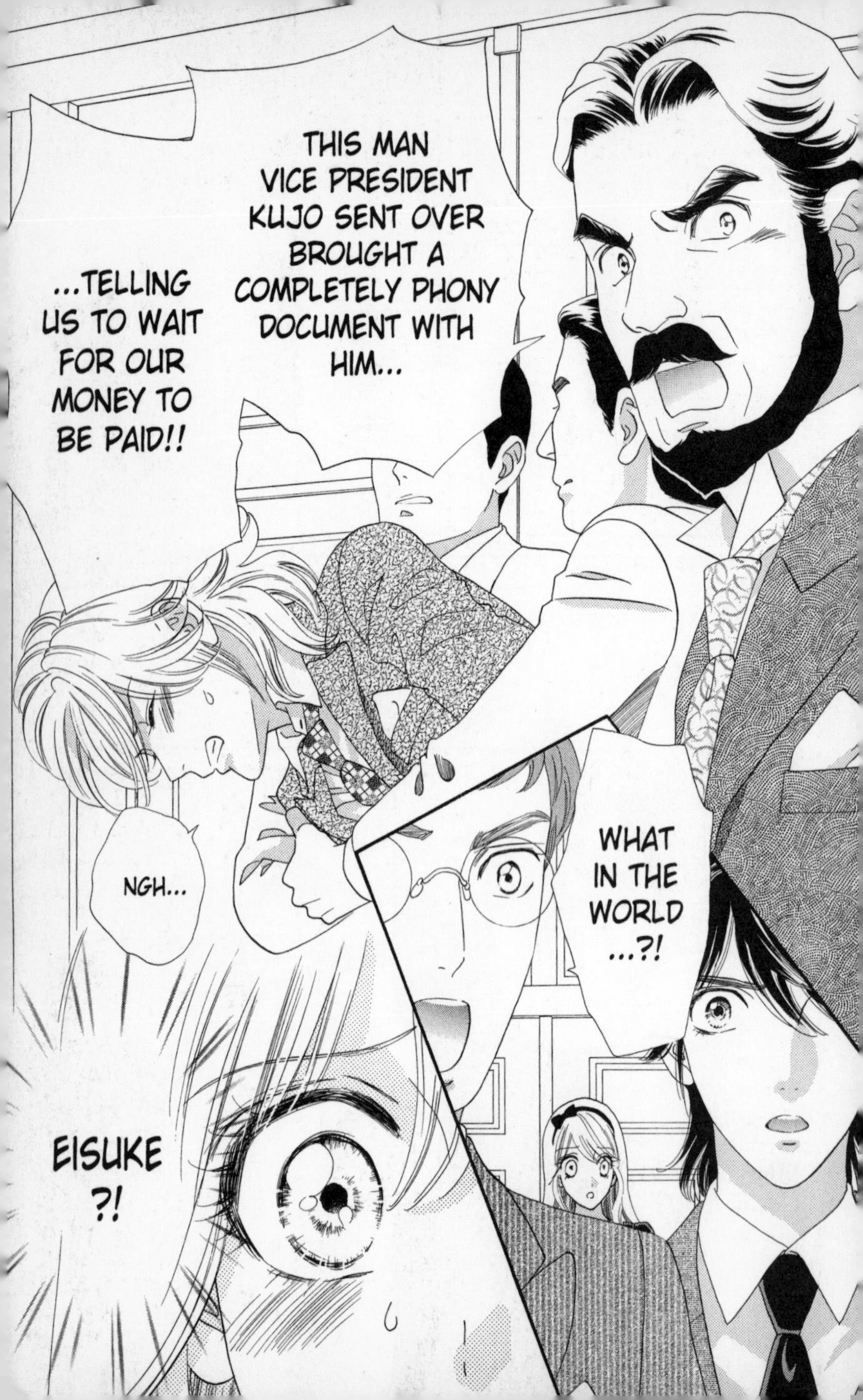
THIS MAN VICE PRESIDENT KUJO SENT OVER BROUGHT A COMPLETELY PHONY DOCUMENT WITH HIM...
...TELLING US TO WAIT FOR OUR MONEY TO BE PAID!!
NGH...
WHAT IN THE WORLD ...?!
EISUKE ?!

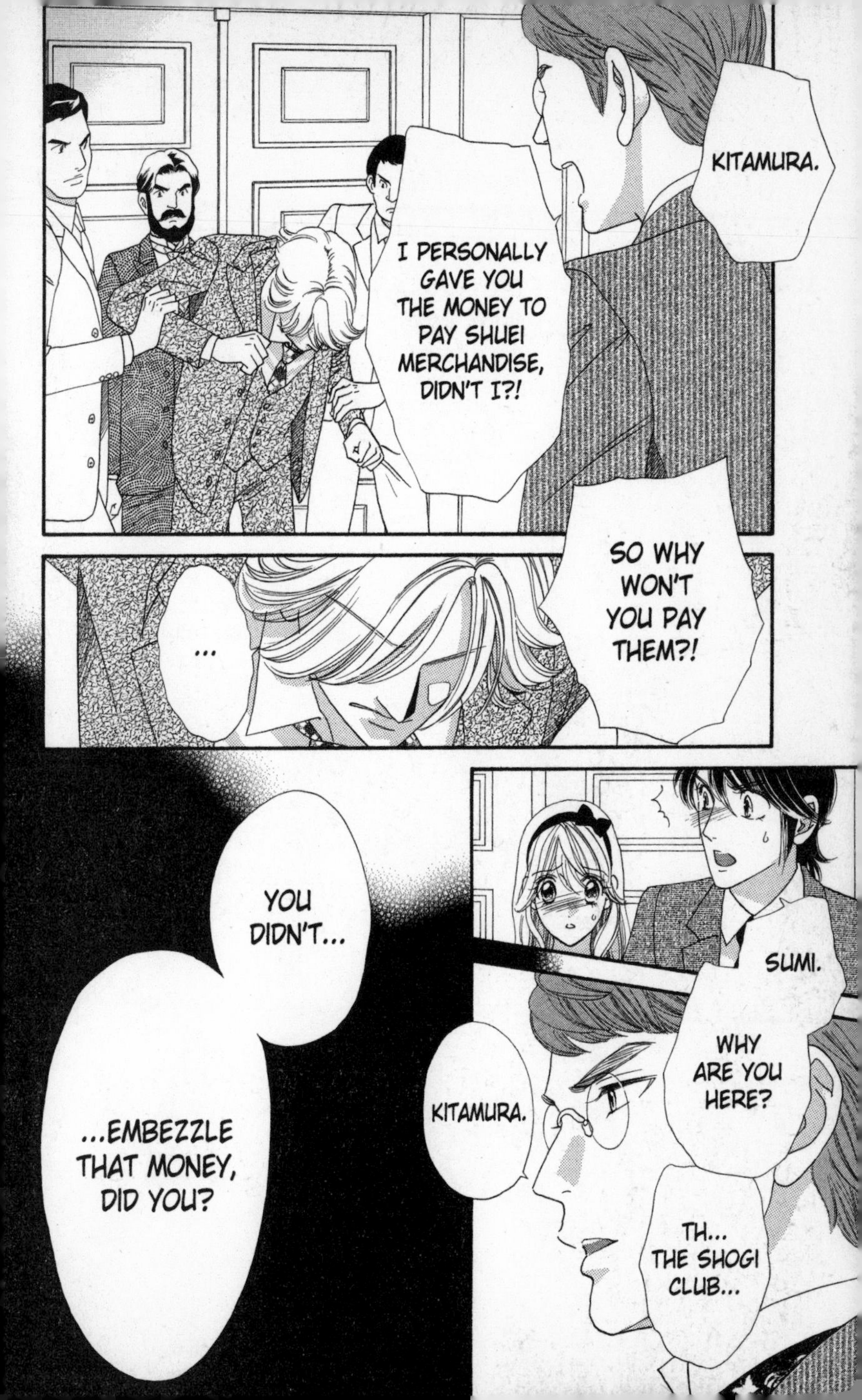
KITAMURA.
I PERSONALLY GAVE YOU THE MONEY TO PAY SHUEI MERCHANDISE, DIDN'T I?!
SO WHY WON'T YOU PAY THEM?!
...
SUMI.
WHY ARE YOU HERE?
KITAMURA.
TH... THE SHOGI CLUB...
YOU DIDN'T...
...EMBEZZLE THAT MONEY, DID YOU?

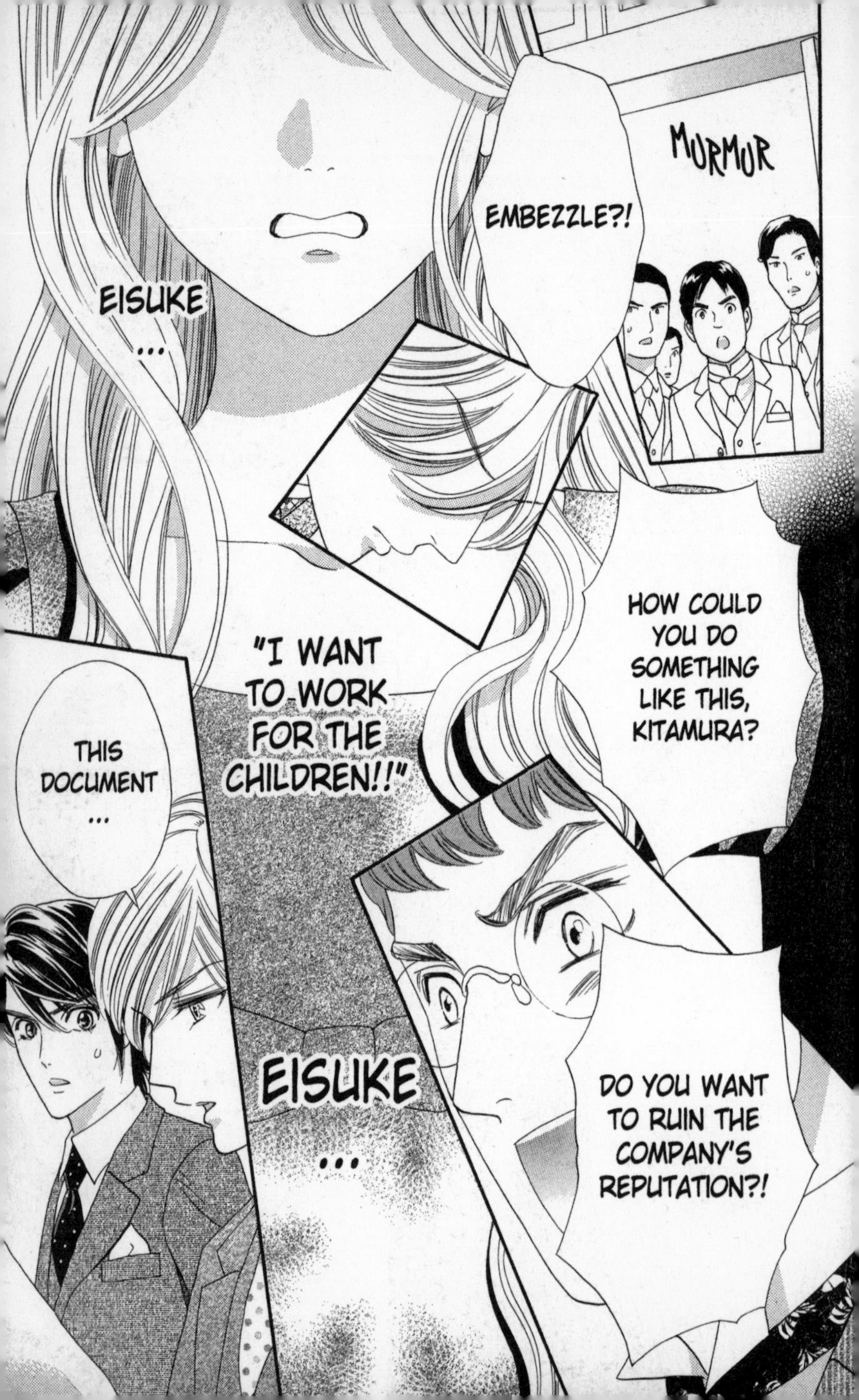
MURMUR
EMBEZZLE?!
EISUKE ...
HOW COULD YOU DO SOMETHING LIKE THIS, KITAMURA?
DO YOU WANT TO RUIN THE COMPANY'S REPUTATION?!
"I WANT TO WORK FOR THE CHILDREN!!"
THIS DOCUMENT ...
EISUKE ...

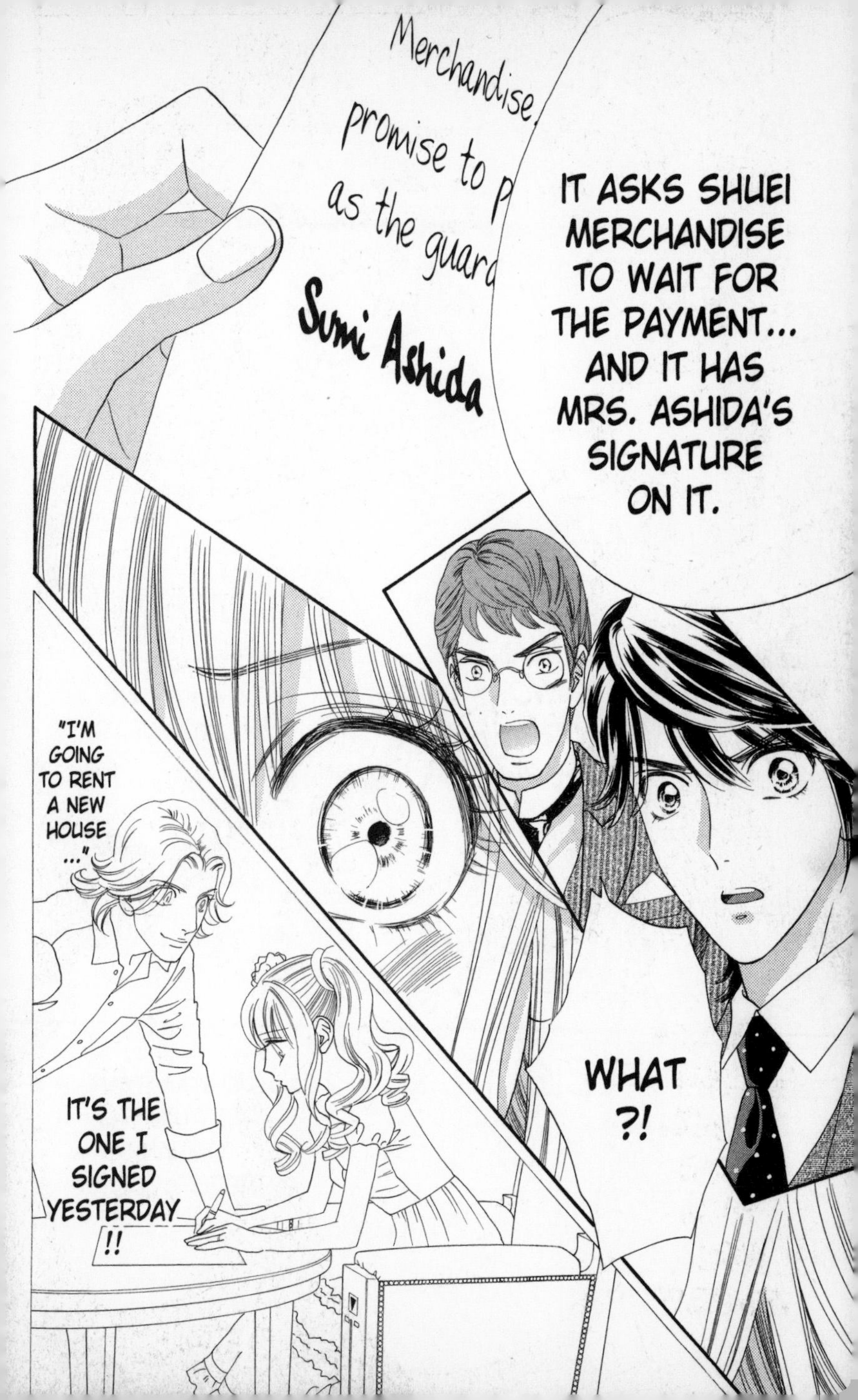
Merchandise,
promise to p
as the guard
Sumi Ashida
IT ASKS SHUEI MERCHANDISE TO WAIT FOR THE PAYMENT... AND IT HAS MRS. ASHIDA'S SIGNATURE ON IT.
WHAT?!
"I'M GOING TO RENT A NEW HOUSE..."
IT'S THE ONE I SIGNED YESTERDAY!!

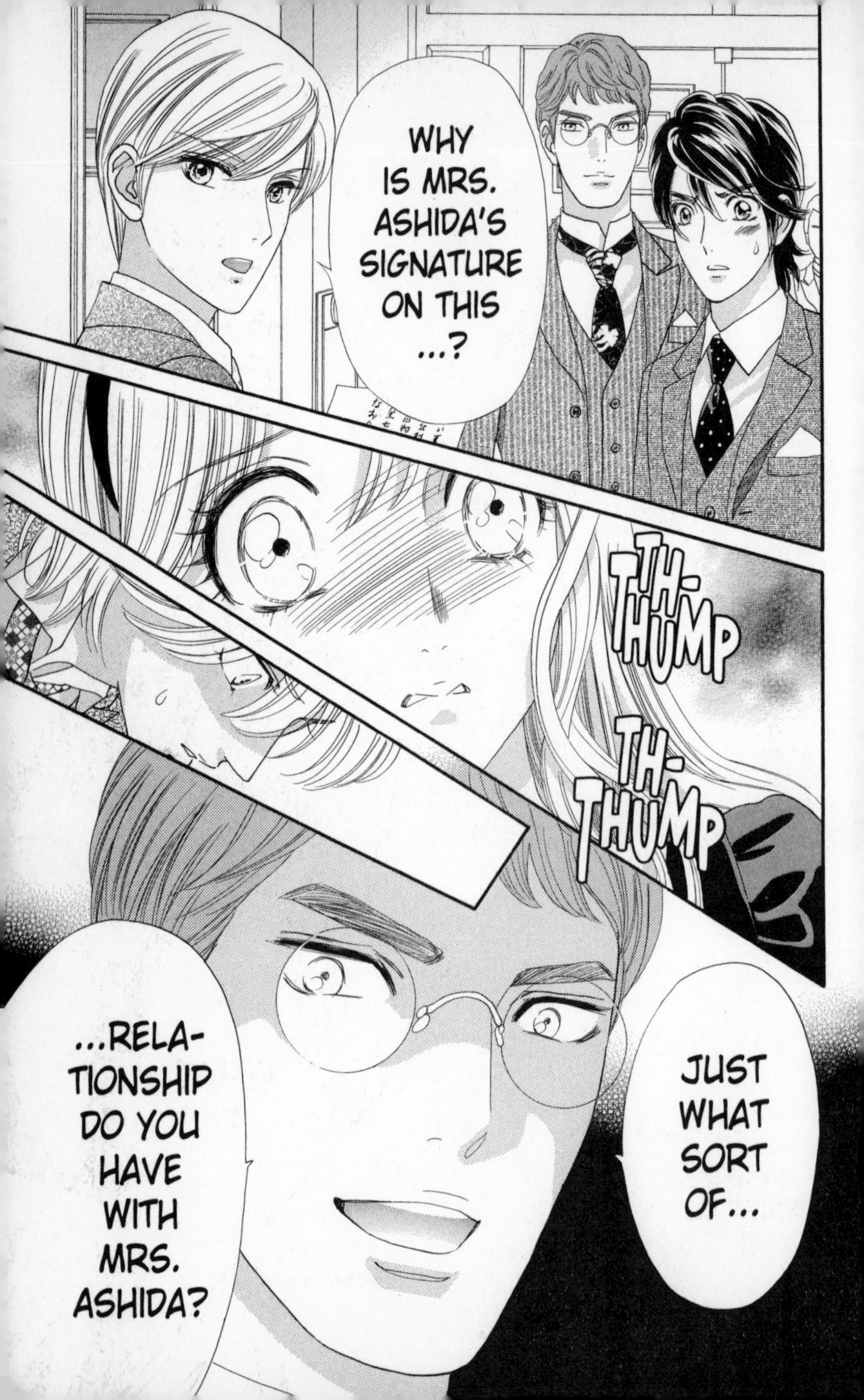
WHY IS MRS. ASHIDA'S SIGNATURE ON THIS ...?
TH-THUMP
TH-THUMP
JUST WHAT SORT OF...
...RELA-TIONSHIP DO YOU HAVE WITH MRS. ASHIDA?

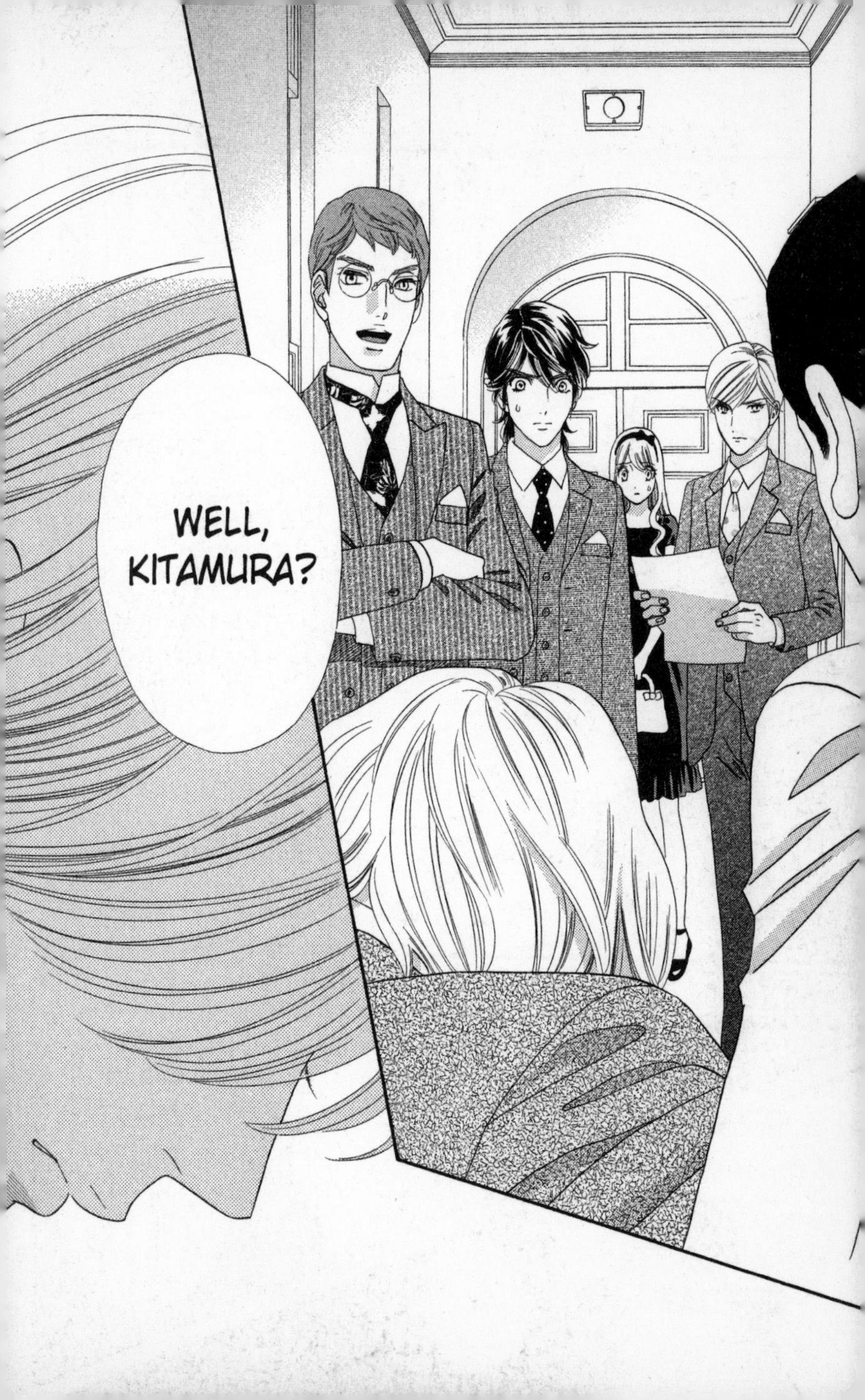
WELL, KITAMURA?

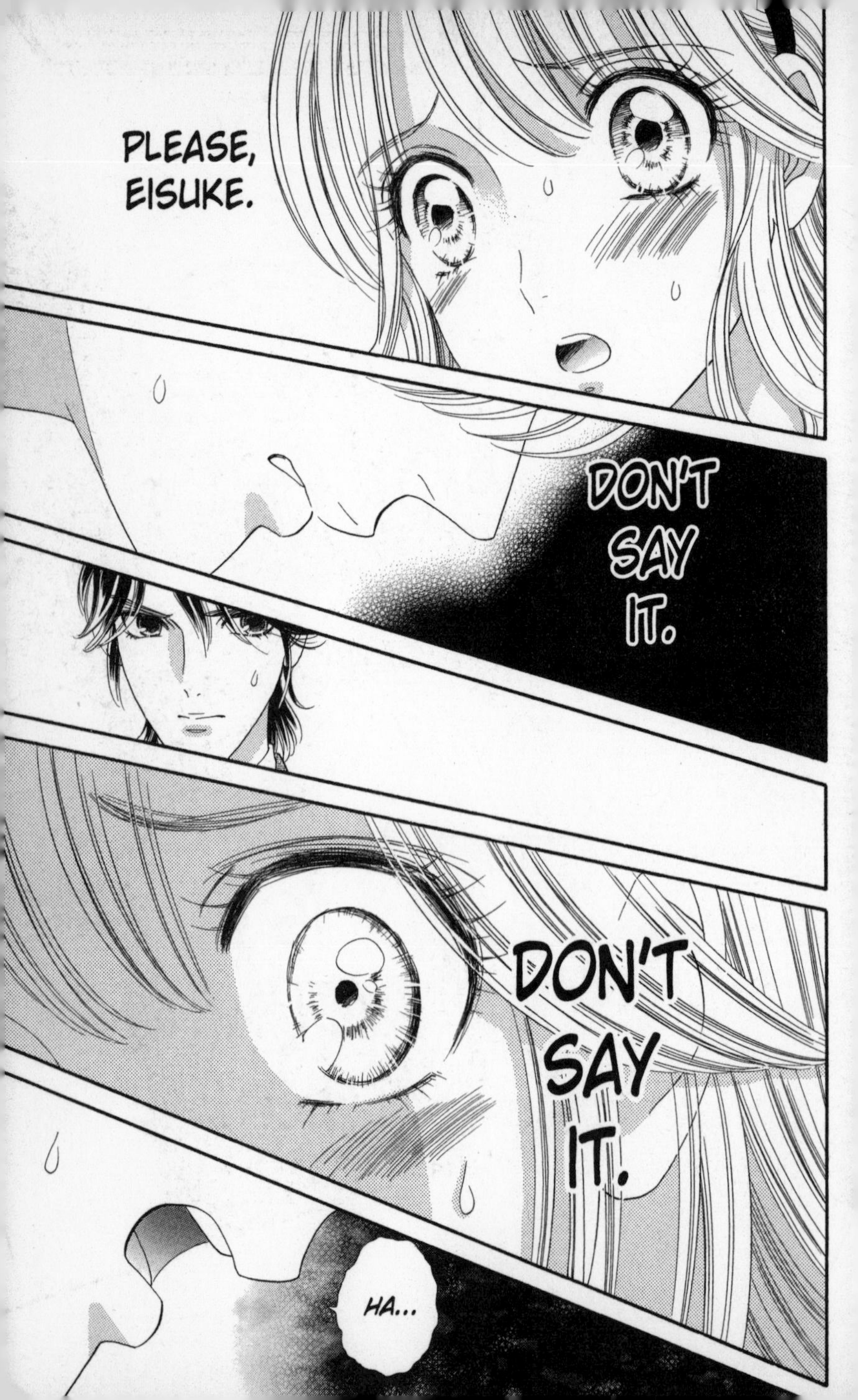
PLEASE, EISUKE.
DON'T SAY IT.
DON'T SAY IT.
HA...

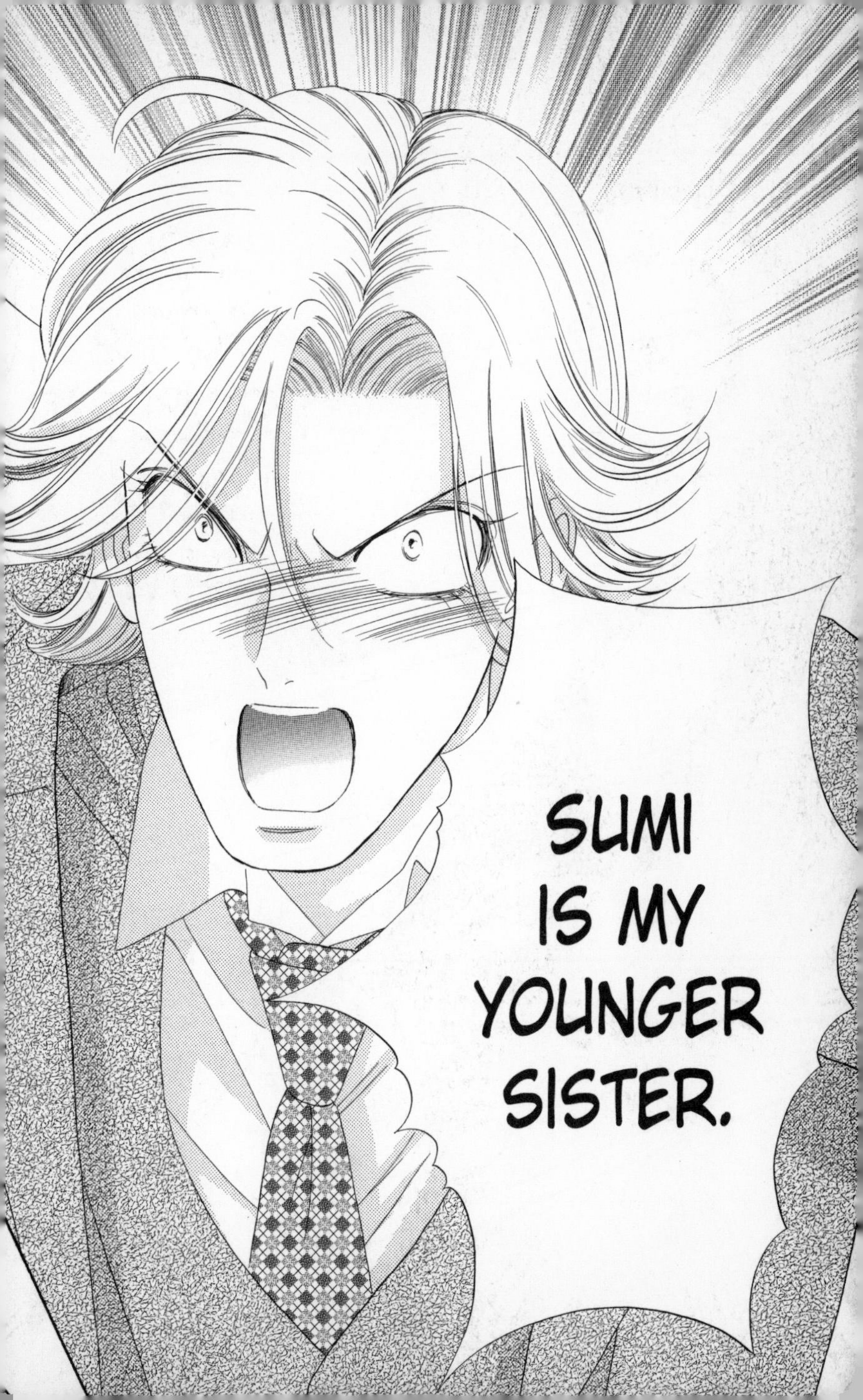
SUMI IS MY YOUNGER SISTER.

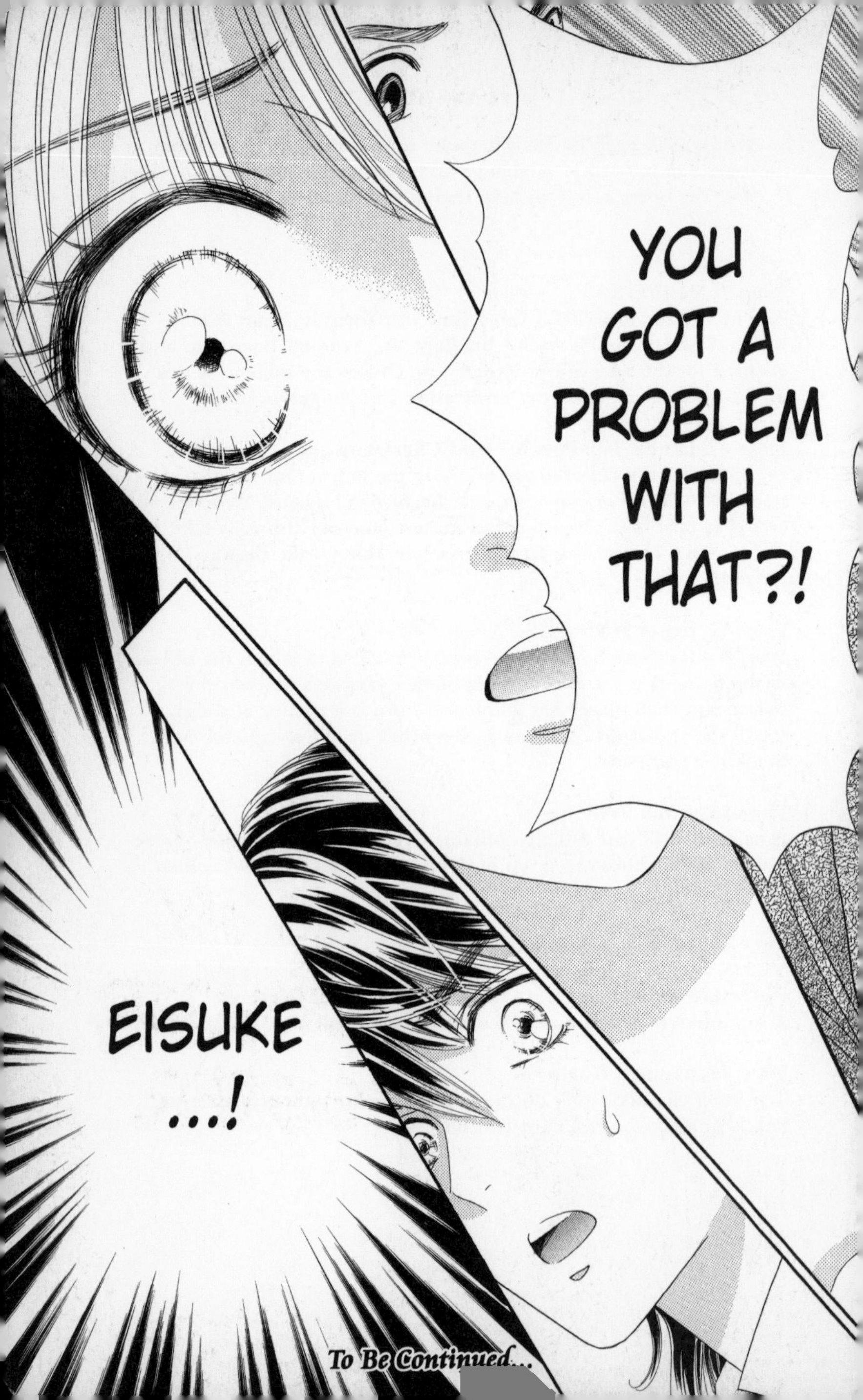
YOU GOT A PROBLEM WITH THAT?!
EISUKE ...!
To Be Continued...

Glossary

The setting of *Stepping on Roses* plays an important part in the story, as it showcases a unique time of change and transformation in Japan. Check out the notes below to help enrich your reading experience.

Page 2: Meiji Era
The Meiji Era (1868–1912) was a time of reform in Japan during which Western models and technology were studied, borrowed and adapted for the sake of modernization. One of the slogans of this period was *bunmei kaika*, or "civilization and enlightenment."

Page 41, panels 1–2: Peaches and Chestnuts…
In this scene, the children are finishing the idiom that the teacher started. "*Momo kuri san-nen, kaki hachi-nen*" means, "Peaches and chestnuts take three years to mature, and persimmons take eight years." This saying emphasizes how things take time to come to fruition.

Page 52, panel 2: Shogi
Shogi is a Japanese board game similar to chess in which the object of the game is to capture the opponent's king. It's played on a board, and each player has 20 pieces. Sumi is a master at shogi, a skill she revealed in volume 3. She heads up the shogi club at Soichiro's company.

Page 55, panel 7: Bento
A packed meal that usually contains rice and an assortment of side dishes. Some choose to wrap bento boxes in cloth called *furoshiki*, as Sumi does.

Page 66: Yamate, Yokohama
Yamate is an area in Yokohama, the capital city of Kanagawa Prefecture and a major port city located south of Tokyo. Yokohama's port was one of the first to be opened to foreign trade.

Page 76, panel 1: Kuruwa
The kanji character (廓) on the lantern means "an enclosed area," and it signifies the red-light district.

I love to draw, but every now and then, I'm overcome with a strong feeling of dislike toward my artwork. I'm just not satisfied with what I draw, and I can't find a way around it. I feel so hopeless at my inability to reproduce the images inside my head. I'll have to work harder and harder at it.

-Rinko Ueda

Rinko Ueda is from Nara Prefecture. She enjoys listening to the radio, drama CDs and Rakugo comedy performances. Her works include *Ryo*, a series based on the legend of Gojo Bridge; *Home*, a story about love crossing national boundaries; and *Tail of the Moon (Tsuki no Shippo)*, a romantic ninja comedy.

STEPPING ON ROSES
Vol. 6
Shojo Beat Edition

STORY AND ART BY
RINKO UEDA

Translation & Adaptation/Tetsuichiro Miyaki
Touch-up Art & Lettering/Mark McMurray
Design/Yukiko Whitley
Editor/Amy Yu

HADASHI DE BARA WO FUME © 2007 by Rinko Ueda
All rights reserved. First published in Japan in 2007 by SHUEISHA Inc., Tokyo.
English translation rights arranged by SHUEISHA Inc.

Printed in the U.S.A.

Published by VIZ Media, LLC
P.O. Box 77010
San Francisco, CA 94107

10 9 8 7 6 5 4 3 2 1
First printing, July 2011

www.viz.com   www.shojobeat.com

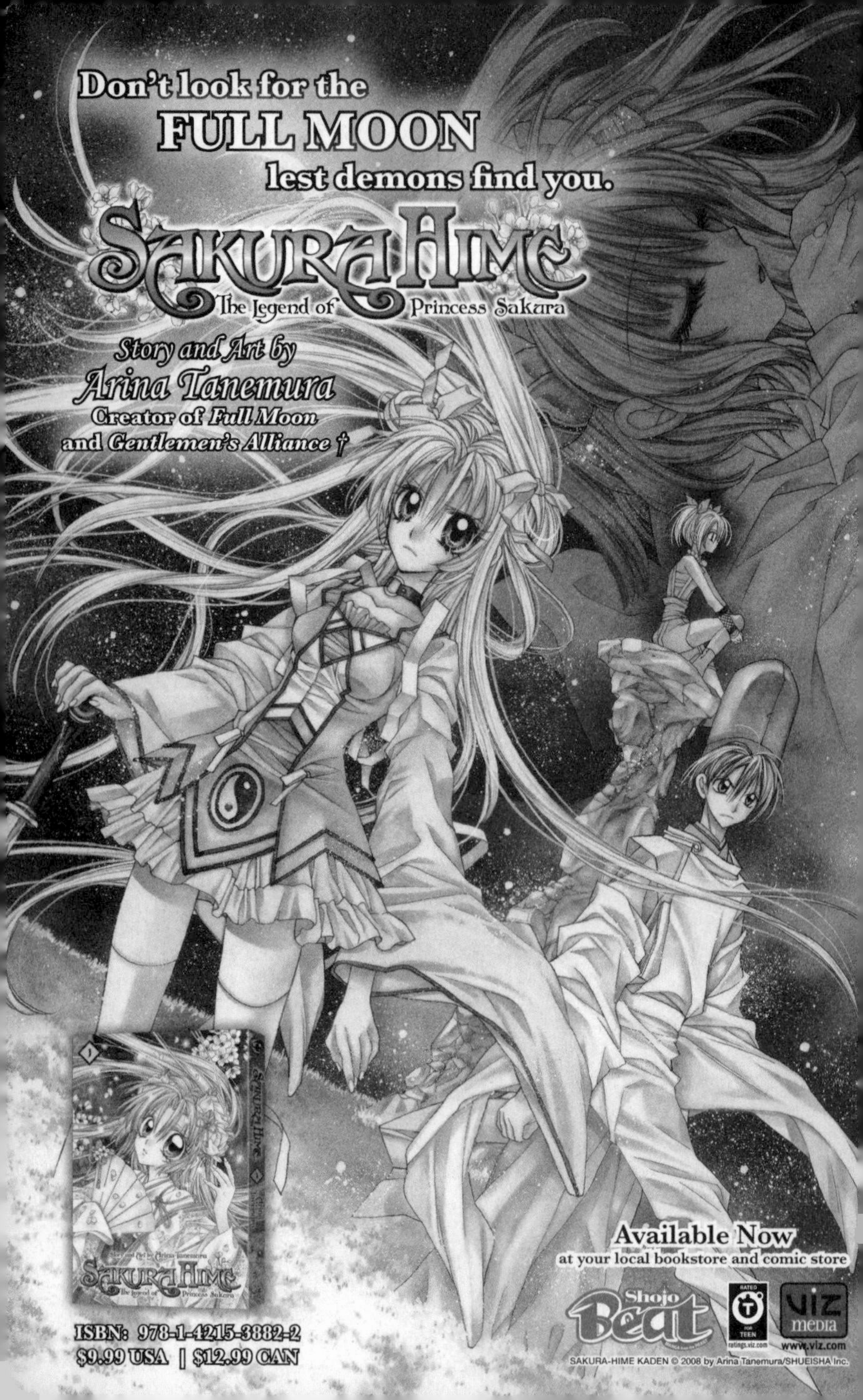

WELCOME to a priva
where trying to become S
can make you feel INFERIOR

THE GENTLEMEN'S ALLIANCE CROSS

Story and Art by Arina Tanemura
Creator of *Full Moon, I•O•N, Short-Tempered Melancholic, Time Stranger Kyoko*

When Haine's father decides to repay a debt by giving her to the Otomiya family, she starts attending the exclusive, aristocratic Imperial Academy. Though she's of proper lineage, will Haine ever really be considered one of the elite?

†

THE GENTLEMEN'S ALLIANCE CROSS
Arina Tanemura
1
THE GENTLEMEN'S ALLIANCE CROSS
Arina Tanemura
11

$9.99 USA | $12.99 CAN *

Read a **FREE** preview at **ShojoBeat.com**
and order the complete manga series at **store.viz.com**
Also available at your local bookstore or comic store.

Shojo Beat

RATED T+ FOR OLDER TEEN ratings.viz.com

VIZ media
www.viz.com